Christianity and Genocide in Rwanda

Although Rwanda is among the most Christian countries in Africa, in the 1994 genocide, church buildings became the primary killing grounds. To explain why so many Christians participated in the violence, this book looks at the history of Christian engagement in Rwanda and then turns to a rich body of original national- and local-level research to argue that Rwanda's churches have consistently allied themselves with the state and played ethnic politics. Comparing two local Presbyterian parishes in Kibuye before the genocide demonstrates that progressive forces were seeking to democratize the churches. Just as Hutu politicians used the genocide of Tutsi to assert political power and crush democratic reform, church leaders supported the genocide to secure their own power. The fact that Christianity inspired some Rwandans to oppose the genocide demonstrates that opposition by the churches was possible and might have hindered the violence.

Timothy Longman is director of the African Studies Center at Boston University, where he also serves as associate professor of political science. From 1996 to 2009, he served as associate professor of political science and Africana studies at Vassar College. He has also taught at the University of the Witwatersrand in Johannesburg, South Africa; the National University of Rwanda in Butare; and Drake University in Des Moines. He has served as a consultant in Rwanda, Burundi, and the Democratic Republic of Congo for USAID and the State Department, the International Center for Transitional Justice, and Human Rights Watch, for whom he served as director of the Rwanda field office 1995–1996. From 2001 to 2005, he served as a Research Fellow for the Human Rights Center at the University of California, Berkeley, directing research on social reconstruction in post-genocide Rwanda. His articles have appeared in *African Studies Review, The Journal of Religion in Africa, Journal of the American Medical Association, Comparative Education Review, Journal of Genocide Research,* and *America,* and he is currently completing a book manuscript titled *Memory, Justice, and Power in Post-Genocide Rwanda.*

AFRICAN STUDIES

The *African Studies Series*, founded in 1968, is a prestigious series of monographs, general surveys, and textbooks on Africa covering history, political science, anthropology, economics, and ecological and environmental issues. The series seeks to publish work by senior scholars as well as the best new research.

EDITORIAL BOARD

A list of books in this series will be found at the end of this volume.

Christianity and Genocide in Rwanda

TIMOTHY LONGMAN

Boston University

CAMBRIDGE UNIVERSITY PRESS
Cambridge, New York, Melbourne, Madrid, Cape Town,
Singapore, São Paulo, Delhi, Tokyo, Mexico City

Cambridge University Press
32 Avenue of the Americas, New York, NY 10013-2473, USA

www.cambridge.org
Information on this title: www.cambridge.org/9780521269537

First published 2009
Reprinted 2010 (thrice)
First paperback edition 2011

A catalog record for this publication is available from the British Library.

Library of Congress Cataloging in Publication Data

Longman, Timothy Paul.
Christianity and genocide in Rwanda / Timothy Longman.
p.   cm. – (African studies)
Includes bibliographical references and index.
ISBN 978-0-521-19139-5 (Hardback)
1. Genocide–Rwanda–History–20th century. 2. Genocide–Religious aspects–
Christianity. 3. Rwanda–History–Civil War, 1994–Atrocities. 4. Rwanda–
History–Civil War, 1994–Religious aspects. 5. Ethnic relations–Religious
aspects–Christianity. I. Title. II. Series.
DT450.435.L66 2010
967.57104'31–dc22   2009023321

ISBN 978-0-521-19139-5 Hardback
ISBN 978-0-521-26953-7 Paperback

To my parents, who have always supported me.
To Jacolijn Post and Isaac Nshimiyimana who made my
research in Rwanda possible.
To Alison Des Forges whose friendship and insight will be
deeply missed.
And to those many Rwandans who lost their lives in the
events of 1994. May your sacrifice never be forgotten.

"What we saw in this country surprised us, too. These were things commanded by the devil...."

– Hutu man, Gisovu, Kibuye

Contents

Acknowledgments

I was never supposed to have gone to Rwanda. In September 1991, with plane tickets purchased and research clearance in hand, I was two weeks away from flying to Kinshasa to spend a year researching church–state relations in Zaire, when troop rioting forced most foreign nationals to flee and made my research plans impossible. After waiting a few months to see if things might calm down in Zaire, one of my professors suggested that I consider shifting my dissertation focus to Rwanda, "a nice peaceful little country." Thus, in May 1992, after a quick crash course on Rwandan history and culture, I found myself arriving in Kigali for a year, with little inkling of the extraordinary events that were about to come crashing down around me. During the initial year that I spent studying religion and politics in Rwanda, I watched as conditions in the country declined precipitously. Though I could never have predicted the extent of the coming violence, nor that it would take an overwhelmingly ethnic rather than political form, I left Rwanda in mid-1993 quite concerned over the probability of imminent violence.

During the next several months, as I toiled away on my dissertation, news trickled in from friends and the media about deteriorating conditions in Rwanda. I was nearly halfway through writing the text when a fellow student called on the morning of April 7 to ask if I had heard that the president of Rwanda had been killed in a plane crash. Over the next weeks, my writing halted as I struggled to find out what had happened to friends and colleagues and to deal emotionally with the devastation that had befallen a country that had become so precious to me. Gradually I received information – sometimes partial, sometimes inaccurate – of friends who had been killed, some who had survived and were in exile, others who were still in Rwanda. In August, I took up a one-year teaching position at Drake University while I completed my dissertation. After defending in May 1995, I began looking for full-time academic employment, but a few months later I received a call from Alison Des Forges about my potential interest in returning to Rwanda to work in the field office of Human Rights Watch (HRW) and the International Federation of Human Rights Leagues (FIDH). While I had some trepidation about returning to Rwanda with all of the sad memories it contained, I eventually agreed, and in the fall of 1995, I headed back to Kigali. My primary task for HRW and FIDH was to conduct research on the 1994 genocide, primarily in Butare and Gikongoro, for the book _Leave None to Tell the Story_. I was also able to follow up on the three case studies that I had conducted in Butare, and Alison also allowed me to return to Kibuye, where I gathered documentary evidence in government offices and interviewed people about how the genocide took place in Kirinda and Biguhu. During the course of the year, I gradually reconnected with friends and colleagues I had known before the genocide and learned their stories of suffering and survival. When I left Rwanda again to take up a teaching position at Vassar College, I had a rich new body of data. Drawing both on my dissertation research and on the additional year of fieldwork, I worked on this book over the next several years, the completion of the text often delayed by new projects in Burundi, Congo, and Rwanda.

Having taken more than a decade to complete this book project and having undertaken two extended periods of field research, I am indebted to a large number of individuals. Jacolijn Post met me at the airport on my arrival in Kigali, provided me with a place to stay, and helped me get started on my first case study; her help, insight, and – above all – friendship, made my first year in Rwanda both successful and enjoyable in ways that would otherwise not have been possible. Through Jacolijn, I met Isaac Nshimiyimana, who became a valuable research assistant and close friend, traveling with me to conduct interviews in various parts of the country, helping me improve my Kinyarwanda, and sharing his deep insights about his country. A number of others assisted me as translators or interviewers, particularly a number of students at the Protestant Faculty of Theology in Butare. Among my colleagues at the Faculty, Rina and Marius Joosten helped me with housing, warm meals, and medical care. Fellow student researchers Jennifer Olson and Christof den Biggelaar were of great help in getting me started on research in Butare. I owe a great debt to Alison Des Forges, who allowed me to follow up on my case studies while I worked under her supervision for HRW and

FIDH. Her mentoring, insights, and inspiration over the years have been invaluable, and she is already sorely missed. The HRW/FIDH researchers and translators, JoJo and Faustin, were a great help in this second period of research. I also am grateful to Bosco Nduwimana for his assistance and friendship during this period. Anysie, Aaron, and Oswald were particularly generous in sharing their stories of survival during the genocide.

My dissertation committee, Crawford Young, Michael Schatzberg, Joanne Csete, Aili Tripp, and Booth Fowler, provided helpful guidance on the earliest versions of this manuscript. Professor David Newbury provided careful, extensive comments on a later version. I am indebted to my colleagues at Vassar College, who always provided support. I must particularly thank my parents, William and Lee Longman, for the patient support that they have provided over the years, encouraging my graduate studies and helping to fund my research. I wish to thank my partner, Tracy Keene, for his patience and support over the years.

Finally, I am indebted to the people of Butare, Save, Kirinda, Biguhu, and Kinigi for welcoming me into their communities, allowing me to observe and interview, and making me feel at home. Some individuals, like Géras Mutimura and Obed Niyonshuti, did not survive the 1994 genocide. This book owes a particular debt to them, and to the millions of other Rwandans who have suffered from war and violence.

Christianity and Genocide in Rwanda

INTRODUCTION

"People Came to Mass Each Day to Pray, Then They Went Out to Kill"

Christian Churches, Civil Society, and Genocide

The small East African state of Rwanda gained sudden international attention in the spring and summer of 1994 when an explosion of deadly violence shook the country. The death of Rwandan President Juvénal Habyarimana in a fiery plane crash on April 6, 1994, served as the pretext for a circle of powerful government and military officials to launch a long-planned offense against opponents of the regime. Within hours after Habyarimana's death, the Presidential Guard and other elite troops spread out into the capital, Kigali, with lists of opposition party leaders, human rights activists, progressive priests, journalists, and other prominent critics of the Habyarimana regime to be eliminated. During the next few weeks, government officials, soldiers, and civilian militia carried the violence into other parts of the country, focusing it more narrowly on one minority ethnic group – the Tutsi, whom regime supporters viewed as a primary threat to their continued dominance. By early July, when the remnants of the Habyarimana regime fled into exile in Zaire, the violence had devastated political and civil societies, killed as many as one million people, and almost completely annihilated the country's Tutsi minority. In a century that has known many atrocities, the genocide in Rwanda was remarkable for its intensity – more than one-tenth of the population of Rwanda was killed in only three months.[1]

---

[1] For details regarding the genocide, the definitive source is Alison Des Forges, *Leave None to Tell the Story: Genocide in Rwanda* (New York: Human Rights Watch, and Paris: Fédération Internationale des Ligues des Droits de l'Homme, 1999), written by a long-time student of Rwanda based on research by a large team of investigators, including myself. Gerard Prunier, *The Rwanda Crisis: History of a Genocide* (New York: Columbia University Press, 1995) is also useful. It is not my purpose here to enter into the debate

Rwanda is an overwhelmingly Christian country, with just under 90 percent of the population in a 1991 census claiming membership in a Catholic, Protestant, or Seventh-Day Adventist Church.[2] In the aftermath of the 1994 genocide, journalists, human rights activists, scholars, and even some church officials condemned Rwanda's Christian churches for their culpability in the shocking violence that ravaged the country.[3] Not only were the vast majority of those who participated in the killings Christians, but the church buildings themselves also served as Rwanda's primary killing fields. As African Rights claims, "more Rwandese citizens died in churches and parishes than anywhere else."[4] Organizers of the

---

over use of the term "genocide." The carnage in Rwanda clearly qualifies as genocide by even the most restricted definitions, for example, Irving Louis Horowitz, *Taking Lives: Genocide and State Power* (New Brunswick: Transaction Publishers, 1997, 4th edition). For useful critical evaluations of various definitions of genocide, see Frank Chalk and Kurt Jonassohn, *The History and Sociology of Genocide: Analyses and Case Studies* (New Haven: Yale University Press, 1990), pp. 8–32; and Helen Fein, *Genocide: A Sociological Perspective* (London and Newbury Park: SAGE, 1993), pp. 8–31.

[2] Government of Rwanda, "Recensement General de la Population et de l'Habitat au 15 Aout 1991" (Kigali, April 1994) reports that 62.6 percent of the population declared themselves Catholic, 18.8 percent Protestant, 8.4 percent Seventh-Day Adventist, 1.2 percent Muslim, and 1.1 "traditional" (p. 146).

[3] "Archbishop Carey's Visit to Rwanda: Rwanda Church Voice 'Silent' During Massacres, Carey Says," *Ecumenical News International*, May 16, 1995; Julian Bedford, "Rwanda's Churches Bloodied by Role in Genocide," *Reuters*, October 18, 1994; Jean Damascène Bizimana, '*Église et le Génocide au Rwanda: Les Pères Blancs et le Négationnisme*, Paris: L'Harmattan, 2001; Raymond Bonner, "Clergy in Rwanda is Accused of Abetting Atrocities: French Church Gives Refuge to One Priest," *The New York Times*, July 7, 1995, p. A3; "Churches in the Thick of Rwandan Violence," *The Christian Century*, November 8, 1995, pp. 1041–2; Joshua Hammer, "Blood on the Altar: Rwanda: What Did You Do in the War Father?," *Newsweek*, September 4, 1995, p. 36; Gary Haugen, "Rwanda's Carnage: Survivors Describe How Churches Provided Little Protection in the Face of Genocide," *Christianity Today*, February 6, 1995, p. 52; Lindsey Hilsum, *Rwanda: The Betrayal*, Blackstone Films, Channel 4; Donatella Lorch, "The Rock that Crumbled: The Church in Rwanda," *The New York Times*, October 17, 1994, p. A4; Tom Ndahiro, "The Church's Blind Eye to Genocide in Rwanda," in Carol Rittner et al., *Genocide in Rwanda: Complicity of the Churches?* St. Paul: Paragon House, 2004; Thomas O'Hara, "Rwandan Bishops Faltered in Face of Crisis," *National Catholic Reporter*, September 29, 1995; Faustin Rutembesa, Jean-Pierre Karegeye, and Paul Rutayisire, *Rwanda: L'Église catholique à l'épreuve du génocide*, Greenfield Park: Les Editions Africana, 2000; Wolfgang Schonecke, "The Role of the Church in Rwanda," *America*, June 17, 1995; Dominique Sigaud, "Genocide: le dossier noir de l'Eglise rwandaise," *Le Nouvel Observateur*, February 1–7, 1996, pp. 50–1; "Sin and Confession in Rwanda," *The Economist*, January 14, 1995, p. 39; Henri Tincq, "Le fardeau rwandais de Jean Paul II, *Le monde*, May 23, 1996; Alan Zarembo, "The Church's Shameful Acts: Many Rwandans Refuse to Return to Sanctuaries Where Blood Was Spilled," *Houston Chronicle*, January 29, 1995.

[4] African Rights, *Rwanda: Death, Despair, and Defiance*, revised edition (London: African Rights, 1995), p. 865.

genocide exploited the historic concept of sanctuary to lure tens of thousands of Tutsi into church buildings with false promises of protection; then Hutu militia and soldiers systematically slaughtered the unfortunate people who had sought refuge, firing guns and tossing grenades into the crowds gathered in church sanctuaries and school buildings, and methodically finishing off survivors with machetes, pruning hooks, and knives.

In Nyakizu commune in the far south of Rwanda, for example, after instigating massacres along the Burundi border to prevent Tutsi from fleeing the country, the burgomaster (leader of the local government) traveled through the commune to encourage local Tutsi, as well as the thousands of refugees from violence in neighboring communes who were passing through Nyakizu, to gather at the Roman Catholic parish of Cyahinda, promising to protect them as Tutsi had been protected in the church from ethnic attacks in the 1960s. The burgomaster subsequently personally supervised gendarmes and civilian militia who surrounded the parish complex and, over a four-day period, systematically slaughtered more than 20,000 people. The church sanctuary, the last building to be attacked, still bears the marks of bullets and grenades and the stains of blood and brains on its floors and walls. According to local officials, 17,000 bodies were exhumed from one set of latrines beside the church, only one of several mass graves at the site.[5] Research by Human Rights Watch, African Rights, and other groups suggests similar numbers killed at parishes throughout the country.[6]

The involvement of the churches, however, went far beyond the passive use of church buildings as death chambers. In some communities, clergy, catechists, and other church employees used their knowledge of the local population to identify Tutsi for elimination. In other cases, church personnel actively participated in the killing. The International War Crimes Tribunal for Rwanda convicted Elizaphan Ntakirutimana, a pastor in the Seventh-Day Adventist Church, for encouraging Tutsi to assemble at his church in Kibuye Prefecture, then leading to the church a convoy of soldiers and civilian militia, who slaughtered some 8,000 Tutsi.[7] In April 1998, a Rwandan court condemned to death two Catholic

---

[5] The information in this paragraph is based on interviews I and several other researchers conducted in Nyakizu in 1995 and 1996 under the auspices of Human Rights Watch. For a more detailed discussion of events in Nyakizu see Des Forges, *Leave None to Tell the Story*, pp. 353–431, the two chapters that I drafted for the book.

[6] African Rights, *Death, Despair, and Defiance*, pp. 258–572.

[7] Marlise Simons, "Rwandan Pastor and His Son Are Convicted of Genocide," *New York Times*, February 20, 2003.

priests, Jean-François Kayiranga and Eduoard Nkurikiye, for luring people to Nyange parish, where soldiers and militia subsequently massacred them, then bringing in a bulldozer to demolish the church and bury alive any survivors.[8] Prosecutors in Rwanda have accused Father Wenceslas Munyeshyaka, the curé of Sainte Famille parish in Kigali, of turning over to death squads Tutsi who had sought refuge in his church. Survivors report that Munyeshyaka wore a flack jacket and carried a pistol and that he helped to select out sympathizers of the Rwandan Patriotic Front to be killed. According to some witnesses, he offered protection to women and girls who would sleep with him and turned over to death squads those who refused his advances.[9]

In my own research, I discovered similar stories. For example, a Tutsi woman who worked at a Catholic primary school in Kaduha parish in Gikongoro Prefecture testified that her priest, Robert Nyandwe, had himself come to take her out of hiding and turn her over to a death squad:

The priest, Nyandwe, came to my house. My husband [who is Hutu] was not there. Nyandwe asked my children, "Where is she?" They said that I was sick. He came into the house, entering even into my bedroom. He said, "Come! I will hide you, because there is an attack." …He said "I'll take you to the CND." He grabbed me by the arm and took me by force. He dragged me out into the street, and we started to go by foot toward the church. But arriving on the path, I saw a huge crowd. There were many people, wearing banana leaves, carrying machetes. I broke free from him and ran. I went to hide in the home of a friend. He wanted to turn me over to the crowd that was preparing to attack the church. It was he who prevented people from leaving the church.[10]

National church leaders were slow to speak publicly, and they never condemned the genocide, instead calling on church members to support the new regime that was carrying out the killing. Based on the past close collaboration of church leaders with the organizers of the genocide and their failure to address specifically the massacres of Tutsi, many church members concluded that the church leaders endorsed the killing.[11] Believing that their actions were consistent with the teachings of their

---

[8] Emmanuel Goujon, "Two Rwandan Priests Given Death Sentences over Rwanda Genocide," Agence France Presse, April 18, 1998; "Priests Sentenced to Death for Rwanda Massacre," Associated Press, April 20, 1998.

[9] Bonner, "Clergy in Rwanda Is Accused of Abetting Atrocities"; Hammer, "Blood on the Altar."

[10] From interview conducted in Kaduha by the author on June 12, 1996, in French and Kinyarwanda.

[11] Des Forges, *Leave None to Tell the Story*, pp. 245–6.

churches, the death squads in some communities held mass before going out to kill. In Ngoma parish in Butare, a Tutsi priest who was hidden in the sanctuary by his fellow Hutu priests reported to me that, "People came and demanded that my fellow priest reopen the church and hold mass. People came to mass each day to pray, then they went out to kill."[12] In some cases militia members apparently paused in the frenzy of killing to kneel and pray at the altar.[13] According to a report by a World Council of Churches team that visited Rwanda in August 1994, "In every conversation we had with the government and church people alike, the point was brought home to us that the church itself stands tainted, not by passive indifference, but by errors of commission as well."[14]

Apologists for the churches have responded to accusations of church complicity in various ways. The official Catholic response has denied institutional responsibility, blaming the participation of Christians in the genocide on individual sinfulness. In a 1996 letter, Pope John Paul II stated that participation in the genocide was clearly against church teachings, and thus clergy and other Christians who participated were personally culpable, without implicating the wider church. According to the pope, "The church itself cannot be held responsible for the misdeeds of its members who have acted against evangelical law."[15] Father André Sibomana, who himself offers a number of criticisms of the Catholic Church, offers a similar defense. "I don't accept the language of generalization which states that the Roman Catholic Church participated in the genocide.... It is not the Church as such which is called into question, but its members."[16]

Others have emphasized the mixed response of the churches to ethnic violence, countering the examples of involvement by some clergy and church leaders with examples of bravery and resistance by others. These authors pointed out that, although the Catholic and Anglican archbishops strongly supported the regime that carried out the genocide, other people

---

[12] Interview conducted by the author March 26, 1996, in Ngoma in French.

[13] This claim, made by Laurient Ntezimana in Lindsey Hilsum's documentary on the churches and the genocide, *Rwanda: The Betrayal* (London: Blackstone Pictures, 1996), was corroborated by other Rwandans with whom I spoke.

[14] "Rwandan Churches Culpable, Says WCC," *The Christian Century*, August 24–31, 1994, p. 778.

[15] "Pope Says Church Is Not to Blame in Rwanda," *New York Times*, March 21, 1996, p. A3.

[16] André Sibomana, *Hope for Rwanda: Conversations with Laure Guilbert and Hervé Deguine* (London: Pluto Press, and Dar es Salaam: Mkuki na Nyota Publishers, 1999), p. 123.

in the churches were actively involved in the democracy movement that emerged to challenge the regime in the early 1990s. The Catholic newspaper *Kinyamateka* played an important role in criticizing governmental corruption and helped to spark an explosion of free press, while the paper's editor, Father Sibomana, was among a number of Catholic and Protestant leaders who became involved in founding a Rwandan human rights movement. The president of the Catholic conference of bishops, Thadée Nsengiyumva, frustrated at his fellow bishops' quiescence, published an open letter in 1991 not only condemning human rights abuses and ethnic violence and calling for multiparty democracy, but also criticizing the churches for their refusal to show leadership. In November 1993, the Catholic bishop of Nyundo publicly condemned the distribution of arms to civilians, an early preparation for the genocide. The churches themselves had a large number of Tutsi priests and pastors, and during the genocide many clergy were killed. According to Ian Linden, emphasizing the role of church people who supported the genocide gives an unbalanced portrait of the churches:

And it would be a simple matter to attempt to balance the record by itemising the many incidents of martyrdom, heroic self-sacrifice, courage and the kind of stubborn unwillingness to take the easy way out and deny their faith.... The death toll of Church leaders, bishops, priests, ministers, and sisters was very high, between a quarter and a third of leadership. This is mostly to be explained by the way Tutsi people had not been blocked from advancement in the Churches as they had been in the rest of society, and their disproportionate presence amongst the clergy.... But a great number of Hutu Church leaders also died opposing the massacres or were killed as intellectual opponents of the Habyarimana regime.[17]

According to the new archbishop of Kigali, Thadée Ntihinyurwa, "Perhaps some priests behaved badly, but we have not carefully figured accounts; I deny the global responsibility of the institution." As an editorial in the Catholic journal *Tablet* states, if the church was complicit, it was also a Church of martyrs.[18] If the church itself suffered in the genocide, the reasoning goes, how could it be truly complicit?

A third defense of the churches emphasizes institutional weaknesses that rendered them incapable of opposing the genocide. According to this argument, the churches were themselves deeply divided along ethnic, regional,

---

[17] Ian Linden, "The Churches and Genocide: Lessons from the Rwandan Tragedy," *The Month*, July 1995, 28, pp. 256–63, citation pp. 261, 263.
[18] "The martyrs of Rwanda," *The Tablet*, June 25, 1994, p. 791.

and ideological lines, creating a "fragmented" religious authority, unable to speak publicly on issues of national importance. As Linden states,

By the early 1990s the Church had no recourse against a propaganda machine that preached exclusive Hutu identity defined over and against the threat of a Tutsi invader, and, indeed, defined being Hutu ultimately as being the killer of Tutsis....It was hopelessly divided at a leadership level as well as parish level.[19]

Saskia Van Hoyweghen claimed that this fragmentation arises from the minimal impact that Christianity has had on Rwandan society. Despite the high rates of conversion and the magnitude of the churches' presence in Rwanda, they lacked "intensive" power, having attracted many members for social and economic reasons without significantly shaping their beliefs. "One should not therefore be blinded by the strong side of the Church, namely its omnipresence in Rwandese social and economic life. We have to look behind membership statistics; the accounts of mass baptisms have no meaning as such."[20] Drawing on Mbembe,[21] Van Hoywegen suggested that the churches have reflected rather than shaped Rwandan society, as Christian symbols have been adapted to Rwandan culture. "[T]here are plenty of indications to suggest that despite the powerful outlook of the Church, the re-appropriation of Catholic symbols has always fermented uncontrolled."[22] The implication of this argument is that Christianity bears no responsibility for the genocide, because at base Rwandan society was not truly Christian. Agatha Radoli, a Catholic sister writing in the preface to a book called, *The Rwanda Genocide and the Call to Deepen Christianity in Africa*, makes a similar claim:

If Rwanda, a country where 70% of the people claimed to be Christians, exhibited such an unchristian attitude in time of crisis then Christ's message of love and fellowship has fallen on deaf ears completely. In spite of a century of evangelization, Christianity has not taken root in Rwanda and many other parts of Africa.[23]

---

[19] Linden, "The Churches and Genocide," p. 262.
[20] Saskia Van Hoyweghen, "The Disintegration of the Catholic Church of Rwanda: A Study of the Fragmentation of Political Religious Authority," *African Affairs*, July 1996, 95, no. 380, pp. 379–402. Van Hoyweghen surprisingly cites my own work in this section implying agreement with this argument.
[21] Achille Mbembe, *Afrique Indocile* (Paris: Karthala, 1988).
[22] Van Hoyweghen, "The Disintegation of the Catholic Church in Rwanda."
[23] Agatha Radoli, "Preface" in Mario I. Aguilar, *The Rwanda Crisis and the Call to Deepen Christianity in Africa* (Nairobi: AMECEA Gaba Publications, 1998), Spearhead Nos. 148–50, p. viii.

As I demonstrate in this book, contrary to the claims of their defenders, the complicity of Rwanda's Christian churches in the 1994 genocide was profound, going well beyond the actions of a few individuals. An analysis of the historical role of Christianity in Rwanda reveals that, far from simply adapting to and reflecting Rwandan society, the churches actively shaped the ethnic and political realities that made genocide possible by acting to define and politicize ethnicity, legitimizing authoritarian regimes, and encouraging public obedience to political authorities. Since by any measure of participation and personal piety, Rwandans were devout and active believers, who, although not necessarily renouncing indigenous religious beliefs, nevertheless accepted many of the principles of Christian faith, Christian involvement in the genocide cannot reasonably be attributed to insufficient conversion. Rather, something in the nature of Christianity in Rwanda made it unable or unwilling to restrain genocide. The Christian message received in Rwanda was not one of "love and fellowship," but one of obedience, division, and power. Far from exonerating the churches, the resistance that some Christians presented to the genocide – and my own research indicates that a number of people were indeed inspired by their faith to challenge authoritarianism and oppose ethnic violence – demonstrates that the churches potentially *could* have opposed the genocide. If the churches were, as I contend, powerful and influential institutions that were in fact being pressured from within and without to take a stand against authoritarianism and ethnic violence, why, then, were they so deeply inculpated in the genocide? It is this question that I hope to resolve in the course of this book.

GENOCIDE AND RELIGION

That the Christian churches in Rwanda should be implicated in genocide is, of course, not exceptional. Religious institutions have unfortunately been involved in a number of shameful acts, including genocides, in which they provided both ideological and institutional support for those seeking to scapegoat vulnerable minorities. The long history of anti-Semitism among Christians in Europe, dating back to the Roman era and inspiring repeated massacres and expulsions from countries, created the preconditions for genocide against Jews and provided the ideological background for the Nazi doctrines of racial supremacy. Anti-Semitism practiced by Christians in Europe implicated Jews as the killers of Christ, in league with the devil, and as child murderers who poisoned wells and degraded society.[24]

Though Nazi leaders were themselves often hostile to Germany's Christian churches, Christianity nevertheless provided ideological support that made the Holocaust possible. As Doris Bergen contended, "[I]t would be inaccurate and misleading to present the Christian legacy of hostility toward Judaism and Jews as a sufficient cause for Nazi genocide. Christianity, however, did play a critical role, not perhaps in motivating top decision makers, but in making their commands comprehensible and tolerable."[25] Most Christians in Germany did not go as far in seeking to reconcile Christianity with National Socialism as the German Christian movement, a radical anti-Semitic faction that gained control of the Protestant churches in 1930s,[26] but the leadership of the major Christian denominations supported the Nazi regime and assisted in the process of genocide by, for example, supplying baptismal records that by exclusion helped identify Jews. The Vatican signed a Concordat with Hitler shortly after his rise to power in 1933, and although the German Catholic bishops challenged the regime on specific issues, such as eugenics, they, like their Protestant counterparts, maintained cordial relations with the regime until the end of the war and never spoke out against the Holocaust.[27]

Christian churches played a particularly important role in supporting the identification, isolation, and deportation of Jews in a number of countries under German occupation during World War II. In Croatia,

---

[24] See Richard L. Rubenstein and John K. Roth, *Approaches to Auschwitz: The Holocaust and Its Legacy* (Atlanta: John Knox Press, 1987), pp. 23–89; John G. Gager, *The Origins of Anti-Semitism: Attitudes Toward Judaism in Pagan and Christian Antiquity* (Oxford: Oxford University Press, 1983); Henry Zuiker, "The Essential 'Other' and the Jew: From Antisemitism to Genocide," *Social Research*, 63, no. 4 (Winter 1996): 1110–1154; Helmut Walser Smith, "Religion and Conflict: Protestants, Catholics, and Anti-Semitism in the State of Baden in the Era of Wilhelm II," *Central European History*, 27, no. 3 (Summer 1995): 283–314.

[25] Doris L. Bergen, "Catholics, Protestants, and Christian Antisemitism in Nazi Germany," *Central European History*, 27, no. 3 (Summer 1995): 329–349, citation p. 329.

[26] Doris L. Bergen, *Twisted Cross: The German Christian Movement in the Third Reich* (Chapel Hill: The University of North Carolina Press, 1996).

[27] Guenter Lewy, *The Catholic Church and Nazi Germany* (New York: McGraw Hill, 1964); Gordon C. Zahn, *German Catholics and Hitler's Wars: A Study in Social Control* (New York: Sheed and Ward, 1962); George Zahn, "Catholic Resistance? A Yes and a No," in Franklin H. Littell and Hubert G. Locke, *The German Church Struggle and the Holocaust* (Detroit: Wayne State University Press, 1974), pp. 203–37; Bergen, "Catholics, Protestants, and Christian Antisemitism."

after World War I, Catholic priests pushed for an independent Croatian state, equating Croatian nationalism with Catholicism.[28] Church leaders embraced the independent Croatian state created by the Germans and Italians after their occupation, and they enthusiastically supported persecution of Jews.[29] Catholic involvement in the murder of Jews, as well as Serbs, was not limited to ideological support, as a number of priests were active in the nationalist movement and nearly half of Croatia's extermination camps were headed by priests. The Vatican was repeatedly informed of the atrocities occurring in Croatia, but refused to condemn them, at one point responding to evidence of crimes that they "are the work of the Communists, but maliciously attributed to the Catholics."[30] Catholics played a similar role in Slovakia, where a priest founded and led the main nationalist party, which regularly employed anti-Semitic rhetoric, and another priest became head of state after the Germans created a Slovakian state. A number of priests served in the Slovak parliament, and all voted in favor of the deportation of Slovakia's Jews.[31]

In the Ottoman Empire as well, religion served as a basis of solidarity for the majority population and a means of singling out minorities, ultimately serving to justify genocide. Although officially Islamic, the Ottoman Empire formally recognized certain rights for non-Muslim "people of the book," the "tolerated infidels." While Muslims were governed by Islamic law, Jews and two Christian communities – Orthodox and Armenian – were organized in separate *millets*, distinct religious communities that were allowed a degree of autonomy, but that paid special taxes and did not enjoy full citizenship rights. As the Ottoman Empire became increasingly weak in the late 1800s, Greek, Romanian, Serbian, and Bulgarian nationalist movements fought successfully for independence, while a nationalist movement emerged among Armenians. A nationalist movement emerged among Turkish Muslims as well, who sought to convert the Ottoman Empire from a multiethnic empire into a nation-state, based on Islam and the Turkish language. As Christians and non-Turkish speakers, Armenians by their existence challenged Turkish nationalist

---

[28] According to Menachem Shelah, even before the war, "clergy taught Croatian nationalism to the faithful, telling them that it was identical with Catholicism." Shelah, "The Catholic Church in Croatia, the Vatican and the Murder of Croatian Jews," *Holocaust and Genocide Studies*, 4, no. 3, (1989): 323–339.

[29] Shelah, "The Catholic Church in Croatia," p. 327.

[30] Helen Fein, *Accounting for Genocide: National Responses and Jewish Victimization during the Holocaust* (New York: The Free Press, 1979), pp. 102–5, quotation p. 104.

[31] Fein, *Accounting for Genocide*, pp. 99–102.

ideologies, and with the Armenian homeland situated as it was in the midst of the Turkish-speaking and Muslim populations of the Ottoman and Russian Empires, Turkish nationalists regarded the Armenians as a threat to their aspirations for a pan-Turkic nation.[32]

During World War I, as Russia threatened to advance on its eastern border, the Ottoman government, dominated by Young Turks, decided to eliminate the Armenian threat by moving the entire Armenian population to the Syrian desert. Beginning in April 1915, Ottoman police and troops arrested Armenians, including those who did not live in the supposedly vulnerable border area. They killed many outright, while thousands of others died en route to or after arriving at the concentration camps. The identification of Armenians as infidels, already used to motivate massacres in the 1890s, made the Armenians an effective scapegoat for the struggling Ottoman state and garnered public support and participation for the massacres and deportations.[33]

More recently, religion has served as an important factor in the conflicts in the former Yugoslavia. Serbian ethno-nationalist rhetoric identified Slavic Muslims, who are today concentrated in the state of Bosnia-Herzegovina and the Kosovo region of Yugoslavia, as traitors who allied themselves with the Turkish conquerors. Serbian myths hold the Muslims responsible for the death of Serbia's historic hero, Prince Lazar, in a 1389 battle with the Ottoman Empire that marked the end of Serb independence. As Michael Sells writes, "Christoslavism – the premise that Slavs are by essence Christian and that conversion to another religion is a betrayal of the people or race – was critical to the genocidal ideology being developed in 1989."[34] The ideology that defined Muslims as "other" served as justification for Serbs and Croats to slaughter Muslims and to drive hundreds of thousands from their homes in Bosnia in 1992–93

---

[32] Robert Melson, *Revolution and Genocide: On the Origins of the Armenian Genocide and the Holocaust* (Chicago: The University of Chicago Press, 1992), pp. 43–69, 141–70; Erik J. Zürcher, *Turkey: A Modern History* (London: IB Taurus and Company, 1993), pp. 75–137; Fein, *Accounting for Genocide*, pp. 3–30; Arnold J. Toynbee, "A Summary of Armenian History Up to and Including 1915," in Viscount J. Bryce, *The Treatment of Armenians in the Ottoman Empire: Documents Presented to Viscount Grey of Falloda, Secretary of State for Foreign Affairs* (London: H.M.S.O., 1916), pp. 593–653. Bryce offers an exhaustive collection of documents regarding the Armenian genocide, a notable early example of a human rights report.

[33] Ibid.

[34] Michael A. Sells, *The Bridge Betrayed: Religion and Genocide in Bosnia* (Berkeley: University of California Press, 1996), p. 51.

and later led to the expulsion of more than a million Albanian-speaking Muslims from Kosovo.

In Africa, religious institutions also have a long record of supporting authoritarian governments that, even if they did not carry out genocide, have oppressed their populations and fostered or engaged in ethnic discrimination and violence. Christian missions were an integral part of the "colonial project," promoting Western culture while undermining indigenous cultural systems. They often developed close and cooperative working relationships with colonial authorities and remained silent or even openly supported colonial repression, torture, displacement of peoples, and other violations of fundamental human rights.[35] Since independence, religious institutions have remained major political and economic players in most African countries, commonly working in close collaboration with the state. The shared material and institutional interests of state and religious institutions are reinforced by close personal relationships between religious leaders and government officials. Religious institutions have provided important legitimization to many autocratic rulers and have generally encouraged obedience to authority rather than standing up for the rights of oppressed populations.[36]

Rather than challenging the ethnic divisiveness that has led to bloodshed in many African countries, churches have commonly reflected ethnic divisions. In the Democratic Republic of Congo (formerly Zaire), for example, the ability of the Catholic Church to challenge the state has been impeded by ethnic conflict within the church.[37] In Tanzania, even as ethnic conflict has been limited within the state sphere, the Lutheran Church has been deeply divided by ethnic competition.[38] In Burundi, which has

---

[35] C.f., Jeff Haynes, *Religion and Politics in Africa* (London: Zed Books, 1996), pp. 23–52; Goran Hyden, "Religion, Politics, and the Crisis in Africa," *UFSI Reports*, 1986, no. 18, pp. 2–3. Cases such as King Leopold's Congo where missionaries defended the human rights of local populations were rare. Adam Hochschild, *King Leopold's Ghost: A Story of Greed Terror, and Heroism in Colonial Africa* (New York: Houghton Mifflin, 1998).

[36] Jean-François Bayart, "Les Églises chrétiennes et la politique du ventre: le partage du gâteau ecclésial," *Politique Africaine*, no. 35 (October 1989): 3–26; Reginald Herbold Green, "Christianity and Political economy in Africa," *The Ecumenical Review*, 30 (1978): 3–17. After reviewing relations between mainstream religious groups and governments throughout Africa, Haynes, in *Religion and Politics in Africa*, concludes that, "the normal role of mainstream religious hierarchies is to support the government of the day" (p. 102).

[37] Timothy Longman, "Congo: A Tale of Two Churches," *America*, April 2, 2001, pp. 12–13.

[38] Catherine Baroin, "Religious Conflict in 1990–1993 Among the Rwa: Secession in a Lutheran Diocese in Northern Tanzania," *African Affairs*, 95 (1996): 529–54.

strong historic and cultural ties with Rwanda, the churches remained silent even after ethnic massacres killed 200,000 in 1972. As in many other countries, in Burundi church leaders such as Catholic and Anglican bishops have been named disproportionately from the same ethnic group as the president and other political officials.[39]

Given the number of genocides and ethnic massacres carried out in the name of God[40] – and the long and inauspicious history of specifically Christian support for bigotry and violence, ranging from the Crusades to slavery to missionary involvement in the colonial project – one might justifiably question whether explaining church involvement in the Rwandan genocide is in fact necessary. Perhaps religious belief and practice are predisposed toward exclusiveness and the type of fanaticism that supports communal violence and genocide. This assumption, however, is refuted by the cases in which religious groups have opposed authoritarian governments, ethnic violence, and genocide. In an extensive statistical analysis of factors that explain the divergent levels of participation in the Holocaust in various countries occupied by Germany during World War II, Helen Fein found that religious opposition was key in the lower levels of Jewish victimization in Belgium, Romania, Bulgaria, Athens, France, Italy, and Denmark. According to Fein's findings:

Where the state or native administrative bureaucracy began to cooperate [with Nazi Germany], church resistance was critical in inhibiting obedience to authority, legitimating subversion and/or checking collaboration directly. Church protest proved to be the single element present in every instance in which state collaboration was arrested – as in Bulgaria, France, and Rumania. Church protest was absent in virtually all cases in which state cooperation was not arrested. Church protest was also the intervening variable most highly related to the immediacy of social defense movements that enabled Jews successfully to evade deportation. The majority of Jews evaded deportation in every state occupied by or allied with Germany in which the head of the dominant church spoke out *publicly* against

---

[39] Philippe Chamay, "L'Eglise au Burundi: un conflit peut en cacher un autre," *Etudes* 266, 2 (February 1987): 159–70; Ephraim Radner, "African Politics and the Will to Silence," *The Christian Century* (November 7, 1984): 1034–8; André Guichaoua, *Les Crises Politiques au Burundi et au Rwanda (1993–1994)*, Lille: Université des Sciences et Technologies de Lille, 1995, p. 750; Christian Thibon, "La démocratisation en crise: Les occasions manquées de l'Eglise catholique au Burundi," in François Constantin et Christian Coulon, eds., *Religion et transition démocratique en Afrique* (Paris: Karthala, 1997), pp. 337–61.

[40] For an overview of religious involvement in genocides, see Omer Bartov and Phyllis Mack, eds., *In the Name of God: Genocide in the Twentieth Century* (New York and Oxford: Berghahn Books, 2001).

deportation before or as soon as it began....The greater the church resistance, the fewer Jews became victims.[41]

The role of religion in Africa is similarly more complex than the history of close cooperation between states and religious institutions might suggest. In recent years, religious groups have become a key source of opposition to authoritarian governments in a number of countries, and in some places they have increasingly organized against ethnic violence and division.[42] The involvement of Christian church leaders such as Anglican Archbishop Desmond Tutu and Reformed Church leader Allen Boesak in the anti-apartheid movement in South Africa is well known.[43] Religious opposition was key to the successful replacement of authoritarian rulers in Zambia, Benin, Congo, Kenya, and Malawi, and even where power has not changed hands, as in Cameroon, religious groups have been key in pressuring governments to accept reforms.[44] Catholic church leaders became an important source of opposition to President Mobutu in Zaire, and in interviews I conducted in April 1996 with refugees from anti-Tutsi violence in Eastern Zaire, a number of refugees claimed that church personnel had protected them and helped them escape. Tutsi refugees reported that in several locations Hutu priests had barred the doors of their churches to death squads, claiming that they could not kill in a church and, in at least one case, paying the mob to leave.[45]

Even where religious institutions and leaders have allied themselves with authoritarian governments and racist ideologies, they generally face dissent from within their own faith communities. Members of Germany's "Confessing Church," although not necessarily opposed to the Hitler regime, fought efforts to give the Nazi state primacy over the

---

[41] Fein, *Accounting for Genocide*, p. 67.

[42] Paul Gifford, "Some Recent Developments in African Christianity," *African Affairs*, 93 (1994): 513–534; J.N.K. Mugambi, "African Churches in Social Transformation," *Journal of International Affairs*, 50, no. 1 (Summer 1996): 194–221.

[43] C.f., Peter Walsh, *Prophetic Christianity and the Liberation Movement in South Africa* (Pietermaritzburg: Cluster Publications, 1995); Tristan Anne Borer, *Challenging the State: Churches as Political Actors in South Africa, 1980–1994* (South Bend, IN: University of Notre Dame Press, 1998).

[44] C.f., Paul Gifford, ed., *The Christian Churches and the Democratisation of Africa* (Leiden: E.J. Brill, 1995); Haynes, *Religion and Politics in Africa*.

[45] See the report that I wrote for Human Rights Watch and the Fédération Internationale des Ligues des Droits de l'Homme, "Zaire: Forced to Flee: Violence Against the Tutsis in Zaire," Human Rights Watch Short Report. New York: Human Rights Watch, 8, no. 2 (A), July 1996.

Protestant churches.[46] Although the number of German Christians who actively resisted the Nazi regime was quite small, resistance by people such as Dietrich Bonhoeffer, Ewald van Kleist-Schmenzin, and Friedrich Siegmund-Schultze nevertheless clearly was inspired by religious faith. Groups such as the Catholic resistance circle in Berlin worked to save Jews, despite the lack of support from the church hierarchy. In fact, many of those recognized as "Righteous Gentiles," non-Jews who saved Jewish lives in Germany and other countries occupied by or allied with Germany, often risking their own lives, acted out of a belief that their religious obligations required them to oppose genocide.[47]

The facts that religious institutions have in some cases opposed genocidal violence and that even where religious leaders support genocide and opposition is hazardous, religious belief may still serve as an important reason for some people to resist bigotry and violence suggests the degree to which the involvement of religious institutions in genocide is contentious. Hence, why religious institutions become allied with authoritarian governments and implicated in ethnic violence and genocide, far from being inevitable, demands explanation and warrants serious investigation. As research such as Fein's demonstrates, the involvement or resistance of religious institutions in genocide can have a profound impact on the success or failure of genocidal movements. By explaining why Christian churches in Rwanda became so deeply implicated in the genocide, I hope to further the understanding of the factors and conditions that encourage and allow religious institutions to oppose authoritarianism, violence, and institutionalized bigotry.

The involvement of Christian churches in the genocide in Rwanda demands explanation for another reason as well. As discussed in subsequent chapters, the 1994 genocide in Rwanda resembles the Holocaust

---

[46] Robert P. Ericksen, "A Radical Minority: Resistance in the German Protestant Church," in Francis R. Nicosia and Lawrence D. Stokes, eds., *Germans Against Nazism: Nonconformity, Opposition and Resistance in the Third Reich* (New York: Berg, 1990), pp. 115–35; Bergen, *Twisted Cross.*

[47] Peter Hoffman, "Problems of Resistance in National Socialist Germany," in Franklin H. Littell and Hubert G. Locke, eds., *The German Church Struggle and the Holocaust* (San Francisco: Mellen Research University Press, 1990), pp. 97–113; John S. Conway, "Between Pacifism and Patriotism – A Protestant Dilemma: The Case of Friedrich Siegmund-Schultze," in Nicosia and Stokes, *Germans Against Nazism*, pp. 87–113; Michael Phayer, "The Catholic Resistance Circle in Berlin and German Catholic Bishops during the Holocaust," *Holocaust and Genocide Studies*, 7, no. 2, fall 1993, 216–29; Rubenstein and Roth, *Approaches to Auschwitz*, pp. 199–228; Ericksen, "A Radical Minority."

and the genocides of Armenians and Bosnian Muslims in many ways, but the Rwandan case differs from these other genocides – and from the violence among Hindus, Muslims, and Sikhs in South Asia, between Christians and Muslims in Lebanon, and against the Christian and animist minority in Sudan – on one key point: In Rwanda, religion did not serve as an ascriptive identifier to demarcate a social group as an essential "other." Although, as I argue, Christian churches were deeply implicated in the genocide, religious affiliation did not coincide with ethnic identity. Both Catholic and Protestant churches were multiethnic, and the genocide in Rwanda occurred within religious communities. Hutu who attacked the churches where Tutsi sought refuge were themselves often members of the very churches they attacked, and in a number of cases, Tutsi priests and pastors were killed by their own parishioners. The question thus arises over why religious identity failed to inhibit ethnic massacres. Why, in other words, did loyalty to their church and to their fellow believers not prevent Catholics from killing fellow Catholics and Protestants from killing fellow Protestants?

CHURCHES AND CIVIL SOCIETY

To understand why Christian churches in Rwanda failed to impede public participation in genocide requires a complex analysis of churches as institutions. In discussing church and society or church and state, social scientists commonly speak of "*the* Church" in a given country, as if Christians were unified in a single, coherent religious organization clearly distinct from "the State." Although this may be good theology, reflecting the belief that God acts on Earth through a single, universal Church that unites all Christian believers,[48] it is bad social science, ignoring not only the confessional divisions between Catholic and Protestant churches, but also the divisions – which in the Rwandan case I argue are more significant – within each confession.

The vast majority of works on the social and political engagement of Christian churches focus on the highest levels of church hierarchies, looking at the official declarations and activities of bishops and other leaders

---

[48] St. Augustine of Hippo, for example, describes the Church as the heavenly community of which Christ is the head. The earthly institutional church, while merely a reflection of this invisible Church, was founded by Christ himself, and stands indivisible, encompassing diversity of cultures and nations, uniting the elect across the globe. C.f., Herbert A. Deane, *The Political and Social Ideas of St. Augustine* (New York: Columbia University Press, 1963).

of a church and assuming that they represent the entire church.[49] While national church leaders certainly possess significant influence and power, wielding considerable moral authority and maintaining substantial control over their churches through the power to hire and fire and to distribute funds, drawing conclusions about an entire church from the actions and statements of the leadership exaggerates the coherence of churches as institutions. A mere recitation of the sermons, official letters, and other statements of church leaders ultimately says very little about the engagement of churches in society, because it ignores the degree to which these declarations are known and accepted by church members and says nothing about their real impact on the society.[50]

Churches are, I contend, diffuse organizations that contain under their institutional umbrellas a wide range of groups and individuals only nominally controlled by their superiors. While according to church polity (particularly in the more ecclesiastical churches such as the Roman Catholic and Anglican churches), national and international church leaders officially represent their churches, standing at the pinnacle of neatly organized hierarchies, in actual practice, much happens in the churches that is not within the control of church leaders and may in some cases be in direct contradiction of official policy. Each level of the church hierarchies – international, national, regional, and local – acts with considerable autonomy, while many groups that fall under the church umbrella, such as Catholic religious orders, informal pietistic movements, and national or regional youth and women's associations, do not fit neatly into the hierarchical structure. To contend that churches are diffuse institutions is not to suggest that they are chaotic, but rather to argue that gaining a more complete picture of how the churches relate to their societies and states requires a complex, multileveled analysis that explores how the various groups and individuals acting in the name of any church connect to one

---

[49] This is particularly true in African studies. C.f., Jean-François Bayart, "La Fonction Politique des Eglises au Cameroun," *Revue Française de Science Politique*, 23, no. 3 (June 1973): 514–36; Adrian Hastings, "Christianity and Revolution," *African Affairs*, 74 (July 1975): 347–61; Haynes, *Religion and Politics in Africa*; Hyden, "Religion, Politics, and the Crisis in Africa;" Richard Joseph, "The Christian Churches and Democracy in Contemporary Africa," in John Witte, ed., *Christianity and Democracy in Global Context* (Boulder: Westview, 1993), pp. 231–47; J. S. Pobee, *Religion and Politics in Ghana: A Case Study in the Acheampong Era, 1972–1979* (Accra: Ghana Universities Press, 1992).

[50] Michael Schatzberg, *Political Legitimacy in Middle Africa: Father, Family, Food*, Bloomington: Indiana University Press, 2001, makes a strong case for viewing both church and state as institutions that are neither monolithic nor distinctly separated, c.f., pp. 71–101.

another and how power is organized and authority exercised within the churches. A brief discussion of the concept of civil society as a location of political contestation between society's weak and powerful can help lay a framework for this analysis.

The concept of civil society has gained considerable attention since the early 1990s as social scientists have attempted to explain challenges to authoritarian governments and reconfigurations of state–society relations, particularly in Eastern Europe and Africa. States in these two regions had for a number of decades sought to dominate all of social, political, and economic life. In Eastern Europe, the Communist Party absorbed into their structures nearly all social organizations, such as women's groups and labor unions, while the states, which were under communist control, owned most industries and controlled most production. In Africa, similarly, most regimes became increasingly authoritarian during the 1960s and 1970s, and many adopted single-party political systems, ostensibly to prevent ethnic conflict and facilitate economic development. These parties, like parties in Eastern Europe, were used as instruments of social control, subsuming nearly all organizations under their umbrella. States became the primary actors in African economies, in some countries because of an acceptance of socialist principles, but more commonly out of necessity, because the lack of an indigenous capitalist class left the state as the only source of capital for investment.[51] As a result of the growth of the state in both regions, those who dominated the state and party were able to dominate the entire society, because the masses of the population, lacking any independent organizations and independent sources of capital, had few means to challenge their domination.[52]

By the 1980s, however, states in both Africa and Eastern Europe had become "overextended." They were pervasive, but they had a declining capacity to conduct the activities typically associated with modern states.[53] States provided fewer services, focusing their energies on collecting revenue and on maintaining control through coercive force.[54] As part

---

[51] Richard Joseph, "Class, State, and Prebendal Politics," *Journal of Commonwealth and Comparative Politics*, 21, no. 3 (November 1983).

[52] Moshe Lewin, *The Gorbachev Phenomenon: A Historical Interpretation*, expanded edition (Berkeley and Los Angeles: University of California Press, 1988 and 1991; Michael Schatzberg, *The Dialectics of Oppression in Zaire* (Bloomington, IN: University of Indiana Press, 1988).

[53] Joseph, "Class, State, and Prebendal Politics."

[54] On the nature of the state in modern Africa, see Crawford Young, *The African Colonial State in Comparative Perspective* (New Haven: Yale University Press, 1995). Catharine Newbury points out that in Zaire, although the state had "gone underground," some

of their coping strategies in response to the declining economy and weakness of the state, which also included engaging in the informal economy,[55] people increasingly joined together in a wide variety of new independent associations, ranging from economic groups, such as rotating credit societies and producers cooperatives, to more social or even spiritual associations. With their declining capacities, party-states could no longer impede the proliferation of spontaneous social and economic groups, permitting the population to carve out a social and economic space independent of state control. In the context of an intrusive yet ineffective state, Moshe Lewin noted, "The societal maze finds new ways to 'keep private' what it wishes to remain private, and to 'socialize' what it does not want to have fully subject to statism."[56]

Scholars have labeled the emergent area of autonomous social action "civil society."[57] While the associations that make up civil society are not necessarily hostile to the state, their very existence compromises the capacity of party-states to monopolize all social space and to establish total control over their societies. According to Lewin:

By "civil society," we refer to the aggregate of networks and institutions that either exist and act independently of the state or are official organizations capable of developing their own, spontaneous views on national or local issues and then impressing these views on their members, on small groups and, finally, on the

---

people were still getting rich through state power, while "the repressive and security organs of the state are...quite visible and relatively effective at dampening dissent." M. Catharine Newbury, "Dead and Buried or Just Underground? The Privatization of the State in Zaire," *Canadian Journal of African Studies*, 18, no. 1 (1984): 112–14.

[55] Janet MacGaffey, *Entrepreneurs and Parasites: The Struggle for Indigenous Capitalism in Zaire* (Cambridge: Cambridge University Press, 1992); Nelson Kasfir, "State, Magendo, and Class Formation in Uganda," in Nelson Kasfir, ed., *State and Class in Africa* (London: Frank Cass, 1984), pp. 1–21.

[56] Lewin, *The Gorbachev Phenomenon*, p. 90. Lewin noted in 1988 that in the Soviet Union "unofficial, spontaneous, often large-scale activities and initiatives are becoming an important fact of national life."

[57] I do not at this point in the text wish to enter into the debate over how, exactly, civil society should be defined. Celestin Monga cautions that "any attempt to define the forces rather hastily grouped together under the label 'civil society' appears problematic and doomed to failure" ("Civil Society and Democratisation in Francophone Africa," *The Journal of Modern Africa Studies*, 33, no. 3 (1995):359–79, citation p. 359). For purposes of discussion, the definition Peter Lewis offers for the origins of the concept in the West will suffice: "Civil society was delineated as the arena of private and particular concerns within a given polity, institutionally separate and autonomous from the formally constituted public authority of the state" ("Political Transition and the Dilemma of Civil Society in Africa," *Journal of International Affairs*, 46, no. 1 (Summer 1992): 31–54. I will return to definitional questions in the final chapter.

authorities. These social complexes do not necessarily oppose the state, but exist in contrast to outright state organisms and enjoy a certain degree of autonomy. The possibility of serious dissidence from various levels of society cannot be excluded.[58]

The expansion of civil society creates an autonomous space in which people are able to envision alternatives to the existing order, and it creates possibilities for those who lack access to state power to empower themselves through other means. In both Africa and Eastern Europe, the emergence of independent economic and social activity helped to create the possibility for greater resistance to regimes, eventually giving rise to democracy movements and, in many countries, political transition.

Religious groups are an important element of civil society in most states and have been actively involved in democratic transitions in many locations. Samuel Huntington, in fact, identified the expansion and reform of Christian churches, the Catholic Church in particular, as a major causal factor in explaining the "third wave" of democratization that began in the 1970s and spread across Europe, Latin America, Asia, and eventually Africa.[59] Because they have generally retained institutional autonomy, even in the officially atheistic states of the former communist bloc, religious groups have been able to offer physical and ideological support for efforts to challenge the hegemonic control of autocratic rulers. They have offered protection and resources to dissidents, and they have created a space outside the reaches of state control where challenges to the status quo could be formulated and launched. As Mary Gautier noted looking at churches and the fall of communism in Central Europe, churches both served as central institutions of civil society and shaped public opinion and values.[60] Similarly, in his analysis of civil society and democracy in Africa, Celestin Monga identified the growth of the religious sector as a major force behind ongoing social change on the continent and argued that religious activities "are the most regular activities of a significant fraction of the population."[61]

---

[58] Lewin, *The Gorbachev Phenomenon*, p. 80.
[59] Samuel Huntington, *The Third Wave: Democratization in the Late Twentieth Century* (Norman: University of Oklahoma Press, 1991).
[60] Mary L. Gautier, "Church Elites and the Restoration of Civil Society in the Communist Societies of Central Europe," *Journal of Church and State*, 40, no. 2 (Spring 1998): 289–317.
[61] Célestin Monga, *The Anthropology of Anger: Civil Society and Democracy in Africa* (Boulder: Lynne Rienner, 1996), p. 127.

The mere existence of public space autonomous from the state does not, however, guarantee a democratic state and society, as the mixed record of religious groups aptly shows. While recognizing religious institutions' centrality to civil society and their contributions to democratization and political transformation in some settings, both Gautier and Monga raised a cautionary note. According to Guatier, whereas churches helped promote a democratic awakening in East Germany and Poland, the churches in Hungary were too closely associated with the state and actually served as a brake on transition.[62] Monga similarly noted that, "Every major social player has desperately tried to gain politically from the explosion of the religious and the parareligious,"[63] including politicians, whom he claimed have tried to co-opt religious institutions to increase their popular support. In other words, although religious groups enjoy a degree of autonomy from the state, their relationship to political power varies from one location to the next and from one religious group to another. While religious institutions, like other elements of civil society, may support political restructuring, they may also help to organize support for the status quo. In Rwanda, as I hope to demonstrate, religious groups played both roles, helping to create support for democratic reform but also defending the entrenched interests of the elite.

The mixed record of religious institutions in relationship to political reform reflects a wider problem with the easy equation of civil society with democracy. Even though the expansion of civil society created possibilities in Eastern Europe, Africa, and elsewhere for subordinate classes to challenge the ruling classes, the transitions that ultimately took place in many countries failed to redistribute significantly either economic or political power. As John Saul pointed out, popular pressures for reform in Africa pushed for both liberal democracy and popular democracy, not just the right to vote, but also a substantial redistribution of power, a goal that transitions did not produce.[64] The work of Antonio Gramsci, the theorist who first popularized the concept of civil society, helps explain why the emergence of civil society has failed to bring about a fundamental redistribution of power. According to Gramsci, in capitalist society the ruling class maintains its dominance both through control of the coercive

---

[62] Gautier, "Church Elites and the Restoration of Civil Society."

[63] Monga, *The Anthropology of Anger*, p. 135.

[64] John Saul, "Liberal Democracy vs. Popular Democracy in Southern Africa," *Review of African Political Economy*, no. 72, pp. 219–36; John Saul, " 'For Fear of Being Condemned as Old Fashioned': Liberal Democracy vs. Popular Democracy in Sub-Saharan Africa," *Review of African Political Economy*, no. 73, pp. 339–53.

force of the state and through creating voluntary consent on the part of the governed by manipulating the various non-state institutions, such as churches, schools, and the media, that he labeled "civil society." While in ordinary circumstances, civil society provides ideological justification for the status quo, during periods of crisis, the control of the ruling classes may be loosened, and alternative configurations of power may attempt to assert themselves within the civil society in a "war of position." The ruling classes respond to this "disequilibrium between classes" by seeking to reconfigure their own power, attempting to co-opt and divide those who challenge them, offering limited political or economic concessions and where necessary turning to coercive force.[65]

In other words, while the emergence of civil society creates a possibility for social groups to resist state control and to craft explicit challenges to the ruling classes and existing structures of domination, the ruling classes will attempt to prevent challenges to their power by extending their control over the civil society. According to Gramsci, civil society is not an inherently democratic or egalitarian space but rather a site in which the ruling classes seek to organize consensual domination and the subaltern classes seek to organize their resistance.[66] Civil society, put simply, is a site of contestation between classes.

In both Eastern Europe and Africa, civil societies emerged during periods of economic and political decline to challenge the totalizing projects of the party-states. By creating economic alternatives, the civil society reduced public dependence on the state, and by developing systems of mutual support, the civil society provided refuge from the predation of the state. Within the autonomous space of civil society, the population was able to articulate critiques to the regime and to organize resistance. In response, leaders in many states implemented political and economic reforms to appease the population – for example, holding elections and allowing greater freedom of press and association – but they failed in general to redistribute power significantly. Even where public protest or elections drove leaders from office, the new leaders came from a similar class background and did not behave in a fundamentally different manner

---

[65] Antonio Gramsci, *Selections from the Prison Notebooks* (New York: International Publishers, 1971), especially Part II, sections 2 and 3. For a useful explanation of Gramsci's main political ideas, see Joseph V. Femia, *Gramsci's Political Thought: Hegemony, Consciousness, and the Revolutionary Process* (Oxford: Clarendon Press, 1981).

[66] For Gramsci, in fact, in most societies civil society is the most important source of domination: "The state was only an outer ditch, behind which there stood a powerful system of fortresses and earthworks ..." (*Selections from the Prison Notebooks*, p. 238).

than their predecessors, while the deposed leaders often continued to enjoy considerable influence and economic opportunity. In a number of countries as well, new ideologies emerged (or old ones reemerged) – often within the civil society – to legitimize the domination of the ruling classes, such as xenophobic attacks on foreigners and foreign influence and ethnically based scapegoating. From a Gramscian perspective, the subaltern classes were able in civil society to challenge the ruling classes, but the ruling classes responded by providing limited benefits to the general population, by reconfiguring power to include – and co-opt – leaders of civil society, and by reformulating the ideological principles that justified their power.

This conceptualization of civil society as a site of class conflict is highly useful for understanding conflicts within the churches in Rwanda and, ultimately, why the churches failed to oppose the genocide. In Rwanda, as in most African countries, civil society was extremely weak in the colonial era, and the first decades after independence. Colonial rule disrupted many existing social relationships, and after independence, even those social organizations that were encouraged by the colonial state, like economic cooperatives, were subsumed under direct party-state control. Under President Habyarimana, the ruling party sought to bring all women's groups, youth groups, and economic organizations under its management. Yet the emphasis on economic development by policy makers and encouragement from the international community ultimately led to the creation of numerous development cooperatives, women's groups, and other associations, particularly from about 1985. Although often closely allied with the regime and controlled by elites, these groups ultimately allowed a degree of autonomous space to emerge and contributed in important ways to Rwanda's democracy movement.[67]

Churches were the one exception to the general rule of state-party control, as they remained formally autonomous throughout the colonial and post-independence periods. At the same time, like other civil society groups, churches were closely linked to the state. Dating back to the beginnings of the colonial era, church leaders in Rwanda sought to maintain a close and cooperative relationship with political leaders, believing that an alliance with the state created the optimum setting for

---

[67] Peter Uvin, *Aiding Violence: The Development Enterprise in Rwanda* (West Hartford: Kumarian Press, 1998), pp. 163–71; Catharine Newbury, "Rwanda: Recent Debates Over Governance and Rural Development," in Goran Hyden and Michael Bratton, eds., *Governance and Politics in Africa* (Boulder: Lynne Rienner Press, 1992), pp. 193–219.

a church to flourish. They sought to contain dissent within the churches in order to avoid tensions with the state, and they actively participated in political power struggles, including those that occurred along ethnic lines. Church leaders organized patrimonial structures within the churches to maintain their power, and these structures were linked to patrimonial structures in the state. Nevertheless, the relative autonomy of the churches and their loose internal organization offered the possibility for some members to develop challenges to the status quo, challenging structures of power both within the state and within the churches. Churches became a major source of support for the emerging civil society in Rwanda in the 1980s and early 1990s. They played a vital role in the creation of women's and human rights groups and supported development organizations, some of which, like the Iwacu Center, articulated a vision of Rwandan society in conflict with that of state officials. Coalitions developed within the churches of those supporting a reorganization of power not only in the state but in the churches as well. The leadership of the churches responded by seeking to reorganize their own support and to rein in opposition.

In other words, churches, like other civil society organizations, became sites of class conflict. While, given their diffuse organizations, churches embraced a considerable diversity of ideas and served a diversity of interests, broad coalitions formed within this complexity, cutting across institutional levels and even denominational lines. As they developed, these coalitions contained an ethnic component, as Tutsi felt they faced limited opportunities within the churches, despite the large number of Tutsi pastors and priests, and supported reform. Leaders of both the churches and the state had a shared interest in preserving the status quo, and both sought means to appease their critics without giving up real power. As the Habyarimana regime turned to ethnic politics as a means of regaining public support, the leaders of the churches, because of their close association with the regime and the long history of church entanglement in ethnic politics, offered little or no opposition but instead engaged in their own brand of ethnic politics. By the time the genocide began, the majority of church leaders had already clearly associated themselves with Hutu ethno-nationalism. They had made their support for the regime clear, and they had offered no condemnation of previous attacks on Tutsi, even when those attacks included targeting church property and personnel. Participation in the genocide, thus, seemed quite consistent with the policies and principles previously articulated by church leaders.

OVERVIEW OF THE ARGUMENT

The purpose of this book is not simply to explain *how* the churches were involved in the 1994 genocide in Rwanda but also to attempt to explain *why*. The book is based primarily on original data collected during two extended periods of field research in Rwanda, first in 1992–93, during the time of transition just before the genocide, then again in 1995–96 after the genocide had taken place, when I returned to Rwanda as head of the Human Rights Watch office there. The research project included interviews with bishops and other church leaders at the national and regional levels as well as collection of official church documents, but the bulk of the data came from case studies of six local parishes, three Protestant and three Catholic, where I conducted both participant observation and extensive interviews during my first period of field work and research in local government archives, as well as additional interviews, during my second period of field work. The combination of research on different churches and on various levels of each church allows a richer, more complex analysis of the engagement of churches in society than a more limited focus on either the national or local level would allow.

The first part of the book presents a broad overview of church engagement in Rwandan history. In Chapters 2 and 3, I review the involvement of Christian missionaries in the colonial project in Rwanda. It is my contention that the nature of missionary activity profoundly affected the particular character of Christian churches in Rwanda. The White Fathers, the missionary society that brought Catholicism to Rwanda, vigorously sought to ally the church with the political establishment, believing that Christianity would most easily flourish where the ruling elite supported the church. While from the earliest days there were dissenting voices that called for the Catholic Church to ally itself with the poor and disenfranchised, church leadership repeatedly reiterated the commitment to alliance with the powerful. The ultimate success of this strategy in winning converts proved to many, both Catholics and Protestants, the efficacy of maintaining close ties to the state. As I discuss in Chapter 3, missionaries and indigenous priests also played an important role in redefining ethnicity within Rwanda. The missionaries regarded Hutu, Tutsi, and Twa as clearly distinct, homogeneous, and mutually antagonistic racial groups, and this erroneous interpretation became a basis for colonial policy and, ultimately, shaped the nature of ethnic identity in the country. Whether missionaries supported the Tutsi, as they initially did, or the Hutu, as many did in the late colonial period, they set a precedent of active engagement of churches in ethnic politics.

In the Chapter 4, I turn to the postcolonial period, in which the churches continued to seek a close relationship with the state, now dominated by Hutu. The churches and the state cooperated extensively on social engagements such as health care, education, and development, and while conflicts occasionally arose, such as over family planning, they were rare and easily resolved. Leaders of the churches and the state developed close personal ties, and the patrimonial structures that they erected to maintain their authority were interconnected and mutually reinforcing. At the same time, structural, theological, and programmatic changes within both Catholic and Protestant churches created opportunities for a wider range of people and helped to foster challenges to perceived injustices in both the state structures and the churches. The churches played an important role in encouraging the growth of civil society – human rights groups, the media, women's associations – out of which eventually emerged challenges to established structures of power, not only within the state but within the churches as well.

In Chapter 5, I turn to the mixed engagement of the churches in the process of democratic reform that emerged in Rwanda in the early 1990s. While some groups and individuals within the churches were at the center of the reform movement, others were closely tied to the regime and saw reform efforts as a threat to their own power. Popular pietistic movements within both Catholic and Protestant churches challenged the authority of established church leaders and claimed spiritual power on the part of the masses, and a general movement within churches called for greater democracy within church structures. Seeking both to remain relevant within the changing political context and to respond to internal pressures, church leaders offered mild endorsements of political reform, but like their counterparts in the state, church leaders were primarily concerned with preserving their personal power and undermining their opponents. To this end, as I suggest in Chapter 6, leaders of both church and state turned to ethnic arguments as a means of regaining popular support. I argue that the genocide was a strategy organized by political and military leaders seeking to eliminate challenges to their power and regain popular support. While they were not central to the planning of the genocide, the churches and their leaders helped make genocide possible by encouraging obedience to authority and making ethnic prejudice seem consistent with Christian teachings. Ultimately the genocide served the interests of church leaders who felt their own power was being threatened by the movement for reform and were, thus, not willing to condemn the violence once it had begun.

In Part 2 of the book, I turn from the broad view of the relationship between churches and the state to a more localized analysis of how churches came to be implicated in genocide. I look in depth at the case studies of two Presbyterian parishes in the west-central province of Kibuye that best illustrate the contrasting roles that religion played in Rwandan society. These two parishes effectively demonstrate the contrasting tendencies for churches that I saw in all six of the parishes I studied, as well as in various other places where I conducted research. In communities throughout Rwanda, churches helped to create a local elite and to organize its hegemonic control while at the same time they created the possibility for challenges to the existing hegemony. In the Presbyterian parish of Kirinda, which I discuss in Chapter 7, the church played a central role in the creation of an elite, which included church employees, politicians, and business people in a unified bloc who cooperated in their exploitation of the local population. In contrast, in the neighboring parish of Biguhu, which I discuss in Chapter 8, the church had become a force for social change, supporting the masses in their efforts to resist exploitation and hindering the formation of a unified elite bloc. As I discuss in Chapter 9, this difference was key in determining the role of each parish in the genocide. In Kirinda, the church was at the center of the slaughter of Tutsi, with church buildings used as a location for killing and church personnel actively involved in the organization and execution of the genocide. In contrast, in Biguhu, although the Tutsi in the community were still killed, the church presented a hindrance to genocide and was itself targeted. While killing occurred in both places, the contrast suggests that greater church resistance might have had some impact in slowing or lessening the extent of the genocide.

In the concluding section of the book, I discuss the implications of the Rwandan case both for understanding religious involvement in ethnic violence and genocide and for the analysis of civil society. To understand the involvement of religious institutions in ethnic violence may require not simply discerning the links between religious institutions and the state, but also an appreciation of power struggles within the religious institutions themselves. The democracy movement that swept Rwanda focused not just on the state sphere but on the religious as well, and church leaders failed to condemn the growing ethnic conflict in the country, not simply because they were too closely associated with the state officials who were orchestrating it but also because heightened ethnic tensions helped to undermine the reform movement and thus served their interests just as they served the interests of the state authorities. The Rwandan example calls for a broader understanding of the process of democratization and also warns against too romantic an assessment of the relationship between civil society and democracy. The struggle for greater democracy may not simply pit the civil society against the state but may also involve a struggle within the civil society itself. Churches, like other institutions of civil society, can play an important part in fostering a more open society where power is widely distributed, but their relationship to power is not predetermined, and they may also help to preserve an oppressive status quo. The example of Rwanda demonstrates that civil society, although potentially progressive, does not necessarily promote democracy and, in fact, may be involved in actions that are distinctly uncivil.

PART I

"RIVER OF BLOOD"

Rwanda's National Churches and the 1994 Genocide

On that day, the Virgin appeared to the children, each in turn, sad, frustrated, the seers even said that she was angry. It was nevertheless the day where on earth we celebrate her triumph in the sky. Alphonsine saw the Mother of God crying. The seers sometimes cried, chattered their teeth, or trembled. They collapsed several times with all the weight of their body during the apparitions, which continued for eight hours, without stopping. The children saw terrifying images, a river of blood, people who killed one another, cadavers abandoned without anyone to bury them, a tree all on fire, a wide open chasm, a monster, decapitated heads. The crowd present that day, around 20,000 people, kept an impression of fear, even of panic and sadness.

– Gabriel Maindron, discussing the apparition of the
Virgin Mary at Kibeho on August 15, 1982

2

"Render Unto Caesar and Musinga ..."

Christianity and the Colonial State

To explain how churches came to be so deeply implicated in the Rwandan genocide requires reviewing the history of Christian involvement in Rwandan society and politics. In the earliest days of Christian missionary activity, a conflict arose between the missionaries who believed that the expansion of Christianity was best promoted through a close alliance of churches with the state and others who believed that the Christian message required the churches to ally themselves with the poor and marginalized. The fact that the first group prevailed in both the Roman Catholic and most Protestant churches has had a determinative impact on the nature of Christianity in Rwanda, where, despite consistent voices of dissent, a close collaboration between churches and the state has been the norm. The entanglement of churches in ethnic politics also has roots in the earliest days of the Christian presence in Rwanda and has profoundly shaped the nature of Christianity.

In this chapter, I present an historical overview of Christian church history in Rwanda from the appearance of the first Catholic missionaries in 1900 to the deposition of King Musinga, an event over which the missionaries had great influence and after which the church entered into a period of exceptional expansion. As I attempt to demonstrate, Catholic Church leaders committed themselves from their arrival in Rwanda to becoming important political players. They interpreted Rwandan power relations in ethnic terms and set as their primary goal gaining the support and ultimately the conversion of the Tutsi group. To this end, they consciously avoided defending the interests of the Hutu masses against the chiefs and other Tutsi, for fear that the chiefs would view them as rivals for power. By focusing on reaching out to the Tutsi youth through education and by relying on the support of the colonial state, particularly after the transfer to Belgian control in 1916, the missionaries eventually achieved their goal, the conversion of the Tutsi elite and the subsequent conversion of much of the populace. As I argue in later chapters, the success of the strategy of building up political power and developing strong alliances with state leaders (success in terms of rates of conversion and ease of operation for the church) led church officials in subsequent decades to seek to maintain a close alliance with the state. The value placed on popular obedience to civic authorities and the acceptance of church involvement in ethnic politics have also shaped subsequent church social engagement in Rwanda.

RELIGION, SOCIAL IDENTITIES, AND THE STATE IN PRECOLONIAL RWANDA

The modern state of Rwanda, like other African states, owes its origins to the colonial division of Africa in the late nineteenth century, but it had an antecedent in the precolonial kingdom of Rwanda, which included much of the territory now contained within the boundaries of the modern state. The kingdom of Rwanda began expanding from a core kingdom in the central Rwandan region known as Nduga in about the sixteenth or seventeenth century, bringing neighboring kingdoms and chieftancies under varying degrees of control through conquest or alliance.[1] While political power became relatively centralized in the nuclear kingdom, where the royal family dominated a complex system of chieftancies with overlapping and competing authorities, the central government exercised little control in more peripheral areas. A number of small kingdoms lying within what is today Rwanda, such as Bukunzi and Busozo in the south and Kibari, Bushiru, and Buhoma in the north, were effectively independent. In the late nineteenth century, however, after a period of rapid territorial expansion, the Rwandan monarch Kigeri IV Rwabugiri sought to consolidate and centralize his rule by placing close supporters in positions of power in areas formerly relatively autonomous and by expanding systems of

---

[1] For discussions of the creation and expansion of the Rwandan kingdom, see Jan Vansina, *Le Rwanda ancien: Le royaume* nyinginya (Paris: Karthala, 2001); Jan Vansina, *L'évolution du royaume rwanda des origines à 1900* (Brussels: Académie Royale des Sciences d'Outre-Mer, 1962), and J. K. Rennie, "The precolonial kingdom of Rwanda: a reinterpretation," *Transafrican Journal of History*, 2, no. 2, 1972, pp. 11–54. Vansina's recent work provides a shortened chronology for the Rwandan kingdom that suggests a more recent foundation than either he or Rennie previously thought.

clientship, such as *ubuhake*, cattle clientship, and *ubutaka*, land client-ship. After colonial rulers arrived in 1898, they assisted the Rwandan royal court in the consolidation and centralization of its rule.[2]

One effect of the centralization of political power was, as Catharine Newbury stated, a "heightened awareness of ethnic differences"[3] in regions where ethnic differentiation was minimal. While the precise meaning of the terms "Hutu," "Tutsi," and "Twa" in precolonial Rwanda is a subject of considerable academic debate,[4] most scholars agree that the terms did not refer to ethnic groups in the modern sense, as all three groups spoke the same language, shared common religious practices, and lived interspersed throughout the region. Many observers claim the division between the groups was occupational, as Tutsi tended to be more dependent on cattle, while Hutu depended more on cultivation and Twa on hunting and the sale of pottery, but the distinction is not sufficient to explain the terms, as most Tutsi did cultivate and many Hutu owned cattle. The terms appear to have been above all a status distinction because Tutsi tended to dominate the social and political hierarchy. The relative flexibility of the terms reinforces this conclusion, as the children of Hutu who became sufficiently powerful would be considered Tutsi and would marry Tutsi, while Tutsi families that lost power eventually became Hutu.[5]

---

[2] Catharine Newbury's *The Cohesion of Oppression: Clientship and Ethnicity in Rwanda, 1860–1960* (New York: Columbia University Press, 1988) convincingly demonstrates that the southwestern Rwandan region of Kinyaga was only nominally integrated into the Rwandan kingdom until the late 1800s, when the central kingdom began to extend its control more effectively over the region, introducing new forms of clientship. After the arrival of colonial authorities, Kinyaga experienced a "dual colonialism," as both the Germans (later Belgians) and the Rwandan king expanded their control. See also Alison L. Des Forges, " 'The drum is greater than the shout': the 1912 rebellion in northern Rwanda," in Donald Crummey, ed., *Banditry, Rebellion, and Social Protest in Africa* (London: James Currey, and Portsmouth, NH: Heinemann, 1986), pp. 311–31; and Vansina, *Le Rwanda ancien*, pp. 61–78.

[3] Newbury, *Cohesion of Oppression*, p. 51.

[4] French historian Jean-Pierre Chrétien (c.f., " 'Vrais' et 'faux' Negres: L'idéologie hami-tique," in Jean-Pierre Chrétien, *Burundi, L'Histoire retrouvée: 25 ans de métier d'historien en Afrique* (Paris: Karthala, 1993, pp. 335–41) argued that the terms were little more than occupational categories with limited social significance in precolonial Rwanda, whereas most other scholars, such as René Lemarchand, Filip Reyntjens, and Catharine Newbury, argued that the terms denoted status differences even before the arrival of European colonizers.

[5] The process of becoming Tutsi was known as *kihutura*, to lose Hutu-ness. (C.f., René Lemarchand, *Burundi: Ethnocide as Discourse and Practice* (Cambridge: Cambridge University Press, 1994), p. 8. Pierre Bettez Gravel, *Remera: A Community in Eastern Ruanda* (The Hague and Paris: Mouton, 1968), presents a fascinating analysis of how the

Although Hutu, Tutsi, and Twa existed as social identities in most regions of Rwanda, the process of centralization of political power that began under Rwabugiri in the late 1800s increased their importance, diminishing the significance of previously salient identities such as lineage and clan. What Newbury noted for Kinyaga in southwestern Rwanda – that the centralization of political power gave the distinction between Hutu and Tutsi "new hierarchical overtones"[6] – was true for most of Rwanda. New and more exploitative forms of land and cattle clientage increased social inequalities, helping to solidify the division between Hutu and Tutsi and to raise the status of Tutsi. In the late 1800s, chiefs began to require farmers (overwhelmingly Hutu), but not pastoralists (overwhelmingly Tutsi), to engage in *uburetwa*, a form of forced labor, which added to the ethnic distinction and contributed to tensions between the groups.[7] The process of ethnic differentiation continued under colonial rule, as the codification and racialization of divisions increased the rigidity of the categories and made them increasingly associated with status and opportunity. As I argue below, the Christian churches played an important role in supporting the centralization of political power and in increasing the importance and transforming the nature of the differentiation between Hutu and Tutsi.

Although religious beliefs and practices showed some variation throughout what is today Rwanda, many aspects of the indigenous religion were common throughout the territory – and indeed throughout most of the Great Lakes Region of East Africa. In the Rwandan cosmology, the high god Imana was an omnipotent being who created the world and gave life to humans. No worship of Imana was necessary, because Imana needed nothing and was understood simply to be the source of all life. A myriad of spirits, however, the *abazimu*, had more immediate relationships with humans, acting as links between the living and the supernatural world, and they required regular supplication. The spirits of dead ancestors and members of the lineage could bring illness or other difficulties upon a family if they felt slighted, or they could protect a family against other spirits if properly appeased.[8]

---

process of changing identities worked in a local community, where powerful Hutu lineages could develop clients and would be absorbed into the Tutsi elite within three generations.
[6] Newbury, *The Cohesion of Oppression*, p. 51.
[7] Vansina, *Le Rwanda Ancien*, pp. 171–8.
[8] André Karamaga, *Dieu au pays des mille collines* (Lausanne: Editions du Soc, 1988); Gerard van't Spijker, *Les Usages Funéraires et la Mission de l'Eglise* (Kampen: Uitgeversmaatschappij J.H. Kok, 1990), pp. 16–22; Bernardin Muzungu, *Le Dieu de nos*

In addition to ancestral spirits, Rwandans and other peoples of the Great Lakes Region turned for assistance to the spirits of powerful heroic figures, the *imandwa*. Two of the *imandwa* – Lyangombe and Nyabingi – had significant followings in Rwanda. *Kubandwa* involved rituals of spirit possession practiced in secret to obtain the intercession of the *imandwa* (what Gravel called "a centralization, so to speak, of the cult of the ancestors").[9] When a family experienced a tragedy or faced some crisis, they might call a *kubandwa* ceremony to initiate one of their children into the society. The cult of Lyangombe was practiced in the south and central regions of Rwanda, in Burundi, and in the Bushi and Buha regions of modern Zaire and Tanzania, while Nyabingi developed more recently in northern Rwanda and southern Uganda.[10]

Among the means the Rwandan court used to expand its influence was the promotion of a royal ideology that emphasized the ritual significance of the king. According to the royal ideology, the king served as a link between Imana and humans, helping to ensure the flow of rain and milk and other signs of fertility.[11] According to Iris Berger, the cult of Lyangombe originally presented a symbolic challenge to the authority of the Rwandan court, but it was gradually integrated into the system of state rule and, thus, was practiced most widely in areas where control of the Rwandan king was most firmly established. The cult of Nyabingi developed later in Ndorwa and neighboring areas that resisted incorporation into the large, centralized kingdoms. As the Rwandan rulers and, later, colonial authorities attempted to exert control over the Kiga, the people of the north, the cult of Nyabingi served as a channel for the expression of resistance and dissent. Resistance movements centered on Nyabingi mediums arose in northwestern Rwanda in 1912

pères (Bujumbura: Presses Lavigerie), in three volumes, 1974, 1975, and 1981, see especially, 2:115–41 and 3:11–134; Jean-Baptiste Bigangara, *Le Fondement de l'Imanisme ou Religion Traditionelle au Burundi: Approche Linuistique et philosophique* (Bujumbura: Expression et valeurs africaines burundaises, 1984).

9 Gravel, *Remera*, p. 147.

10 Iris Berger, *Religion and Resistance: East African Kingdoms in the Precolonial Period* (Butare: Institute National de Recherche Scientifique, 1981); Jim Freedman, *Nyabingi: The Social History of an African Divinity* (Butare: Institute de Recherche Scientifique, 1984); Centre de Recherches Universitaires du Kivu, *Lyangombe Mythe et Rites: Actes du Deuxieme Colloque du CERUKI* (Bukavu: Editions du CERUKI, 1976); van't Spijker, *Les Usages Funéraires*, pp. 20–2.

11 Christopher C. Taylor, *Milk, Honey, and Money: Changing Concepts in Rwandan Healing* (Washington: Smithsonian Institution Press, 1992), pp. 24–50; Newbury, *The Cohesion of Oppression*, pp. 38–9; Vansina, *Le Rwanda ancien*, pp. 75–80, 119–23.

and in the Kiga regions of southern Uganda and northern Rwanda in 1915.[12]

When King Rwabugiri, who worked during his thirty-five-year reign to consolidate Rwandan control over regions conquered by his predecessors and to centralize the power of the royal court over Rwanda, died in 1895, a crisis of succession ensued for several years, during which his designated successor was dethroned. When the Germans arrived in 1897, the new king, Yuhi V Musinga, had only recently succeeded to the throne, and the advances made by Rwabugiri in extending the power of the royal court were under challenge. Hence, the German offer of support for the king, after a demonstration of fire-power, was warmly welcomed.[13]

With the institution of indirect rule, the Germans came to play an important role in the further centralization of political power in Rwanda. Through a series of treaties, the colonial powers established fixed borders for the Rwandan kingdom, and they supported efforts by the court to bring all areas within those boundaries under control of the king (and by extension the colonial administration). In the first decades of the twentieth century, the Germans and, after 1916, the Belgians, assisted the Rwandan monarchy in subduing independent regions, particularly in the north. The colonial authorities supported the court's efforts to increase its direct control over the population by enacting reforms that eliminated much of the complexity of the precolonial political structures, regularizing the institutions of chieftancy and extending hierarchical systems of clientship throughout the territory.

The Missionaries and Political Authority

After several failed attempts at starting missions in Burundi, the Society of Missionaries of Africa, better known as the White Fathers, established their first permanent mission near Bujumbura in 1898, and two years later, in February 1900, the first White Fathers arrived at the Rwandan

---

[12] Ian Linden with Jane Linden, *Church and Revolution in Rwanda* (New York: Africana Publishing Company, 1977), pp. 21–2, 81–2, 104–9; DesForges, " 'The Drum is Greater than the Shout' "; Berger, *Religion and Resistance*.

[13] Louis de Lacger, *Le Ruanda: Aperçu historique* (Kabgayi, 1939 and 1959), pp. 358–9, 361–9.

capital in Nyanza to request permission to begin mission work in Rwanda. Monsignor Jean-Joseph Hirth, the apostolic vicar of the Catholic region known as Nyanza Meridional, insisted that land be granted for a mission in the heavily populated south, near the supply stations in Burundi, and despite some resistance within the court, a site was granted on Save, a large hill near what is today Butare. Within a year, the king granted two other stations, Zaza in the east near the Tanganyika border and Nyundo in the north, and two years later another northern mission was founded at Rwaza and one in the southwest, Mibirizi.[14]

Certain characteristics that marked mission work in Rwanda from the beginning appear in hindsight to have shaped indelibly the nature of Christianity in Rwanda. The founder of the Missionaries of Africa, Cardinal Charles Lavigerie, believed that conversion of non-Christian peoples would be most successfully accomplished by focusing evangelistic efforts on political leaders. Lavigerie believed that, as happened in Rome after the conversion of Emperor Constantine, once the chiefs and kings were converted, they would create an accommodating environment for the conversion of the masses and that where tension existed between missionaries and civil authorities, the church would never develop a firm footing.[15]

Although Lavigerie died nearly a decade before Catholic mission work began in Rwanda, the idea that gaining the support of state leaders was essential to successful missionary work remained a central principle for leaders of Lavigerie's order, who consistently called on the missionaries working in Rwanda to gain favor with the indigenous leadership. While the ultimate goal of the White Fathers was to convert Rwanda's ruling class, given the initial hostility of many officials, the superiors of the order set as an immediate goal gaining favor with the king and other political leaders by offering them unconditional support.[16] As early as

---

[14] The best source for information on Catholic mission work in colonial Rwanda is Linden and Linden, *Church and Revolution in Rwanda*. See also Justin Kalibwami, *Le catholicisme et la société rwandaise, 1900–1962* (Paris: Présence Africaine, 1991).

[15] See the useful discussion of Lavigerie's ideas in Kalibwami, *Le catholicisme et la société rwandais*, pp. 174–81.

[16] An entry in the Diaire de Rwaza, February 1904, p. 3, quoted in Paul Rutayisire, *La christianisation du Rwanda (1900–1945): Méthode missionaire et politique selon Mgr. Léon Classe* (Editions Universitaires Fribourg Suisse, 1987), p. 29, demonstrates the impression the leaders of the White Fathers hoped to present: "We want only to raise and affirm the authority of the king ..., we want to be always his friends ..., we will have people pay tribute." This and all other translations from the French by the author, unless otherwise noted.

1901, Mgr. Hirth reprimanded the missionaries in Rwanda for challenging the authority of the local chiefs in the regions where they worked,[17]
and he and other superiors repeatedly urged the missionaries to placate
local and national leaders, even when their policies were offensive to
missionaries' sensibilities.[18] Whenever the actions of missionaries alienated local authorities, the superiors of the order called on the missionaries to reassure the chiefs of their loyalty. For example, when Rwandan
officials complained that the missionaries at Rwaza were settling disputes, a traditional prerogative of local chiefs, Mgr. Hirth ordered that
the practice cease:

Hasten to clear up as completely as possible all trials and litigation that have
nothing to do with your entirely spiritual jurisdiction. Render unto Caesar and
Musinga all that can be returned to Caesar and Musinga. As a result, you will be
accordingly more free to fulfill the requirements of the priest and more certain
to make yourselves loved and to win the confidence of all for the welcoming of
souls.[19]

As the German colonial administration and the royal court worked
together to consolidate rule over the entire territory defined by the colonial
powers as Rwanda, they met with resistance, particularly in regions where
independent Hutu kingdoms had existed until the advent of Musinga's
reign. Hirth and other superiors of the White Fathers demanded of the
missionaries that wherever conflict arose, they side with the Rwandan
king, whom they judged to be the legitimate authority in the country,
and the support of the missionaries proved essential to efforts to consolidate rule. Musinga strategically granted the right to establish missions
in regions only recently brought into Rwanda where royal authority was
weakest – Nyundo in Bugoyi in the northeast, Rwaza in Mulera in the
north, Zaza in the kingdom of Gisaka in the east, and Mibilizi in Bukunzi

---

[17] In a December 31, 1901, letter to the superior general of the White Fathers Hirth complained that "The missionaries of Rwanda do not sufficiently look after good relations
with the authorities." Quoted in Rutayisire, *La christianisation du Rwanda*, pp. 28–9.

[18] In a letter dated March 16, 1911, to the superior of Rwaza mission, Father Leonard, a
regional church official, urged the missionaries to support the king and his chiefs, despite
legitimate complaints by the local population that led them to revolt: "Regarding the
injustices ... that are committed around you in a revolting fashion, you see and note
that we cannot remedy them. All that we can do, we can do by our patience, by acceptance, and by love of the humiliations that come from our absolute abstention. Quoted in
Rutayisire, *La christianisation du Rwanda*, p. 52.

[19] Mgr. Hirth in letter to Rwaza mission, 1911, quoted in Rutayisire, *La christianisation
du Rwanda*, p. 52.

in the southeast – and the missionaries dutifully helped to integrate these regions into the kingdom. For example, the White Fathers at Zaza refused to support a revolt seeking to restore the independent monarchy of Gisaka in 1901, earning thanks from Musinga (though he quickly ran into conflict with the missionaries of Zaza on other issues).[20] Similarly, when a major revolt broke out in the north in 1911, the missionaries in Rwaza urged their followers to support their king, despite entreaties from the rebel leaders.[21] Shortly thereafter, the German colonial administrator Dr. Richard Kandt acknowledged the contributions of the missionaries to extending royal and colonial authority in a letter to Mgr. Hirth, thanking him for the work of the church and requesting that mission stations be opened in another region that had yet to be fully brought under colonial control:

Sir,
The missions that you have founded in the north of Rwanda contribute a good deal to the pacification of that district. They facilitate substantially the task of government. The influence of your missionaries has saved us the necessity of undertaking military expeditions....[22]

By appeasing Rwanda's rulers, the White Father superiors hoped not simply that the order would be allowed to function in Rwanda without interference but ultimately that some of the ruling elite would convert to Catholicism. The Catholic leaders feared that if they failed to convert the indigenous elite, the elite might be drawn to Protestantism, particularly because the German colonial authorities were predominantly Protestant, and this would permanently impede Catholic missionary efforts in the country. As Father Leon Classe, vicar delegate, wrote to the Superior General of the White Fathers in 1911, "Without the chiefs we will not have the people in a serious manner. Without them, that is, without the social regime that will be fortified, we will give to Catholicism a situation of inferiority, of slavery, condemning it to face continually the difficulties of oppression."[23]

---

[20] Linden and Linden, *Church and Revolution in Rwanda*, pp. 29–45; Kalibwami, *Le catholicisme et la société rwandaise*, pp. 149–54, 165–71.
[21] Des Forges, "The Drum Is Greater than the Shout," pp. 321–7; Rutayisire, *Le christianisation du Rwanda*, pp. 45–52.
[22] Des Forges, "The Drum Is Greater than the Shout," pp. 321–7; Rutayisire, *Le christianisation du Rwanda*, pp. 45–52.
[23] Father Classe in a letter to Superior General, April 28, 1911, quoted in Rutayisire, *La christianisation du Rwanda*, p. 44.

Realizing that they would be unlikely to convert the older chiefs, the Catholic missionaries focused their evangelistic attentions on the young men in the royal court. According to Rwandan tradition, leading families in the country sent their young men to the royal court to receive training as *intore* warriors and to be indoctrinated into court traditions before they themselves became chiefs. Believing that these youths would be more open to persuasion, the missionaries sought to establish a school in the capital, Nyanza, as early as 1900, hoping that they could attract the youths by providing a European-style education, a key to gaining access to the colonial administration, and in the process of teaching literacy and other skills, convert the youths to Christianity. While the school project met with little success in the first decade, attracting few students and meeting only sporadically, by the beginning of World War I, a core of youths from the court had begun to receive instruction.[24]

The Missionaries and the Construction of Ethnicity

One aspect of missionary engagement that ultimately had profound consequences for Rwandan society was the missionaries' definition of power relations in ethnic terms. The principles of the White Fathers exhorted the missionaries to understand the indigenous cultures within which they worked, learning local languages and customs so that they could more effectively convert the population. In their efforts to understand Rwanda and Burundi, the White Fathers applied contemporary European ideas about race and ethnicity, which assumed that the peoples of the world could be neatly divided into distinct racial categories and subcategories. Early European travelers to East Africa who encountered complex societies with a hierarchical organization theorized that such a high level of political development could not have been the creation of Negroid populations, whom modern theories considered savage and anarchic, but must have been the result of earlier Caucasoid influences on Africa. John

[24] The first attempt at establishing a school occurred in 1900 but quickly foundered and was stopped. In December 1904, a catechist began teaching the king Swahili, and in 1905 a second arrived who began working with fifty *intore*, but by 1906, the numbers had dwindled to three. In 1909, the school at Nyanza was wrecked by a gang of Tutsi youths, but by 1911, there were again fifteen *intore* studying in the mission school, and attendance in the school increased steadily. R. Heremans, *L'éducation dans les missions des Pères Blancs en Afrique centrale (1879–1914)* Bruxelles: Editions Nauwelaerts 1983; Linden and Linden, *Church and Revolution in Rwanda*, pp. 50–114; Rutayisire, *La christianisation du Rwanda*, p. 45.

Hanning Speke, who visited Buganda and other kingdoms in what is today Uganda in the 1860s, speculated that the political systems there had been created by a pastoralist Hamitic group, probably the Galla of Somalia, that had migrated to the region some centuries before, and Speke's "Hamitic hypothesis" became the basis for later European interactions with peoples of the region.[25] Harry Johnston, the first British administrator of Uganda, elaborated on the hypothesis, theorizing that the Hima of Nkole and other rulers of the kingdoms of Uganda were descendants of Hamitic peoples from Ethiopia who had conquered the inferior local populations and brought them civilization.[26]

The White Fathers had worked in Uganda for several decades before founding missions in Burundi and Rwanda, and several of the early missionaries in Burundi and Rwanda had previous experience in Uganda. Hence, the missionaries encountered the populations of Rwanda and Burundi with the Hamitic hypothesis already in mind, and they seem to have played an important role in transferring the hypothesis to the

[25] Speke's speculations are found in John Hanning Speke, *Journal of the Discovery of the Source of the Nile* (London, 1863). For a useful discussion of the origins of the Hamitic hypothesis, see Edith R. Sanders, "The Hamitic Hypothesis: Its Origin and Functions in Time Perspective," *Journal of African History*, 10, no. 4 (1969), pp. 521–32; and Chrétien, *L'histoire retrouvée*, pp. 335–41. In the early 1800s, the term Hamitic came to be applied to "races" of people in Africa, such as Egyptians and Somalis, who had "superior" cultures and bore greater physical resemblance to Europeans than other Africans. The Hamites, it was theorized, were the lowest level of Caucasoid people. As Sanders writes, the theory held that "everything of value ever found in Africa was brought there by these Hamites, a people inherently superior to the native populations" (p. 532).

[26] In cataloguing the different "races" in Uganda, Sir Harry Johnston, *The Uganda Protectorate* (London: Hutchinson, vol. 2, 1902) wrote, "The fifth and last amongst these main stocks is the Hamitic, which is negroid rather than Negro. This is the division of African peoples to which the modern Somali and Gala belong, and of which the basis of the population of ancient Egypt consisted. ... [T]he ancestors of the Bahima were probably only the last in a series of Hamitic invaders of Negro Africa. Yet though in this way superior races coming from the more arid countries of Southern Abyssinia and Galaland have continually leavened the mass of ugly Negroes pullulating in the richly endowed countries between and around the Nile lakes, it is very doubtful whether the ancient Egyptians ever penetrated directly up the Nile beyond the vicinity of Fashoda .... Rather it would seem as though ancient Egypt traded and communicated directly with what is now Abyssinia and the Land of Punt (Somaliland), and that the Hamitic peoples of these countries facing the Red Sea and Indian Ocean carried a small measure of Egyptian culture into the lands about the Nile lakes. In this way, and through Uganda as a half-way house, the totally savage Negro received his knowledge of smelting and working iron, all his domestic animals and cultivated plants (except those, of course, subsequently introduced by Arabs from Asia and Portuguese from America), all his musical instruments higher in development than the single bowstring and the resonant hollow log, and, in short, all the civilisation he possessed before the coming of the white man ..." (pp. 484–6).

division between Hutu and Tutsi. In their earliest writings, the missionaries demonstrated that they regarded the division between Hutu and Tutsi not only as the fundamental social division in the two countries but also as a division between distinct racial groups. Because they regarded Hutu and Tutsi as distinct races, one Hamitic and one Negroid, the missionaries failed to recognize the regional variations in the application of the terms, the flexibility in the categories, and the serious divisions within each category. Other social divisions within Rwanda and Burundi were interpreted through a racial prism, producing an oversimplified and distorted understanding of Rwandan society. The missionaries assumed that all chiefs were Tutsi, while their subjects, "the people," were Hutu, ignoring the persistence of Hutu kingdoms and the presence of Hutu chiefs even in the Rwanda kingdom proper, as well as the numbers of Tutsi who were not chiefs, such as the poor nomadic Tutsi in northern Rwanda. Similarly, the missionaries ignored the fact that in Burundi, the rulers were drawn from the Ganwa, a group that was considered neither Hutu nor Tutsi.[27] The missionaries assumed that clientelistic institutions, such as *ubuhake*, divided neatly along racial lines as well, and their analysis exaggerated the level of exploitation, rather than the reciprocal ties, of many clientage arrangements and ignored the diverse forms of clientage that persisted in Rwanda.[28] In short, the missionaries' interpretations of Rwandan social and political structures were influenced by the Hamitic hypothesis so that they saw in the Tutsi a superior race whose relationship with the Hutu masses was one of conquerors ruling over the conquered.

The interpretations of Rwandan society offered by the priests had a profound impact, as the few German administrators in Rwanda and Burundi relied heavily on the missionaries to explain the local culture.[29] It is not that the missionaries "invented" ethnicity in Rwanda, as some

---

[27] Lemarchand, *Burundi: Ethnocide as Discourse and Practice*, pp. 6–16.

[28] Rutayisire noted, drawing on missionary reports from 1904, "The first missionaries identified very early the relations that united the *bagaragu* (clients) with their *shebuja* (patrons) in 'slavery' and in a 'serfdom with multiple injustices.' They saw in it an instrument of political domination of the Batutsi (assimilated into the patrons) over the Bahutu (assimilated into the clients) and an instrument of economic servitude of the last by the first." *La christianisation du Rwanda*, p. 82.

[29] According to Linden and Linden, *Church and Revolution in Rwanda*, p. 52, there were five times as many White Fathers as German administrators in Rwanda in 1904. David Newbury and Catharine Newbury, "Rethinking Rwandan Historiography: Bringing the Peasants Back in," paper prepared for Colloquium Series, Program in Agrarian Studies, Yale University, April 3, 1998, claimed that in 1913, there were still only five German administrators, compared to 41 missionaries, of whom 34 were Catholic.

have claimed.[30] Rather, the missionaries took existing social categories and transformed their meaning. The division between Hutu and Tutsi had become increasingly important in Rwanda and increasingly unequal at least since the reign of Rwabugiri. By imparting a racial significance to the difference between Hutu and Tutsi, the missionaries helped to strengthen the rigidity of the division, because race is regarded as a fixed aspect of individual identity, and they gave ideological support to the exclusion of Hutu from opportunity and power. Their own practices exacerbated the inequalities between the two groups and helped to increase the power and prestige of the Tutsi at the expense of the Hutu.

Because they defined political power in Rwanda as divided along racial lines, the White Fathers' charge to convert the rulers first meant that evangelistic efforts were to be directed above all at Tutsi. Initial Christian conversions, however, occurred almost exclusively among Hutu, particularly poor and otherwise marginalized Hutu who viewed the priests as potential patrons whose power could be called on to protect them from exploitation by existing powerful patrons.[31] The failure to convert Tutsi in the first decades of missionary work caused considerable consternation among White Father superiors, who feared that if the Protestants won over the Tutsi, the Catholic Church would be crippled. In his 1912 *Instructions*, Mgr. Hirth stressed the importance of reaching out to the Tutsi:

Will we, without reacting through all possible means, allow the country to become divided into two confessions, the one of the Protestants with the chiefs and the Batutsi for it, the other of the Catholics with the people? That the apostolate with the people be more comforting, more rapid, one should hope not. ...God who preferably goes to the humble does not push away the rich.... To neglect the conversion of the chiefs is to reduce Catholicism to servitude, it is to paralyze its action if not to destroy it completely.[32]

---

[30] Didier Goyvaerts, "The Hutu-Tutsi Divide in Burundi," (in Goyvaerts, ed. *Conflict and Ethnicity in Central Africa*, Tokyo: Institute for the Study of Languages and Cultures of Asia and Africa, 2000, pp. 263–86), for example, argues that "ethnicity in Ruanda-Urundi, as in much of the rest of Africa, was created by the colonizer" (p. 281).

[31] Linden and Linden, *Church and Revolution in Rwanda*, chapter three, convincingly makes the argument that the missionaries were integrated into Rwanda's clientage structure and came to be viewed early on as powerful patrons to whom those without patrons could turn for support. Because most of those at the bottom of the social hierarchy who lacked access to the protection of patronage were Hutu, they were the group initially most drawn to the church.

[32] Mgr. Hirth in *Instructions*, quoted in Rutayisire, *La christianisation du Rwanda*, p. 69.

Similarly, in a letter to the Superior General of the White Fathers dated April 28, 1911, Father Classe warned of the need to convert the Tutsi:

It is a serious error to say that here the people will be Catholic without the chiefs, more serious than anywhere else, since the chiefs and the people are not of the same race here. There is an antagonism of races, of conquerors and the conquered.... [Since] Protestantism is the religion of the [German colonial] government, it will enjoy favors. Should the chiefs throw themselves toward it with their policy, the Tutsi race will have the support of the government, and because of this policy, it [the Protestant Church] will have to help this race govern.... The other race, Catholic, will seek us out despite ourselves. Now already they say that we make of ourselves the defenders of the Bahutu. It is not far from there to a political antagonism.[33]

The White Father superiors, thus, repeatedly warned the missionaries against allowing the Catholic Church to become too closely associated with the Hutu, and they instructed the missionaries whenever conflicts arose that they should side with the Tutsi.

Dissension within the Church

From the beginning of the missionary endeavor in Rwanda, there were missionaries who objected to the church's alliance with the powerful against the weak, who believed that Christian principles called on the church to side with those who were being exploited rather than with their exploiters. Although they did not challenge the basic analysis of Rwandan society that regarded Tutsi and Hutu as distinct and antagonistic groups, the dissenters objected to the decision to ally the church with the Tutsi minority against the Hutu majority. Several missionaries who worked in Save, the first Rwandan mission, encountered significant resistance from the Tutsi chiefs. They developed an antipathy for Tutsi and became defenders of the rights of the Hutu.[34] The superior of the mission, Father Brard, wrote in 1902, "It will be necessary perhaps to limit the rights of the chiefs over the Bahutu. Because through their pillaging, they kill the initiative of the workers and ruin the prosperity of the country."[35] Brard and his fellow priests used well-armed Baganda *askari* to support

---

[33] Quoted in Rutayisire, *La christianisation du Rwanda*, p. 44.

[34] In 1901, Father Barthélémy wrote in the Save Diary that the Tutsi were "real Jews; they are rapacious flatterers and above all hypocrites." Quoted in Linden and Linden, *Church and Revolution in Rwanda*, p. 38.

[35] Quoted in Rutayisire, *La christianisation du Rwanda*, p. 36.

the mission, and did not shy away from allowing the *askari* to humiliate local chiefs who offered resistance.[36]

Because the initial converts to Catholicism were marginal individuals who regarded the priests as potential protectors, they regularly called on the priests to defend their interests against chiefs who demanded excessive taxes or powerful individuals who sought to claim their land or livestock. The White Father superiors, however, urged the missionaries to avoid alienating the chiefs and other Tutsi and encouraged them, accordingly, to avoid supporting challenges to their authority. For example, in the region of Mulera where the Rwaza mission was located, there were few Tutsi until 1905, when an onslaught of Tutsi from Nduga, the heart of the Rwandan kingdom, settled in the area to establish the authority of the crown. They sought an acknowledgment of their authority from the missionaries, and, although even Mgr. Hirth grumbled about the excessive and unfair new taxes being levied against the local population (including against some poor local Tutsi), the missionaries acquiesced, making clear their allegiance to the Tutsi chiefs and the court.[37]

A number of priests on the ground in Rwanda objected to decisions of this sort, and the superiors had a difficult time maintaining control of their subordinates. The records from the early years of missionary work in Rwanda reveal regular conflict between the missionaries and their superiors, who consistently called on the missionaries to practice the principles of the order, no matter how difficult.[38] As Ian Linden pointed out, the conflict reflected not simply a contrast between those working in administration and those active in the field, but also important differences in background, because leaders of the White Fathers, including leaders of the Rwanda mission, were from the upper class or were treated as though they were, while the missionaries themselves were often from humble rural backgrounds.[39]

Faced, then, with a challenge to the basic principle of seeking favor with civil authorities, which in Rwanda they interpreted as supporting

---

[36] Linden and Linden, *Church and Revolution in Rwanda*, pp. 38–9, 57–61.

[37] Linden and Linden, *Church and Revolution in Rwanda*, p. 63.

[38] C.f., R. Heremans and Emmanuel Ntezimana, eds., *Journal de la Mission de Save, 1899–1905* (Ruhengeri, 1987); Rutayisire, *La christianisation du Rwanda.*

[39] Linden and Linden, *Church and Revolution in Rwanda*, pp. 66–7. According to Linden, "Hirth and Classe remained missionaries yet became honorary members of the colonial ruling group. Similarly, the missionaries who spent much of their day with Africans, the Pougets and Brards, came to identify with their interests and sometimes to see the world through their eyes ..." (p. 67).

the Tutsi, the superiors of the White Father order acted forcefully to reassert their authority and quash dissent. In 1906, Father Brard was sent back to Europe, while Father Classe, who had distinguished himself by his faithfulness to the directives of his superiors, was named superior of Save.[40] Despite Classe's unpopularity among other missionaries, who regarded him as having limited skills, in 1907 the order appointed him Vicar Delegate, assistant to the Apostolic Vicar Mgr. Hirth, and he took over the quotidian activities of managing the Rwanda mission.[41] The message to the missionaries working in Rwanda was clear: the policy of allying the church with the leaders of the country and supporting the Tutsi over the Hutu was to remain in force. As a result, the missionaries resigned themselves to following the proscribed line. As Paul Rutayisire noted:

[A]fter 1906, a very clear change is perceptible in the behavior of the missionaries with regards to the authorities. Conforming to the directives, the fathers adopted a more submissive attitude, preaching obedience to the chiefs to all the inhabitants and above all to their adepts, taking care not to take sides, as in the past, with the subjects against their chiefs.[42]

While the intervention of the superiors did not entirely eliminate missionary challenges to the chiefs and support for the Hutu, it clearly restrained those who disagreed with official church policy.

CHRISTIAN MISSIONS DURING BELGIAN COLONIAL RULE

During the disruptions of World War I, mission expansion was put on hiatus, but after the war, the establishment of the Belgian protectorate offered the White Fathers a more favorable environment for conducting their work. While the Catholic missionaries had regularly consulted

---

[40] The following quote demonstrates Classe's acceptance of the principles of focusing mission on the Tutsi and his loyalty to his superiors: "Unfortunately ... we have not always listened to the wise counsel of Mgr. Hirth. A little prejudiced, we have often left in the background the Batutsi: Too rich, too hostile, we say, they are not yet mature for our holy religion. We forget that in leaving them to the side we develop a powerful party against us, all the more powerful since it holds authority. ... We must absolutely busy ourselves with them, if not we will come to this fatal division: the people can become Catholic, but the chiefs Protestant." Father Classe in letter to the Superior General, March 24, 1907, quoted in Rutayisire, *La christianisation du Rwanda*, p. 41.
[41] Linden and Linden, *Church and Revolution in Rwanda*, pp. 65–7; Rutayisire, *La christianisation du Rwanda*, pp. 29–40.
[42] Rutayisire, *La christianisation du Rwanda*, p. 45.

and cooperated with the German colonial administration, the relationship between the church and the colonial state had always been uneasy. The missionaries, who were primarily French, believed that the German administrators favored the Protestant churches and worried that their favoritism would allow Protestant missionaries to win over the Tutsi elite and place the Catholics in a disadvantaged position. The Germans, for their part, saw the missionaries as a frequently disruptive element that impeded their efforts to maintain cordial relations with the royal court.[43]

After the Belgians assumed control of Rwanda in 1916, however, the Catholic missionaries found themselves facing a much more congenial regime. The Belgian administrators were themselves Catholic, and, like the White Fathers, they spoke French. Because the White Fathers were the only Europeans remaining in Rwanda after the German retreat, the new Belgian authorities depended heavily on them for advice and information.[44] Further, they perceived much more thoroughly than their German predecessors did the assistance that the fathers could offer in subduing the population and the advantages to be gained from Christian conversion of the masses. One of the early Belgian policy changes was to force Musinga to sign a decree guaranteeing religious liberty, and, although the overwhelming power the White Fathers enjoyed immediately after the Belgian victory was curtailed by 1918 as the Belgians realized their need to maintain the support of the royal court, the missionaries found in the new colonial regime a strong ally.[45]

The White Fathers' policy of winning over the civil authorities needed consistently to be reemphasized. Immediately after the Belgian occupation of Rwanda in 1916, with the court significantly weakened, a number of the priests once again took on significant secular authority that challenged the power of local chiefs, adjudicating disputes and seeking economic advantages for the Hutu Christian converts. As in the past, Father Classe instructed his priests to avoid assuming a political role, and once

---

[43] Linden and Linden, *Church and Revolution in Rwanda*, pp. 39, 96–122; Kalibwami, *Le catholicisme et la société rwandaise*, pp. 167–79.

[44] According to Linden and Linden, *Church and Revolution in Rwanda*, p. 125, "When the Belgian commanders came to consider problems beyond the immediate needs of their advancing columns they could turn to no one but the White Fathers for advice. Their experience in the Congo had little relevance to the problems of ruling a kingdom like Rwanda. Armed with only the vague notion of supporting the local chiefs, all but the most militantly atheist of administrators welcomed the priests' services … ."

[45] de Lacger, *Le Ruanda*, p. 463; Kalibwami, *Le catholicisme et la société rwandaise*, pp. 169–71; Linden and Linden, *Church and revolution in Rwanda*, pp. 125–51.

again a priest who had overstepped the bounds, setting himself up as a virtual chief, was sent out of Rwanda. The policy of deference to Tutsi hegemony began to achieve results, as in December 1917 the first Tutsi nobles were converted to Christianity.[46] Father Classe noted in a letter to the superior general of the White Fathers, "All around Rwanda the Hutu people have for a long time cherished the illusion that the missionaries were going to deliver them from the Tutsi state. Today, it seems that they are getting over this hope and that they are finally beginning to see the fathers in their true light."[47]

As Justin Kalibwami pointed out, Cardinal Lavigerie, in the principles he developed for missionizing, did not insist that missionaries show blind obedience to civil authorities but rather advised missionaries to gain the support, and ultimately the conversion, of political leaders. While this required showing deference to the indigenous elite, it also meant becoming involved in local politics and using the power of the church to ensure the ascendancy of chiefs who supported the church.[48] Hence, as the White Fathers in Rwanda found themselves in an increasingly powerful position, with the numbers of Christian converts expanding and a more supportive colonial regime, their political engagement began to shift. As the missionaries began to gain allies and converts among the Tutsi nobles, they used their influence to help these nobles advance politically and they felt increasingly empowered to challenge those nobles they viewed as the enemies of the church.

The position of the White Father order in Rwanda, then, was not a principled deference to earthly authorities but rather a calculated effort to gain support from state leaders, what Kalibwami called a "rather Machiavellian policy."[49] As Linden stated, "The question was not whether the Fathers would become politically involved but how they would become involved."[50] While the superiors of the White Fathers did not wish the individual missionaries to set themselves up as theocrats, exercising secular

---

[46] Linden and Linden, *Church and Revolution in Rwanda*, pp. 130–3.
[47] Letter from Classe to the Superior General, March 2, 1917, quoted in Rutayisire, *La christianisation du Rwanda*, p. 103.
[48] Kalibwami, *Le catholicisme et la société rwandaise*, pp. 174–81. In Tanganyika, for example, where there were a large number of small chieftancies, Lavigerie counseled the White Fathers to work "to create more important political entities by supporting, in their struggles against their adversaries, whichever African chief judged particularly advantageous. This one, seeing his power grow and consolidate with the aid of the missionaries, could not but be an ally in the evangelization of the region" (p. 179).
[49] Kalibwami, *Le catholicisme et la société rwandaise*, p. 173.
[50] Linden and Linden, *Church and Revolution in Rwanda*, p. 59.

power in a fashion that challenged the power of the indigenous elite, they were more than willing for the church leadership to become embroiled in court politics, allying themselves with those they felt would best support the spread of Christianity and applying the influence of the church as an institution not only to support their allies but to attract supporters who hoped to gain power through an association with the church.

One means that the missionaries used to promote their interests was through appealing to the colonial state. Given their uneasy relationship with the administration, the White Fathers appealed to colonial authority only sparingly under the Germans, such as when, after attempting for six years to convince Musinga to grant a site for a mission in the center of the country, Mgr. Hirth appealed to Kandt, who convinced Musinga to permit the opening of a mission at Kabgayi.[51] Directly after World War I, the White Fathers found themselves at odds with the Belgian administration, but within a few years, they came to work much more closely with the colonial administration than they had under the Germans. Father Classe, who replaced Hirth as Apostolic Vicar in 1922, became an important advisor to the colonial leaders, who regularly consulted him regarding colonial policies, and Classe used his influence to further the cause of developing a Christian government.[52]

As always, the missionaries in the interwar years sought to win over the Rwandan elite, as well as retain the support of the colonial administration, by encouraging popular obedience and promoting the interests of national leaders. Classe played a leading role in the effort to return to Rwanda and the Belgians a large area of eastern Rwanda turned over to the British in the post-World War I treaties. The British regarded the region as essential to their plans for a Cape-to-Cairo railroad, and they planned to govern the territory by reviving the monarchy of Gisaka, conquered by Rwanda in the 1800s. During a sojourn in Europe in 1920–22, Classe argued forcefully for Rwanda's historic rights to the territory claimed by the British and for the importance of the region to the leading families of Rwanda, many of whom kept cattle in the region and had claims to land. While the region was officially transferred to Britain in 1922, it was returned to Rwanda in 1924, with both the Belgian administration and the Rwandan nobles crediting Classe for his efforts.[53]

---

[51] Kalibwami, *Le catholicisme et la société rwandaise*, pp. 153–4.
[52] Rutayisire, *La christianisation du Rwanda*, pp. 150–2; Linden and Linden, *Church and Revolution in Rwanda*, pp. 135–55.
[53] Kalibwami, *Le catholicisme et la société rwandaise*, pp. 181–95.

The Catholic Church also played an important role in the 1920s in helping to eliminate remnants of Hutu political power and to increase the concentration of power in Tutsi hands. When the administration in the early 1920s sought to increase central government control over Bushiru and Buhoma, regions historically governed by Hutu kings, they turned to the missionaries for assistance. According to Rutayisire, "They responded to this call in several ways: in preaching submission 'in the *inama* [chapels] and in the Church;' in founding branches in areas qualified as turbulent; and even in assisting in territorial justice."[54] When the Belgians implemented reforms in 1926 to streamline indigenous administration, eliminating the multiple, overlapping chieftancies that were the norm throughout most of Rwanda, they eliminated many positions held by Hutu, but at the same time they experimented with naming Hutu to the new, more powerful chieftancies. Mgr. Classe counseled against placing Hutu in positions of authority and instead urged that the young, educated Tutsi be moved into the new chieftancies. In a 1927 letter to the Belgian resident Mortehan, who sought advice from the apostolic vicar, Classe wrote:

Currently, if we take a practical point of view and consider the interest of the country, with the Tutsi youth we have an incomparable element of progress, which all who know Rwanda cannot overestimate.... If one asked of the Hutu if they preferred to be commanded by commoners or by nobles, the response is not in doubt; their preference goes for the Tutsi, and for good reason: born chiefs, they have the sense for commanding. That is the secret of their installation in the country and of their seizure of it.[55]

Within a few years, the Hutu chiefs were removed, and Tutsi came to occupy virtually all political offices in Rwanda.[56]

The White Father leaders continued to emphasize the importance of schools for attracting young Tutsi and providing a forum for winning their support. In 1925, Mgr. Classe wrote to the missionaries at Rulindo:

Encourage the movement of Tutsi into the mission, it is the future of the religion that is in play. These young people who are the future chiefs: it is important that

---

[54] Rutayisire, *La christianisation du Rwanda*, p. 136. Hutu kings were deposed in the early 1920s in Bukunzi and Busozo in the south as well.

[55] Letter from Mgr. Classe to Resident Mortehan, September 12, 1927, quoted in Kalibwami, *Le catholicisme et la société rwandaise*, p. 200.

[56] A. Van Overschelde, *Mgr L.P. Classe* (Kabgayi 1945), wrote "Already indebted to Mgr. Classe for the conservation of Gisaka, country where they possessed their primary family goods, the Tutsi owed to him moreover a much larger benefit still: their traditional hegemony and their hereditary privilege in the country" (p. 130).

we gain hold of them. Even if they are not instructed and baptized, their relations with us give more stability and activity to our work. The chiefs are and will be our great force against the actions and projects of the Protestants. The people will also have more confidence to come to us. Therefore, develop the Tutsi school, giving it the greatest attention and real support, this will be the means of keeping this youth with us, even if the government realizes the project of secular schools in all the chieftancies.[57]

In the 1920s, the White Fathers' strategy of appeasing the chiefs and courting the Tutsi finally began to pay off. The competing factions within the royal court, most of which had previously opposed the expansion of the missions and refused to cooperate with the missionaries, began to appeal to the missionaries for support in their struggles for power. Important Tutsi families began to send their sons to Catholic schools (while strategically sending other sons to the secular Belgian schools in Nyanza, Gatsibo, and elsewhere), and large numbers of young Tutsi signed up as catechumens and began to be baptized as Catholics. Classe and other missionaries now began to intervene to increase the power of the Catholic Tutsi, for example, by recommending baptized Christians or catechumens for the positions created in the administrative restructuring of 1926.[58]

By the early 1930s, the White Fathers found themselves in a particularly powerful position, with the Catholic Church playing an increasingly significant role in supplying education and other services, many Catholic converts having taken up important political positions, and favorable relations with the Belgian administration. Hence, Mgr. Classe felt sufficiently confident to confront the major remaining obstacle to the dream of establishing a Catholic kingdom: King Musinga himself. Since the White Fathers first began working in Rwanda in 1900, relations with the king had frequently been tense. Musinga had used the missionaries to help extend government control over peripheral regions and had periodically appealed to the White Fathers for support in his struggles against competing factions in the court, but he had remained suspicious of the missionaries and often demonstrated contempt for their religion. As the White Fathers gained in power, Musinga increasingly sought to appease them, but by then the missionaries already viewed Musinga as an enemy of the church, and they rebuffed his appeals. In 1927, in a terrible

---

[57] Letter from Classe to Rulindo mission, March 1925, quoted in Rutayisire, *La christianization du Rwanda*, p. 294.
[58] Rutayisire, *La christianisation du Rwanda*, pp. 150–2; Linden and Linden, *Church and Revolution in Rwanda*, pp. 135–64.

political miscalculation, Musinga began to court the Protestant missionaries who had recently renewed mission work in Rwanda. Unfortunately for Musinga, the Adventists and Anglicans had few converts and little influence, and his overtures to the Protestants solidified Catholic opposition to his rule.[59]

As early as 1927, Classe began a campaign against Musinga, denouncing the king in letters to the governor and resident and publishing an article in Europe in 1930 explaining his opposition to Musinga. Classe claimed that Musinga was the single greatest obstacle to economic development and social progress in Rwanda, and accused him not only of irresponsible leadership but of sexual immorality, including homosexuality and incest.[60] In the annual report for 1930–31, Classe wrote:

From a political point of view, the situation is becoming more difficult. Our sultan, Musinga, backtracks more and more: anti-European, anti-Catholic, he confides more and more in sorcerers, old regime, very convinced that the hour will sound where he will be able to boot out of his kingdom all the loathed Europeans who impede him to reign as he pleases. ... Throughout recent times, he has tried to turn to the Adventists; at base, he is mistaken about them, but they give largely and, through that, he thinks to hit us. His animosity against us is so much that the Tutsi youth is avid to be instructed and comes to us in large numbers. These young people subsequently refuse to serve the shameful royal pleasures, and, in this genre our Musinga has nothing to envy a Mtésa or a Mwanga of old Uganda. Even his sons, his daughters, are born for his pleasure. His hatred was accentuated the day when his second son and his sister, who in hiding were being instructed by people of their entourage, refused to lend themselves to his criminal pleasures. In an instant we became his declared enemies![61]

Although some priests viewed Classe's claims as exaggerated and dishonest, his campaign against Musinga had a profound impact on the colonial administrators who began to look for means to replace the king, and Classe played a central role in laying the groundwork for this action.[62]

---

[59] Alison Des Forges, "Defeat Is the Only Bad News: Rwanda under Musinga (1896–1931)," Ph.D. dissertation, Yale University, 1972; Linden and Linden, *Church and Revolution in Rwanda*, pp. 167–71; Rutayisire, *La christianisation du Rwanda*, pp. 177–87; Kalibwami, *Le catholicisme et la société rwandaise*, pp. 202–7.

[60] C.f., Kalibwami, *Le catholicisme et la société rwandaise*, pp. 207–10; Rutayisire, *La christianisation du Rwanda*, pp. 178–80; Ferdinand Nahimana, *Le blanc est arrivé, le roi est parti* (Kigali: Printer Set, 1987), pp. 172–9.

[61] *Rapports annuels des Missionaires d'Afrique*, no. 23, 1930–31, cited in Nahimana, *Le blanc est arrivé, le roi est parti*, pp. 175–6.

[62] Linden and Linden, *Church and Revolution in Rwanda*, p. 174.

While Musinga's son Rwigemera was the first prince to receive Catholic instruction, Classe doubted his sincerity and abilities and instead began to cultivate Rudahigwa who in 1930 became chief of Marangara, where Kabgayi is located. Rudahigwa met with Classe several times and became a Catholic catechumen, and Classe offered him to the Belgian administration as an alternative to his father. On November 14, 1931, the Belgian governor, with Mgr. Classe at his side, gathered together the chiefs of the country at Nyanza to announce that Musinga had abdicated in favor of his son, Rudahigwa, and two days later Rudahigwa was crowned under the dynastic name supplied to him by Classe, Mutara IV.[63]

As Musinga began to lose his grip on power, particularly after the administrative reforms of 1926, the Tutsi elite began to turn to the Catholic Church in massive numbers. Tutsi came to realize that conversion to Christianity was a requirement for advancement under the new system. As Linden stated, "The conversion of the Tutsi was a corporate recognition that the source of power within the State had shifted away from the mwami [Musinga]."[64] With the kingship in crisis, many of the elite were also looking for alternate sources of ritual legitimation that Catholicism promised to provide. The resulting rates of conversion were remarkable: while in the annual report for 1929–30, the White Fathers counted 4,937 baptisms, the number for 1930–31 jumped to 9,014 and to 16,527 in 1931–32, a large portion of these being Tutsi.[65] Just as the principles of Lavigerie predicted, once the chiefs converted, the masses followed in large numbers. While in 1930, the Catholic Church counted fewer than 100,000 baptized members, by 1940 the church had more than tripled in size to more than 300,000 adherents.[66] Some missionaries objected to the mass conversions, arguing that Cardinal Lavigerie had called for a long period of postulancy before allowing people to join the church. They complained that the mass conversions would, given the lack of a rigorous catechism, produce mediocre members, inadequately instructed in the principles of the faith, believers in name only.[67] But after

[63] Des Forges, "Defeat Is the Only Bad News"; Linden and Linden, *Church and Revolution in Rwanda*, pp. 167–75; Kalibwami, *Le catholicisme et la société rwandaise*, pp. 210–12; Rutayisire, *La christianisation du Rwanda*, p. 182; Ferdinand Nahimana, *Le blanc est arrivé, le roi est parti*, pp. 172–9.

[64] Linden and Linden, *Church and Revolution in Rwanda*, p. 173.

[65] Nahimana, *Le blanc est arrivé, le roi est parti*, p. 153.

[66] Kalibwami, *Le catholicisme et la société rwandaise*, p. 261.

[67] Rutayisire, *La christianisation du Rwanda*, p. 327. A lengthy period of training before being allowed to become a member was one of Lavigerie's central principles, since it

three decades of effort, the work of the White Fathers was finally paying off, and Mgr. Classe was not about to change strategy. Observers of the church in Rwanda in the 1930s wrote of a "tornado" where the "breath of the spirit" was blowing, as the churches filled with believers and thousands of Rwandans converted.

SUMMARY

In this chapter, I have not attempted to offer a comprehensive account of the relations of the White Fathers with the Rwandan court and the colonial administration during the early colonial period, but rather I have highlighted a few key characteristics of the implantation of the Catholic Church in Rwanda that have shaped the subsequent engagement of Christian churches in Rwandan society. From their earliest involvement in Rwanda, the leaders of the White Fathers attempted to become important political players and to use their political connections and influence to create a propitious environment for the expansion and successful operation of the Catholic Church. While they sought to increase the political power of the church, building up bases of support and manipulating their personal connections, the church leaders encouraged obedience to civil authorities on the part of their converts. The goal of the White Father leadership was not to set the church up as an alternative to the state but rather to make the church an indispensable partner of the state, with the state depending on the church to help maintain an orderly and prosperous society.

The church leaders did not offer unconditional support for civil authorities but sought to gain access to the centers of power, which they could use to influence the nature of policy. Some of the missionaries were critical of this approach, because they felt that the church should ally itself with the exploited of the society rather than with those who were exploiting them, but the leadership of the order acted forcefully to quash such dissent. Challenging the regime from below, they argued, would produce a weak and ineffective church and an unruly population and disorderly society. As I expand upon in Chapter 3, such views were influenced in no small part by the attitudes of the leadership toward the various ethnic groups – their sense that the Tutsi were more closely related to Europeans and, thus, destined to rule, while the Hutu were savages who could not

would discourage shallow conversion for political reasons. Over time in Rwanda, however, the period of time required in catechism classes had been gradually reduced.

be trusted with power. While expanding the power and influence of the church was their primary goal, the leaders of the order also appreciated the conservative values of obedience and social order. If the Catholic Church was to become an important center of political power and a partner with the state, the leaders did not want the population to challenge the structures of power. If reforms needed to be made, the church would help to bring them about in an orderly fashion from the top.

3

The Churches and the Politics of Ethnicity

Over the course of the six decades of colonial rule in Rwanda, the attitudes of the White Fathers and other missionaries toward Rwanda's ethnic groups shifted, but their belief in the centrality of ethnicity to social and political relations in the country never wavered. The White Fathers sought as a fundamental goal of their mission to build an alliance between the Catholic Church and the dominant political class in society, and they understood political power in Rwanda in primarily ethnic terms, ignoring or downplaying important divisions of class, region, lineage, clan, and political faction. Working together with the colonial administration and the indigenous elite, the missionaries helped to make this interpretation reality, so that by the end of the colonial period, the division among Hutu, Tutsi, and Twa had indeed become the predominant cleavage in Rwandan society.

In this chapter, I analyze the change in the Catholic missionaries' sympathies from a belief in the superiority and natural dominance of the Tutsi to a commiseration with the Hutu and support for their political rights. Although this shift had a profound impact on Rwandan society, helping to make possible the rise to power of the Hutu majority, it did not mark a major shift in the engagement of the Catholic Church in Rwanda. The church continued to support the centrality of ethnicity to Rwandan politics, and individuals within the church continued to use their political power to influence the selection of political leaders. As I also argue in this chapter, despite important theological differences and considerable antagonism between Catholic and Protestant missionaries, most Protestant missionaries did not differ substantially from the White Fathers in their attitudes toward political power and ethnicity. Like the White Fathers, Anglican, Seventh-Day Adventist, and Presbyterian missionaries all sought to promote their churches by gaining the favor of state leaders, and they held many of the same attitudes as the White Fathers toward ethnicity and civil obedience. The entanglement of church and state and the involvement of churches in ethnic politics in Rwanda are factors that have been consistent across denominational divides as well as across time, and they are at the root of explaining why the churches became so heavily implicated in the Rwandan genocide.

CHRISTIANITY AND THE CONSTRUCTION OF ETHNICITY

In the introductory essay to his edited volume on the construction of ethnicity in Southern Africa, Leroy Vail argued that European Christian missionaries played a crucial role in the development of ethnic ideologies in Africa. According to Vail:

In addition to creating written languages, missionaries were instrumental in creating cultural identities through their specification of "custom" and "tradition" and by writing "tribal" histories.... Once these elements of culture were in place and available to be used as the cultural base of a distinct new, ascriptive ethnic identity, it could replace older organizing principles that depended upon voluntary clientage and loyalty and which, as such, showed great plasticity. Thus firm, non-porous and relatively inelastic ethnic boundaries, many of which were highly arbitrary, came to be constructed and were then strengthened by the growth of stereotypes of "the other"....[1]

Vail argued that missionaries "incorporated into the curricula of their mission schools the lesson that the pupils had clear ethnic identities," and claims that they "educated local Africans who then themselves served as the most important force in shaping the new ethnic ideologies."[2] Combined with the policies of colonial administrators and the popular acceptance of ethnic ideas as a means of coping with the disruptions of modernity, the actions of missionaries helped to create the deep social divisions that are at the root of ethnic conflict in many African countries.

The Rwandan case is quite consistent with Vail's analysis. As discussed in Chapter 2, from their arrival in Rwanda the White Fathers regarded the divide among Hutu, Tutsi, and Twa as a racial divide, and

---

[1] Leroy Vail, "Introduction: Ethnicity in Southern African History," in *The Creation of Tribalism in Southern Africa*, edited by Leroy Vail (Berkeley and Los Angeles: University of California Press, 1989), pp. 1–19. Citation from p. 12.

[2] Ibid, p. 12.

their observations of the groups were shaped by their assumptions about the racial categories to which they believed each group belonged – the Tutsi to the Hamitic, the Hutu to the Bantu or Negroid, and the Twa to the Pygmoid. Based on highly selective observation, the missionaries developed an ideal physical type for each group. They saw the Tutsi phenotype as tall and thin, with narrow facial features and light skin; the Hutu as short and stocky, with wide facial features and darker skin; and Twa as very short, very dark, with very wide noses. Although certainly some people within each group fit the phenotype, looking stereotypically "Tutsi" or "Hutu" or "Twa," there were also many short and stocky Tutsi and tall, thin Hutu. In actual fact, the definitions revealed more about the preconceptions of the missionaries and other observers than they did about the actual physical appearance of the groups, which had after all been defined quite flexibly prior to colonial rule based on social status and occupation rather than on physical type or racial origin. The definition of the Tutsi phenotype in particular was shaped by the Hamitic hypothesis, which contended that the Hamites were distant relatives of Europeans.[3] Even some observers who have accepted the ideas of a racial divide between the groups could acknowledge the degree to which the definition of the Tutsi type was developed less out of scientific observation than out of the desire to confirm the Tutsi relationship to Europeans. For example, a discussion of physical anthropology in an official government publication from late in the colonial period noted:

The Tutsi's [narrow] nose made such an impression on the first observers that, referring unconsciously to the European physique, they ascribed thin lips to them as well. In fact, the Tutsi have, on the average, thicker lips than the Hutu and it is the Twa who have by far the thinnest lips. ... There is hardly any difference in the skin color of the groups ... .[4]

Despite the quite arbitrary nature of the definition of physical types, the conclusions of the earliest missionaries have shaped subsequent understandings of what it means to be Hutu, Tutsi, and Twa. As one survivor of the 1994 genocide told me, "So many people died because of their morphology."[5]

---

[3] Sanders, "The Hamitic Hypothesis"; Jean-Pierre Chrétien, *L'histoire retrouvée*, pp. 335–42.

[4] Information and Public Relations Office, Belgian Congo and Ruanda-Urundi, *Ruanda-Urundi: Geography and History* (Brussels, 1960), pp. 19–20.

[5] Private conversation with author in Butare, Rwanda, March 1996.

According to sociobiological theories widely accepted at the time that missionaries began working in Rwanda, various races had developed through an evolutionary process that left different races endowed not only with distinct physical traits but also with distinct capabilities. Races could be ranked hierarchically, with northern Europeans being the most highly evolved group with the most highly developed capabilities. More highly evolved races were considered more civilized, being biologically better equipped to create orderly and prosperous societies, and thus where more than one race existed in a country, the more highly evolved race would naturally dominate. Even before publication of Charles Darwin's *Origin of Species* in 1859 popularized the concept of evolution, ethnographers had identified a variety of distinct racial groups supposedly present in Africa. As Europeans encountered additional African groups, they placed the groups within the existing racial hierarchy that regarded Hamitic and Semitic peoples as the most highly evolved African groups, Bushmen and Pygmies most degenerate, and Negroid or Bantu peoples in between.[6]

Influenced by these sociobiological theories, most missionaries believed that the apparent physical differences among Hutu, Tutsi, and Twa were matched by their distinct personalities and psychological traits. The missionaries and other colonialists regarded the Tutsi as destined to rule Rwanda because of their superior intellect, refinement, and natural gifts for commanding, while they considered the Hutu simple and solid, naturally fit for physical labor and service. They viewed the Twa as savage, dirty, and dishonest. A passage from *Un Document, une épopée* demonstrates the attitude shared by many:

The Tutsi possess know-how, tactful manners that the Hutu, more uncouth and more timid, do not have. They have moreover a real sense of command that one notices even among children of fourteen or fifteen years of age. The Hutu is a worker, more tenacious, but more coarse.[7]

The support of the White Fathers for the Tutsi, then, derived not only from a pragmatic belief in the necessity of winning over the elite but also

---

[6] Sanders, "The Hamitic Hypothesis," pp. 523–8. The classic arguments for the hierarchical nature of racial differentiation include Arthur de Gobineau's *The Inequality of Human Races* (New York: G.P. Putnam's Sons, 1915), originally published in 1854, and Francis Galton's *Inquiries Into Human Faculties* published in 1883, in which he coined the term "eugenics." A number of excellent histories of racial ideas are available, including the 1933 classic by Eric Voegelin, *The History of the Race Idea: From Ray to Carus* in *The Collected Works of Eric Voegelin*, vol. 3 (Baton Rouge: Louisiana State University Press, 1998).

[7] Quoted in Rutayisire, *La christianisation du Rwanda*, p. 423, n. 155.

a belief in the natural superiority of the Tutsi. The missionaries, particularly the missionary superiors, supported the Tutsi not simply because
they ruled the country, but because they believed they *should* rule the
country according to the natural order of things and the talents that
God had given them. A 1927 letter from Mgr. Classe to Belgian Resident
Mortehan reflects this sentiment that God had ordained Tutsi to rule:

> As for ourselves, from a religious point of view, since that is our perspective, we
> think from experience that the Tutsi element is for us better, more active, more
> committed, more capable of playing the role of inspiring the masses, and those
> who exercise the happiest directing influence on the masses. ... This good element
> that we already have in hand, all we have to do is to use it for the material devel-
> opment of Rwanda.[8]

In a 1930 letter, Classe warned Mortehan against replacing the Tutsi
political elite, an idea considered because of frustrations with Musinga
and his supporters.

> A revolution of that nature would lead the entire state directly into anarchy and
> to bitter anti-European Communism. Far from furthering progress, it would nul-
> lify the government's action by depriving it of auxiliaries who are, by birth, capa-
> ble of understanding and following it. This is the view and the firm belief of all
> superiors of the Ruanda mission, without exception. Generally speaking, we have
> no chiefs who are better qualified, more intelligent, more active, more capable of
> appreciating progress and more fully accepted by the people than the Tutsi.[9]

The White Fathers did not, of course, single handedly create ethnicity in
Rwanda. The categories of Hutu, Tutsi, and Twa existed before the arrival
of Europeans in Rwanda, and the process of centralization, particularly
under Rwabugiri who established Tutsi as chiefs in various peripheral
areas of the kingdom, had already increased the significance of the categories, endowed them with status distinctions, and limited their flexibility. Missionary conclusions about race relations in Rwanda were based to
some extent on existing social categories and the inequalities that existed
in at least some parts of the colony, and they were confirmed by both
colonial administrators and academics. Further, the Tutsi quickly perceived the advantages of feeding European stereotypes and misconcep-
tions. Not surprisingly, Tutsi did not dissuade the missionaries from their
belief in natural Tutsi superiority, which not only implied their natural

---

[8] Classe in letter to Resident Mortehan, September 12, 1927, quoted in Rutayisire, *La christianisation du Rwanda*, pp. 175, 177.
[9] Cited in Lemarchand, *Rwanda and Burundi*, p. 73.

right to rule, but also provided evidence to support the conclusions. As Alison DesForges wrote, "In a great and unsung collaborative enterprise over a period of decades, Europeans and Rwandan intellectuals created a history of Rwanda that fit European assumptions and accorded with Tutsi interests."[10]

While they did not create ethnicity, the missionaries did have a profound impact on the nature of identities in Rwanda, particularly by infusing them with racial significance. Using oral traditions from the royal court as evidence, several Catholic priests, including White Fathers such as Albert Pagès and Louis de Lacger, and above all Alexis Kagame, a Rwandan Tutsi of royal lineage, published histories that played an important role in shaping perceptions of the Rwandan past.[11] These histories ignored the complexity of precolonial political arrangements, the often-limited nature of central court authority over territories, and the flexible character of ethnic identities and instead reinforced royal claims to a right to control Rwanda by arguing that Tutsi were indeed a Hamitic people who had conquered Rwanda through their superior military and political organization. J.K. Rennie summarized the history developed by Pagés, de Lacger, Kagame, and a few others:

> The "court interpretation" holds that into a fragmented congeries of tiny Bantu chieftaincies came a cohesive group of pastoral "Hamitic" Tutsi from the north. ... By diplomacy, by settlement, by economic power deriving from their control of cattle, but above all by conquest, they built an expansionist state with an organized army which by the end of the nineteenth century had expanded throughout and even beyond present Rwanda. The chief means by which the conquered Bantu ("Hutu") were assimilated into this state was by a system of vassalage in which they received the use of cattle in return for services and loyalty.[12]

Far from being of merely academic interest, these histories served to confirm the racial nature of the three groups in Rwanda and the

---

[10] Alison Des Forges, "The Ideology of Genocide," *Issue: A Journal of Opinion*, 23, no. 2, 1995, p. 45.

[11] C.f., A. Pagès, *Un Royaume Hamite au centre de l'Afrique: Au Rwanda sur les bos du lac Kivu* (Brussels: Van Campenhout, 1933); de Lacger, *Le Ruanda*; Alexis Kagame, *La Poésie Dynastique au Rwanda*, (Brussels: Institute Royal du Congo Belge [IRCB], 1951); Kagame, *Le code des institutions politiques du Rwanda précolonial* (Brussels: IRCB, 1952); Kagame, *Les organisations socio-familiales de l'ancien Rwanda* (Brussels: IRCB, 1954); Kagame, *L'histoire des armées bovines dans l'ancien Rwanda* (Brussels: ARSOM, 1963).

[12] Rennie, "The precolonial kingdom of Rwanda," p. 12. For an assessment of the significance of these histories, in addition to Rennie, see Claudine Vidal, *Sociologie des passions* (Paris: Karthala, 1991), in which she discusses Kagame as a person and his impact on the development of ethnic identities in Rwanda.

superiority of the Tutsi, whose origins were outside Rwanda and who had subjugated local populations, and thus justified the further exclusion of Hutu from power and opportunity. The White fathers actively discriminated in their schools in favor of Tutsi whom they believed would, as "natural" leaders, make better priests and administrators. They favored Tutsi for entrance in the Catholic seminaries, producing a large group of Tutsi priests with significant social and political influence.[13] The early general education offered by the Catholic Church served primarily the children of Tutsi chiefs, and as the numbers of schools increased and Hutu gained admittance, they offered separate programs of education for Hutu and Tutsi. The students who enrolled in Group Scolaire d'Astrida, the preeminent secondary school in Rwanda established in the town now known as Butare by the church with government funds in 1929 (the first students enrolled in 1932), were almost exclusively Tutsi, even though officially the school was open to "all castes." From the school's foundation, graduates of Groupe Scolaire dominated Rwandan public life, being the primary group out of which the Belgian regime chose chiefs and administrators and the source of nearly all Rwandan professionals, such as teachers, agronomists, and medical personnel.[14]

Under the system of indirect rule applied by the Belgians, the myths of ethnicity that church personnel had helped to create became a basis for law. In administrative reforms that began in the 1920s, chieftancies were reserved for Tutsi. "Native tribunals," a court system designed to be consistent with indirect rule, became, in the words of René Lemarchand:

> the instruments through which the ruling Tutsi oligarchy not only retained but abused its privileges. Their function was not so much to dispense justice as to legitimise abuses and wrong-doings. Since they were in every case headed by Tutsi chiefs it is difficult to imagine how they could have served a different purpose.[15]

As the colonial state sought to privatize and legally define property rights, Tutsi were in a position to benefit disproportionately, in part

---

[13] René Lemarchand, *Rwanda and Burundi* (New York: Praeger, 1970), pp. 136–7.

[14] Gamiliel Mbonimana, "Christianisation indirecte et cristallisation des clivages ethniques au Rwanda (1925–1931)" *Enquêtes et Documents d'Histoire Africaine*, 3 (1978), pp. 125–63; Lemarchand, *Rwanda and Burundi*, pp. 74–5, 134–9; Rutayisire, *La christianisation du Rwanda*, p. 316. Rutayisire wrote, "[E]thnic segregation was ... one of the dominant traits of this educational system. This aggravated the inequalities between the Hutu and Tutsi, in monopolizing cultural and political power in the hands of the educated Tutsi elite and in this manner arousing ethnic cleavages that did not previously exist" (p. 316).

[15] Lemarchand, *Rwanda and Burundi*, pp. 75–6.

because they could use the native tribunals to make successful claims over land, cattle, and other property for which their rights of ownership were questionable. Other policies also enhanced the position of Tutsi while increasing the subjugation of Hutu. The *Uburetwa* system that required labor and tribute from those of low status for chiefs and others of high status had expanded in the late precolonial period as the monarchy used ethnic differentiation to increase its power, but under the Belgians, forced labor under *uburetwa* was assigned to all Hutu men by law, codifying the status differentiation.[16]

The conceptions of ethnicity and of Rwandan history propagated by the missionaries, colonial administrators, and indigenous elite and the discriminatory practices of both church and state ultimately affected how Rwandans perceived their own identities. Regardless of where authors fall in the academic debate over whether in precolonial Rwanda the terms Hutu, Tutsi, and Twa referred to mere occupational categories or reflected a status difference, they almost universally recognize that the colonial experience endowed the terms with expanded significance. Under colonial policies, political, economic, and even religious opportunities were reserved for Tutsi, while individual identities lost their previous flexibility. By issuing identity cards in the 1930s that registered each individual's ethnic identity and by codifying the principle that children automatically take their father's identity, the administration eliminated the possibility for Hutu families to become Tutsi through the accumulation of power. As Alison Des Forges states, "These administrative measures made it almost impossible for Hutu to become Tutsi just at a time when being Tutsi brought all the advantages."[17] While academics might debate the historical meaning of the terms, in the experience of individual Rwandans, whether they were Hutu or Tutsi came to be of great importance, since it determined to a substantial degree their life chances. Since the first academic account to significantly challenge the official version of Rwandan history was not published until 1962,[18] Rwandans heard no alternatives to the history they were taught in schools, and the image it presented of a clear ethnic division coincided with their contemporary

---

[16] Newbury, *The Cohesion of Oppression*, pp. 140–7.
[17] Alison DesForges, "Rwanda," in Cynthia Brown and Farhad Karim, eds., *Playing the Communal Card: Communal Violence and Human Rights* (New York: Human Rights Watch, 1995), pp. 1–17, quotation p. 2.
[18] Vansina, *L'évolution du royaume Rwanda*, challenged a number of the assumptions of the work of Kagame, Pagès, and de Lacger, proposing a shorter history of the Rwandan kingdom, in which central control was extended less steadily and with less thoroughness.

experience of ethnic inequality. It is not surprising, then, that Rwandans came to understand their ethnicity in the terms developed largely by the churches. Within a few decades of the arrival of the first German administrators and the first Catholic missionaries, the fiction of ethnicity had, in a practical sense, become a reality, a political and social fact of primary importance.[19]

FROM TUTSI TO HUTU

In the decades after World War II, attitudes toward ethnicity among both Catholic missionaries and, eventually, colonial administrators began to shift. Affected by changing ideas about race, justice, and equality, a number of newer missionaries were offended by the terrible contrast between the growing poverty of the Hutu masses and the wealth and opportunity of the Tutsi elite. These missionaries created opportunities for Hutu within church institutions, fostering a new Hutu elite who challenged the injustices of the Rwandan system and eventually, after a popular revolt in 1959 drove Tutsi chiefs from office, assumed political power. Despite the highly consequential shift in missionary support from Tutsi to Hutu, the principles of church–state engagement in Rwanda remained substantially unchanged. The churches continued to engage actively in ethnic politics without challenging the central principles at the root of Rwanda's ethnic conflict. Furthermore, the Catholic Church once again played kingmaker, helping to bring to office politicians with strong ties to the church; the close alliance between church and state was never in doubt.

From the beginning of the White Father mission in Rwanda, some priests believed that the Catholic Church should challenge the perceived injustices of the Rwandan socioeconomic system and support the rights of the Hutu against the Tutsi whom they believed oppressed and exploited the Hutu, but the order's leadership intervened to quash such sentiments and reassert the church's conservative support for the existing structures of power. By the 1940s, however, the White Fathers had accomplished

---

[19] Filip Reyntjens, *L'Afrique des Grands Lacs en Crise: Rwanda, Burundi: 1988–1994* (Paris: Karthala, 1994) argued that the attempts to understand the historical anthropological nature of ethnicity in Rwanda and Burundi neglect ethnicity as it is experienced by the population: "The anthropological definitions that have so often been given to demonstrate the existence or not of ethnicity in the two countries, when all is said and done have little importance for understanding the conflicts of today. ... It is thus necessary to extend the anthropological definition and search for a politically operational definition based on the sentiments of attributed membership, real or ideal" (p. 10).

their primary goals – making the Catholic Church a powerful presence in Rwandan politics and society, converting the political elite, and attracting large numbers of the masses. With the death in 1945 of Mgr. Classe, the chief architect of Catholic policy for nearly forty years, church leaders were freed to consider new strategies and priorities for the church. For example, concerned that many of the new Catholic converts showed little understanding of church teachings, the superiors of missions decided in a 1945 meeting to return to one of Cardinal Lavigerie's main principles previously neglected in Rwanda and extended substantially the duration of the period of catechism required before conversion.[20]

Mgr. Classe's successor, Mgr. Laurent Deprimoz, was relatively conservative and did not radically change the direction of the church, but while he was bishop, a new breed of missionary began arriving in Rwanda who questioned the church's alliance with the Tutsi. In the aftermath of World War II, attitudes toward race, human rights, and colonialism were changing internationally, and although the Catholic Church leadership and many older missionaries were slow to react to these changing ideas, many of the younger missionaries had links to the European working class and were influenced by social democratic ideas. They saw in the Hutu an exploited class whose interests the church should be championing, and they began to create opportunities for Hutu, increasing Hutu enrollment in church schools and cultivating educated Hutu. For example, in 1950 Father Arthur Dejemeppe took Grégoire Kayibanda, a young Hutu school teacher who had attended the junior seminary at Nyakibanda, with him to a Young Catholic Worker (Jeunesse Ouvriere Catholique, JOC) conference in Belgium, where he spent two months living with Dejemeppe's family and made contacts with Christian socialists and trade unionists.[21]

The new missionaries were critical of the colonial nature of the Catholic Church in Rwanda, with nearly all leadership positions still held by whites, but they were also uncomfortable with the predominance of Tutsi among the clergy. The Tutsi clergy were a particularly conservative lot; generally strong royalists, they developed a close alliance with the Tutsi chiefs, and they objected increasingly to the continuing domination of the church by the White Fathers. Sympathies among the missionaries for Hutu only exacerbated the tensions with the Tutsi clergy. By 1951, indigenous clergy outnumbered the White Fathers, eighty-nine to eighty-seven – numbers that do not include the members of the two indigenous

---

[20] Linden and Linden, *Church and Revolution in Rwanda*, p. 220.
[21] Ibid, pp. 220–9.

religious orders, the Josephite Brothers and Benebikira Sisters – and in response to growing tensions, the church hierarchy began to appoint Rwandans to various ecclesiastical positions. In 1947, the church sent the first Rwandan to study abroad, Déogratias Mbandiwimfura, a Tutsi. In 1952, Aloys Bigirumwami, a descendent of the royal family of Gisaka, was named bishop of the new vicariate in the northwest of the country, Nyundo, which quickly became a center for dissident Tutsi clergy.[22]

As Rwandan clergy expanded their presence in the Catholic Church, they deepened the alliance between political and religious authorities. While the leadership of the White Fathers had sought to make the Catholic Church a player in national politics, the indigenous clergy translated these principles to the local level, integrating parishes into local structures of power. As Linden wrote,

Both Tutsi and Hutu priests were able to translate their spiritual authority into a temporal sway over their parishioners. Members of an Abbé's family tended to settle around his mission or find employment there, and as Father Superior he was able to build up a network of clients, often becoming a confidant of the local chief; several Astridiens [graduates of Group Scolaire] passed through minor seminaries in the company of future Abbés, and school ties remained strong. False modesty or pretence that authority should be shorn of material expression was generally lacking; the priest was a local leader.[23]

Kalibwami made a similar observation:

The priests, religious brothers, sisters, new elite of Rwanda, benefited thus, and in all localities, from a special prestige. The people allowed them the socio-economic and cultural advantages they enjoyed, because Rwanda considered social hierarchies as natural. People waited only for the privileged, well dressed, and highly placed person to show himself useful and kindly. And the people had no doubt that the clergy and members of religious congregations would prove useful ... .[24]

The Catholic Church of course remained an important power at the national level as well. In 1943, King Rudahigwa and the queen mother were baptized, and in 1946 Rudahigwa consecrated Rwanda to Christ the King. In 1950, the Rwandan Catholic Church celebrated its fiftieth

---

[22] Linden and Linden, *Church and Revolution in Rwanda*, wrote, "No clear-cut split occurred among the clergy but it would be truer to say that Nyundo became the Tutsi, rather than the Rwandan, vicariate, with a powerful caucus of anti-colonial Abbés intent on championing ruling-class culture" (p. 230). See also, Kalibwami, *Le catholicisme et la société rwandaise*, pp. 290–311.

[23] Linden and Linden, *Church and Revolution in Rwanda*, pp. 223–4.

[24] Kalibwami, *Le catholicisme et la société rwandaise*, p. 276.

anniversary with great ceremony. Most chiefs and administrators were Catholic, and association with the Catholic Church (or to a lesser degree a Protestant church) had become essential for social advancement.[25]

Facing increasing public discontent, the colonial administration, like the Catholic Church, began in the 1950s to implement a variety of reforms. In 1952, they created representative councils in each subchieftancy, chieftancy, and province to act as a check on the power of the chiefs, and in 1953, they created a Conseil Supérior for the country to advise the king.[26] In 1954 the king and the Conseil Supérior issued a decree to dissolve the *ubuhake* system of cattle clientship progressively and allow the distribution of cows between patrons and clients.[27] The impetus for reform increased after Jean-Paul Harroy was named Vice-Governor General for Ruanda-Urundi in 1955, since he became convinced of the necessity of confronting Rwanda's ethnic tensions.[28] Rather than appeasing Rwandan critics of the colonial regime, however, reforms raised public expectations, particularly among Hutu, who were quickly disappointed by the failure of the changes to improve their material and political conditions. The "representative" councils were not in fact representative and tended to increase the power of the chiefs, while the abolition of *ubuhake* did little to open up economic possibilities for the Hutu peasants.[29]

The church became deeply embroiled in the growing ethnic strains in Rwanda in the 1950s. As Lemarchand noted, "As an instrument of socialisation, nowhere else in Africa did the Church play a more critically important role than in Rwanda."[30] The Catholic church had played an important role in creating the class of educated and Westernized Tutsi elite who dominated nearly all positions of power in the country from the early 1930s and in developing an ideology to support their domination, but after World War II, the church also played the primary role in creating what Lemarchand called a Hutu "counter-elite." While Tutsi clergy remained closely tied to Tutsi political officials and helped to develop anti-European and nationalist ideas, advocating independence from the

---

[25] Ibid, pp. 279–86.

[26] Linden and Linden, *Church and Revolution in Rwanda*, pp. 230–1.

[27] Newbury, *The Cohesion of Oppression*, pp. 144–7; Lemarchand, *Rwanda and Burundi*, pp. 127–33.

[28] Harroy's autobiography offers an interesting window into the activities of the Belgian administration in the decade prior to independence. Jean-Paul Harroy, *Rwanda: De la féodalité à la démocratie, 1955–1962* (Brussels: Hayez, 1984).

[29] Lemarchand, *Rwanda and Burundi*, pp. 119–33; Linden and Linden, *Church and Revolution in Rwanda*, pp. 230–1.

[30] Lemarchand, *Rwanda and Burundi*, p. 133.

Belgians, whom they accused of manufacturing the ethnic tensions in the country, the younger missionaries began cultivating a class of educated Hutu who would eventually oversee a transformation of the Rwandan political system, particularly after one of these young White Fathers, André Perraudin, succeeded Deprimoz as bishop of Kabgayi in 1956. Beginning in 1956, Group Scolaire began to increase significantly its Hutu enrollment. With administrative and political posts closed to Hutu, however, the new graduates had difficulty finding suitable employment; Rwanda's first university graduate was forced to take a job as a typist, after being rejected for employment by the king and various colonial agencies. The churches provided some of the only opportunities for educated Hutu, and the missionaries actively sought to promote the Hutu they considered to have greatest potential. Kayibanda became editor of the Catholic newspaper *Kinyamateka* in 1954 and later served as Mgr. Perraudin's personal secretary and as head of Trafipro, a Catholic consumers' cooperative. Calliope Mulindihabi, a Hutu who also subsequently became an important political figure, also served as Perraudin's secretary.[31]

In the late 1950s, the Hutu counter-elite began to express criticisms of the Rwandan state. Given the conservatism of much of the Tutsi elite, which resisted Belgian initiatives for reform and supported national independence as a means of protecting Tutsi hegemony, Hutu anger was directed not primarily at the Belgians, who had assisted the Tutsi concentration of power and wealth, but at the Tutsi themselves, whom the Hutu viewed as their primary obstacle to gaining political power. Such a position should not be surprising, given the fact that the Tutsi themselves had promulgated a version of Rwandan history that claimed that the subjugation of the Hutu had begun long before the arrival of the Europeans. As editor of *Kinyamateka* from 1954 to 1956, Kayibanda published articles that analyzed the injustices of Rwandan society through the prism of Catholic social teachings, and *Kinyamateka* quickly became a mouthpiece for Hutu resentments.[32] Although Perraudin replaced him as editor in 1956, Kayibanda became an important figure among the Hutu counter-elite. In March 1957, Kayibanda joined with Perraudin's secretary, Mulindahabi; Maximilien Niyonzima, an editor at *Kinyamateka*;

---

[31] Lemarchand, *Rwanda and Burundi*, pp. 133–45; Linden and Linden, *Church and Revolution in Rwanda*, pp. 231–9; Kalibwami, *Le catholicisme et la société Rwandaise*, pp. 298–311.

[32] Linden and Linden, *Church and Revolution in Rwanda*, pp. 235–7; Kalibawmi, *Le catholicisme et la société rwandaise*, pp. 268–373.

Claver Ndahayo, an employee of the Catholic printers at Kabgayi; Aloys Munyangaju, an active Catholic who worked for a Belgian company; and several other prominent Hutu, with the assistance of at least two White Fathers, to publish the *Bahutu Manifesto* from Kabgayi. This document decried indirect rule, the political monopoly of Tutsi that had allowed them to gain a social and economic monopoly as well, and the persistence of *ubuhake*, and it laid out a series of demands regarding private property, workers' rights, and the promotion of Hutu to political office.[33]

Three months later, Kayibanda founded the Muhutu Social Movement (Mouvement Social Muhutu, MSM), a party that he planned to use to launch a campaign for Hutu equality. Although the MSM initially had very little popular support, Lemarchand noted:

> The main asset of the Hutu leadership was the almost unconditional support they received from the Catholic Church, which enabled them, among other things, to gain control over the vernacular press and to use the daily newspaper *Temps Nouveaux d'Afrique*, published in Bujumbura, as a vehicle for the diffusion of their ideas among Europeans and literate Africans.[34]

Another Hutu party, the Association for the Social Promotion of the Mass (Association pour la Promotion Social de la Masse, APROSOMA), was founded shortly later by a former seminary student, Joseph Gitera, who was a signatory of the *Manifesto* but believed that Kayibanda and the MSM were too moderate. Gitera and his party were motivated by a type of Christian radicalism and based at the Save parish.[35]

The Belgian administration was slow to react to the *Manifesto*, but as Hutu complaints and political organization expanded, an opinion grew among administrators that significant change was taking place in response to the Hutu–Tutsi conflict. The Tutsi elite, in contrast, responded both defensively and dismissively to Hutu criticism, believing that the Hutu counter-elite did not represent the masses. A May 1958 letter signed by the elders in the king's court asserted that since the founder of the king's Banyinginya clan had defeated the Hutu and reduced them to servitude, "there could be no basis for brotherhood between Hutu and Tutsi. ... Since our king conquered the country and the Hutu and killed their petty kings, how can they claim to be our brothers?"[36] Tensions were raised

[33] Lemarchand, *Rwanda and Burundi*.
[34] Ibid, p. 151.
[35] Linden and Linden, *Church and Revolution in Rwanda*, pp. 251–4; Lemarchand, *Rwanda and Burundi*, pp. 151–3.
[36] Bagaragu b'ibwami bakuru, quoted in Lemarchand, *Rwanda and Burundi*, p. 154.

significantly after King Rudahigwa died in Bujumbura in July 1959 under mysterious circumstances that led many Tutsi to conclude that he had been murdered. In August, a group of prominent Tutsi chiefs founded the National Rwandan Union (Union Nationale Rwandaise, UNAR) as a party to defend Tutsi supremacy, adopting an anti-Belgian, pro-monarchist platform. In October, Kayibanda converted the MSM into a more effective political party, the Party of the Movement for Hutu Emancipation (Parti du Mouvement pour l'Emancipation Hutu, PARMEHUTU), which quickly gained a large following in Kayibanda's home region, Gitarama. UNAR denounced the formation of the party as an orchestration of the Belgian administration and the Catholic Church.[37] Mgr. Perraudin responded by denouncing UNAR in a confidential circular to all priests and later in a joint letter with Mgr. Bigirumwami claiming that the party was "ultra-nationalist" and anti-Church, influenced by communism and Islam.[38]

Tensions in Rwanda had mounted to a point where violence became likely. The spark that set it off came in early November 1959, when UNAR militants beat a Hutu subchief in Gitarama and it was erroneously reported that he had died. Hutu who gathered at the local chief's house to protest were insulted, and they responded with violence, killing four Tutsi leaders. Over the next week, violence spread throughout Gitarama and to neighboring provinces. Small groups of Hutu traveled through the countryside looting and burning Tutsi homes, in an apparently spontaneous uprising.[39] Attacks drove thousands of Tutsi from their homes, many fleeing Rwanda for refuge in neighboring countries. UNAR responded with targeted attacks against politically active Hutu, sometimes accompanied with improvised trials at the royal court in Nyanza.[40]

---

[37] UNAR claimed in a circular, "This movement will be said to have come from Christ and to preach charity. Its first meeting was held in Kigali, on September 1. Its adherents went to pay homage to Mgr. Perraudin on September 15." Quoted in Lemarchand, *Rwanda and Burundi*, pp. 160–1.

[38] Linden and Linden, *Church and Revolution in Rwanda*, pp. 254–67; Lemarchand, *Rwanda and Burundi*, pp. 153–61.

[39] Lemarchand, *Rwanda and Burundi*, wrote: "Despite the striking uniformity of the methods used, there is every reason to believe that the revolt was more in the nature of a spontaneous uprising, triggered off by the force of example, than the result of a master plan" (p. 163).

[40] Lemarachand, *Rwanda and Burundi*, p. 165, reports the testimony of a Hutu who survived a trial at the court because of administrative intervention. During his interrogation, "... Sendanyoye asked me to write down on a piece of paper that Mgr. Perraudin was the President of APROSOMA. I answered that this was false and that I would not write such a statement." (p. 166). The testimony suggests the degree to which Tutsi leaders

Finally, two weeks into the violence, Belgian paratroopers arrived from Congo to restore order.[41]

In the aftermath of the *jacquerie*, the colonial administration, under the direction of Colonel Guy Logiest, who was sent in as Special Resident at the beginning of the violence, moved quickly to change the face of Rwandan politics. Twenty-one Tutsi chiefs and 332 subchiefs were killed, arrested, or driven from office during the crisis, and the Belgian administration replaced nearly all of them with Hutu. In some cases, the administration merely declared that a chief or subchief lacked popular support and named a replacement. Almost immediately after the violence, the administration began to devise a new administrative structure, replacing subchieftancies with communes headed by an elected burgomaster and communal council. The first elections were held in June and July, allowing Hutu their first opportunity to elect their local leaders, though the elections were heavily regulated by the administration and were surrounded by violence, perpetrated by Hutu, Tutsi, and colonial security forces. In the council elections, PARMEHUTU won 2,390 of 3,125 seats, with UNAR winning only 56. On January 28, 1961, following the failure of a conference held at Ostend to develop a solution agreeable to the Belgian government, Hutu leaders, and the royal court, Logiest and the leaders of PARMEHUTU brought together the communal councilors from throughout the country for a meeting at which Joseph Gitera announced the abolition of the monarchy and Kayibanda was introduced as the new prime minister.[42]

CHURCH AND STATE IN THE AFTERMATH OF THE REVOLUTION

When Rwanda gained independence on July 1, 1962, a large portion of the country's new leaders were Hutu who had risen to prominence through support from Catholic missionaries. While most avenues of advancement had remained closed to Hutu, regardless of their abilities and qualifications, the Catholic Church had provided a select group of Hutu with education and jobs, and offered the institutional backing that

---

believed that the Hutu were being driven to revolt by the Catholic church and the colonial administration.

[41] Lemarchand, *Rwanda and Burundi*, pp. 159–69.

[42] Prunier, *The Rwanda Crisis*, pp. 48–54; Lemarchand, *Rwanda and Burundi*, pp. 170–96.

allowed them to challenge Tutsi hegemony over Rwandan society and politics. In the aftermath of the ethnic violence and the rise to political office of many of the Hutu who had been encouraged by the church, both Hutu and Tutsi alike credited the Catholic Church with encouraging the revolution. Many Hutu came to view the Catholic Church as their champion, while many Tutsi, particularly those living in exile, turned away from the church, accusing it of being anti-Tutsi.[43]

In reality, the position of the Catholic Church in the independence process was much more complex and divided. As Lemarchand noted,

[I]t is important at the outset to call explicit attention to the dual role played by the Church in Rwanda. Insofar as it lent its support to the principle of indirect rule and deliberately favoured the ruling caste in matters of education and evangelisation, the Church has undoubtedly contributed to the preservation of the status quo; but to the extent that there were significant exceptions to this rule, as was the case after the Second World War, its role has been just the opposite.[44]

The duality of the Catholic Church persisted even at the time of the violence and transfer of power. While a number of the younger missionaries actively sought to promote a group of Hutu protegés in the hopes of eliminating the injustices they saw in Rwandan society, other missionaries continued to hold a romanticized vision of the noble Tutsi who dominated the Hutu masses because of their superior capacities. The vast majority of the indigenous clergy were Tutsi, who condemned not only the Belgian administration but the White Fathers as well. While Kabgayi became a center for Hutu activism, conservative Tutsi churchmen looked to Nyundo for support. As Linden argued convincingly, however, although Tutsi accused Mgr. Perraudin of personally encouraging the revolution, the archbishop's position was in fact much more ambivalent. Perraudin opposed the anti-European, anti-Catholic rhetoric of UNAR but refused to endorse PARMEHUTU, replacing Kayibanda as editor of *Kinyamateka* with a moderate Tusti, Justin Kalibwami, and later with a more hard-line Tutsi, and seeking to maintain some neutrality for the church. Mgr. Bigirumwami should also not be characterized as a

---

[43] Linden and Linden, *Church and Revolution in Rwanda*, pp. 270–86. The Tutsi's belief that the Catholics were responsible for the Hutu revolt inspired many Tutsi refugees to convert to Protestantism or even to Islam. Among the Tutsi who have returned to Rwanda since 1994 are a large number of Anglicans, Pentecostals, and Muslims.

[44] Lemarchand, *Rwanda and Burundi*, pp. 133–4.

Tutsi hard-liner, as his political activities were few.[45] In a complex reality, the church harbored both European missionaries and Hutu priests who sympathized with the Hutu struggle for power and used church institutions to promote the interests of the Hutu and at the same time other missionaries and conservative Tutsi priests who opposed a transfer of power and used church institutions to support the status quo.

While the support that representatives of the Catholic Church offered Hutu activists contributed to a major transformation of Rwandan society, in several key ways the actions by the progressive missionaries – and by extension the Catholic Church – in the 1950s and 1960s were consistent with previous church positions. Just as Mgr. Classe had cultivated Rudahigwa and orchestrated his ascension to power, Father Dejemeppe and others cultivated Kayibanda and other Hutu and influenced the Belgian administration in bringing them to power. The church once again played the role of kingmaker, and after independence in 1962, church leaders were once again well placed to have substantial political influence. Conflicts did occasionally arise in the First Republic as Kayibanda and other leaders fostered by the missionaries struggled to show that they were not mere puppets of the priests, but the links between the new government elite and the church were generally as close as they had been under the previous regime. The Rwandan Catholic Church in fact came under international criticism in the early 1960s for failing, because of the privileged position of the church in the new Rwandan state, to condemn ongoing massacres of Tutsi.[46] Just as the missionaries had never been unanimous in their approval of Classe's alliance with the Tutsi elite, the Catholic Church in the 1950s was not united in its support of the Hutu counter-elite, but in both cases, the conflict was never over *whether* the church should engage in politics but which side it should take; the principle of the church acting as an important political player remained consistent.

Second, although the Catholic Church may have changed sides in Rwanda's Hutu-Tutsi conflict in the 1950s, as clerical advocates for Hutu became more numerous, the principle of Catholic engagement in ethnic politics remained consistent. In contrast to the historical revisionism offered by academics beginning with Jan Vansina's reassessment

[45] Linden and Linden, *Church and Revolution in Rwanda*, pp. 235–73; Kalibwami, *Le catholicisme et la société rwandaise*, pp. 415–47.

[46] Linden and Linden, *Church and Revolution in Rwanda*, pp. 282–4; Lemarchand, *Rwanda and Burundi*, pp. 258–60.

of the dynastic tradition published in 1962, the Catholic missionaries who championed the rights of Hutu did not challenge the basic facts of Rwandan history offered in the "court interpretation" – the Tutsi conquest and subjugation of the Hutu. Instead, they challenged the results of the history. While for an earlier generation of missionaries, influenced by conservative social ideas and racial ideologies, the Tutsi's supposed natural superiority justified their rule, for the younger missionaries, influenced by Catholic social democratic ideas, the Hutu were not an inferior race but an exploited underclass.[47] Neither the old nor the new missionaries, however, questioned the significance of ethnicity as a political issue, nor did either group question the church's involvement in ethnic politics.

The involvement of the church in the 1959 revolution did mark a deviation from the previous engagement of the Catholic church in Rwandan society on one key point: In sharp contrast to the policy of allying the church with the powerful advocated by Mgr. Classe, the newer missionaries encouraged, at least indirectly, rebellion against established authorities. While the White Fathers under Classe became embroiled in internal court politics, supporting a "palace coup," under Perraudin they supported a challenge to the regime from outside, which many Hutu and Tutsi alike saw as a general church endorsement of radicalism. In retrospect, the change was not as profound as it at first appeared, as even the most radical fathers did not truly support the general principle of rebellion but rather the rights of the majority to have a representative government. Once the revolution was achieved and Hutu dominated political office, there was no longer justification for popular insurrection, and the church once again returned to a conservative message of obedience to authorities. In fact, as Linden argued, the Catholic working class activism in Europe that influenced the new missionaries was a strategy for maintaining the loyalty of the masses to the church in the face of the threat of Communism. By supporting the rights of the masses, the church could prevent their movement to an even more radical politics. In the Rwandan case, once the rights of the Hutu were achieved, the masses had no legitimate grounds for opposing the regime, and the priests, foreign

---

[47] The missionaries were not alone in this intellectual evolution. Academics, such as Jacques J. Maquet, *The Premise of Inequality in Ruanda: A Study of Political Relations in a Central African Kingdom* (London: Oxford University Press, 1961), also challenged the exploitation of the Hutu without questioning the nature of ethnic identity. The historical revisionism that challenged the basic ideas about the powerful centralized state under a Tutsi monoploy of power and a clear distinction between Hutu, Tutsi, and Twa did not begin until publication of Vansina's *L'évolution du royaume Rwanda* in 1962.

and indigenous, who had previously been viewed as radicals became a new breed of conservative, closely allied to state leaders and generally uncritical of state policies.

PROTESTANT CHURCHES

To this point in the discussion, I have referred to Rwanda's Protestant churches only in passing, since the Protestant churches got a very late start in Rwanda, attracted few members, and were of limited political significance until quite late in the colonial era. Further, their engagement in Rwandan society did not differ significantly from that of the Catholic Church. Rather than taking a different approach than the Catholics, for example, setting themselves up as churches for the poor and voiceless, the Protestant churches envied the Catholic relationship with both the colonial regime and the indigenous state and sought to emulate it. Because the Protestant churches expanded rapidly after independence, today counting nearly a third of the population as members, and have become important political actors, a brief discussion of the history of the Protestant missions is necessary before entering into an analysis of post-independence church–state relations.

The threat of Protestantism motivated the rapid expansion of Catholic mission activity from the beginning,[48] but the first Protestant missions in Rwanda were established by the Berlin-based Bethel Mission only in 1907 at Kirinda in west-central Rwanda and at Zinga in Gisaka in the east. These were followed by stations at Rubengera on Lake Kivu and a station on the Isle of Idwji in 1909, a station at Remera in central Rwanda in 1912, and another at Cyangugu in 1913. The Bethel missionaries worked closely with the German colonial administration, most of whose officers were Protestant and viewed the White Fathers with some suspicion, and actively sought support from Musinga and his court, with the pastor at Kirinda visiting Nyanza weekly to offer instruction to the king's children. The growth of the Bethel missions, however, was quite slow, with the first baptisms reported at Kirinda only in 1911, and when Rwanda fell to the Belgians in 1916, the Bethel mission stations were abandoned.[49]

---

[48] C.f., the letters of Classe in Rutayisire, *La christianisation du Rwanda.*

[49] Michel Twagirayesu and Jan van Butselaar, eds., *Ce don que nous avons reçu: Histoire de l'Eglise Presbytérienne au Rwanda (1907–1982)* (Kigali: Eglise Presbytérienne au Rwanda, 1982), pp. 15–67; Tharcisse Gatwa and André Karamaga, *La Presence Protestante: Les autres Chrétiens rwandais* Kigali: Editions URWEGO, 1990, pp. 38–40; Linden and Linden, *Church and Revolution in Rwanda*, pp. 73–4, 111–14.

The Protestant missionaries, even early on, shared much of the perspective of their Catholic competitors. The head of the Kirinda mission, Ernst Johanssen, wrote in his memoirs:

The population of Ruanda is organized organically in three races: the Watussi, the Bahutu, and the Batwa. The Watussi are a clan of hamitic pastoralists who, because of their stature, their color, and their intellectual posibilities, are distinguished fundamentally from the two other races, whom they have submitted to their domination, although they constitute without doubt scarcely a tenth of the population.[50]

The renewal of Protestant mission work after World War I came only slowly. Seventh-Day Adventist missionaries from Belgium and Switzerland arrived in Rwanda in 1919 and briefly reoccupied the Bethel stations at Kirinda and Remera, before beginning new stations at Gitwe, near the royal capital Nyanza, and at Rwankeri, in the northwest.[51] In 1920, the Belgian King requested the Belgian Society of Protestant Missions in Congo (Société Belge de Missions Protestantes au Congo, SBMPC), which had begun work in the Belgian Congo in 1914, to take over the stations abandoned by the Bethel Mission, and in 1921, the first SBMPC missionaries arrived in Rwanda to restart missions at Kirinda, Rubengera, and Remera, allowing the other Bethel stations to remain abandoned. From the beginning of its operations, the SBPMC sought close collaboration with both the Belgian administration and the royal court. According to Henri Annet, the pastor who made initial contacts with the court, Musinga expressed enthusiastic support for the SBMPC in their first meeting, declaring, "I want strong Protestant missions to counter-balance the influence of the Fathers. It is like balancing two trays. I am in the middle and the missions are on each side. If the balance leans too much to one side, that does not go well, because I can no longer maintain equilibrium."[52] The Belgian administration also offered greater support to the SBPMC than to other Protestant groups because of its national affiliation, providing the SBMPC with subsidies for educational and medical activities, as they did for the Catholics. Nevertheless, the

---

[50] Quoted in Tharcisse Gatwa, *Rwanda Eglises: Victimes ou Coupables: Les Eglises et l'idéologie ethnique au Rwanda 1900–1994* (Yaounde: Editions CLE and Lomé: Editions Haho, 2001).

[51] Linden and Linden, *Church and Revolution in Rwanda*, pp. 153–4; Gatwa and Karamaga, *Les autres chrétiens rwandais*, pp. 64–7.

[52] Henri Annet, "Report of Voyage of June 10, 1921," quoted in Twagirayesu and van Butselaar, *Ce don que nous avons reçu*, p. 82.

SBMPC was limited by a lack of funding and personnel (largely because of the small number of Protestants in Belgium) and expanded very slowly, maintaining only its three initial stations until after independence, when the church entered into a period of rapid growth.[53]

The Church Missionary Society (CMS), an Anglican group, which had been active in Tanganyika and Uganda for some time, made an initial foray in Rwanda in 1916 but was banned from the country in 1917. After Gisaka fell under British control, the CMS established a mission at Gahini in 1920 and quickly gathered a large following. In contrast to the other Protestant groups, the CMS was well funded and had well educated missionaries, including a Cambridge-educated doctor who began a hospital at Gahini. Under British mandate, Gisakans viewed the mission as a means of gaining access to the British administration, but even after the territory reverted to Rwanda, the mission remained strong, attracting people with its medical services and a substantial number of schools. The CMS later expanded their operations and founded missions at Shyira in the northwest and Kigeme near Gikongoro in 1932 and later Shyogwe near Gitarama in the center of the country.[54]

The relationship between the colonial state and the Anglicans and Adventists was tense from the first, and the CMS and Adventist missionaries frequently complained of the discrimination they faced. Unlike the SBMPC, the CMS and Adventists did not benefit from government subsidies but found themselves barely tolerated by the administration. After a meeting with all the Protestant groups in Rwanda and Burundi held at Kirinda in 1935, a delegation appealed to the office of the governor in Leopoldville for greater religious liberty, after which the situation improved somewhat.[55] The tensions with the Belgians, both the White Fathers and the colonial administration, actually added to the appeal of the Adventists and CMS among those who sought to oppose the expansion of state power. In the 1920s and 1930s, the Adventists gained support among Hutu in the north, as the state extended control over the formerly

[53] Twagirayesu et van Butselaar, *Ce don que nous avons reçu*, pp. 69–137; Gatwa and Karamaga, *La presence protestante*, pp. 40–2; Rutayisire, *La christianisation du Rwanda*, pp. 225–30.

[54] Linden and Linden, *Church and Revolution in Rwanda*, p. 154; Gatwa and Karamaga, *La presence protestante*, pp. 52–4; "L'Esprit et le sel: Rechereches sur l'histoire de l'Eglise au Rwanda par un groupe de travail de l'Ecole de Théologie de Butare," (Butare: Ecole de Théologie, 1978), pp. 14–24.

[55] Rutayisire, *La christianisation du Rwanda*, pp. 226–30; Linden and Linden, *Church and revolution in Rwanda*, p. 154.

independent Hutu kingdoms, continuing the tradition of religious protest associated with the Nyabingi cult in this area, and the Anglicans played a similar role around Gahini in the east.[56] Both churches, however, avoided establishing too strong an association with Hutu protest, ever hoping to mirror the Catholic's road to success. Bowen argues that the CMS's conservative attitudes, "led to an emphasis on evangelism rather than any engagement with the public life of the nation or critique of the sociopolitical context."[57] Hence, the churches continually sought to develop good ties with the court. When Musinga realized he had lost the support of the White Fathers in 1927, he invited a CMS pastor to give Bible lessons and also made contact with the Adventists.[58] As early as the 1940s, as their anger with the White Fathers and Belgian colonial rule increased, Tutsi royalists turned increasingly to the Anglican Church. With their upper class backgrounds, CMS missionaries were both more comfortable with Tutsi aristocrats and uncomfortable with popular rebellion, and the CMS did not experience the same transformation as the White Fathers. In the aftermath of the 1959 revolution, the CMS continued to attract many Tutsi, although its membership remained majority Hutu.[59]

While the level of antagonism between the Protestant and Catholic Churches during the colonial era was quite high, and while the Protestants in general did not enjoy the advantages of a close working relationship with the colonial state, the approach to social and political engagement of the two traditions did not differ substantially. The Adventists, SBMPC, and CMS all actively sought support from the Belgian colonial state, and they complained vociferously when that support was denied. Each of the Protestant groups also became embroiled in Rwanda's ethnic politics, advocating the interests of one group or the other depending on both theological principles and the advantages they expected to gain. In general, they were as supportive of the status quo as their Catholic counterparts.

The Protestant missions experienced divisions similar to those experienced by the Catholic Church. In the 1930s a pietistic movement that began in Uganda, swept through the Anglican church in Rwanda.

---

[56] Linden and Linden, *Church and Revolution in Rwanda*, pp. 161, 202–3.
[57] Roger W. Bowen, "Genocide in Rwanda 1994: An Anglican Perspective," in Carol Rittner, et al, *Genocide in Rwanda: Complicity of the Churches?* (St. Paul: Paragon House, 2004), p. 38.
[58] Ibid, p. 167; Rutayisire, *La christianisation du Rwanda*, p. 183.
[59] Lemarchand, *Rwanda and Burundi*, p. 133; Linden and Linden, *Church and Revolution in Rwanda*, pp. 208–9, 255–9.

The *Abarokore*, or saved, accepted a strict code of conduct, abstaining from alcohol and tobacco, denounced witchcraft, and believed the Second Coming to be imminent, and they challenged the authority of the missionaries, whom they accused of failing to live sufficiently by the Christian principles they preached. It was with considerable difficulty that the CMS missionaries were able to reassert their authority and bring the movement under control. For the CMS missionaries, the intensity of the faith engendered by the movement could not compensate for the challenge to authority that it represented, and thus it had to be contained.[60]

Three other Protestant groups expanded into Rwanda during the colonial period from their bases of operation in Burundi or Congo. Danish Baptist missionaries began working in Burundi in 1928, and they began evangelizing in southern Rwanda in 1936, founding a station at Nyantanga, near Kigeme. The Union of Baptist Churches (Union des Eglises Baptiste au Rwanda, UEBR) spread primarily in southern Rwanda. The Free Methodist Church, based in the United States, also came to Rwanda from Burundi, where it began working in 1937. The Free Methodists established a mission station at Kibogoro on Lake Kivu in 1942. Finally, the Pentecostal Church, today probably the largest Protestant community,[61] was brought to Rwanda in 1940 by Swedish missionaries based in Congo. In contrast to the other Protestant missionaries, the Pentecostals had little interest in cooperation with the government, in part because their evangelical theology regarded political activity with suspicion, as corrupting and diversionary from the key activity of winning souls to Christ. This disdain for political activity and consequent distance from political authorities gave the Pentecostal Church a certain appeal among those at the margins of society, initially poor Hutu, then after the revolution, poor Tutsi. None of these churches, however, was very large before colonialism, and none of them played an important political role.[62]

[60] Linden and Linden, *Church and Revolution in Rwanda*, pp. 203–5.
[61] It is difficult to obtain accurate statistics on the membership in Protestant churches, because statistics provided by the government and other sources conflate all the Protestant groups. Historically, the Anglicans were the largest Protestant group, but the Pentecostals have experienced incredible growth since independence.
[62] Gatwa and Karamaga, *La presence protestante*, pp. 57–64; Tharcisse Gatwa, "Eglises protestantes," *Vivant Univers*, no. 357, May–June 1986, pp. 40–1.

4

"Working Hand in Hand"

Christian Churches and the Postcolonial State (1962–1990)

The active involvement of church leaders in struggles for political power, the engagement of churches in ethnic politics, and the development of local parishes as centers of power during the colonial era set the pattern for church–state relations in postcolonial Rwanda. Many officials in the First Republic, including President Kayibanda, were protégés of the Catholic Church who, while occasionally clashing with church leaders as they sought to assert their political independence, maintained close personal and official ties with the Catholic hierarchy. The military personnel who assumed power in a 1973 coup did not owe the same political debt to the Catholic Church as their civilian predecessors, but appreciating the power of the church, the new president, Juvénal Habyarimana, made clear his own position as a devout Catholic and quickly sought to develop strong ties between his regime and both Catholic and Protestant church leaders. Church leaders, for their part, embraced the new regime and continued to teach obedience to political authorities.

Just as in an earlier generation some missionaries challenged the decision of the Catholic leadership to ally the church with the Tutsi and the royal court, during the Habyarimana regime some segments of the churches objected to the alliance of the churches with an authoritarian state and the integration of churches into structures of power that benefited the rich. During the 1980s, the influence of liberation theologies, church institutional reforms, the expansion and reconceptualization of church-sponsored development activities, and the emergence of new church-related organizations and movements fostered the growth of a democratic sentiment within the churches. These developments within the churches helped to undermine the Habyarimana regime's efforts to maintain total control over the society and eventually helped give rise to a movement in support of democratic political reform in Rwanda. They also created an increasing challenge to the authority of church leaders at both the national and local levels. As I discuss in Chapters 5 and 6, the desire of church leaders to reassert control over their churches and to defend their personal privileges explains in large part their ultimate resistance to democratic reforms and their support for genocide.

THE CHURCHES AND THE RISE OF HABYARIMANA

Grégoire Kayibanda came to power in Rwanda as the leader of a movement that was both revolutionary and ethnic. Because of the discrimination against Hutu practiced by the colonial administration, during the colonial period being Tutsi became equivalent in the popular imagination with being elite, even though many Tutsi in fact enjoyed neither wealth nor political power. PARMEHUTU (which officially became PARMEHUTU-MDR [Mouvement Démocratic et Républicain]) attracted the Hutu masses not only by appealing to ethnic loyalties but also by espousing a populist rhetoric, promising opportunities and development for the common people who had previously been excluded from the political, social, and economic realms. The 1962 constitution, written by PARMEHUTU activists, promised that "all the citizens are, by right, equal before the law, without distinction of race, origin, sex or religion" and assured that "the privileges of caste are abolished and cannot be restored."[1]

During the first decade of independence, however, the rhetoric of the regime assumed an increasingly ethnic character, as the ideology of the regime equated democracy with rule by the majority ethnic group.[2] Between 1961 and 1965, after incursions into Rwanda by bands of armed Tutsi refugees based in Burundi, Rwandan political officials encouraged attacks by Hutu militia that killed thousands of unarmed Tutsi civilians, increasing ethnic tensions in the country and leading many more Tutsi to flee into exile.[3] While Rwanda officially remained a multiparty state, PARMEHUTU became a *de facto* single party by 1965, as the government

---

[1] Quoted in Filip Reyntjens, *Pouvoir et Droit au Rwanda: Droit Public et Evolution Politique, 1916–1973* (Butare: Institut National de Recherche Scientifique, 1985), p. 338. According to Reyntjens, the constitution sought to mark a clear rupture with the *ancien régime*.

[2] Jean Paul Kimonyo, *Rwanda: Un Génocide Populaire* (Paris: Karthala, 2008).

[3] Lemarchand, *Rwanda and Burundi*, pp. 197–286; Reyntjens, *Pouvoir et Droit*, pp. 455–71.

suppressed the activity of other parties (particularly the largely Tutsi UNAR) and acted in an increasingly authoritarian manner. The economic and social development promised by PARMEHUTU failed to occur, and most Hutu found themselves with no more political power and in no better economic situation than before the revolution. As discontent with the regime mounted, Kayibanda relied increasingly for support on trusted associates from his home region in central Rwanda, Gitarama, increasing the public impression that the government had become autocratic and further weakening popular support.

Events in neighboring Burundi with its similar ethnic makeup ultimately contributed to the downfall of Kayibanda. The 1959 revolution in Rwanda had a profound impact in neighboring Burundi, pushing Burundians to ignore the intragroup divisions that had moderated ethnic conflict during the colonial period and instead to define their interests increasingly in ethnic terms. Tutsi refugees from Rwanda played a radicalizing role in Burundi, warning Burundi's Tutsi of the danger of ceding power to Hutu, while Hutu were inspired by the model of Rwanda to demand greater political power. After an uprising in 1965 by Hutu army officers, hundreds of Hutu were killed, and Hutu were purged from the army and government. After King Rwagasori, who had acted as a moderating force on ethnic issues, died in 1966, the son who became king was unable to maintain popular unity, and in November 1966, a group of Tutsi army officers took power under the leadership of new president Michel Micombero, a member of the lower status Hima group of Tutsi who had historically been excluded from power.[4] Hoping to avoid a Rwandan-style revolution, Burundi's new leaders moved to exclude Hutu from any positions of power that might provide them with a platform for rebellion. After an attack in May 1972 on southern Burundi by a group of rebels supported by Mulelist Congolese rebels, the Burundian military responded by systematically slaughtering as many as 200,000 Hutu, targeting in particular intellectuals, professionals, and any others the military perceived as holding the potential to organize rebellion, what Lemarchand has termed a "selective genocide."[5]

[4] Lemarchand, *Burundi: Ethnocide as Discourse and Practice*, pp. 58–75.

[5] For information on the 1972 massacres in Burundi, see René Lemarchand and David Martin, *Selective Genocide in Burundi* (London: Minority Rights Group, 1973); René Lemarchand, "The Hutu-Tutsi Conflict in Burundi," in Jack Nusan Porter, ed., *Genocide and Human Rights: A Global Anthology* (University Press of America, 1982), pp. 195–217; and Lemarchand, *Burundi: Ethnocide as Discourse and Practice*, pp. 76–105.

The massacres in Burundi drove thousands of Burundian Hutu refugees into Rwanda and significantly exacerbated ethnic tensions in Rwanda, contributing to a new wave of ethnic unrest that swept Rwanda in 1973. Growing initially out of a movement of students from northern Rwanda at the National University in Butare who objected to the southern Rwanda bias of Kayibanda's government and the continuing dominance of the educational system by Tutsi, a purge of Tutsi swept across the country. In January and February 1973, Hutu students, often with the assistance of armed groups, drove their Tutsi colleagues from schools, seminaries, and convents. In several parts of the country, most notably in Gikongoro, mobs attacked Tutsi, killing several thousand and driving many more to flee the country. The movement grew into general disorder until it was eventually halted by Kayibanda's intervention.[6] In this atmosphere of instability, Kayibanda sought to further consolidate his power over the next several months by replacing key northern politicians and military officers, but a group of military officers, led by army chief Major-General Juvénal Habyarimana, himself from Gisenyi prefecture in the north, ousted Kayibanda in a July 5, 1973, coup d'état, apparently seeking to protect their jobs.[7]

The churches offered little effective response to the waves of violence that took place in Rwanda between 1959 and 1965 and again in 1973, even though the churches were directly affected. During the ethnic attacks that swept Rwanda in 1973, the violence focused predominately on schools, where the attackers believed Tutsi continued to hold unfair advantage over Hutu, and the vast majority of the schools attacked at this time were church schools. The failure of the churches to address ethnic violence was due in part to the uncertain position of the churches as they sought to negotiate their role in the post-independence societies. The churches experienced massive growth during the period immediately following independence. The Catholic Church in Rwanda doubled its size in a decade, from 698,000 baptized members and 435,000 catechists in 1960 to 1,439,000 baptized members and 385,000 catechists in 1971.[8] Yet

---

[6] Reyntjens, *Pouvoir et Droit*, wrote that "It seems now highly probable that the flame that traversed the schools was set off at the initiative of the president himself" (p. 502).

[7] Reyntjens, *Pouvoir et Droit*, pp. 501–9; Jean Rumiya, "Ruanda d'hier, Rwanda d'aujourd'hui," *Vivant Univers*, no. 357 (May–June 1985), pp. 2–8; Chrisophe Mfizi, *Les lignes de faîte du Rwanda Indépendant* (Kigali: Office Rwandais d'Information, 1983), pp. 48–55.

[8] Baudouin Paternoste de la Mairieu, *Le Rwanda: son effort de développement: Antécédents historiques et conquêtes de la révolution rwandaise* (Brussels: Editions A. De Boeck, 1981), pp. 354–5.

despite their popular appeal, the churches remained vulnerable to charges of neo-colonialism because of their legacies as missionary churches and the continuing presence of large numbers of foreign pastors and priests – which was ironically made necessary in part because of the growth in membership. The churches were more interested in establishing cooperative relationships with the new regimes than they were in becoming a voice for society, and criticizing the new leaders could open the churches to charges that they were influenced by foreign interests.

The perceived role of the Catholic Church in the Rwandan Revolution caused problems for that church. State officials in Rwanda regarded as burdensome the legacy of church support in their rise to power. As in many African countries, the churches' ever expanding involvement in health care, education, and development made them rivals to the state as the central institutions in public life. Conflict arose in Rwanda in the mid-1960s over control of schools, as the state attempted to exercise greater authority over hiring, firing, and curriculum that had hitherto been directed by the churches, even though the state had been providing substantial financial support to the schools. After a series of bitter public exchanges between church and party leaders, the government briefly suspended the publication of *Kinyamateka*, the paper once edited by Kayibanda, and repatriated its Belgian editor. The churches eventually backed down, granting the state increased control over education, but relations between church and state were strained.[9]

Ethnic politics was also an important factor in explaining the inaction of the churches in the face of violence. Because of the decades in which the churches had discriminated against the Hutu, the majority of indigenous clergy were Tutsi in both countries. Church officials maintained close personal ties to state officials during the Kayibanda regime, but their relationship was sometimes contentious, as government officials sought to demonstrate their independence from their former mentors. Although the Catholic Church gained a degree of goodwill because of its role in the shift of power, the predominance of Tutsi among the clergy made the church suspect and opened it to accusations of anti-revolutionary sentiment. The situation was similar for Protestant churches.

Having failed to address the ethnic violence after it began in 1959 and subsequently encouraging no process of dialogue or reconciliation, Catholic and Protestant leaders in Rwanda were not well situated to

---

[9] Lemarchand, *Rwanda and Burundi*, pp. 258–61.

respond to the renewed ethnic attacks when they broke out. What Gatwa and Karamaga wrote about the Protestant churches in was equally true of Catholics: "History had not given its lesson. No reflection on that which occurred in 1959–1961 had taken place."[10] Several Presbyterian leaders told me two decades after the 1973 violence that their church's failure to intervene remained a point of shame for the church and continued to haunt the leaders themselves, but at the time, they were concerned about the church's becoming direct targets of public anger because of the predominance of Tutsi clergy.[11]

Despite the churches' public silence, as attacks against Tutsi in Rwanda expanded in 1973 from their original focus on schools and other public institutions to include Tutsi civilians, as in parts of Gikongoro, those threatened fled to churches, where they received sanctuary.[12] The Catholic Episcopal Conference eventually did issue a pastoral letter in February condemning the ethnic nature of the attacks. In the next several months, groups of attackers targeted Catholic parishes themselves, particularly in the Nyundo (Gisenyi) diocese, which was regarded as a pro-Tutsi diocese. A number of Tutsi priests and lay workers fled into exile, and in Nyundo an army major was put in charge of the seminary.[13] The failure of the Kayibanda government to support the churches and its delay in halting the violence further alienated church leaders from the regime. As a result, when Habyarimana's coup took place a few months later, church leaders – like most Rwandans – greeted it with enthusiasm.[14]

---

[10] Gatwa and Karamaga, *La présence protestante*, p. 71. They add, "it is to be regretted that the Protestant church had not profited from the situation [following the revolution] to unleash a process of ethnic reconciliation or at least to alert the attention of the public power to the danger of sleeping on an active volcano, relying on false signs of the period of calm" (pp. 70–1).

[11] Interviews in Kigali, July 31, 1992.

[12] The fact that Tutsi who fled to churches in 1973 received sanctuary and that the sanctity of churches was generally accepted assured many Tutsi when the genocide broke out two decades later that they would again be safe in churches. Leaders of the genocide actually exploited this belief in order to gather their intended victims in a central location to facilitate their slaughter.

[13] Linden and Linden, *Church and Revolution in Rwanda*, pp. 282–6. Lemarchand noted discontent in the schools in Nyundo as early as 1965 (*Rwanda and Burundi*, p. 239).

[14] As just one indication of church sympathies, the Catholic journal *Dialogue* published by the Episcopal Council of Bishops began immediately to publish President Habyarimana's speeches, such as his "Discours du 1 août 1973," *Dialogue* no. 4, September–October 1973, pp. 2–17.

Church Support for Habyarimana

Although his immediate reasons for seizing power were personal,[15] Habyarimana as president soon adopted a forcefully articulated political program, under the motto "peace, unity, and development." He promised to complete the transformations begun in 1959 by effecting a "moral revolution," referring to the misuse of political authority by Kayibanda and his associates for their personal benefit. Habyarimana moved quickly to bring order to the country by banning political activity for two years and, to mitigate the causes of the most recent round of ethnic violence, by establishing ethnic quotas for education and employment. He reorganized the state administrative apparatus, centralizing political authority and strengthening state capacities, and in 1975 he founded a single political party, the Mouvement Révolutionaire National pour le Développement (National Revolutionary Movement for Development, MRND), to help maintain order, ensure support for the regime, and organize popular participation in economic development. MRND membership was compulsory for all citizens, and the party oversaw the local implementation of national government programs, such as *animation*, ritualized expressions of support and loyalty to the regime, and *umuganda*, a program of weekly community service, such as planting trees, building bridges, and repairing roads. By halting overt ethnic conflict and by emphasizing a commitment to development, Habyarimana was able to attract substantial international development assistance, which allowed the economy to grow at a respectable rate.[16]

---

[15] The 1973 coup in Rwanda well fits Samuel Decalo's observation that although they are justified in ideological terms as bringing order and development, coups generally occur for more immediate and proximate reasons, in this case, Habyarimana's fear that he and his northern associates were soon to be replaced. Samuel Decalo, *Coups and Army Rule in Africa: Motivations and Constraints* (New Haven: Yale University Press, 1990).

[16] Newbury, "Recent Debates Over Governance and Rural Development," pp. 197–199; Mfizi, *Lignes de faîte*, pp. 54–67; Rumiya, "Ruanda d'hier, Rwanda d'aujourd'hui," pp. 5–7.

Habyarimana's favorable international image is suggested by a 1979 United States Department of State report, "Although remaining one of the world's poorest, the Rwandan economy has made encouraging progress in recent years. ... A moderate, development-oriented government has fostered good relations with neighbors – Burundi, Zaire, Uganda, and Tanzania – and has attracted economic aid from a variety of donors. ... The challenge for Rwanda is to make the most of the present favorable conjunction of trade and political developments, and to provide a base for long term growth" (American Embassy, Kigali, "Rwanda," Foreign Economic Trends and Their Implications for the United States, November 1979), p. 1.

Even though the churches played no role in the military's rise to power, the Habyarimana regime quickly developed strong ties with the churches. Realizing the power and influence of the churches, Habyarimana actively sought to develop alliances with church leaders and to strengthen formal links between church and state. President Habyarimana presented himself as a devout Catholic. He sought to gain the support of religious leaders by including them publicly in political activities. He went beyond simply inviting religious leaders to appear jointly with him at public events to formally involving them in political institutions, particularly the MRND. Vincent Nsengiyumva, who became Catholic archbishop of Kigali in 1976,[17] was named to the central committee of the MRND. When Michel Twagirayesu became president of the Presbyterian Church in 1977, he assumed a seat on the Kibuye prefecture committee of the MRND.

The churches responded to the government's overtures by elevating leaders who were sympathetic to the president. All the major denominations named Hutu as their leaders. (The only Tutsi Catholic bishops were named before independence.) Archbishop Nsengiyumva was, like Habyarimana, a northern Hutu, originally from Ruhengeri, and he became known as Madame Habyarimana's personal confessor. When Tutsi bishop of Nyundo Bigirumwami retired in 1984, he was replaced by a Hutu. Joseph Ruzindana, who was named bishop of Byumba, was a relative of President Habyarimana's wife. All of the Anglican bishops were Hutu, and the bishop of Kigali, Adonia Sebununguri, was vocally supportive of the regime. The Catholic Church moved the seat of its archbishop from Kabgayi (a few minutes walk from ex-president Kayibanda's home) to Kigali in 1976 to facilitate cooperation between the church and the government; the Presbyterian Church similarly moved its headquarters to Kigali, even though its membership was concentrated overwhelmingly in Kibuye and Gitarama prefectures. Leaders such as Nsengiyumva, Sebununguri, and Twagirayesu maintained close personal relationships with the president and often dined at the president's home.[18] Similar ties existed at the regional and local levels, as prefects and burgomasters (the leaders of the communes) generally developed strong ties with religious

[17] Nsengiyumva was initially named bishop in 1974 and became archbishop in 1976 when Perraudin retired and the seat of the archbishop was moved to Kigali.
[18] Guy Theunis, "Le rôle de l'église catholique dans les événevments récents," pp. 289–98; André Karamaga, "Les églises protestantes et la crise rwandaise," pp. 299–308; and "Institutions et Personnalités," pp. 774–5, in André Guichaoua, ed., *Les crises politiques au Burundi et au Rwanda (1993–1994)* (Lille: Université des Sciences et Technologies de Lille, 1995).

leaders in their communities. As Guy Theunis wrote, "This 'collaboration' between the Church and the State existed at all levels of the hierarchy: hence, often, the bishops were part of the prefecture council of development, the curés of the communal council of development, councils that prepared the programs of development in the country."[19]

The relationship between church and state elites went beyond simple fraternal ties. As in most other African countries, the government in Rwanda assured its power not only through control of coercive force and ideological arguments but also by linking itself to the population through a system of patron–client ties.[20] Political positions and government resources were distributed through a patrimonial structure that rewarded individuals and communities for their loyalty to the regime. In a similar manner, church leaders assured their personal power through their own patrimonial structures. Church officials placed their allies in key church posts and rewarded communities that supported them and respected their authority with money for development projects, scholarships for local students, and other benefits, while they punished their enemies by placing them in undesirable positions and denying access to church funds. These parallel patron–client systems within church and state were generally mutually reinforcing (as I describe in greater detail in Part II of this book through an analysis of church–state relations at the local level). Government officials helped to increase the status and wealth of church personnel and sometimes used their influence to support their allies in decisions about promotion and leadership within the churches, while church officials helped to organize public support for the regime and to increase the status of government officials. Rumors of illegal activities, such as smuggling and kickbacks, frequently accused church and state leaders of collaboration.

The personal ties between church and state elites were complemented by significant institutional links. The government and the churches as institutions cooperated closely on many of their activities, particularly in the provision of social services. The ultimate authority of the state over education and health care had been largely established by the time Habyarimana came to power, with the state instituting national educational and medical standards and in exchange providing funding to pay salaries for teachers, doctors, and nurses. Any remaining doubts about

---

[19] Theunis, "Le rôle de l'église catholiques dans les événements récents," p. 291.
[20] On patrimonialism, see Michael Bratton and Nicholas van de Walle, "Neo-Patrimonial Regimes and Political Transitions in Africa." *World Politics*, 46, no. 4. (1994): 453–89.

the state's authority had been laid to rest when the military intervened to restore calm in schools during the 1973 crisis, an action that church leaders generally supported. Habyarimana thus felt that he could appeal to the churches for their assistance in providing social services without unduly threatening the dominant position of the state within society. With the regime's emphasis on economic development, the support of the churches was essential, as they could draw on international church connections for financial support and could help to organize development projects at the grassroots level, while the government focused on attracting major donors and instituting large-scale development projects, such as building highways and tea plantations.[21]

As during colonial times, both church and government leaders regarded the cooperative relationship that prevailed between their institutions under Habyarimana as beneficial. The Habyarimana regime gained a degree of legitimacy through its public association with the churches, whom they believed had substantial influence over the population. Church documents often openly supported state goals and praised state achievements. In addition, the churches' provision of social services eased the state's financial and administrative burden and helped appease the population. As the missions had done in earlier times, the churches in independent Rwanda helped to maintain order, integrating the population into the social system and teaching obedience to authority. With their close links to the population, particularly in rural areas, churches served as centers of public life, assisting the government in administration. Church services frequently included announcements from government agencies or political leaders, and clergy assisted in such secular tasks as marriage registration and organizing participation in *umuganda* and *animation*.

For their part, churches found that their relationship with the state facilitated their operations, making it easier to access the population and maintain the support of their membership and eliminating competition. State support for church work in education, health care, and development, financial and otherwise, helped the churches attract members, because people coming to receive social services could also be exposed to

---

[21] The government instituted its first five-year plan for economic and social development in 1977, laying out development goals and appealing for international donor support to improve the transportation network, control overpopulation, increase industry, and develop exploitation of mineral resources. C.f., Ministry of Planning, Republic of Rwanda, "3ème Table Ronde des Aides Exterieures au Rwanda," Kigali 1982.

the Christian message. The government left churches largely free to seek out new members, provide services, and collect funds.

The churches also benefited from the coercive power of the state, which helped to eliminate new religious movements that might challenge their support within the population. Officially, the Constitution of the Republic of Rwanda of 1962 guaranteed religious liberty.[22] The new constitution that Habyarimana presented for public referendum in 1978 did not change the provisions that guaranteed the principle of religious liberty. In practice, however, while not officially established, the Catholic Church clearly enjoyed a privileged position in society. As Kalibwami wrote:

Catholicism, without being an official religion (the State recognizing religious liberty equally for all religious confessions), remains nevertheless the religion that in practice occupies the first position. Most members of the ruling class in all domains are Catholics, educated by the Catholic Church; Catholics constitute the most dynamic group in the country given the already favorable circumstances in which Catholicism is constantly found in Rwanda.[23]

Mainstream Protestant groups occupied a secondary position vis-à-vis the state, but they still enjoyed a generally cordial relationship with those in power and received support from the government for their operations. In contrast, the government actively intervened to quash newer religious movements that attempted to gain a following in Rwanda. The government required all religious groups to register, thus requiring the permission of the state to function. Those groups that refused to recognize state authority and objected to registration could not legally operate, while licensed religious groups had to respect state authority or face revocation of their registration. The government forcefully suppressed unregistered groups.[24]

In 1986, the government brought to trial three hundred members of four unregistered Christian "sects" – the Jehovah's Witnesses, the *Abarokore* (the Saved), the *Abatempera*, Temperants of Central Africa,

---

[22] *Constitution de la République Rwandaise* (Kigali: service de la Législation de la Présidence de la République Rwandaise, November 24, 1962), see Chapter IV, Articles 37 and 38.

[23] Kalibwami, *Le catholicisme et la société rwandaise*, p. 551.

[24] These regulations seem never to have been applied to the indigenous religious groups such as Kubandwa and Nyabingi, which the government apparently viewed as failing to pose a threat to their power. This is ironic, given the history of these religions as sources of rebellion (see Berger, *Religion and Resistance*, and Freedman, *Nyabingi*), but in the modern era, the spirit of religious rebellion seems to have been expressed more through radical syncretic Christian movements.

a sect that broke away from the Seventh-Day Adventist Church, and the *Abantu b'Imana bihana* (the Repentant People of God). These groups were cited "for inciting the population to rebellion against the established powers, for insulting the flag or official symbols of sovereignty of the Republic, for calling for disobedience."[25] The members of these religious groups refused to pay party membership fees in the MRND and to participate in *umuganda* and *animation*, because they considered these obligations idolatrous, a veneration of the state that affronts the commandment to worship only one God. Smaller numbers of followers of unregistered religious movements had been tried in the preceding years, but the large number tried and the severity of the penalties made this case particularly notorious. Those found guilty (all but two who recanted) were sentenced to between five and fifteen years in prison.[26]

This much-publicized case sent a message to the population that they needed to keep their religious expressions within the established churches; radical religious movements and schisms from the registered churches would not be accepted. At the same time, the case sent a message to the established churches to reign in their own extremes. The government instituted this case at a time when public discontent with the regime was growing. By targeting minor religious movements, the state asserted its own supremacy over religious institutions and clearly indicated that it would not tolerate religiously inspired challenges to its authority.

In general, however, the leadership of the mainstream churches needed little encouragement to toe the official line. Keeping conflicts between church and state to a minimum served the interests of both religious and political elites. Hence, cooperation and compromise tended to characterize relations between the government and the churches. Conflicts did occasionally arise, because of the different institutional imperatives of church and state, but leaders of each institution sought to find common ground quickly and to diminish inter-institutional tensions.

A conflict that arose in the 1980s over family planning between the Catholic Church and the state demonstrates effectively this tendency toward compromise. As the most densely populated country in Africa,

---

[25] "Carnet: Septembre–Octobre 1986," *Dialogue*, no. 120 (January–February 1987);
[26] "Rwanda: Entre la peur et l'anathème," *Dialogue*, no. 125 (November–December 1987): 3–7; Théophile Malyomeza, "Ces sectes religieuses qui nous interpellent," *Dialogue*, no. 125 (November–December 1987): 8–21; Joseph Ntamahungiro, "Sectes ou mouvements religieux?" *Dialogue*, no. 125 (November–December 1987): 22–41; François-Xavier Mfizi, "Les Temoins de Jehovah," memoire Ecole de Théologie de Butare, 1985–1986; "Rwanda: Defiant Protestants jailed, *Africa Report*, January–February 1987.

with an overwhelmingly rural population and one of the highest birth rates in the world, Rwanda was forced by pressure from international donors to integrate control of population growth into its development planning and in 1981 established the Office National de la Population (ONAPO). Unfortunately for the government, the Catholic Church's teachings against artificial contraception complemented the conviction in Rwandan social thought that large families are a sign of wealth and male virility and that only God/Imana should control birth. By ignoring the depth of this belief and aggressively promoting the use of artificial birth control, ONAPO alienated many people and raised the ire of the Catholic leadership, which condemned the use of contraceptives and spread warnings in church publications about the unknown health risks of using contraceptive devices. The government reacted by requiring by law that all health centers in the country, including those run by the churches, establish a family planning office and make contraceptives available.[27]

While this conflict could potentially have exploded into a major confrontation between church and state, instead officials from ONAPO opened a dialogue with church leaders and were able to design a compromise. The Catholic Church agreed to commit itself to the same principles as ONAPO – spacing births and keeping population growth at manageable levels – but by regulating pregnancy through natural means. In 1986, a commission that included representatives of ONAPO and the Catholic Church developed a plan for the church to create a Service of Natural Family Planning to work with ONAPO, and Action Familial committees were subsequently established in each parish. ONAPO for its part agreed to broaden its approach to family planning, by showing greater sensitivity to Catholic moral precepts and expanding its focus beyond encouraging artificial contraception.[28]

While Catholic Church policy continued to regard artificial contraception as immoral, in the interests of maintaining cordial relations with the

---

[27] Etienne Mvukiyehe, "Sensibilisation au problème démographique rwandais," *Dialogue*, no. 45 (July–August 1974): 47–58; François Funga, "Espacement des naissance... et après?" *Dialogue*, no. 104 (May–June 1984): 56–64; Emmanuel Semana, "Politiques et programmes de population dans le monde et au Rwanda," *Imbonezamuryango*, no. 12 (August 1988): 5–11; Viateur Rwabukwisi, "Relations juridiques entre l'Etat rwandais et les confessions religieuses en matiere socio-sanitaire," *Imbonezamuryango*, no. 12 (August 1988): 17–20.
[28] Rwabukwisi, "Relations juridiques," p. 19.

state, church leaders were willing to silence their vocal opposition.[29] The fact that a sharp difference between the official policies of the government and the Catholic Church did not lead to a breakdown in church–state relations demonstrates less the ability to find common ground on this issue than the willingness of leaders of both institutions to overlook even major disagreements for the sake of preserving their cooperative relationship. Authorities in both church and state had a common vested interest in preserving the existing structures that had permitted them to gain power, status, and wealth. Allowing disagreements between church and state to intensify could undermine the patrimonial system that kept both secular and sacred leaders in office.

Rwandan Churches and Ethnic Politics

Church and state leaders, then, cooperated in efforts to maintain the social, political, and economic status quo, and they used similar methods. As they had since their earliest days, the churches continued to play ethnic politics. During the Habyarimana regime, even though the majority of priests and pastors were Tutsi, most leadership positions were reserved for Hutu.[30] As André Karamaga stated:

It is shameful to recall, but it is true that the ethnic discrimination that characterized the actions of the government of Rwanda existed in the Church as well. Ethnic equilibrium, for example, that bizarre manner of protecting the majority against the minority, far from being condemned by the Church was rather practiced at its very heart. Furthermore, all nominations or promotions to leadership posts obeyed ethnic criteria, certainly with a discretion skillfully hidden by sweet, correct words in ecclesiastical millieux.[31]

In the Catholic Church, a minor scandal erupted in 1988 when a priest named by the Vatican to be elevated to bishop withdrew himself for

---

[29] See, for example, the November 1987 letter from the bishops in which they acknowledge the government's legitimate interest in controlling population and urge people to have only the number of children they can support but insist that they regulate births through natural methods, while condemning policies that are "anti-child and anti-life." Les Evêques du Rwanda, "Lettre pastorale sur la parenté responsable," reproduced in *Dialogue*, no. 129 (July–August 1988): 6–26.

[30] Guy Theunis estimates that 70 percent of Catholic priests were Tutsi, while 90 percent of church members were Hutu (Le rôle de l'Eglise catholique, p. 293). Between 1962 and 1991, not a single Tutsi was named bishop. In 1992, Frédéric Rubwejanga was named bishop of Kibungo, making him one of only two Tutsi bishops, the other being Jean-Baptiste Gahamanyi, bishop of Butare, named on the eve of independence.

[31] Karamaga, "Les églises protestantes et la crise rwandaise," p. 302.

"personal reasons" just two days before his installation. Word spread first through the public rumor mill, then later in the press, that Abbé Felicien Muvara, a respected scholar and priest, had been forced to withdraw by Archbishop Nsengiyumva who, apparently under pressure from the president, did not want another Tutsi bishop.[32] Similarly, in the Presbyterian Church, most key posts were reserved for Hutu. Karamaga had long been in conflict with Twagirayesu and had chosen to work for the All Africa Conference of Churches in Nairobi, where his Tutsi identity was not a barrier to his career advancement. After the civil war broke out in 1990, the Tutsi head of the Theology Department was demoted from that prestigious position to a minor parish. The only Tutsi who served as a regional president in the Presbyterian Church represented the newest and least significant church region.

The facts that church leaders protected their power through patrimonial structures parallel to and linked to state patrimonial structures and that they based their power at least in part on ethnic solidarity are essential to understanding how the churches became implicated in the genocide. Just as political leaders felt threatened by democratization and turned to ethnic violence as a means of reasserting their control, church leaders found their own power under threat and found a similar appeal in a policy that forcefully defended the established structures of power. As the population of Rwanda mobilized in the 1990s to demand greater personal autonomy, a decentralization of power, an end to ethnic discrimination, and greater accountability, their attentions focused not simply on the state but also on the centralized, autocratic, discriminatory, and sometimes corrupt church institutions.

CONTENDING CURRENTS WITHIN THE CHURCHES

Before turning in the next two chapters to the role of the churches in the period of democratization and civil strife in the early 1990s, we need to explore the factors that were transforming the churches and creating a growing challenge to structures of church power and calls for democratization of the churches. From the advent of Christianity in Rwanda, though the dominant powers in the churches chose to ally themselves and their institutions with political authorities, voices of dissent within the churches challenged this decision and called for an alternative vision

---

[32] Straton Gakwaya, "L'Eglise catholique au Rwanda, 1962–1987," *Dialogue*, no. 123 (July–August 1987): 46–58.

of the churches as social institutions. Missionaries such as Father Brard objected from the earliest days of Christian mission work in Rwanda to the decision of the White Father superiors to side with the Tutsi chiefs and called instead on the Catholic Church to ally itself with the socially marginal, while the mission superiors repeatedly reasserted their decision to seek the support of the state. After World War II, this approach again came into question when missionaries influenced by social democratic ideas championed the interests of the Hutu majority, eventually helping to bring about a transfer of political power. The assumption of power by Hutu did not, however, create a fundamentally different social situation for the majority of people in the country, who remained poor and continued to have little political power. The churches found their relationship with the Kayibanda regime strained, but they were not well situated to offer a critique, having supported his rise to power and feeling themselves politically vulnerable. When Habyarimana came to power, church leaders were happy to once again develop a close alliance with the state.

During the 1980s, however, a variety of developments within the churches create the conditions for a renewed challenge to the churches' association with political power – and to a challenge of the structures of power within the churches themselves. New theological ideas, structural changes within the churches, increased church involvement in grassroots economic development programs, and a proliferation of lay church movements and organizations all contributed to a reassessment of the role of churches in society, the empowerment of laity within the churches, and, for some people, a rethinking of the very nature of Christianity, its central ideas, and its organization.

Theologies of Liberation and Empowerment

International theological developments in both Catholic and Protestant churches influenced the churches in Rwanda beginning in the 1970s and challenged the established relationship of church and state in the country. Historically in Africa, the Roman Catholic Church's theology paid little attention to social issues, focusing instead on an other-worldly salvation that considered material conditions in this life of little importance. Because bringing people into the church was their fundamental mandate, church leaders sought alliances with political officials and worked with the state to extend their influence throughout society. The social services they provided helped attract people to the church. As one regional Catholic official told me, "The church said, we are here to serve the soul. This was especially true in those countries like Rwanda that were predominantly Catholic. The church gave no thought of taking the message of the Gospel and translating it into material life."[33] As early as 1891, when Pope Leo XIII published his first social encyclical, *Rerum Novarum*, the church's theological focus began to expand to embrace social themes. In the early decades of the twentieth century, fears about the expanding influence of communism encouraged the church to advocate social reform and to create lay social organizations, known as Catholic Action. It was not, however, until the Second Vatican Council (known as Vatican II) from 1962 to 1965 that the Catholic Church as a whole committed itself to active social engagement. The policies that came out of Vatican II in documents such as *Gaudium et Spes* sought to modernize the church by making it more responsive to the local contexts within which it operated, symbolized by the change of mass to vernacular languages. Vatican II called on Catholic churches around the globe to concern themselves with the material conditions of their societies. It legitimized and emphasized the church's social ministry and committed the church to defending the interests of those marginalized by either political or economic conditions. In his 1971 encyclical *Octogesima Adveniens*, Pope Paul VI continued this emphasis on social engagement, encouraging local church hierarchies to take independent initiative to respond to the particular needs and conditions of their communities.[34]

While Catholic churches, including the church in Rwanda, had already been extensively involved in social programs, Vatican II provided a theological foundation for these activities. No longer simply a method of attracting new members to the church, nor mere charity, assistance to the needy became a means of expressing the Gospel on Earth. The emphasis shifted from merely helping the suffering to transforming the world according to God's perceived plan. Thus, the church's work expanded to include development programs as well as more overtly political activities, such as advocacy for human rights and democracy. Episcopal councils of Catholic bishops have adopted the practice of issuing pastoral letters to address issues of public concern on subjects ranging from more clearly

[33] Father Peter Lwaminda, secretary of AMECEA, interviewed in Nairobi, July 13, 1999.
[34] J. Bryan Hehir, "Catholicism and Democracy: Conflict, Change, and Collaboration," in John Witte, Jr., ed., *Christianity and Democracy in Global Context* (Boulder: Westview, 1993), pp. 15–30.

social concerns such as family life to more directly political concerns such as civil rights and constitutional reform.[35]

The best known theological response to Vatican II was the Latin American movement that came to be known as Liberation Theology. In the spirit of collegiality inaugurated by Vatican II, the Catholic bishops of Latin America gathered in 1968 at a meeting in Medellín, Colombia, in which they expressed the support of the Catholic Church for social and economic changes that could bring "authentic liberation" to the people of Latin America. Taking their cue from Medellín, Latin American theologians such as Gustavo Gutierrez and Leonardo Boff began arguing for a new biblical interpretation that recognized God's support for the liberation and empowerment of the poor. They called on the church to make a "preferential option" for the poor and demanded radical political transformations. They criticized the church itself for its hierarchical and elitist nature and, building on Vatican II's call for greater lay involvement, demanded a restructuring of the church and a radical decentralization of church authority. They urged that theology become more based in real lived experience and upheld the right of average church members to engage in theological reflection.[36]

Within Africa, Catholic theologians responded to the call to contextualize their faith primarily by developing "theologies of inculturation," reflections on possible connections between African culture and Christianity. Many of these theologies of inculturation remain quite abstract, often accepting African traditions unconditionally, and rarely addressing political issues.[37] Liberation theologies, however, with their greater emphasis on political engagement, advocacy of the poor and

---

[35] For a comprehensive analysis of the impact, particularly the theological impact, of Vatican II on the Catholic Church, see the massive three volume text, René Latourelle, ed., *Vatican II: Assessment and Perspectives Twenty-five Years After (1962–1987)* (New York: Paulist Press, 1989).

[36] Paul E. Sigmund, *Liberation Theology at the Crossroads: Democracy or Revolution?* (New York and Oxford: Oxford University Press, 1990); Phillip Berryman, *Liberation Theology: The Essential Facts about the Revolutionary Movement in Latin America and Beyond* (New York: Pantheon Books, 1987), pp. 9–62, 80–137; Penny Lernoux, *People of God: The Struggle for World Catholicism* (London: Penguin Books, 1989), pp. 15–27. Gustavo Gutierrez, *A Theology of Liberation: History, Politics, and Salvation* (Maryknoll, NY: Orbis Books, 1988) and Leonardo Boff, *Ecclesiogenesis: The Base Communities Reinvent the Church* (Queson City, Philippines: Claretian Publications, 1986) are two of the most important contributions to liberation theology in Latin America.

[37] There are numerous examples of theologies of inculturation. Among the best is Benézét Bujo, *African Theology: Its Social Context* (Nairobi: Paulines Publications, 1999).

oppressed, and focus on church structures, have gradually influenced African churches. As John Parratt wrote:

Outside the Republic of South Africa, African theologians have, until comparatively recently, seemed surprisingly little concerned to relate their Christian faith to political systems. Within the last decade or so, however, it has become evident – possibly because of the influence of South African black theology, possibly due to the wider emergence of liberation theology on the ecumenical scene – that we are beginning to witness a new interest in political issues.[38]

Some Protestant churches in Africa have actually embraced liberation themes more quickly than their Catholic counterparts. The active involvement of the World Council of Churches and the All Africa Conference of Churches in the political struggle against apartheid in South Africa and consideration of liberation themes in these organizations influenced member churches, pushing them to confront the forms of injustice that existed in their own countries. During the 1980s, African Catholic theologians began to discuss liberation themes as well.[39]

In Rwanda, the liberation theologies began to have some impact on theological discussions in the churches by the late 1980s. Many expatriate clergy were influenced by liberation theologies, and in the Catholic Church, expatriates constituted nearly half of the priests, brothers, and nuns. In the Protestant churches, expatriates were fewer in number, but they had considerable control over the distribution of funds from international church partners, and many of these foreign churches based their activities in Rwanda on liberation principles. Some Rwandan Christians, even if they had not read the formal theologies, had independently developed similar ideas about the church's social responsibility and the need to reform church structures, often because of their work with the poor and destitute. As churches expanded their social work, an increasing number of those involved in that work became convinced that corrupt and authoritarian government prevented the empowerment and development of the population, and they placed pressures on church leaders to become more politically engaged.

New theological ideas, thus, created pressures on church leaders in Rwanda from both above and below to rethink their relationship to political power and, ultimately, to consider how the church itself was

---

[38] John Parratt, *Reinventing Christianity: African Theology Today* (Grand Rapids, MI: William B. Eerdmans Publishing and Trenton, NJ: Africa World Press, 1995), p. 137.
[39] Parratt, *Reinventing Christianity*, pp. 137–62.

organized and exercised its power. As I discuss in greater detail in the next chapter, these pressures did force the church leaders to modify their principles somewhat. Most noticeably, nearly all church leaders embraced the need to engage in development work. On the whole, however, church leaders resisted major revisions to their theological principles, never shying from an open alliance with the regime or amending their counsel to obey authority. Struggles for power in the churches became, at some level, struggles over theology.

Structural Changes

Within the Catholic Church, the Second Vatican Council initiated changes to the church structures. Two major concerns of Vatican II, the role of lay people in the church and their relationship to the clergy and the renewal of church institutional structures,[40] combined to inspire innovations in church organization. In Latin America, gatherings of small neighborhood groups within parishes evolved in some areas into a structure of sub-parish units known as Basic Christian Communities or Basic Ecclesial Communities. At the 1968 Medellín Conference, the bishops advocated the formation of the basic communities as a location where consciousness raising of the population could take place.[41] Many liberation theologians embraced basic communities as a way of supporting the poor by breaking down the hierarchical and elitist nature of the church. Brazilian theologian Leonardo Boff discussed basic communities as "a new way of being church," that allowed lay people to take greater responsibility for their own religious life and could become vehicles for combating poverty and exploitation.[42]

In both Catholic and Protestant churches in Rwanda, *Communautés Ecclesiales de Base* (Basic Ecclesial Communities, CEBs) first grew out of

---

[40] Louis Ligier, "'Lay Ministries' and Their Foundation in the Documents of Vatican II," in René Latourelle, ed., *Vatican II: Assessment and Perspectives Twenty-five Years After (1962–1987)*, vol. II (New York: Paulist Press, 1989), pp. 160–76; Giovanni Magnani, "Does the So-Called Theology of the Laity Possess a Theological Status," in Latourelle, ed., *Vatican II: Assessment and Perspectives*, vol. I, pp. 568–633; Angel Antón, "Postconciliar Ecclesiology: Expectations, Results, and Prospects for the Future," in Latourelle, ed., *Vatican II: Assessment and Perspectives*, vol. I, pp. 407–38.

[41] Berryman writes, "The exact starting point for base communities themselves cannot be determined with precision," but he suggests several relevant developments in the 1950s and early 1960s. Berryman, *Liberation Theology*, pp. 63–79; Sigmund, *Liberation Theology at the Crossroads*, pp. 14–39.

[42] Boff, *Ecclesiogenesis*.

the process of evangelization. Historically, when a parish sought to expand into an adjacent area, catechists and evangelists, trained lay employees of the church, who would enter the area, gather people together, and preach the message of the church. They would begin a Bible study or a catechism class, and eventually a pastor or priest would baptize the people from the community as members of the church. As it grew, the community often retained a separate identity within the parish, and one of the catechists or evangelists might continue to work with the community. Eventually some of these communities, particularly those with a concentration of members or far removed from the parish center, would become independent parishes, but others remained within the parish.[43]

These fields of evangelism generally followed the historic social division of Rwandans into *imisozi* (hills). Nearly all of Rwanda is covered by high, rolling hills, and families have historically farmed or raised livestock on the hillsides, living in isolated household units in an enclosure of one or more buildings surrounded by the family fields. In the place of villages, families living together on a hill (*umusozi* or *umurenge*[44]) formed a community. People from a common hill shared a loyalty and expectation of mutual assistance, and people in Rwanda continue to identify themselves by their hill of origin. The royal court adopted *imisozi* as an administrative unit, and the churches followed suit, with parishes and communities generally taking the names of the hills upon which they were based.[45]

The distinct communities growing out of the fields of evangelization served as an important antecedent to the system of Basic Ecclesial Communities that were adopted in both Catholic and Protestant parishes in the 1970s and 1980s. The idea for basic communities probably came to Rwanda initially from Congo (the former Zaire), where the church hierarchy decided in 1961 to begin establishing small communities as a means of responding to a shortage of priests.[46] In Rwanda, pastors and priests initially organized CEBs to serve administrative functions

---

[43] Michel Donnet, "Les C.E.B., lieu de liberation des pauvres?" *Dialogue*, no 141 (July–August 1990): 33–50; Twagirayesu and van Butselaar, *Ce don que nous avons reçu*, pp. 152–66.

[44] *Umusozi* (pl. *imisozi*) is the general word meaning "hill." *Umurenge* (pl. *imirenge*) literally means foothill but has also been used to mean a portion of hill and has been applied to the subchieftaincies and administrative sectors. Some hills, such as Save, are quite large and therefore were divided into several communities.

[45] See Newbury, *The Cohesion of Oppression*, pp. 108–9, 219, for discussion of Rwandan social divisions. Donnet, "Les CEB," discusses the development of base communities.

[46] "Les Communautés ecclésiales de base: Une Eglise communion de communautés, missionaire et authentiquement africaine," *Missi*, no. 508 (February 1989): 52–57; René

in organizing large and unmanageable parishes and to integrate church members more effectively into parish life. Many parishes cover large territories, and many have huge memberships – for example, two Catholic parishes I studied, Butare and Save, had 31,638 and 45,529 baptized members respectively.[47] By dividing the parish along the lines of the existing *imisozi*, pastors and priests could better manage their parishes. The lay people selected to lead each of the units, called *inama z'imisozi* or *inama z'imirenge* (hill councils) in the Catholic Church and "chapels" in most Protestant churches, could keep in closer contact than the clergy with the membership and could help to communicate the needs and concerns of parishioners to the clergy. In some places, the CEBs could provide many aspects of church life – for example, community prayers, Bible study, hymn singing, Sunday school, and catechism classes.[48]

Beginning in the 1980s, the example of the vibrant base communities in Latin America came to influence the organization of CEBs in Rwanda. Beginning in 1983, the Archdiocese of Kigali began a program to reform the CEBs in all of its parishes to become a more essential part of church life and more independent. Using the model of communities in Latin America, large *inama z'imirenge* were broken into smaller groups, called *inama-remezo*,[49] that gathered together a limited number of families in an area. Leaders of the *inama* were elected by group members rather than appointed by the priest, and the transformed groups were given greater responsibilities, such as overseeing the distribution of Caritas assistance and initiating development projects. The groups met weekly for Bible study, prayer, and discussion of community needs and problems. This program of revitalizing CEBs was eventually extended to Catholic parishes throughout the country, and many Protestant parishes followed the Catholic lead, giving their own basic communities greater autonomy and responsibility.[50]

In contrast to those in Latin America, CEBs in Africa have generally been created under the initiative of the hierarchy, and the clergy

Luneau, *Laisse aller mon peuple! Eglises africaines au-delà des modèles?* (Paris: Karthala, 1987), chapter 2.

[47] Diocèse de Butare, "Statistiques Annuelles Diocèse de Butare, 1990."

[48] Donnet, "Les C.E.B."

[49] Officially, the new CEBs were called *umulyango remezo wa kiiziya*, literally "basic ecclesial communities," but they were known as *inama-remezo* (base councils) or simply *inama*.

[50] Protais Safi, "La formation du laicat chrétien," in *L'Eglise du Rwanda vingt ans après le Concile Vatican deux* (Kigali: Edition Pallotti-Presse, 1987), pp. 153–66; Donnet, "Les C.E.B.;" interviews in Butare, December 15, 1992, and in Save, January 9, 1993.

have continued to oversee their activities closely. My own research in Rwanda confirmed the impression of observers of the churches in Kenya, Tanzania, and Uganda that CEBs in East Africa rarely addressed political issues overtly and were much less likely than their Latin American counterparts to expose unjust socioeconomic structures in their discussions.[51] Nevertheless, the establishment of CEBs throughout the country and their transformation into more autonomous institutions was significant, because it provided Christians with concrete experience in democracy and suggested that they themselves had a right to organize and control their own religious lives. Even without providing a fundamental critique of social structures, the CEBs did help raise the consciousness of participants, creating connections between community members, and encouraging them to believe in their own power to effect change.

From Charity to Sustainable Development

From their earliest days in Rwanda, missionaries provided education and medical care, famine relief, and other forms of assistance,[52] and over the decades, the involvement of the Catholic and most Protestant churches in these activities steadily increased. Two primary interests motivated this work. First, missionaries hoped to attract people to the missions and win converts by offering people the benefits of Western technology and learning. In the 1920s and 1930s, the Catholic schools played a vital part in the conversion of the Tutsi nobility.[53] In the Presbyterian Church, the first converts were children who attended the church schools and worked for the parish.[54] The Anglican Church had early success in attracting converts by offering medical services. Second, missionaries had a charitable concern for the well-being of people. They believed that they had a biblical

---

[51] Joseph Kelly, "The Evolution of Small Christian Communities," *AFER* 33, no. 3 (June 1991): 108–20; Patrick A. Kalilombe, "Cry of the Poor in Africa," *AFER* 29 (1987): 202–13; Fritz Lobinger, "Christian Base Communities in Africa and Brazil," *AFER* 29, no. 3 (1987): 149–53; Hastings, "Christianity and Revolution," pp. 347–61.

[52] The journal of the Save mission, the first mission station in Rwanda, indicates that upon their arrival in 1900, the Catholic missionaries began to construct the station and to recruit students for catechism, and within their first month in place they began to dispense medical care. The sick arrived "by the hundreds," according to the missionaries' account. *Journal de la Mission de Save, 1899–1905,* notations and comments by Heremans and Ntezimana, p. 35.

[53] Linden and Linden, *Church and Revolution in Rwanda,* pp. 152–85.

[54] Twagirayesu and van Butselaar, *Ce don que nous avons reçu,* pp. 31–8.

mandate to assist the poor and to heal the sick, according to the model of charity displayed by Jesus Christ himself.

These two motivations, attracting new members and the obligation to provide charity, continued to inspire church involvement in health, education, and development after independence. Nearly all of the church leaders I interviewed, both at the local and the national levels, justified church social work with these two explanations. The secretary general of the EPR, for example, explained to me his support for social programs in the following terms:

All that we have is a gift from God, and so we must care for it. We must manifest the word of God in our everyday activities. This involves not simply the development of the earth. Anyone can do that. When you are a Christian, there is more. The Gospel calls you to help those poorer than you.

There are criticisms by some people [in the church] today of church development work. There are people who criticize the work as forgetting evangelism. But you have to attempt to mix the two. You cannot have one without the other. You can bring people [to the church] through development projects. People who only preach without providing service forget people's lives.[55]

The archbishop of the Eglise Episcopale au Rwanda (EER) offered a similar sentiment:

"Evangelism" says everything; it touches the body, the heart, and the mind. Evangelism by necessity contains the diaconate [charitable Christian service]. As Christians we have to see the problems people face. If a man lives in misery, how can you be with him? Evangelization is not something theoretical but practical. And when it is practical, it touches every part of a person's life. How can someone hear the word of the Gospel if he has to worry about finding food to eat?[56]

Or again the Butare *Économe général*, the financial director for the Butare Catholic diocese:

Why does the church do development work? For me it is a conviction of faith. If you speak of God, you speak of man. Simply. That is my faith. All that concerns man must concern the church. The law of God is the duty of men.[57]

Although most early church social service work concentrated on education and health care, even in the early years of mission work some attention was given to rural economic development. Both Protestant and

---

[55] Interview in Kigali, July 31, 1992.
[56] Interview in Shyira, Gisenyi, August 6, 1992.
[57] Interview in Butare, March 25, 1993.

Catholic missions introduced into Rwanda a wide variety of new agricultural products that increased crop diversity, including wheat, potatoes, cabbage, tomatoes, coffee, and pigs, and new techniques for building homes and making bricks.[58] Efforts to address economic issues specifically as part of the church mission, however, began only in the last years of colonial rule. The Catholic Church began organizing rural producers' cooperatives in the 1950s, with the intention, according to Pierre Sirven, of creating economic opportunities in rural areas that could discourage youths from migrating to the cities where they might fall under the influences of Islam and urban immorality.[59]

After independence, church economic development activities continued to expand. In addition to the interest in attracting members and providing charity, involvement in economic development became an important element of the relationship of churches with the government. The Habyarimana regime in particular placed great emphasis on rural development and received substantial international assistance to launch economic development initiatives. While many development projects were large scale, such as the conversion of farmland into tea plantations, the regime also undertook many smaller projects, such as the Popular Banks set up throughout the country and various producer cooperatives.[60] Rural development programs often depended on close cooperation with the churches, and many were implemented by the churches.

Both Catholic and Protestant churches invested considerable energy and funding into instituting economic development programs. Within the Catholic Church, while Caritas focused on providing emergency relief to victims of famine and war and regular assistance to widows, orphans and the handicapped, the church established a new related agency, the Bureau Episcopal de Développement (BED), with offices in each diocese, that focused on programs that created economic opportunities and combated poverty in the long term. Various religious orders organized their own development programs, such as assisting street children, people with HIV/AIDS, and single mothers. The Presbyterian, Anglican, Free

---

[58] Pierre Sirven, *La sous-urbanization et les villes du Rwanda et du Burundi* (Published by the author, 1984); Twagirayesu and van Butselar, *Ce don que nous avons reçu*, p. 56.

[59] Sirven, *La sous-urbanization et les villes*, p. 118. According to Sirven, the Catholic Church's active social work in the rural areas was one of the primary contributing factors to Rwanda's continuing low level of urbanization prior to the chaos of 1994.

[60] Direction Générale de la Politique Economique, *L'Economie rwandaise: 25 ans d'efforts (1962–1987)*, Kigali: Ministère des Finances et de l'Economie, 1987; Uvin, *Aiding Violence*, pp. 19–102; Newbury, "Recent Debates," pp. 199–204.

Methodist, and Baptist churches all established offices of development and instituted a range of programs. Both Catholic and Protestant lay organizations also took up economic development as a primary area of concentration. For example, the Jeunesse Ouvrière Chrétienne (Young Christian Workers, JOC) was originally organized to encourage urban youth to retain Christian moral standards, but beginning in 1977, JOC became active in supporting the formation of worker cooperatives, projects to provide employment to youth.[61] Women's groups, youth groups, and other church organizations took up similar development work during the 1980s.

The types of programs initiated by the churches in the 1970s and 1980s ranged widely. In rural areas, the churches instituted programs that sought to increase food production by fighting erosion, introducing high-yield crops, and developing inputs to improve soils and to create new possibilities for earning income by making baskets, honey, jellies, charcoal, woodcarving, and other products, and by forming farmers' cooperatives. Even though Rwanda remained an overwhelmingly rural country, urban areas experienced a large growth in population due to declining fertility, dwindling available land, and increased rural poverty leading to an increase in homeless street children, unemployed youth, crime, prostitution, and other problems associated with urban poverty. The churches responded by establishing a number of urban development programs, particularly for children and youth. In both urban and rural areas, churches sponsored *tontines*, rotating credit societies, and provided small low interest loans, both of which could provide capital for individuals and groups to initiate economic ventures.[62]

The philosophy of development that undergirded economic programs in Rwanda gradually began to change, and this had a particularly profound impact within the churches. Beginning in the 1970s, a variety of scholars offered profound criticisms of the paternalistic and ineffective manner in which economic development programs were being carried

---

[61] Jean Casas, "L'Action Catholique," in Commission Episcopale pour le clergé, *L'Eglise au Rwanda vingt ans après le Concile Vatican II* (Kigali: Edition Pallotti-Presse, 1987), pp. 179–217; and Jean Casas, *L'enfant des milles collines* (Paris: Les Editions du CERF, 1991).

[62] C.M. Overdulve, *Le defi des pauvres: De la fonction diaconale de l'Eglise au Rwanda* (Butare: Faculté de Théologie Protestante, 1991) offers an excellent analysis of the problems of poverty in Rwanda and the responsibility of the churches to offer an effective response. Casas, *L'enfant des milles collines* analyzes the work of the Catholic Church in combatting poverty in Kigali.

out in the Third World and in Africa in particular. Seeing Africa as "backward," stuck at an earlier stage on the road to development, Northern governments and international development agencies ignored the degree to which the continent was already integrated into world markets in an exploited position. Under the belief that they knew better what was needed to drive economic growth, development experts designed programs without consulting local populations and without adequate consideration of local conditions and cultures.[63] As a result, the development programs failed to respond to what Africans themselves perceived as their needs, ignored knowledge that local populations had about their own environment and conditions, and often exacerbated existing social, economic, and political problems. For example, the emphasis on production of cash crops for an international market led in many places to food shortages and decreased nutritional intake, while the emphasis on industrial development exacerbated the existing expenditure differential between urban and rural areas. Many development projects had negative environmental ramifications. The transfer of large sums to governments fueled corruption and reinforced patrimonial structures that propped up unpopular, undemocratic leaders. Development expenditures focused on large-scale projects, such as dams, roads, factories, and plantations, which required importation of personnel and technology. African economies often lacked the base to support these programs, so their operation required continued international inputs, and they often failed once these inputs were withdrawn. While many development projects produced only minimal income, they created massive debt, and they made African governments and economies heavily dependent on continued support from the international community.[64]

---

[63] While development agencies did consult African governments before implementing programs, these governments were rarely representative, and their priorities rarely coincided with those of the population. Furthermore, the agencies allowed African governments only minimal influence. In Rwanda, the country representative of the World Bank told me that in small countries like Rwanda, the World Bank presented its program to the government 90 percent concluded, allowing the government only to modify the details. (Interview in Kigali, July 20, 1992.)

[64] Critiques of international development are numerous. Goran Hyden's influential *No Shortcuts to Progress: African Development Management in Perspective* (Berkeley and Los Angeles: University of California Press, 1983) criticizes the emphasis on large-scale projects that African economies cannot support. Paul Harrison, *The Greening of Africa: Breaking Through in the Battle for Land and Food* (New York: Penguin, 1987) discusses the negative environmental impact of development policies. Bill Rau, *From Feast to Famine: Official Cures and Grassroots Remedies to Africa's Food Crisis* (London: Zed Books, 1991) discusses the negative impact of development policies on rural populations

Based on these critiques, some scholars and development workers have offered alternative models of development, commonly grouped together under the label "sustainable development" or "grassroots development." They emphasize respecting and building upon the knowledge that local communities have about their own resources and needs rather than relying on outside "experts." They encourage small-scale, predominantly rural projects that are locally controlled, environmentally sensitive, require little if any outside funding, and use local materials and personnel, so as to discourage the development of dependence. Sustainable development programs seek to empower the poor and marginalized to take charge of their own development. Many programs are designed intentionally to protect the economically marginal from exploitation by both the international market and domestic elite, and the programs emphasize the meeting of basic needs as a primary goal. The formation of cooperatives, which gather together individuals and families within a community to organize self-development, is a primary tool of this approach. The predominant role of development workers and aid organizations is to act as a catalyst and facilitator, sometimes providing seed funds, appropriate technologies, and information where requested by local communities, but seeking to do so in a way that does not encourage dependence.[65]

The new philosophies of sustainable development began to have an impact in Rwanda in the 1980s. Within the churches, development had initially been viewed as a charitable activity. Money to buy goats or to build a model field or to erect a silo, usually donated by international partner churches, came to local communities from the central church offices as gifts. The initiative for projects came from the national office, and little local input was sought in design and implementation. Local populations as a result generally felt little personal connection to projects. Development expenditures furthermore helped reinforce the patrimonial system within the churches. As I illustrate in Chapter 7 through analysis of one local community, in many cases the local elite were able

---

and food security. For the Rwandan case, Peter Uvin's *Aiding Violence*, provides a damning critique of the role that development programs in Rwanda played in exacerbating inequality and contributing to the conditions that made genocide possible.

[65] C.f., Rau, *From Feast to Famine*, pp. 145–202; Harrison, *The Greening of Africa*; Alan B. Durning, "Action at the Grassroots: Fighting Poverty and Environmental Decline," World Watch Paper 88 (Washington: World Watch, 1989); Michael Cernea, "Farmer Organizations and Institution Building for Sustainable Development," *Regional Development Dialogue* 1987, 8; Peter Uvin, *Human Rights and Development: Translating Rights-Based Approaches from Theory into Practice* (Hartford: Kumarian Press, 2004).

to enrich themselves by diverting funds intended for the poor. Even when money arrived to its intended goal, it was treated as spoils in the system of patronage, as a reward to the faithful for participating in the church and for supporting church leaders. Rather than empowering communities, rather than augmenting the capacity of local communities to organize themselves to address their economic needs, the patrimonial nature of church expenditures encouraged a "dependency mentality," an expectation among the peasantry that their economic advancement would come through outside intervention rather than through local initiative and effort.[66]

International church development organizations were among the first to embrace the ideas of sustainable development and to attempt to implement them in their programs. Churches already had a stronger connection to the population than other organizations engaged in development, they worked extensively with rural inhabitants, and their projects tended to be modest in scope. Their development work was also already closely linked to education and health care, essential cofactors in improving the quality of life for the poor. But many church development workers became concerned that church programs were fostering dependency and reinforcing patronage systems. By the early 1990s, the philosophy of sustainable development had been accepted by most international church development agencies working in Rwanda, most Rwandan church development offices, most church development workers, and many other church personnel. The archbishop of the EER explained to me in 1992 why he was pushing his church to change its approach to development:

Following colonization, particularly in our country Rwanda, there was a mentality that believed all assistance should come from the exterior. The colonizers and missionaries and others from outside appeared very powerful economically, intellectually, culturally. People were taught to simply expect everything from them. When the churches worked in this environment, they did the same thing. ...

After developing this mentality, simply continuing aid was not a good method [of bringing development]. People, the population in general, do not benefit from this type of assistance. These programs are not well directed, because the people here are not responsible for them. When the foreigners leave, the project is finished. Thus foreign donor groups, like Christian Aid, the United Fund, ITO, have changed the method [of sponsoring development projects]. It was necessary to change the method. The church is there among the people, but it is not there to

---

[66] Uvin, *Aiding Violence*, provides a devastating – and convincing – analysis of the way that development expenditures ostensibly intended to fight poverty actually ended up augmenting inequality.

work *for* the people. Rather, it is there to work *with* the people. That is to say, now in most cases, if you do a project, it is initiated by the participants and does not come out of an office....

To aid effectively, the church must change the mentality of people. Many people [in the church] still don't understand this. ...It is a new philosophy of running things. That is why we have started to have seminars to educate all the workers, all the pastors, even the catechists who run the base communities. We have encouraged all the divisions of the church to initiate this sort of new philosophy. The workers should be among the people as counselors.[67]

While many people within the churches embraced sustainable development programs because they more effectively combated poverty, these programs also had an important, often unforeseen, impact on the churches themselves, as they subverted patronage systems and empowered people to defend their interests. By no longer allowing local pastors and national church leaders to distribute development aid as rewards for their supporters, the new development programs eliminated an important resource for the patron–client system. By bringing poor people together and creating economic opportunities for them, sustainable development programs decreased their vulnerability to exploitation and made them less susceptible to manipulation by elites. People successfully empowered for purposes of development were unlikely passively to accept limitations in other spheres of life. As people became increasingly aware that their hard economic conditions were not inevitable but resulted at least in part from corruption, mismanagement, and exploitation, they became increasingly critical of authorities, both within the state and within the churches.

Lay Movements and Organizations

The theological embrace of social issues, commitments to improving the material conditions of Christians, the reconsideration of the role of laity within church life, and other trends within the churches led to the creation of a large number of lay organizations in Rwanda in the 1980s and 1990s. Development cooperatives and basic Christian communities were but two of the myriad lay organizations, both formal and informal, that proliferated during the decades preceding the 1994 genocide. This significant expansion of lay movements under the auspices of the churches challenged the ability of church leaders to maintain control over their institutions.

---

[67] Interviewed in Shiyra, Gisenyi, August 6, 1992.

Lay groups are, of course, not a novel phenomenon in the churches. Catholic concerns in Europe early in the twentieth century over a declining appeal among the working class and the threat that workers would leave the church for communist organizations, with their anti-church tenets, inspired the foundation of Catholic Action groups, lay organizations that could appeal to workers outside the traditional confines of the mass. Belgian priest Joseph Cardijn founded the Young Christian Workers after World War I, followed by the Young Catholic Students (Jeunesse Etudiante Catholique [JEC]) in 1929 and Young Agricultural Catholics (Jeunesse Agricole Catholique [JAC]) in 1932. Under the motto "See, Judge, Act," Cardijn formed the groups to help personalize the Christian faith, foster community among believers, and help Christians concretely transform their material reality in order to live in dignity. This method of organizing the Catholic laity was given papal approval by John XXIII in *Pacem in Terris* and was promoted by Vatican II as a means of "preparing the way for the Lord."[68]

As Catholic officials sought to address the concerns of the politically excluded Hutu masses in Rwanda beginning in the late 1950s, they inaugurated a number of Catholic Action groups. Bishop Perraudin himself oversaw the establishment of JOC in 1958. He also oversaw the formation of the consumers' cooperative TRAFIPRO (Travail, Fidelité, Progrès; [Work, Faith, Progress]) in 1957. Many of the social action groups, such as JOC, JEC, and JAC, remained relatively small in Rwanda, while more pietistic Catholic Action groups such as the Xaverian Movement, the Legion of Mary, and Charismatic Renewal gained wider followings. Throughout the 1960s and 1970s, these groups tended to be heavily dominated and controlled by the clergy, but in the 1980s, they began to assert increased autonomy, while many parishes formed new groups for women and youth and other segments of the parish.[69]

Lay organizations have a much deeper history in the Protestant churches. Associations composed predominantly of laity, such as the Christian Missionary Society in the Anglican Church, played a key role in the implantation of Protestant churches in Rwanda, and groups such as the Anglican Mothers' Union were created early in the history of the churches in Rwanda. Each of the mainline Protestant churches had offices for youth and women, and nearly every local Protestant parish sponsored

---

[68] Casas, "L'Action Catholique," pp. 179–86; Berryman, *Liberation Theology*, pp. 64–6.
[69] Casas, "L'Action Catholique," pp. 187–205; Sirven, *La sous-urbanization et les villes du Rwanda et du Burundi.*

groups for women, youth, and, in many cases, men. While the clergy have specific functions reserved to them, the laity holds primary responsibility for organizing the Protestant churches, serving on councils at the parish, regional, and national levels and overseeing the selection of church leaders. As in the Catholic Church, however, Protestant clergy exercised strong influence over lay organizations, and only in the 1980s did lay groups begin to act with increased independence.

In addition to these formally recognized lay church groups, there were other officially autonomous organizations that were, nevertheless, founded and sponsored by the churches. Many of the development cooperatives founded and supported by the churches were officially autonomous. Trafipro was one of the first church-launched projects to become independent of church authority, run entirely by a committee of its members, and other church-sponsored cooperatives followed suit. Church leaders sponsored other types of organizations as well. Michel Twagirayesu, president of the Presbyterian Church, created the Association pour le bien-être de la Famille (Rwandan Association for the Well-Being of the Family [ARBEF]) to provide a Protestant response to the problem of overpopulation. ARBEF sought to respond to the inadequacies of ONAPO, taking better into account local attitudes and Christian moral concerns.[70] The Catholic Church provided the personnel and some funding to found Iwacu (meaning "our place"), a center in Kigali that supported the work of cooperatives. Iwacu provided training and logistical support to cooperatives throughout the country. While an initiative of the Catholic Church, Iwacu was an independent association controlled by member associations that were themselves nearly all member controlled.[71]

In addition to the officially recognized church associations, more informal movements emerged in both the Catholic and Protestant churches in the 1980s. An evangelical movement known as *Abarokore*, "the Saved," first emerged in the Anglican Church in the 1930s. While in Rwanda the missionaries successfully suppressed the movement, it spread to Uganda, Kenya, and Tanzania, where, known as the East African Revival, it had a lasting impact on the Protestant churches.[72] In the 1980s, a new *Abarokore*

---

[70] Interview with ARBEF director, Butare, February 26, 1993.

[71] IWACU, Centre de Formation et de Recherche Cooperative, "Rapport d'Activités 1992," (Kigali 1993); interviews in Biguhu, July and December 1992, February 1993. While written like an acronym, IWACU is rather the Kinyarwanda word for "our place."

[72] Linden and Linden, *Church and Revolution in Rwanda.*

movement emerged in the Protestant churches in Rwanda. Drawing inspiration from both the East African Revival and North American charismatic and fundamentalist churches,[73] the new *Abarokore* movement that spread through the various established Protestant churches called on people to have a personal relationship with Jesus Christ and preached a strict code of morality that forbade consumption of alcohol and cigarettes, sexual immorality and participation in bribery, corruption, and other illegal behavior. The *Abarokore* met informally under the direction of lay leaders after Sunday church services for prayer, hymn singing, personal testimonials, and speaking in tongues.

In the Catholic Church, a similar charismatic movement, Charismatic Renewal, came to Rwanda from the United States in the 1970s. Theologically, the ideas of Charismatic Renewal were quite similar to those of the *Abarokore*, and their prayer meetings involved singing hymns, prayers, and speaking in tongues, activities more common to Protestant churches. By 1987 it had an estimated 15,000 members in Rwanda.[74] Another movement that gained a much larger following emerged in 1981, when a young woman, a student at a Catholic high school in the poor rural parish of Kibeho, claimed to have been visited by the Virgin Mary. Over the next several years five other young women and one young man claimed to have had similar visitations from Mary or, in a few cases, Jesus. Being alerted by a revelation that Mary or Jesus would appear, the youth would spread the word, and on the appointed day, thousands of people from throughout Rwanda and beyond would descend on Kibeho. The messenger would be struck by a trance in which he or she would be able to speak to Mary or Jesus. Sometimes the messenger would answer questions from the crowd; other times she would bring a statement for the Church in Rwanda and beyond, sometimes dark visions of violence and suffering if the population of Rwanda did not repent and draw closer to God. These events inspired a massive religious revival in the Rwandan Catholic Church, and even among some Protestants.[75]

---

[73] Rwanda's Pentecostal Church, though founded by Swedish missionaries, grew out of the Pentecostal movement that originated in the United States. It was the fastest growing church in the country and influenced most other Protestant churches.

[74] Smaragde Mbonyintege, "Mouvements de spiritualité et récent dévotions populaires au Rwanda," in *L'Eglise du Rwanda vingt ans après le Concil Vatican deux* (Kigali: Editions Pallotti-Presse, 1987), pp. 311–20; Casas, "L'Action Catholique," pp. 200–1.

[75] Gabriel Maindron, *Des Apparitions à Kibeho: Annonce de Marie au Coeur de l'Afrique,* (Paris: O.E.I.L., 1984); Augustin Misago, *Les Apparitions de Kibeho au Rwanda* (Kinshasa: Faculté Catholique de Kinshasa, 1991).

CHANGING CHURCHES IN RWANDA

These theological and structural changes in the churches in Rwanda challenged the ability of church leaders to maintain control over their institutions. While early missionary leaders had been able effectively to preserve their vision of the churches against challenges – as Msgr. Hirth had done in quelling dissent among the White Fathers and the Anglican missionaries did in quashing the first *Abarokore* movement – Catholic and Protestant leaders in the 1980s and 1990s found it increasingly difficult to quiet dissent and to point the churches in the direction they saw fit. A growing number of people within the churches were becoming critical of the close association between the churches and the government. Both evangelicals and social activists increasingly called on the church leaders to distance themselves from the state and to use their influence to promote an independent agenda. Gatwa and Karamaga, two Protestant intellectuals, articulated the opinion of many Catholics in the early 1990s:

[T]he Catholic Church maintains a preponderant position not only because of the number of members and highly qualified apostolic workers, but also because of its works. When one perceives that the relationship with the government is particularly cordial, as the two institutions work hand in hand in all domains with the sole exception of family planning, one asks oneself if there has not been a tendency for the Catholic Church to yield to triumphalism.... Considering that which passes under other skies – the increasing role of the Church in favor of the majority of the population in Latin America, in South Africa, and more recently in Benin, Gabon, even in Burundi under the Bagaza regime – the Rwandan population asks itself some questions. When will the powerful Catholic Church establish the necessary distance vis-à-vis temporal power to play its prophetic role in society?[76]

Father Straton Gakwaya made a similar plea in 1987, one that could equally have applied to the Protestant churches:

What people seem to be waiting for from the Church is that it become a *sign* for them, a *prophetic sign*.... The important thing is not to be standing high, but to undertake the road of men and women, with men and women. The Church still seems to enjoy a considerable audience. But it is necessary not to act too late. We have enormous potential in lay and clerical personal at our disposal. It would be a shame to waste it.[77]

---

[76] Gatwa and Karamaga, *La prèsence protestant*, p. 37.
[77] Gakwaya, "L'Eglise catholique au Rwanda," p. 58.

As I discuss in Chapter 5, this changing sentiment placed demands on church leaders, pushing them to present themselves increasingly as an independent voice in society. However, the church leaders were not willing to sacrifice their close relationship with political authorities, nor to cede their control over the churches. The democracy movement that shook the political system in Rwanda in the early 1990s shook the foundations of power in the churches as well, driving church leaders to support drastic means to preserve the status quo.

5

"Giants with Feet of Clay"

Christian Churches and Democratization
(1990–1992)

In the brief period from 1990 to 1992, popular activism inside Rwanda combined with both diplomatic and military pressures from abroad to force the Habyarimana regime to accept limited political reforms. Growing out of the theological and organizational changes discussed in the previous chapter, church personnel and institutions played an essential part in fostering the growth of civil society in Rwanda and the emergence of the democracy movement that pushed for reform. At the same time, diverse elements within the churches challenged the authority of church officials themselves. Just as Habyarimana found it necessary to respond to public criticism both by offering limited reforms and by seeking to undercut his critics through intimidation and appeals to ethnic loyalty, church leaders, from the national to the local level, felt compelled to respond to their own critics by offering limited support for political and social reforms while simultaneously both continuing to back the regime and reasserting their authority within the churches. Ultimately, church officials, fearing the loss of their own power, offered tacit support to the policy that state officials used to regain the political initiative – scapegoating of Tutsi – a policy that finally culminated in genocide.

POLITICAL REFORM AND WAR

Seeds of Discontent

By preventing ethnic conflict, attracting international investment, and bringing economic growth, the Habyarimana regime was able to maintain strong popular support during its first decade in office. During the

mid-1980s, however, a deteriorating economic situation, growing awareness of official corruption and the divide between the rich and poor, and
increasing weariness with authoritarian rule undermined public support
for the regime and ultimately gave rise to a democracy movement. Despite
the economic growth posted under Habyarimana, Rwanda remained
among the poorest countries in Africa – a fact obscured by discussions
of economic achievement. Further, two factors served to enlarge the gap
between rich and poor in the country. First, Rwanda's economic expansion in the 1970s and 1980s benefited primarily a limited bourgeoisie, a
small group of military, administrative, commercial, and technocratic personnel who managed under Habyarimana to enrich themselves substantially, to accumulate land, construct homes, and buy businesses. Second,
population growth significantly outpaced economic growth, so that the
per capita national product actually declined, even as the economy grew.[1]
From 1980 to 1990, gross national product (GNP) increased at an average annual rate of 1.0 percent in real terms, but GNP per capita declined
by an annual rate of 2.2 percent.[2] Taking into account the increased concentration of wealth, the standard of living for the majority of Rwandans
– already quite low in 1973 – declined seriously under Habyarimana.

Overpopulation was a major source of Rwanda's declining standard of
living. From a population of 1 million at the turn of the century, Rwanda
grew to an estimated 7.7 million in 1994, on a territory approximately the
size of the U.S. state of Vermont.[3] With an average in 1990 of 290 people
per square kilometer, Rwanda ranked behind only Bangladesh in population density, while it had the highest rate of fecundity in the world, with
8.4 children born on average per woman by the end of her childbearing
years.[4] The overwhelming majority of Rwanda's population continued to
live in rural areas, with 91 percent of the labor force occupied in the agricultural sector and 80 to 95 percent of agricultural production devoted to
subsistence farming. A 1984 study by the Ministry of Agriculture found
that 63.2 percent of cultivated land had no protection against erosion,

[1] Fernand Bézy, *Rwanda 1962–1989: Bilan socio-économique d'un regime* (Louvain-la-
Neuve: Institut d'Etudes de Développement, January 1990).
[2] Filip Reyntjens, "Rwanda: Economy," in *Africa South of the Sahara: 1993* (London:
Europa Publications, 193), pp. 680–2.
[3] ONAPO, *Le Problème Démographique au Rwanda et le Cadre de sa Solution* (Kigali: la
Présidence du MRND and ONAPO, 1990), pp. 10–11.
[4] Service d'Appui à la Coopération Canadienne, "Profil socio-économique de la femme
rwandaise," (Kigali: Réseau des femmes oeuvrant pour le développement rural, May
1991); Office National de la Population, "Rwanda 1983 Enquête sur la Fécondité, (Kigali:
ONAPO, 1983); ONAPO, *Le Problème Démographique*, p. 13.

though more than 50 percent of cultivated land was at an incline of at least 10 degrees.[5] Overcultivation, deforestation, and overgrazing all contributed to erosion and declining soil fertility. As a result, since at least 1977, increases in food production had not kept pace with increases in population growth.[6] In 1985, 35 percent of Rwandans lacked adequate drinking water, and only 57 percent of daily protein requirements were met.[7]

Socioeconomic factors exacerbated the negative impact of deteriorating farming conditions on poor farmers. Shortfalls in production forced farmers to buy additional food, adding to the need for cash to buy clothes, hoes, cooking pots, salt, and other necessities and to pay for school fees and health care, creating opportunities for those with available cash to capitalize on the situation for purposes of profit. Just before harvest, when food was most scarce, farmers might sell off a portion of their anticipated harvest at a fraction of the market value. While this could produce immediate cash, it diminished the amount of harvest available for consumption or for sale at the market rate.[8] Selling off a parcel of land could also bring in cash, but this would often necessitate renting land in the future to produce sufficient harvest for consumption. The 1984 Ministry of Agriculture study found that 48.9 percent of parcels of cultivated land in Rwanda were rented, with 83.7 percent of those rented to grow food for household consumption.[9]

A small portion of the population with available capital was able to benefit from this system to purchase produce and land and turn it into profit. This system created a cycle of poverty in which a privileged few were able to become increasingly wealthy while the vast majority of the population witnessed declining income and nutrition levels, and it was above all those with government connections who had the necessary available cash to benefit. Government officials had access to funds for their personal investment from both legal and illicit sources, and they could also assist family and friends by naming them to civil service positions,

[5] Government of Rwanda, "Enquête national agricole 1984" (Kigali: Ministère de l'Agriculture, de l'Elevage et des Forêts, September 1985), quoted in Bézy, *Bilan Socio-économique.*

[6] Nezehose Jean Bosco, *Agriculture rwandaise: Problématique et perspectives* (INADES-Formation-Rwanda, 1990); Reyntjens, "Rwanda: Economy," p. 680.

[7] Narciss Munyembaraga, "Développement socio-économique: Problèmes et perspectives," *Vivant Univers,* no. 357 (May–June 1985): 10–15.

[8] Bernard Itangishaka, "Pour la défense du revenu du paysan," *Dialogue,* no. 130 (September–October 1988):26–36. This practice was illegal, but Itangishaka indicates that it was widespread. See also, Newbury, "Recent Debates," p. 209.

[9] Bézy, *Bilan Socio-économique,* pp. 31–2.

which offered not only salaries but opportunities for graft, or by helping them enter into business, providing startup capital, facilitating licensing, overlooking taxes, and providing government contracts.[10] Relatives of the president and his wife and close associates from their home region, Gisenyi, amassed the greatest wealth during this period, but other business, military, and government elites allied to the president throughout the country profited as well. According to Bézy,

> In Rwanda, the revolution [of 1959] literally made a clean slate, on the economic and social level. The new republic was strongly egalitarian, and the ministers of the first government traveled in Volkswagen "Bugs." ... [But] equality has certainly disappeared: a new multi-form bourgeoisie has been constituted to the detriment of the peasantry.[11]

The economic boom that benefited the commercial and administrative sectors began to taper off in 1980, and the economy fell into decline when the price of coffee, Rwanda's primary export, collapsed in the late 1980s. Earnings from coffee dropped from 150 million dollars in 1986 to 70 million dollars in 1989.[12] Coffee dropped from 82 percent of total export earnings (at 12,569 million Rwandan francs) in 1986 to 56 percent of export earnings (at 4,690 million Rwandan francs) in 1989, and overall income from trade diminished by nearly 50 percent.[13] This produced a serious decline in per capita Gross Domestic Product, of 4.3 percent in 1987, 7.1 percent in 1988, and 10 percent in 1989.[14] Since coffee was one of the few reliable sources of cash for small farmers, each of whom was required by law to maintain a few coffee trees, the decline in coffee prices aggravated cash-flow problems, but it also seriously affected the middle class, many of whom found their own incomes dwindling. Adding to the country's economic woes, a serious famine struck parts of Southern Rwanda in 1989, when inclement weather combined with increasing problems of soil degradation and overpopulation to cause severe crop failures.[15] During this period, the production of beans declined by 50 percent,

---

[10] Bézy, *Bilan Socio-économique*, p. 40.

[11] Bézy, *Bilan socio-économique*, p. 4.

[12] Jean-Claude Klotchkoff, "Méfaits d'une dépendance: Une économie dominée par l'agriculture," *Jeune Afrique*, no. 1551 (September 19–25, 1990): 55–6.

[13] Reyntjens, "Rwanda: Economy," p. 680.

[14] Hamza Kaïdi, "Economie quand le café ne paie plus," *Jeune Afrique*, no. 1526 (April 2, 1990): 42–3.

[15] Newbury, " Recent Debates," pp. 212–18; Filip Reyntjens, "Rwanda: Recent History," *Africa South of the Sahara: 1993* (London: Europa Publications, 1993), p. 679.

bananas by 30 percent, and sorghum, sweet potatoes and manioc by 20 percent each.[16]

While declining economic conditions produced deteriorating living standards, even for the middle class, public discontent in Rwanda emerged less in response to actual economic decline than to the impression that its impact was being unequally distributed. In much of the country, people resented what they regarded as the relatively privileged position of the northern prefectures, Habyarimana's home region. The prefectures of Gisenyi and Ruhengeri received a share of public investment vastly disproportionate to their populations. Gitarama, the second most populous prefecture and home to former president Kayibanda, received only 0.16 percent of the government's investments in the rural sector from 1982 to 1984.[17] Northerners also had an advantage in gaining spots in secondary school and university, scholarships, and employment. In 1979, the number of students sent to study abroad included 76 from Gisenyi and 71 from Ruhengeri, compared to 54 from Butare, 32 from Kibuye, and 37 from Cyangugu. In 1985–86, 167 students from Gisenyi and 138 from Ruhengeri studied abroad compared to 84 from Butare, 37 from Kibuye, and 55 from Cyangugu.[18]

Among the people I interviewed in Butare and Kibuye in 1992–93, regional favoritism featured as a prominent complaint against the Habyarimana regime. An employee of Shyanda commune in Butare expressed a typical complaint. "With the *ancien régime* [prior to democratic reforms] they were busy with the problems of their regions while we suffered here. No secondary school studies, no scholarships, no projects to give work to the youth."[19] A farmer and nightwatchman from nearby concurred:

I am for these [political] changes. Before it was like we were colonized by the people from the north. The better places were for them: nightwatchmen, orderlies, gardeners, cooks at the UNR [Université Nationale du Rwanda] were from Ruhengeri and Gisenyi, while our brothers were unemployed or fired to be replaced by people from the north.[20]

Ethnic discrimination similarly led to frustration with Habyarimana, as Tutsi found their opportunities for education and employment restricted

[16] "Carnet: Novembre–Décembre 1989," *Dialogue*, no. 139 (March–April 1990): 94.
[17] Newbury, "Recent Debates," p. 203.
[18] André Sibomana, summarized in *Dialogue*, no. 143 (November–December 1990): 92.
[19] Interview in Butare, January 27, 1993.
[20] Interview in Mbazi-Kabuga, Butare, January 30, 1993.

by Habyarimana's policy of "ethnic equilibrium," a quota system that officially limited the number of Tutsi admitted to schools and hired for positions. In practice, although guaranteed a certain representation by the equilibrium policies, Tutsi were almost entirely excluded from the armed forces and had only a small presence in the civil service. Many Tutsi supported political reform, not only because they felt that they had virtually no political influence in the Habyarimana regime but because they saw the regime as limiting their opportunities for education and employment.

In addition to resentment over Northern favoritism and ethnic discrimination, the public was becoming increasingly angry over abuse of office. Even as the majority of the population suffered from economic decline, government officials became increasingly wealthy. Early in his regime, President Habyarimana had encouraged officials to launch economic ventures, and many officials took this as a sanction to use their office for illegal accumulation, through demanding bribes and embezzling public funds.[21] As officials were in office for longer periods, they developed their patrimonial systems more fully and found increasing means of gaining income. Newbury suggested that younger administrators who did not participate in the revolution were not hindered in their drive to accumulate by a sense of responsibility to revolutionary principles of egalitarianism.[22]

In my interviews in Butare, Kibuye, and Ruhengeri in 1992–93, many witnesses complained of official corruption. As one example, the Catholic relief agency Caritas provided a poor widow in Butare with tiles, nails, doors, and windows to build a home and organized labor for construction, but asked her to request lumber from the communal forest, which had been planted through *umuganda*, public communal labor, ostensibly for the public benefit.

You know how many times I had to bring myself to the commune to have these trees I talked about? The agronomist wanted Primus [bottled beer], the subburgomaster, the councillor, the monitor as well, up to the guardian of the forest. So at the State, it is necessary to give and to receive afterwards. If you have nothing to give, you do not receive anything.[23]

Many people I interviewed expressed a frustration that government officials were growing rich at the expense of the poor. One woman from

---

[21] Bézy, *Bilan socio-économique*, pp. 40–2.
[22] Newbury, "Recent Debates," p. 203.
[23] Interview in Mbazi-Kabuga, Butare, January 19, 1993.

Save parish near Butare complained, "With the commune, it is difficult [to get assistance]. You have to come back day after day without the hope of getting what you're asking for. You have to have money or connections."[24]

Much of the population supported the Habyarimana regime when it first came into office because of its populist rhetoric, but by the mid-1980s many people no longer believed that the government had their best interests at heart. As a program of communal work, in which all citizens, rich and poor, peasants and government officials, worked alongside one another, *umuganda* most exemplified the regime doctrine of "unity, peace, and development." But by the 1980s, state officials and wealthy individuals had ceased participating in *umuganda*, while the masses of poor farmers were still required to spare a block of time each week for this public work. At the same time, the work increasingly benefitted the wealthy and those in power, as peasants were forced to build roads and bridges for the cars of the rich, to plant communal forests they were not allowed to use, and even to work the fields of state officials. In many places, *umuganda* became nothing short of forced labor for the benefit of officeholders and other elite, reminiscent of the *uburetwa* forced labor under the colonial state and monarchy.[25]

With corruption like this becoming widespread in Rwanda, the state appeared increasingly an instrument for the personal enrichment of a few rather than for the development of the whole country, and in a context of general economic privation, this alienated the population from the state. As one person complained, "Even when there was the famine [in 1989], the beans, corn, oil, sorghum that they should have given to us were consumed by the functionaries of the commune and the councilors, when they were intended for us."[26] State officials, even at the communal level, used their offices to accumulate land and cattle, construct homes, and buy shops and other businesses, and they benefited from various forms of preferential treatment outside the financial sphere, such as easier admission to secondary schools for their children. While the government attributed declining economic conditions to the fall in coffee prices, the

---

[24] Interview at Kiruhura, January 28, 1993.

[25] Damien Nyandwi, "Que les Parties Politiques S'interessent Normalement aux Problèmes actuelles du Pays: Que les Partis Nous Disent Ce Qu'ils Vont Faire au Lieu de Nous Tromper," *Imbaga*, no 10–11 (February–March 1992), gives examples of peasants who were forced to work on collective sweet potato fields, but after the harvest they received none of the produce or profits.

[26] Interview in Mubuga, Butare, January 27, 1993.

ostentatious display of wealth by state officials led an increasing number of people to attribute their impoverishment to official exploitation.[27]

Rumors of corruption spread through Rwanda's informal system of communication, known locally as *radio troittoir* ("sidewalk radio") or *radio bouche-bouche* ("mouth-to-mouth radio"), implicating officials ranging from minor local administrators to the highest levels of power. The Habyarimana regime came to office through a coup intended to reverse the consolidation of power by people from Gitarama, Kayibanda's home prefecture in central Rwanda and from the beginning included many northerners from Habyarimana's home region, Gisenyi, and neighboring Ruhengeri. Over time, however, power became increasingly concentrated in the hands of a limited group, particularly relatives of the president's wife, Agathe Kazinga, who was from a prominent Gisenyi family, descended from the royal family of Bushiru, one of the small northern Hutu kingdoms. In the late 1980s, Madame Habyarimana evidently orchestrated a series of government reshuffles that consolidated power in the hands of her relatives and people from her commune.[28] This group, which came to be known as the presidential *akazu*, or "little house," took control of key positions in the government, administration, and military, as well as in parastatal corporations that controlled such things as gas, transportation, banking, and electricity, pushing out rival groups from Gisenyi and Ruhengeri (southerners were almost entirely excluded from the inner circles of power). Catholic and Protestant leaders were drawn in as key allies as well, with leaders of both the Catholic and Anglican churches from Gisenyi and Ruhengeri.[29]

As Prunier accurately points out, the struggles for power within the inner circles of the Habyarimana regime resembled earlier internecine

---

[27] Sibomana, summarized in *Dialogue*, pp. 90–6; Bézy, *Bilan socio-économique*; Newbury, "Recent Debates," pp. 213–14.

[28] Agence France Presse, "Ethnic Rivalry" (November 9, 1989) in *Africa Research Bulletin*, p. 9485; Sandrine Tolotti, "Le Rwanda retient son souffle," Croissance, no. 356 (January 1993): 34–9; Christophe Mfizi, "Le Réseau Zéro," open letter to the President of the MRND (Kigali: Editions Uruhimbi, July–August 1992); Prunier, *The Rwanda Crisis*, pp. 84–90.

[29] According to Prunier, the key members of the *akazu* were Mme. Habyarimana's brothers Colonel Pierre-Célestin Rwagafilita, Protais Zigiranyirazo (prefect of Ruhengeri), and Séraphin Rwabukumba (head of enterprise La Centrale), her cousin Elie Sagatwa (Habyarimana's personal secretary), and "close associates" Colonel Laurent Serubuga and Noel Mbonabaryi (*The Rwandan Crisis*, p. 85). See also Des Forges, *Leave None to Tell the Story*, pp. 43–5.

struggles within the royal court of Rwanda, with intrigue, political manipulation, and violence employed to advance the interests of one faction against another in a competition for control that took little account of the vast majority of the population. These conflicts among the elite exploded into public view with the assassination in April 1988 of a popular army official, Colonel Stanislas Mayuya, who was considered a likely successor to Habyarimana as president but was regarded as a threat by Madame Habyarimana's group. With Mayuya's murder, rumors about palace intrigues came into the open and seriously compromised the notion that the regime was acting in the interests of the population rather than in the interests of those in power.[30]

If the government had been capable of stopping Rwanda's economic decline or seriously addressing other pressing social problems such as overpopulation, AIDS, or the 1988–89 famine, the pursuit of profit by government officials and consolidation of power would perhaps have been tolerated, but given the deterioration of conditions in the country, corruption, nepotism, and *affairisme* elicited increasing public anger in the late 1980s. Emmanuel Ntezimana, professor at the National University of Rwanda in Ruhengeri, writing in the Catholic review *Dialogue*, effectively expressed the sense of frustration with the leaders of state and society that emerged in the Rwandan population in the late 1980s and early 1990s:

Very curiously and quite dangerously, in a very short lapse of time, mutations and ruptures have been produced in Rwanda, notably at the level of "ubupfura" (dignity), "ubugabo" (courage) and "ubudahemuka" (integrity). There have been sudden transformations operating in the name of "development."

Among the elite and people of note, the goal of life, the value of the individual and the quality of society seem henceforth reduced *to the search and fantastic accumulation of goods and material comforts*, at the same time delicious and poisonous. And all means appear good, including those falsely called "political." This poorly thought out seeming ideology of "development" disarticulates and destroys the substratum of our society. It is in its name that, in the absence of a secondary sector, an elitist minority can monopolize the machinery of the state to manipulate and marginalize, otherwise said to exploit and colonize, the popular masses.[31]

---

[30] Marie-Roger Biloa, "Institutions, le président et les autres," *Jeune Afrique*, no. 1526 (April 2, 1990): 36–8; Prunier, *The Rwanda Crisis*, pp. 84–90.
[31] Emmanuel Ntezimana, "Principes essentiels et conditions préalables à la démocratie," *Dialogue*, no. 144 (January–February 1991): 37. Emphasis in original.

The Genesis of Opposition Politics

By the close of the 1980s, the sources of public discontent in Rwanda were manifold – economic decline, a growing disparity between rich and poor, official corruption, a sense of alienation from the state, regional and ethnic resentments. Nevertheless, this discontent need not have produced calls for democratic reform. After all, following similar complaints in 1973 the population welcomed a military coup and greater centralization of power rather than more democracy. The essential factors leading to the development of a democracy movement in Rwanda included changing public attitudes toward authority, a growing civil society, the role of the press, and the changing international political climate.

After almost three decades of independence, the Rwandan public had lost faith not simply in the particular government headed by Habyarimana but in the process of government more generally. People were frustrated with their exploitation by government officials, business people, and other elites and the lack of control they commanded over their lives. The government constrained their economic and social activity, not only demanding taxes and requiring participation in *umuganda*, *animation*, and MRND functions, but also requiring and regulating cultivation of coffee, pyrethrum, and other cash crops by individual farmers. Rwandan people expressed their frustration through growing noncompliance and declining deference to figures of authority, which manifested itself in part in a growing crime rate.[32] Most people I interviewed condemned the rise in crime, but they blamed it on the government, feeling that the corruption of government officials had encouraged lawlessness. People increasingly viewed the state as a threat to their well-being, a tool to enrich a small elite at the expense of the majority. A consensus began to develop in the society that serious political reform was needed to limit the power of the state to work ill. While the public did not anticipate a particular form of government, they wanted more than a mere shuffling of personnel or shift of alliances as the 1973 coup ultimately appeared to have produced. Increasing criticism of the government and growing noncompliance with

---

[32] "Carnet: Novembre–Décembre 1989," *Dialogue*, no. 139 (March–April 1990): 99. A provocative collection of essays edited by Donald Crummey, *Banditry, Rebellion, and Social Protest in Africa* (London: James Currey, 1986), asserts that there is an ambiguous line between crime and social protest. I am convinced that in Rwanda the growing crime rate in the late 1980s reflected in part declining public respect for the government's right to establish and enforce law.

government directives at the local level challenged the authority of the state and helped create political openings for demands for state reform.

Another significant development in Rwandan society that helped spark a democracy movement was the emergence of a number of independent organizations outside the state sphere. While early in the Habyarimana regime the MRND was able to monopolize most social space, creating its own associations for women and youth and preventing rival groups from forming, by the late 1980s people had begun to organize extensively outside the control of the party. Groups like Iwacu, Reseau des Femmes (Women's Network), and Duterembere (Pull Together, a women's association) were ostensibly focused on development, but they gradually became politicized as they determined that the government, rather than supporting their efforts for development, hindered their work through misappropriation of funds and excessive control and interference. Local-level groups proliferated as well, as state development programs actively encouraged the formation of cooperatives, like the numerous small development cooperatives sponsored by the churches discussed in the previous chapter. Churches sponsored many other groups as well, from prayer groups to youth associations. In contrast to the observations of some Africanist scholars who discount the contributions of grassroots and other associations below the national level,[33] I found that in Rwanda social developments at the local level inspired and empowered formal democracy activism. In Rwanda, as in many African countries, the formal democracy movement – those associations and individuals who intentionally organized and attempted to effect changes in government structure and policy – involved primarily educated and elite individuals, those with greater awareness of international trends and greater access to print media. But those formally involved in mobilizing for political reform, such as the media, human rights groups, and associations like Iwacu and Duterembere, drew support from the grassroots groups, which gave people experience in democracy and provided forums for discussion of social problems and political education, helping to create an environment fertile for more formal democracy activism.

I am not trying to argue here that civil society groups, whether national or local, are necessarily in opposition to the state nor necessarily democratic. As I discussed in the introductory chapter, civil society groups are

---

[33] C.f., Claude Ake, "Rethinking African Democracy," *Journal of Democracy*, 2, no. 1 (Winter 1991): 32–44; Naomi Chazan, "Africa's Democratic Challenge," *World Policy Journal*, 9, no. 2 (spring 1991): 279–307.

sites of class conflict and politics. Established powers in societies generally try to co-opt or control societal groups, and many ostensibly independent civil society organizations are closely linked to the state.[34] Nevertheless, civil society does present possibilities for social organization independent of the state. In Rwanda, the expansion of civil society created an arena, a political space, where political alternatives could be formulated. Although the state sought to control social groups, even playing a role in the creation of various groups such as development cooperatives, as the number of groups expanded and policies of liberalization forced on the country by international donors took effect, groups were increasingly able to act with a degree of independence. These groups became a basis of support for those who wished to challenge the political status quo and increasingly provided an alternative for those discontent with state policies.

The press played a particularly important role in channeling public discontent and individual forms of resistance into overt political protest. Since 1973, Habyarimana had closely controlled the media, with the radio and most publications run by the government and other publications kept within the government line through intimidation.[35] Yet from 1988, new independent publications began to appear, and the nongovernmental press began to discuss the problems facing the country and the need for political reform.[36] This helped to coalesce public attitudes and give a more concrete form to the inchoate frustration with official corruption and incompetence.

For a number of years, the Catholic Kinyarwanda-language biweekly *Kinyamateka* was the only independent newspaper in the country. The paper had considerable prestige, not only because it was the oldest paper in the country, but also because it had supported the cause of Hutu nationalism in the 1950s and its editor, Kayibanda, went on to become president. In 1988, under the direction of a new, European-educated editor, Father André Sibomana, *Kinyamateka* began to run stories that openly discussed

---

[34] Stephen Ndegwa, *The Two Faces of Civil Society: NGOs and Politics in Africa* (West Hartford: Kumarian Press, 1996), makes this point convincingly, comparing two groups in Kenya, one in conflict with the state and one largely co-opted. On Rwanda, see Uvin, *Aiding Violence*, pp. 163–79.

[35] Joseph Ntamahungiro, "Se reconcilier avec le Peuple," *Dialogue*, no. 147 (July–August 1991): 35–50; Jean-Marie Vianney Higiro, "Kinyamateka sous la 2e République" *Dialogue*, no. 155 (June 1992): 29–39.

[36] See, for example, Joseph Ntamahungiro, "Sans morale pas de démocratie," *Dialogue*, no. 128 (May–June 1988): 26–38.

previously taboo subjects. The newspaper published accounts of official corruption, nepotism, and land accumulation by government officials, thus legitimizing rumors that had been circulating widely in the country.[37] The most notorious case of official corruption covered in the paper involved a Minister of Finance and Economy, member of the central committee of the MRND, and deputy director-general of PETRORWANDA, the state oil and gas company. *Kinyamateka* exposed him for embezzling 30 million Rwandan francs in the sale of a gas station owned by his relatives. The controversy surrounding his case forced the government to bring legal action in which they found him guilty and sentenced him to six years in prison.[38] This case and others like it publicized by the paper highlighted the corruption of officeholders, their tendency to hold more than one position, and the networks of support they used to benefit their family and friends. These reports confirmed the rumors spread by *radio bouche-bouche* and indicated to people that problems of official corruption were nationwide, not limited to their own community or region.

In addition to exposing corruption, *Kinyamateka* frankly discussed Rwanda's economic problems. It gave details of the drought that ravaged the south of the country in 1989, exposing the inadequacies of government agricultural development programs.[39] The location of the drought in the south reinforced the image that Habyarimana was unresponsive to the needs of the south of the country. The newspaper's coverage of the country's economic problems exposed the government's own newspaper and the state-run radio as unreliable sources of information that glossed over serious challenges facing the country.

The government responded to *Kinyamateka*'s criticisms by arresting several people associated with the paper, including the editor, Father Sibomana. Nonetheless, the willingness of the paper to discuss Rwanda's problems openly – particularly given *Kinyamateka*'s importance for the 1959 revolution – helped unleash the feelings of frustration and resentment that had been building in Rwandan society. The discussions in *Kinyamateka* of corruption and opulent displays of wealth by government officials juxtaposed against the extreme hardship experienced by

---

[37] Charles Mutaganzwa, "La liberté de presse, essai d'interpretation conjoncturelle," *Dialogue*, no. 147 (July–August 1991): 51–61; Newbury, "Current Debates," pp. 212–214; Reyntjens, "Recent History;" Higiro, "Kinyamateka sous la 2e République."

[38] Agence France Presse, "Former Minister Jailed," (December 7, 1989) in *Africa Research Bulletin*, January 1990, p. 9530; "Carnet: Novembre–Decembre 1989."

[39] Catharine Newbury, "The Resurgence of Civil Society in Rwanda," Paper prepared for conference on Civil Society in Africa, Hebrew University, Jerusalem, January 5–9, 1992.

common people exemplified by the drought seem to have spurred many of Rwanda's nongovernmental elite into action. Throughout 1990, a large number of new publications appeared in Rwanda, representing a variety of social interests, both attacking and defending the government.[40] *Kinyamateka* and many of the newer papers, such as *Kanguka*, spoke with increasing forthrightness and openly called for political reforms on the lines of those taking place in other African countries.[41]

Greater freedom of the press became possible in large part because the Rwandan population had already begun quietly to criticize and resist the government, but the explosion of new publications and their frank reportage in turn inspired the public to express itself more freely. With this greater freedom of discussion, the problems of the country and the fault of the government came into clearer focus. As one informant told me, "In years past we lived in fear. We couldn't speak about politics, so everyone thought everything was fine. But we were in torpor. The problems were there before, but we couldn't discuss them."[42] Once people began openly to discuss the problems of the country, public perception – particularly regarding the government – changed rapidly, and anger that had been latent came into the open, encouraging others to air their own complaints.

Within this context of growing criticism of the government, international developments in 1989 and 1990 helped public dissatisfaction in Rwanda develop into concrete demands for political reform. The newly freed and expanded press helped keep Rwandans abreast of developments in Eastern Europe, South Africa, Benin, Congo, Zambia, and elsewhere in Africa. Ngirira Mathieu and Nzitabakuze Jean Bosco attribute the rise of a movement in favor of political reform in Rwanda in part to international factors:

Abolition of the political monolith of the single party in countries of Eastern Europe, a political system that African countries had imitated. ... The retreat of economic and military assistance from Western countries to African governments that do not respect human rights and pluralism. ... End of the Cold War and the bipolarity of two great powers who made intervention by one no longer necessary to counter the other.[43]

---

[40] "Radioscopie de la nouvelle presse rwandaise," *Dialogue*, no. 147 (July–August 1991): 69–80, counts 22 new journals founded between January 1990 and May 1991.
[41] Mutaganzwa, "La Liberté de presse."
[42] Interview in Butare, December 5, 1992.
[43] Mathieu Ngirira and Jean Bosco Nzitabakuze, *Le Rwanda à la croisée des chemins* (Butare, June 1991), pp. 74–5. Ngirira was director of SORWAL, an insurance company, and Nzitabakuze was a professor at the national university in Butare.

Other Rwandan writers likewise acknowledge the influence of changes in Eastern Europe and Africa on events in Rwanda, as well as the changing attitudes of Western powers in light of the end of the Cold War.[44] Antoine Mugesera, a director at Iwacu and one of the important voices in favor of democratic reform in Rwanda, claimed in early 1991 that Rwanda was caught up in a wind of change that could not be stopped, just as the wind of independence that blew across Africa thirty years before had not spared Rwanda. Yet he questioned whether the Rwandan people, the elite in particular, were ready for democracy.[45]

Ready or not, the convergence of economic crisis, growing public dissatisfaction, expanded freedom of speech, greater public awareness of official corruption and government inadequacies, and an international context where democratic reform was the trend of the day inspired calls in Rwanda for political reforms. By autumn 1989, a foreign journalist observed in Kigali an "atmosphere of the end of a regime."[46] Perhaps because it appeared just after the national conferences in Benin and Congo, a mildly worded letter released by the Catholic bishops on February 28, 1990, full of praise for the president but expressing concern over growing ethnic, regional, and class conflicts,[47] helped to inspire other Rwandans to express their own demands publicly. Journals began to demand a national conference for Rwanda like those in Benin and Congo and the establishment of a multiparty system. On May 31, a fight that broke out at a concert in Butare between gendarmes and students from the National University after a student jumped queue ended in the death of one student and the injury of five when gendarmes opened fire. Students in Butare then went on strike, took over the campus, and barricaded the main road to Bujumbura. Students at the university campuses in Ruhengeri and Kigali joined in, until President Habyarimana agreed to meet with a delegation of students on June 6. At the meeting, the president promised them appropriate measures would be taken, and a month later he suspended the Prefect of Butare and the commander of the gendarmes in Butare. Many people in the country interpreted the conflict as

---

[44] C.f., Joseph Ntamahungiro, "Oui au Multipartisme," *Dialogue*, no. 144 (January–February 1991): 59–73, François Funga, "Condamnés au Multipartisme," *Dialogue*, no. 144 (January–February 1991): 51–57.

[45] Antoine Mugesera, "L'Irresistible poussée démocratique," *Dialogue*, no. 144 (January–February 1991): 129–43.

[46] Quoted in Reyntjens, *L'Afrique des Grands Lacs en Crise*, p. 89.

[47] Les Evêques Catholiques du Rwanda, "Le Christ, Notre Unité," (Kigali: Pallotti-Presse, April 1990).

a reflection of a growing tension between students and the government because of the students' support for political reform.[48]

In response to the increasingly open calls for political change and apparent pressure for reform from French President François Mitterrand at the April 1990 Franco-African summit at La Baule, Habyarimana announced on July 5, 1990 that he would begin a process of political reform. He promised to appoint a commission to propose a future political organization for the country, and over a two-year period he pledged to relinquish some of his power and begin the process of moving the country toward multiparty politics. He also promised to reform unpopular government programs such as *umuganda* and *animation*, and to allow free expression of ideas in order to make possible the formulation of political reforms.[49]

Despite the promise that free expression would be tolerated, those who openly expressed ideas unappreciated by the government continued to face harassment. For example, Sibomana and three other employees of *Kinyamateka* were taken to court in September 1990, but they used the case as a forum to publicize criticisms of the regime. To defend themselves they presented considerable evidence to prove the truth of their claims of official corruption.[50] Despite intimidation, a number of Rwandans continued to express their opinions. Thirty leading Rwandan intellectuals, including Sibomana and other church personnel, issued an open letter to the president on September 1, 1990, calling on him truly to allow free debate on political reform by placing himself "above the debate and guaranteeing the neutrality of the State apparatus." They called for the Central Information Service to stop intimidating the press and the depoliticization of the National Radio. The letter continues, "The organization of meetings, debates, and conferences on political subjects ought to be authorized from this point on, in order to permit planning and reflection between people who want it outside the meetings of the MRND."[51] The signatories called on the MRND to renounce its political monopoly

[48] François Misser, "Rumpus in Rwanda," *New African* (August 1990): 20; "Carnet: 1er-15 Juillet 1990," *Dialogue*, no. 142 (September–October 1990): 104.

[49] Alison Des Forges, "Recent Political Developments in Rwanda," unpublished paper, March 1992; Des Forges, *Leave None to Tell the Story*, pp. 47, 51–2; Newbury, "Recent Debates," p. 214; Prunier, *The Rwanda Crisis*, pp. 88–90.

[50] Reyntjens, *L'Afrique des Grands Lacs en Crise*, pp. 89–90; Higiro, "Kinyamateka sous la 2e République;" Des Forges, *Leave None to Tell the Story*, p. 47.

[51] "Pour le multipartisme et la démocratie," *Dialogue*, no. 144 (January–February 1991): 144–50.

and allow free association, to accept the principle of multipartyism, to support the separation of powers within the state, to discontinue *animation politique* and *umuganda*, and to replace automatic party membership and fees with voluntary membership and fees.[52]

Pope John Paul II was scheduled to visit Rwanda in September 1990, and rumors circulated throughout the country that something would unfold after the visit, possibly a coup. Perhaps as a preemptive move, Habyarimana began to act on his promises of July, and on September 24, 1990, he appointed thirty religious, political, and intellectual leaders to a National Commission of Synthesis to draft a new national political charter, a set of reforms that were to be presented for approval to the Comité National de Développement (CND), the national legislature.[53] These promises, however, seemed to do little to quell the unrest in the country, as the Rwandan public received them with great skepticism.[54]

The War of October and Its Political Impact

On October 1, 1990, an invasion of northern Rwanda by a band of mostly Tutsi refugees based in Uganda launched a civil war that drastically changed the political equation in Rwanda. During the violence against Tutsi in 1959–65 and again in 1973, thousands of Rwandan Tutsi fled into exile in neighboring countries where they had been living as refugees ever since. In Uganda, which had the largest population of refugees, estimated at 200,000, the Tutsi fell afoul of President Milton Obote's second regime in the early 1980s. In the wake of systematic attacks on their homes and lives, thousands of Rwandan refugees attempted to flee back into Rwanda in October 1982, but President Habyarimana closed the border, inspiring a great hatred of him among the refugee population.[55]

---

[52] Ibid.

[53] "Avant-projet de la Charte Politique Nationale," *La Relève*, no. 154 (December 28, 1990–January 3, 1991) reprinted in Commission Justice et Paix, "Le Rwanda: Ombres et lumiéres," (Brussels, February 1991); Newbury, "Recent Debates," pp. 214–15; Reyntjens, "Recent History," p. 679.

[54] Reyntjens, "Recent History," p. 679.

[55] Catharine Watson, "Exile from Rwanda: Background to an Invasion," (Washington: The U.S. Committee for Refugees, February 1991; Catharine Watson, "War and Waiting," *Africa Report* (November/December 1992): 51–5; Gerard Prunier, "L'Uganda et le F.P.R.," *Dialogue*, no. 163 (February 1993): 3–18; La Communauté Rwandaise du France, "Memorandum sur la crise politique actuelle au Rwanda," (December 1990). In addition to the Tutsi refugees from violence, there were other Rwandans living in Uganda, many

As a consequence of their persecution, many Rwandans joined a rebel fight to overthrow Obote, the National Resistance Army (NRA), led by Yoweri Museveni. When the NRA swept to power in 1986, several Rwandans who had been with Museveni from the beginning gained important political posts. Major-General Fred Rwigyema served as chief of the army, while Paul Kagame served as head of the military intelligence service. Despite this power, as refugees the position of the Tutsi was vulnerable; thus a plan to regain Rwanda by force emerged among Tutsi in the NRA as early as 1986. When a number of Tutsi were sacked from positions in the NRA in 1989, planning for an invasion became more serious. A group of Rwandans in the NRA, including Rwigyema, secretly organized a rebel force, the Rwandan Patriotic Army (RPA) and its political wing, the Rwandan Patriotic Front (RPF), and drafted plans to invade Rwanda. While some in the group hoped to restore the monarchy, the majority view appeared to coalesce around two goals – gaining the right for refugees to return to Rwanda and driving Habyarimana from office in order to establish a multiethnic democratic government. Several prominent dissidents who fled to Uganda in 1990, including Pasteur Bizimungu, director of Electrogas, a Hutu from Habyarimana's home village, convinced RPF leaders that the time was ripe for an invasion, because Habyarimana's declining popularity and the growing momentum of the democracy movement made the regime vulnerable. Thus, evidently believing that southerners and other opponents of Habyarimana would flock to their cause, a disorganized group of several thousand Rwandans, primarily former NRA soldiers, launched a surprise attack on Rwanda's northeast frontier.[56]

The initial RPA attack was a massive failure, resulting in many deaths and the near collapse of the rebel group. Rwigyema was killed in the second day of combat, apparently murdered by leaders of a rival monarchist faction among his own troops. With the help of Zairian troops, the Rwandan army was able by the end of October to scatter the RPA into the Akagera National Park. Paul Kagame returned from training in the United States to take over as military commander of the RPA and led the rebel army on a retreat across southern Uganda to the Virunga volcanoes that form Rwanda's northwestern border with Uganda and Zaire. Here

of whose ancestors had migrated to the country during the colonial period in search of fertile land. These, too, suffered from Obote's oppressions.

[56] Prunier, *The Rwanda Crisis*, pp. 61–74, 90–2; Prunier, "L'Uganda et le F.P.R.," pp. 9–14; Watson, "War and Waiting," 53–4; Watson, "Exile from Rwanda," pp. 12–14.

he rebuilt the RPA, benefiting from hundreds of volunteers and donations that poured in from the Tutsi refugee communities throughout East Africa.[57]

Despite the swift success of the Forces Armées Rwandaises (FAR) in repelling the RPA invasion, the Habyarimana regime used the attack as a pretense for cracking down on political opponents. The president implemented a curfew and curtailed the freedom to travel, and the army established road blocks throughout the country. On the night of October 4–5, heavy gunfire sounded in the capital, which the government claimed was an attack by RPF infiltrators that the army repulsed. In fact, later investigations by human rights groups revealed that the "attack" was staged by the army for political purposes. In the next several days, soldiers and gendarmes arrested people throughout the country whom they accused of RPF sympathies, primarily Hutu opponents of the regime and prominent Tutsi. As many as 13,000 were ultimately arrested; many were tortured, and many died. These arrests served not only to intimidate regime critics but also to begin to identify Tutsi, as well as moderate Hutu, as suspect.[58] As Alison Des Forges wrote:

> In accusing the Tutsi, authorities reverted to the tactics of the 1960s, but in a departure from the earlier practice, they included Hutu as well among the "accomplices." Unwilling to wait for the scapegoating of the Tutsi to produce solidarity among the Hutu, they sought to hasten the effect by imprisoning Hutu opponents, hoping to silence and perhaps even eliminate some while at the same time intimidating others into rallying to the president.[59]

In the commune of Kibilira, where Bagogwe, a group of forest dwelling Tutsi, had been in conflict with authorities over a World Bank-sponsored program to clear much of the Gishwati Forest Reserve and open it for

---

[57] "Uganda/Rwanda: Picking up the pieces," *Africa Confidential*, 31, no. 23 (November 23, 1990): 5–6; "Rwanda/Uganda: A violent homecoming," *Africa Confidential*, 31, no. 23 (October 12, 1990): 1–3; Reyntjens, "Recent History;" Watson, "War and Waiting;" Reyntjens, *L'Afrique des Grands Lacs en Crise*, pp. 91–103; Prunier, *The Rwanda Crisis*, pp. 93–9, 114–20.

[58] Monique Mujawamaliya, "The Development of the Rwandan Human Rights Movement and Its Collaboration with International Human Rights Associations," paper presented at the African Studies Association meeting, Boston, December 1993; Josette Thibeau, "Le Rwanda: Ombres et Lumières" (Brussels: Commission Justice et Paix, February 1991); Africa Watch, "Rwanda: Talking Peace and Waging War, Human Rights Since the October 1990 Invasion," *Human Rights Watch Short Report*, 4, no. 3, February 27, 1992, pp. 7–11; Reyntjens, *L'Afrique des Grands Lacs en Crise*, pp. 94–5; Des Forges, *Leave None to Tell the Story*, pp. 49–50.

[59] Des Forges, *Leave None to Tell the Story*, p. 50.

grazing, authorities organized a massacre of Tutsi on October 11–13. Hundreds of homes were burnt, and at least 348 people killed. According to investigations by an international human rights commission:

the troubles began with a meeting at the sub-prefecture of Ngororero to which the communal councilors were summoned. The prefect was present at the meeting, but said nothing. The sub-prefect showed two cadavers, saying that they were Hutu killed by Tutsi and ordering the councilors to return to their communities to make the population aware in view of assuring security.[60]

After the initial surprise and disorientation caused by the attack, Habyarimana sought to reassert his authority in the country. On October 4, the night of the faked attack on Kigali, France, Belgium, and Zaire sent troops to Rwanda, ostensibly to protect foreign nationals, but their presence helped to boost public confidence in the president, particularly given the role French troops had recently played elsewhere in Africa to support faltering regimes. After the first few days, the army gained the upper hand, and by November 1, Habyarimana declared the war was over. Although renewed fighting quickly proved this false, the RPA appeared to have been diminished to a guerilla force incapable of sustained attacks and, thus, no immediate threat to national security.[61]

Despite these initial set backs, the War of October did not entirely extinguish momentum for democratic political reform. Whether because of the apparent success of the Rwandan army in containing the rebels, because of international pressure, or because of Habyarimana's political weakness, the regime did not crush all opposition in the wake of the October attack. In fact, despite initial attacks on civil liberties, in some ways the war seemed to add momentum to reform efforts. Several new human rights group formed in response to the mass arrests, newspapers

---

[60] Fédération Internationale des Droits de l'Homme (FIDH), Africa Watch, et al., "Rapport de la Commission Internationale d'Enquête sur les Violations des Droits de l'Homme au Rwanda Depuis le 1er Octobre 1990 (7–21 Janvier 1993): Rapport Finale," (Paris: FIDH, March 1993), pp. 18–22. See also Association Rwandaise pour la Défense des Droits de la Personne et des Libertés Publiques (ADL), "Rapport sur les Droits de l'Homme au Rwanda, Septembre 1991–Septembre 1992" (Kigali: ADL, December 1992), pp. 100–16. The Gebeka project, funded by the World Bank, oversaw massive cutting of the Gishwati Forest, traditional home to many Bagogwe. The land was then used to graze cattle, most owned by the president and other members of the *akazu* (C.f., Prunier, *The Rwanda Crisis*, p. 88).

[61] "Government Declares Victory," *Africa Research Bulletin*, November 1–30, 1990, pp. 9914–16; Reyntjens, "Recent History;" "Picking up the pieces;" Prunier, *The Rwanda Crisis*, pp. 100–8.

continued to discuss democracy, and the Commission of Synthesis began its work.[62] In the wake of his apparent military victory and feeling more confident of his popularity, Habyarimana sought to retake the political initiative. He announced a series of new reforms on November 13, speeding up the timetable for the Commission de Synthèse, and promising to put their plan up for a national referendum in June. He announced an end to the practice started during the 1930s of marking ethnic labels on identity cards, and declared that a multiparty system would be formed. In a speech to the CND he said, "Nothing impedes people from this point from thinking about the parties that they would like to create and the political program that they would like to submit to the people."[63]

As Habyarimana had promised, the Commission of Synthesis released its proposals for public comment in December, recommending a national charter that would separate the government from the ruling party, legalize multiparty politics, depoliticize the police and army, and create a presidency elected by direct popular vote for a five-year term. The Commission presented a final draft constitution in April, which was adopted by the CND on June 10, 1991 (as Habyarimana reneged on his plan to hold a popular vote). With the adoption a week later of a law legalizing the formation of political parties, a number of new political parties quickly formed. Despite the constitutional requirement that all parties be national in character, most parties quickly took on a regional or ethnic character. The Mouvement Démocratique Républicain (Republican Democratic Movement, MDR) signaled its appeal to the former constituency of Kayibanda, Hutu in the central and southern parts of the country, by adopting a name formerly employed by PARMEHUTU. The Parti Social Démocrate (PSD) drew its support from Butare, a region where ethnic attitudes were more liberal, presenting itself as a multiethnic party with a progressive platform. The Parti Libéral (Liberal Party, PL), initially organized as an urban party, representing business interests and professionals, with a Hutu president, but it became associated with Tutsi interests following Habyarimana's declaration that it was a Tutsi party and subsequently attracted many Tutsi, though it continued to seek Hutu support. The MRND, meanwhile, reconstituted itself, changing its

---

[62] Reyntjens, *L'Afrique des Grands Lacs en Crise*, pp. 103–6; "Picking up the pieces," pp. 5–6; Mujawamaliya, "The Rwandan Human Rights Movement."

[63] François-Xavier Munyatugerero, "Oui au multipartisme," *Jeune Afrique*, no. 1560 (November 21–27, 1990):7; François-Xavier Munyatugerero, "Dérapages de moins en moins contrôlés," *Jeune Afrique*, no. 1562 (December 5–11, 1990): 29; Thibeau, "Ombres et Lumières," pp. 13–23; Reyntjens, *L'Afrique des Grands Lacs en Crise*, pp. 105–7.

name to the Mouvement Républicain National pour la Démocratie et le Développement (The National Republican Movement for Democracy and Development). While the new constitution removed its monopoly on power, the MRND retained a strong base of support among Hutu in the north of the country and among political officials throughout the country, who owed their rise to power to the regime. A few smaller parties also formed, but these four had the largest followings.[64]

The MDR, PSD, and PL formed a coalition in September 1991 to lobby Habyarimana to hold a national conference that would establish a "government of national union" as the only possible means to bring the country to democracy and peace. On October 13, Habyarimana named Sylvestre Nsanzimana prime minister and charged him with forming a government that would negotiate peace with the RPF, set up an electoral process, and manage the structural adjustment program that had been launched the previous year. The MDR-PSD-PL coalition declared that they would participate in a government of transition only if the president and prime minister were of different parties, other important posts were distributed between parties, and the government sponsored a sovereign national conference, and in November they organized a march in Kigali that drew 13,000 people in support of a national conference. Without the cooperation of the opposition coalition, Nsanzimana named a cabinet on December 30 that included a member of the Parti Démocrat Chrétien (PDC), a party allied with the MRND, but was otherwise entirely MRND. The opposition responded by organizing protest marches, one of which on January 8, 1992, attracted 30,000 to 100,000 people.[65]

In the first months of 1992, the country entered into a serious political crisis, as much of the public rallied around the opposition. In an effort to resolve the crisis, leaders of the Catholic and Protestant churches formed a Contact Committee (Comité de Contact) that arranged negotiations between the political parties in February and March, eventually culminating in a compromise agreement in which Habyarimana named a new prime minister, Dismas Nsengiyaremye, from the MDR and charged him with forming a government that could bring an end to the

[64] Danielle Helbig, "Rwanda: de la dictature populaire à la démocratie athénienne," *Politique Africaine*, no. 44 (December 1991): 97–101; "Carnet: Avril–May 1991," *Dialogue*, no. 147 (July–August 1991): 136–7; Reyntjens, *L'Afrique des Grands Lacs en Crise*, pp. 104–9; Prunier, *The Rwanda Crisis*, pp. 121–6.

[65] Reyntjens, *L'Afrique des Grands Lacs en Crise*, pp. 108–12; Prunier, *The Rwanda Crisis*, pp. 127–35; "Carnet" section of *Dialogue*, no. 149 (November–December 1991): 89–94, no. 150 (January 1992): 34–9; and no. 151 (February 1992): 50–1.

war, calm tensions within the country, and effectively manage the government. Nsengiyaremye named a government with eight ministers from the MRND, three each from the MDR, PSD, and PL, and one from the PDC.[66]

At the same time that Habyarimana sought to appease his critics by offering political reforms, he and his allies pursued a parallel program of appealing for popular support and undermining regime opponents by reviving ethnic conflict in Rwanda. The massacres of Bagogwe and the arrest of Tutsi and moderate Hutu in October 1990 were only the first in a series of events designed to heighten ethnic divisions and regain support among southern Hutu by scapegoating Tutsi. Immediately after the RPF launched a second major surprise attack on Rwanda on January 23, 1991, sweeping down from the volcanoes on Rwanda's northwestern border and briefly capturing Ruhengeri town, demonstrating that the RPF had regrouped and remained a force to be reckoned with, leaders of several communes in Ruhengeri and Gisenyi organized another massacre of Bagogwe Tutsi, but once again the massacre was kept quiet, denied by government officials, known only to the general population through *radio bouche-bouche*. As with the previous massacres and arrests, the new round contributed to a climate of fear in the country.[67]

Even as the political crisis over multiparty government was being defused in March 1992, the groundwork for the genocide was beginning to be laid. A group of hardline Hutu formed a new political party, the Coalition pour la Défense de la République (Coalition for the Defense of the Republic, CDR), claiming that "in the current political landscape, no party, no institution, no person has been able publicly and consistently to defend the interests of the majority" [i.e., Hutu].[68] The CDR criticized the MRND for conceding too much to the opposition and the RPF, but they were generally close allies of the MRND, helping to articulate a more radical anti-Tutsi line that would be too contentious for the MRND to state publicly.[69] Also in March, a new wave of ethnic massacres took place in

[66] Michel Twagirayesu, "La Politique: La réflection de l'Eglise," speech at the Faculté de Théologie Protestante à Butare, April 2, 1993; Prunier, *The Rwanda Crisis*, pp. 144–50; "Le pouvoir commence à se partager," *Imbaga*, no. 12 (April 1992); Reyntjens, *L'Afrique des Grands Lacs en Crise*, pp. 111–12; "Carnet" section of *Dialogue*, no. 154 (May 1992), no. 155 (June 1992).

[67] Prunier, *The Rwanda Crisis*, pp. 120–39; FIDH, et al., *Rapport de la Commission*, pp. 27–42.

[68] Quoted in Reyntjens, *L'Afrique des Grands Lacs en Crise*, p. 127.

[69] Des Forges, *Leave None to Tell the Story*, pp. 52–4; Reyntjens, *L'Afrique des Grands Lacs en Crise*, pp. 126–8; Prunier, *The Rwanda Crisis*, pp. 128–9.

southeastern Rwanda in the Bugesera region, an area where many Tutsi were resettled after the violence of the 1960s.

THE CHURCHES AND POLITICAL REFORM

The Rwandan churches, as I have described them, had a history of close cooperation with the state. Church leaders had been actively involved in struggles for political power since their arrival in the country, and under Habyarimana the strong alliance between church and state included both personal and institutional links. At the same time, churches were not fully coherent in their attitude toward the state. The churches were complex institutions that contained a wide range of groups and associations under their institutional umbrellas, each acting with a certain degree of autonomy, and church leaders had consistent problems asserting their authority throughout the institution. Within these complex structures, differing theological visions competed for acceptance, and individuals used various church institutions for divergent purposes. During the Habyarimana regime, liberation theologies influenced some individuals to call for a more outspoken church, while expanded involvement in development led others to decry exploitation of the poor by political officials and other elite. Even as a patron–client system helped maintain church leaders in office, new informal alliances began to emerge among reform-minded individuals and groups, both within and outside the churches, and they began to call for a restructuring not only of church–state relations but also of the structures of power within the churches themselves.

It is not surprising, then, that the church reaction to the democracy movement that emerged in the early 1990s was mixed. Groups and individuals affiliated with the churches were among the first to push for reform and were at the heart of the democracy movement. Churches provided essential support to the human rights groups, women's associations, and cooperative centers that articulated the demands for political change, and they influenced many people within the population to support reform. At the same time, many people at all levels who were tied into the patrimonial structures within the churches and benefited from the status quo saw the challenges to the government as a threat to their own power, which was tied so closely to the regime. They searched for ways to resist change even as they felt pressured to appease the growing pro-reform sentiments of church members.

Church Support for Reform

Many of the most visible and influential voices pushing for political reform within Rwandan political society had links to the churches. For example, *Kinyamateka* was published by the Episcopal Conference of Catholic Bishops and contributed significantly to the expansion of press freedom in Rwanda by pushing the limits of government tolerance. For the first decade of Habyarimana's rule, *Kinyamateka* remained highly supportive of the regime, but in the early 1980s, Father Sylvio Sindambiwe, fresh from journalism school in France, took over as editor and began to publish more investigative articles looking at prison conditions, expropriation of land, public finance, and an article questioning *animation* as "idolatry of a chief." The controversy surrounding the journal led to Sindambiwe's resignation in late 1985 and his replacement by a less political editor. In October 1988, however, the Episcopal Council named Sibomana, also trained in France as a journalist, as editor in chief, and the paper began once again to tackle political issues, especially official corruption, administrative mismanagement, and the violation of human rights.[70] The death of Sindambiwe in a suspicious traffic accident in November 1989 was seen as a warning to the current editorial staff, but *Kinyamateka* continued to criticize the regime and soon other journals had begun publication, inspired by *Kinyamateka*'s example.[71] The monthly French-language Catholic journal, *Dialogue*, also enjoyed some influence among intellectuals. As early as 1987 *Dialogue* published an article on "The Sick Rwandan Economy," and in 1988 an article on democracy. During the early 1990s, *Dialogue* served as a forum for discussion of political reform, publishing issues on "Democracy and Multipartyism," "Yes to the National Conference," and "For a True National Conference."[72]

The churches also played an important part in supporting the formation of human rights groups. Monique Mujawamaliya was an active Catholic layperson who, because of her job as a social assistant in a Catholic center, was drawn into helping families of those arrested at the beginning of the War of October. She became inspired to form a

---

[70] Sibomana's *Hope for Rwanda* provides a fascinating personal account of the period from one of its chief actors.

[71] Higiro, "*Kinyamateka* sous la 2e République," pp. 29–39.

[72] *Dialogue*, various issues. Although with a limited circulation, *Dialogue* was avidly read by the elite. I was with a high-ranking military officer in 1993 when he received a copy of *Dialogue* and anxiously looked to see what it had to say about the political situation.

human rights organization, the Association Rwandaise pour la Défense des Droits de la Personne et des Libertés Publiques (ADL), both to assist her and to offer institutional protection for her activities, and she turned to the churches for support. She approached Archbishop Nsengiyumva for assistance but he refused, saying that the state was justified in having security concerns. She received strong support, however, from the Jesuit community, and a number of church people signed on as founding members, including Sibomana; Belgian priest Guy Théunis and Enos Nshimyimana from *Dialogue*; Tharcisse Gatwa, director of the Rwandan Bible Society and former secretary general of the Presbyterian Church; Dominique Nkiramacumu, the president of the Association Rwandaise des Travailleurs Chrétiens; and Etienne Ndahimana, secretary of the YMCA. The ADL received logistical support and information from the churches, as the frequent testimonies from priests in ADL publications indicates.[73] Another human rights group, the Ligue Chrétienne de Défense des Droits de l'Homme au Rwanda (LICHREDHOR), based in the southwestern prefecture of Cyangugu, also drew its support from the churches. Chrysologue Mahame, a Jesuit priest who directed the Jesuit Christus Center in Kigali, founded another group, Association des Voluntaires de la Paix (AVP) in 1992 and served as its legal representative.

The churches supported a variety of other civil society organizations that engaged in the pro-reform struggle. Iwacu worked to represent the interests of the rural populations and to keep them informed about the ongoing reforms. In 1992, Iwacu committed itself to developing civil society and instituted a civic education program that trained 265 peasants in nine five-day sessions to enable them to organize civic education programs in their communities.[74] Many of the community leaders who signed public letters calling for reform worked for the church or were active in church lay organizations.

Perhaps even more important than the influence of the churches in the highly visible and vocal national organizations of civil society was the influence that churches had at the grassroots in helping to create a wider constituency for democratic reforms. As mentioned in the previous chapter, participation in women's groups, development cooperatives, and basic Christian communities helped to create solidarity among church members and to raise their consciousness of their rights and capabilities. While most people in the countryside lacked the ability to become

---

[73] Interview conducted December 6, 1993 in Boston; ADL, *Rapport sur les Droits de l'Homme au Rwanda*.
[74] Iwacu, "Rapport d'Activités 1992."

directly involved in national voluntary organizations, to write articles and sign letters, and otherwise engage in the formal process of lobbying for reform, they nevertheless found ways to express their political opinions. During the early 1990s, the rural population *en masse* began practicing noncompliance with government directives. Even before the law on parties was changed, people refused to attend MRND functions and refused to pay MRND membership dues. Many people stopped participating in *umuganda* and *animation*, and some people protested against government regulations on their farming by uprooting or burning their coffee trees. By late 1992, protests were becoming more serious. In Kibuye and Gikongoro, people protested against *umuganda* and against exploitation by the wealthy by burning forests owned by the commune, rich individuals, and even the churches. Eventually, many people refused to pay their taxes, which they believed were simply going into the pockets of government officials. Many of these people joined opposition parties and became involved in local organization and local protests. It is my contention that churches helped to politicize the rural population and, while not actively endorsing these protests, helped create the connections between people and the consciousness necessaries for these types of action.

Many of the church members I interviewed in 1992 and 1993 expressed strong support for political reforms:

I am for these changes that have delivered us from forced labor that they claimed was for the community although we didn't get anything from it. I hope that we will have the right to express ourselves now.[75]

As for us, we aren't yet in any party, but multipartyism has delivered us from oppression: forced work called *umuganda*, communal assessments. And now we are free to speak.[76]

Previously people were judged in a mean fashion, but for the moment people are judged carefully. Politicians have become very nice, they no longer demand the full tax that they used to.... Each person exploits his land now according to his own means, but before you worked under constraint, following laws you didn't have any control over, working in fields that weren't even your own.[77]

I think that [the changes] are good, because in the time of single party rule, there was forced communal labor, forced *animations* for the president. You couldn't point out the faults of the government. Now everything is changing. We are becoming more and more free.[78]

[75] Interview in Cyarwa, Butare, February 2, 1993.
[76] Interview in Shyanda-Kinteko, December 26, 1992.
[77] Interview in Gituntu, Mwendo, Kibuye, December 26, 1992.
[78] Interview in Shyanda, Mbazi, Butare, December 21, 1992.

As Rwandans both at the grassroots and national level engaged in a struggle to exercise their rights and defend their interests, they did not focus only on government institutions, but also on the churches themselves. At the same time that the wider society was struggling to gain control of the reigns of government, struggles were taking place within a number of Rwanda's churches over theology, ritual, and leadership. In the Episcopal Church, for example, a conflict broke out from 1990 to 1993 over who would become archbishop of Rwanda, which had until then been part of the diocese of Rwanda-Burundi and Goma-Zaire, but was preparing to become a distinct province of the Anglican church. Bishop of Kigali, Adonia Sebununguri, was the first Rwandan Anglican bishop and had served since 1966. He was a close associate of Habyarimana and considered quite conservative. In contrast, Justin Ndandari, who had served as bishop of Butare since the creation of the diocese in 1975, was regarded as more moderate and sympathetic to reform efforts. In 1990, the provincial synod voted to interchange Justin Ndandari with Augustin Nshamihigo, bishop of Shyira, Rwanda's third diocese. Ndandari objected to the transfer, because he saw this as an attempt to undercut his authority by moving him from the largest Anglican diocese (and his home region) to a smaller diocese whose headquarters were located in a remote part of Gisenyi where Ndandari lacked connections and support. In response, the province dismissed Ndandari in mid-1991, but more than sixty pastors and officials of the Butare diocese signed a petition in support of him.[79]

To be recognized as a province of the international Anglican communion, the Rwandan church needed to have four dioceses, so plans were made to create a new diocese of Byumba. Ndandari objected to this, however, because he felt that it would make three of the dioceses in northern Rwanda against one in the south and thereby ensure Sebununguri's power and appointment as archbishop. Refusing to recognize the authority of either the former provincial synod or Sebununguri, Ndandari sought the support of the Archbishop of Canterbury, symbolic head of the Anglican church worldwide, to appoint bishops to three new dioceses in November 1991. Sebununguri, meanwhile, named a new bishop of Butare, thus creating two sets of four competing bishops. Eventually the situation was resolved through a compromise that balanced the power of Sebununguri and Ndandari: Nshamihigo became archbishop, but the

---

[79] "Carnet" section of *Dialogue*, issues 141, 149, 150, 151, 158, and conversations with EER pastors and representatives of the church in Shyira and Butare.

bishops appointed by Ndandari retained their posts, and a new diocese was created for the bishop named by Sebununguri, raising the number of dioceses to eight.[80]

While this may seem an arcane intra-church battle for personal power, many Rwandans interpreted the conflict as a struggle over the future direction and character of the Anglican Church and the nature of its engagement in Rwandan society. With his ties to Habyarimana and the MRND and his autocratic style of leadership, Sebununguri represented to many Anglicans a conservative choice who would continue or even strengthen church ties with the state. In contrast, Ndandari had promoted sustainable development programs and other progressive policies in his diocese and was considered sympathetic to the political reform movement. With Nshamihigo, the church chose a man who was a strong supporter of Habyarimana but whose style of leadership was less autocratic and who was more sympathetic to innovative church programs.

The popular pietistic movements discussed in the last chapter, particularly the Abarokore and devotions to Mary related to Kibeho, challenged the monopoly on religious authority of the clergy. Mainline Protestant leaders found the Abarokore movement problematic, because although those who participated were often inspired to become highly devoted church members, many also felt empowered to openly criticize pastors and other church leaders for failing to follow the appropriate code of conduct – for drinking alcohol or womanizing or participating in corruption. Because the meetings of the Abarokore occurred under the direction of laity without pastoral supervision, they tacitly asserted the right of laity to exercise religious authority and challenged the exercise of authority through the church hierarchy.

Similarly, although the events at Kibeho had created a revival of religious fervor within the Catholic Church, the church hierarchy viewed the supposed visions with suspicion. The popular nature of events, with Mary (and occasionally Jesus) appearing to a common shepherd and to schoolgirls, half of whom were Tutsi, seemed to transfer religious authority to the masses. The visions contained condemnations of the sinfulness of the land, pointing particularly to the selfishness of the rich whose wealth had taken their hearts from God. Such messages seemed to challenge the very structures of power that benefited the bishops and priests.[81] The call to

---

[80] Ibid.
[81] Both Maindron, *Des Apparitions à Kibeho*, and Misago, *Les Apparitions de Kibeho*, contain detailed accounts of the events at Kibeho as well as interpretations of the theological content of the apparitions.

repent and the dark visions of the consequences of a failure to do so seem
eerily to have anticipated the coming violence, as in the vision of a "river
of blood" that Gabriel Maindron reports from an August 19, 1982,
vision: "The children saw terrifying images, a river of blood, people who
killed one another, cadavers abandoned without anyone to bury them, a
tree all on fire, a wide open chasm, a monster, decapitated heads."[82] The
fact that the role of prophet was taken up by poor children in an obscure
corner of the country seemed a threat to the Catholic hierarchy.

In my research in Rwanda in the early 1990s, people openly complained about church leaders. Development offices, peasant cooperatives, women's groups, and others were actively struggling to reshape
the agenda of their church, and they often found themselves in conflict
with the established powers in the churches. Some people demonstrated
their disapproval of the status quo with their feet, either transferring to
another church or dropping out of active participation in any church. As
conflicts over authority within churches have no obvious connection to
state power, many social scientists disregard their political content. Most
Rwandans, however, recognized that churches in their country were political institutions not simply because they could influence the state, but also
because they had control over substantial resources, they could bestow
status on individuals, and they exercised spiritual power, which to many
people was very important.[83] Hence, struggles for increased power within
the religious realm were not divorced from but rather intimately connected to the struggles for state reform. As people sought to gain greater
control over their lives, this included greater control over the religious
sphere of their existence.

The Mixed Reaction of the Church Hierarchies

Like state officials, church leaders reacted in diverse ways to the growing popular democratic sentiment in Rwanda. They felt compelled to
demonstrate a degree of political independence from the regime and to
remain socially relevant by addressing the rapid transformations taking
place in the country, but they did not wish to jeopardize their close relationship with the state nor to undermine a regime whose fortunes were
closely linked to their own. Hence, church leaders expressed support for

---

[82] Maindron, *Des Apparitions à Kibeho*, p. 183.
[83] On spiritual power see Schatzberg, *Political Legitimacy in Middle Africa*, and Ellis end
    Ter Haar, "Religion and Politics in Sub-Saharan Africa."

the general principles of democracy and good governance and sought to act as neutral arbiters in conflicts between political parties and in the civil war, helping to negotiate the new multiparty government, but at the same time, they made clear their continuing strong support for the Habyarimana regime and urged loyalty to the government in the context of the War of October. Many church leaders made little effort to mask their own dislike and distrust of Tutsi, and many Christians interpreted the church leaders' failure to oppose the growing ethnic tension and violence in the country as an endorsement of the regime's policy of ethnic scapegoating. Leaders struggled to quash rebellions within their churches, and, like many state officials, some apparently came to regard the threats to their authority in ethnic terms, which hardened their support for the regime and opposition to the RPF.

In principle, clergy derive their authority from their position as religious leaders. In the Christian tradition, clergy derive legitimacy from apostolic succession, the idea that their religious power has been passed down in direct succession from Christ Jesus, which allows them to claim the right to serve as spiritual leaders and administer sacraments. In practice, however, clergy are constrained by the fact that churches are voluntary organizations. Unlike the state, in which the "exit option," the choice to withdraw ones participation and support, is limited,[84] people can leave a church they do not like with relative ease. With the diversity of churches present in Rwanda after independence, as well as the persistence of indigenous religious practices, residents had multiple options for meeting their spiritual needs. A church's ability to distribute schooling, healthcare, development support, and relief gave churches sway over nearby populations, but the appeal of a church's message was also significant. If a church's ideas were unbelievable or irrelevant, people would turn away, and if church leaders failed to follow the messages they preached, people might doubt the truth of the message. The growth of populist theologies and lay church structures during the 1980s were particularly important in this regard, because they allowed people greater freedom to read the Bible themselves and reflect on its message, and led many people to note

---

[84] Albert O. Hirschman's concept of "exit," (*Exit, Voice, and Loyalty: Responses to Decline in Firms, Organizations, and States* (Cambridge: Harvard University Press, 1970) originally developed to discuss product loyalty and choice, has been widely applied to other institutions as well. Because of the state's monopoly of force within any society and the non-voluntary nature of law, people's choices in the governmental realm are limited. People may try to limit their involvement with the state, but ultimately they can only truly "exit" by uprooting themselves from their homes and going into exile.

the apparent contradictions between the behavior of church leaders and the messages in the Bible. As a result, even the most conservative clergy, those most closely tied to the regime, and those most benefitting from the status quo felt some need to respond to the changing currents of public opinion within their churches.

One important way in which the Rwandan Catholic bishops sought to demonstrate their political engagement and to influence developments was through issuing pastoral letters. Since the letters require the signature of all the bishops, they represent a compromise between divergent ideas, and as a result, as a quick review will demonstrate, they tend to be vague. They nevertheless offer a window into the positions of the Catholic leadership. In February 1990, well before the start of the War of October, the eight Catholic bishops of the country issued the joint pastoral letter "Christ, Our Unity," that addressed the disintegration of the sense of community in Rwanda and the ethnic, regional, and class divisions that were emerging in the country. They wrote that, "the Church, for its part, does not cease to preach unity," but that:

there are some Rwandans who reject these teachings and continue to support ethnic rivalries through all sorts of speeches and maneuvers. One sometimes hears people complain that, for reasons of ethnic origin, they have been refused a job or a place in school, they have been deprived of benefits, or that justice has not been impartial in their regard ....[85]

They claimed that, "The Twa, the Tutsi, the Hutu, the foreign guest, all of us are children of God and we possess one and the same father: God." And they assured their readers that, "Even now the representatives of authority do not cease calming quarrels and hatreds of ethnic origin."[86] The bishops decried "certain wealthy individuals or leaders" who use their property or power only to benefit "those of their parentage or clan" while neglecting those in true need. They called on the population:" Let us rise up against the dishonest schemes and plots of little groups of privilege who, in the exercise of their functions or elsewhere, want to limit their privileges to their friends and relatives, prejudicial against others."[87]

---

[85] Les Evêques Catholiques du Rwanda, "Le Christ, Notre Unité," p. 6. All of the bishops' pastoral letters 1990–1994 are collected in single volume, Sécretariat Général des Evêques Catholiques du Rwanda, *Recueil des Lettres et Messages de la Conference des Evêques Catholiques du Rwanda Publies Pendant la Period de Guerre (1990–1994)* (Kigali: Sécretariat Général, 1995).

[86] Evêques du Rwanda, "Le Christ, Notre Unité," p. 6.

[87] Ibid, p. 10.

The bishops did not, however, give specific examples of the nepotism and ethnic and regional prejudice they discussed, and they insisted that the president as well as most Rwandans were on the side of unity and order. In other words, the problems were merely aberrations rather than systemic. The bishops quoted Habyarimana, praised the policy of ethnic equilibrium, and implied that if only the population would respect the policies of the regime, the problems would evaporate.

In May 1990, a few months before the visit of Pope John Paul II, the bishops issued a second part to "Christ, Our Unity," devoted to "Justice for People." In this letter, they addressed a multiplicity of social problems, arguing that justice and development are inseparable, supporting human rights and the rights of prisoners, criticizing banditry, and defending the right to free means of communication. They particularly targeted corruption:

Another bad habit that has spread now a little everywhere: *nepotism and favoritism*, but above all the *bribes*[88] that are called "sweeteners." Today, many people have difficulty finding quickly that to which they have a right without recourse, to resolve their problems, to the mediation of people better placed. Whoever wants a certificate from the administration or hopes to advance a legal case, give a bribe! Whoever wants schooling for his child, or good recommendations to show to the upper echelon, give a bribe! Whoever wants a sure position of employment, again a bribe! The merchant who wants to import some merchandise passing by customs, or wants a diminution of the tariffs has recourse to a bribe! The car driver in flagrant offense, to free himself from the gendarmes, uses a bribe! Whoever wants to win a lawsuit distributes bribe! ...

That which is revolting is to see a person who, in a very brief time, succeeds in building houses to rent, and who what's more, manages to buy trucks with trailers; and meanwhile one can see that this man lives in peace, worried by nothing, since the authorities responsible in this domain seem not to seek to question the origin of all these goods. How can one tarry when one sees the manner by which the little people tighten their belts to raise money to pay the taxes and all the fees required for everything, while this money passes into the pocket of certain people who pillage the common good without difficulty? Worse still, these grand sums of money that they have just accumulated, they're going to leap across the borders of the country to be deposited in foreign banks![89]

Despite these strong words, the bishops did not directly criticize the government. On the contrary, they again implied that the Habyarimana

---

[88] The term used by the bishops here literally translates as "pots-of-wine." This is a general expression for bribe, but it also refers quite literally to the common demand for calabashes of banana beer, or sometimes other alcoholic beverages, as bribes.

[89] Ibid. Emphasis in the original.

regime was in full accord with them, as when they commended the government for supporting human rights treaties "and working, as much as possible, to put them into application."[90]

Although these letters lacked specifics, pointed no fingers, and in fact praised the regime, they gave comfort to supporters of reform, since the bishops conceded the need to discuss corruption and human rights violations and helped reinforce the growing public sentiment that order was declining and that Habyarimana's government had become clannish and corrupt. To many Rwandans, aware that several bishops strongly supported the regime, the letters indicated that even allies of the president had accepted that a multiparty system was inevitable. Some people even hoped that more moderate bishops were gaining greater influence and that the churches might eventually throw their weight behind the reform movement; after all, the churches had switched sides in Rwanda's conflicts once before.

In their next significant letter, however, the bishops stepped back into the more familiar role of defenders of the regime. Writing a month after the outbreak of the War of October, the bishops issued a pastoral letter, "Happy the artisans of peace, for they will be called sons of God," in which they offered comfort to the population and strong support for the government. They supported government claims that the attack involved Ugandan soldiers, that accomplices had infiltrated even into the capital, and that the RPF was unjustified in attacking, because the refugee problem was on the verge of resolution. In a section addressed to the authorities, the bishops thanked the government for its efforts to restore peace:

Since the attack on our country, we have greatly appreciated the efforts displayed, with great sacrifice, to assure security and peace to our population. ... Knowing that all authority emanates from God (*Rm 13: 1–2*), we entrust you to that same God so that he helps you with your heavy responsibilities. Providence has entrusted you with the charge of watching over Common Good of our Nation. ... We assure you of our close collaboration. ...[91]

---

[90] Secrétariat Général, *Recueil des Lettres et Messages*, pp. 35–73. A third part of *Christ, Our Unity* issued in August focused specifically on spiritual issues, including Kibeho, which the bishops said they could not address definitively until the work of the commissions was complete, but they cautioned Catholics not to become too excessive in the worship of Mary, since "There is one God, there is also one mediator between God and humankind, Christ Jesus" (1 Timothy 2:5) (*Recueil des Lettres et Messages*, pp. 75–118).

[91] Conference des Evêques, *Recuiel des Lettres et Messages*, pp. 119–33, quotation pp. 128–9.

The bishops did address the ethnic tension in the country in general terms, but they said nothing about the specific circumstances of the ethnic situation in the wake of the war, nor did they mention, much less condemn, the massacres in Kibilira, which had already taken place. In fact, in denouncing unspecified "disinformation, savagely and maliciously organized by those who attacked Rwanda," they implied that rumors of massacres were false.[92] Similarly, they did broach the subject of mass arrests and call on leaders to act judiciously, but they made no mention of the ethnic and regional nature of the arrests, nor of the Catholic clergy arrested. While making passing reference to "respect for human rights and dignity of the human person," they did not condemn the bad conditions in prison nor the torture of prisoners, facts of which they were certainly aware.[93]

In a Lenten message, "As I have loved you, so you should love one another," released shortly after the second RPF invasion in January 1991 and the new wave of massacres of Tutsi, the bishops addressed the growing tension and violence in the country in relationship both to the war and to internal security.

Because of the tensions and socio-economic difficulties suffered by our country, we must conduct a common search with the goal of promoting a fraternal coexistence marked by justice and stable and durable peace.... Ancestral Wisdom reassures us of the benefits of a harmonious dialogue: *"Abajya inama Imana irabasanga"* ("God reunites those who hold counsel"). We launch a pressing appeal to each Rwandan, whatever his ethnicity, his region, his social group: that he be engaged resolutely on the path of constructive dialogue in the framework of the socio-political changes in process, in particular the announced multipartyism and the promotion of the mass-media.[94]

They called on the Rwandan population to unite to address the problems of the country:

Dear members, the Savior demands us to conquer courageously all the temptations inspired by ethnic prejudice and regionalism threatening to plunge our

---

[92] They write, "In troubled periods, we are threatened with temptations of hatred and racism susceptible to engender murder, vengeance, robbery, and slander. We should be unanimous in disapproving of such acts that go against God, Father of all: "Love your neighbor as yourself" (*Lv 19:18; cf. Mt 22:29*). ... At the ethnic level, our Christian solidarity ought to manifest itself in good understanding, tolerance and complementarity. Every Rwandan, whatever ethnicity he is, has the right to live and to flourish undisturbed" (p. 123).

[93] Mujawamaliya was only one among others who personally informed the archbishop of the problems of imprisonment.

[94] Les Evêques Catholiques du Rwanda, "Comme je vous ai aimés, aimez-vous les uns les autres" (Kigali: Conférence Episcopale du Rwanda, March 2, 1991), p. 5.

people into a destructive civil war. "Those who will take the risk of fomenting such confrontations, always prejudicial to the innocent, will be criminals."[95]

And to "socio-political leaders" they wrote:

Because you are the first actors in the promotion and safeguard of the common good and of socio-economic development of our people, it is up to you to put in honor the virtues of justice and professional conscience, in place of letting yourself be taken by "the exclusive desire for profit," as well as "the thirst for power with the goal of imposing on others (your) will." ... Apply yourself with ardor to preparing the terrain for the consolidation of democracy and the imminent coming of multiparty rule.[96]

Once again, while condemning ethnic and political conflict in general terms, the bishops provided no specifics, ignoring the hundreds of people killed in massacres in October and January, and the thousands still languishing in prison and suggesting strong continuing confidence in the government. The population was left to decide for itself what constituted a "temptation ... to plunge our people into a destructive civil war." For many, this was a condemnation of the RPF for launching an attack on the country.

In a May 1991 letter, "The truth will make of you free men," written just before the adoption of the new constitution, the bishops provided guidance for the transition to democracy.

Here are some of the democratic attitudes: the respect of the liberty of the person, the defense of the common good, the election of leaders, the separation of the three powers, the liberty of thought and of speech for each individual.... Our Rwanda will be authentically democratic the day when it will be governed "by a State of law and on the basis of a correct conception of the human person." ...[97]

Turning to the new constitutional provisions to be implemented in the following months, they forbid bishops, priests, members of religious orders, and deacons from participating "in the direction of a party," and they stated that "The authority of the Church is never entangled with the power of the state." They instructed church members:

Dear laity, support a party that has a constructive program, that is to say, not founded on the exclusions of ethnic, regionalist, and religious inspiration, with a program that does not separate the rich from the poor, but combats the divisions

---

[95] Ibid.
[96] Ibid., p. 8.
[97] Sécretariat Général, *Recueil des Lettres et Messages*, pp. 151–69, quote p. 157.

and the intrigues, the intolerance and the oppression threatening to drive people to murder....[98]

By issuing public letters and messages, the bishops sought to maintain a high profile for the Catholic Church in the transitions the country was undergoing, but disagreements among the bishops prevented their presenting a clear position, either in complete support of the regime or in favor of reform. Archbishop Nsengiyumva and other bishops steadfastly blocked efforts to discuss specific human rights violations or articulate a clear stand in favor of democratic elections. A few more moderate bishops, such as Thadée Nsengiyumva[99] of Kabgayi and Wenceslas Kalibushi of Nyundo, pressured their fellow bishops to back reform efforts and speak up for human rights, and they received support from the papal nuncio, Giuseppe Bertello, who arrived in Rwanda in April 1991 with a mandate to urge the church to assume a more prophetic role.[100] To most Rwandans, however, the letters did not represent a marked shift in the position of the bishops. As one person I interviewed said, "The bishops write all these letters, but we know that they don't really believe them." While the letters formally endorsed democratic reforms, what most people read between the lines was continuing strong support for Habyarimana and his Hutu ethno-nationalist policies.

Many people within the Catholic Church became frustrated with the continuing close alliance between the bishops and the state and the lack of democratic practice within the church. Although the Vatican had forced Archbishop Nsengiyumva to resign from the Central Committee of the MRND in 1985, he remained informally closely associated with the party and regime. Progressive elements in the church produced public letters of their own to challenge the conservatism of the hierarchy. In April 1989, a group of Catholic priests from Kibuye wrote a letter to the Episcopal Council:

In future, we would like more transparency in the work of the Episcopal conference in general and of our bishops in particular. We would like our bishops not to work alone but that they share with their close collaborators the pastoral

---

[98] Ibid., p. 165.
[99] No relation to Archbishop Nsengiyumva. In Rwanda, there are no family names. A Kinyarwanda name is generally given at birth, while a Christian name is usually given at baptism.
[100] Prunier, *The Rwanda Crisis*, p. 132; Carnet section, *Dialogue*, July–August 1991, no. 147, pp. 137–8.

charge of a diocese of the church of Rwanda, that they work with their priests, the faithful, that they show proof of transparency.[101]

In April 1990, a group of priests from Nyundo issued a letter in response to "Christ, Our Unity."

[I]t is regrettable that in their letter the bishops take first as their point of departure political slogans... The church should dare to say to the Rwandese State that it should agree to consider citizens without applying considerations of ethnicity or region. The maintenance of this discrimination gives rise to many problems and casts doubt upon the most beautiful speeches concerning unity. A nation in search of unity cannot continue to base everything on ethnic and regional identity.

If the church was not committed to supporting to the letter the policy of the country, but was prepared to dare to suggest firmly to the State the true principles of social justice, then it would have assumed its prophetic mission. But alas![102]

The head of the Episcopal Council, Thadée Nsengiyumva, himself frustrated with the reluctance of his fellow bishops to distance themselves from the state, brought together the priests of his diocese to issue a letter on December 1, 1991, "Convert us to live together in peace," to call the church to action. The letter, apparently written with the encouragement of the papal nuncio first bluntly laid out the problems confronting Rwanda:

Rwandan society currently knows a recrudescence of theft, armed aggression, and other reprehensible acts that are not prosecuted in the justice system. One would think that the people qualified to create respect for the law have resigned or that they are accomplices of their partners. The agents of the state no longer do their work conscientiously. The development projects are deteriorating. Here and there, the population refuses to work, to pay taxes, and to participate in communal works for development, the pretext being of course the advent of multipartyism which is believed to abolish all that which has been imposed.[103]

The letter went on to accuse the Catholic Church of being "a giant with feet of clay," failing to respond adequately to the myriad problems facing Rwanda: ethnic and regional conflict, corruption, social injustice, violations of liberty, the war, and AIDS. The church had compromised its credibility. According to the letter, "The Church lives in a continual lie, because its submission to temporal power impedes it from being

---

[101] Quoted in African Rights, *Death, Despair, and Defiance*, p. 870.
[102] Quoted in African Rights, *Death, Despair, and Defiance*, pp. 870–1.
[103] Sandrine Tolotti, "Le Rwanda retient son souffle," *Croissance*, no. 356 (January 1993): 34–9.

critical toward this power and from denouncing the numerous violations of human rights." The letter called on the church to offer a message
of liberation and to support the implementation of a sovereign national
conference to help solve the current problems and map a new future for
the country. The letter finally addressed the government, demanding a
negotiated settlement to the war and a rapid move toward democratic
rule.[104]

Given the many criticisms leveled against them, not only in these letters but also in the media and in many informal venues, the bishops
felt pressured to respond. The pastoral letters were an attempt to show
political independence, but given their vagueness and ambivalence, most
people read them cynically. Apparently under pressure from the nuncio,
the bishops issued a message for the new year 1992 in which they signed
on to Nsengiyumva's call for a national conference. Attributing the war
to the struggle for power, they called on political actors to allow power
to be decided through democratic means, and they offered their support
to negotiations. They asked all parties to come together in a government of transition, and "If it should prove necessary, after consultation
with the people, this government should convoke a national conference
that would assemble delegates from all the stratums of Rwandan society, including those residing outside." This advocacy of a concrete political proposal, one already publicly rejected by Habyarimana, marked
something of a departure for the bishops. At the same time, the call was
included in a section titled, "Support the authorities for the interest of
the country."[105]

In addition to seeking to appease their critics through their pastoral
letters, the bishops sought to limit dissent and independence within the
church. In particular, they sought to bring the growing pietistic movements under control. A few church leaders recognized the value of these
movements in revitalizing the faith and drawing people to the church.
Augustin Misago, for example, identified both Charismatic Renewal and
the piety surrounding Kibeho as instances of "spontaneous inculturation," that indicated the public desire to have a church and liturgy more
relevant to their culture:

What is done on the occasion of the prayer meetings organized at the initiate
of Christians in the group Charismatic Renewal or the apparitions of Kibeho
reveals that our Rwandan Christians have need of something other than this

---

[104] "Carnet: Decembre 1991," *Dialogue*, no. 151 (February 1992): 52.
[105] Secrétariat Général, *Recueil des Lettres et Messages*, pp. 195–214.

Roman liturgy all cerebral, cold, and stripped of signs and symbols, in smothering the exuberant expression of the body.[106]

Most Catholic leaders, however, saw both Charismatic Renewal and the movement surrounding Kibeho as a threat to their authority and sought to reign them in as early as the mid-1980s. In July 1983, the bishop of Butare (whose diocese then included Kibeho) issued a pastoral letter reminding the faithful that it was for the church leaders to determine the truth of the apparitions. The bishop explained that he had already named a theological and a medical commission to study the incidents. He cautioned Catholics to practice the adoration of Mary only through the established and approved rituals and urged priests and catechists to ensure that their parishioners knew the orthodox teaching about the Virgin Mary.[107] In a follow up letter in 1986, the bishop reminded people that, though the number of incidents had continued to expand, the two commissions had yet to reach any conclusions about the validity of the apparitions. He acknowledged the reinvigoration of the church the events have produced but cautioned believers against unwittingly accepting heresy.

Certain people ask themselves if it is permitted to meet at Kibeho for prayer at the place where the seers claim to have had apparitions. Yes, Christians always have the right to meet for prayer while respecting public order and the general framework of the life of the diocese. This is what one calls private worship (*culte privé*) not to be confused with public worship (*culte public*).

This latter requires an explicit approbation from the bishop, it is directed by people legitimately deputized (canon 834.2) and it contains, among other things, the administration of the sacraments, notably the celebration of the Eucharist and, eventually, the erection of a sanctuary....

We must mistrust the assimilation of the practices of piety to the rites of magic, as if by our words or our gestures, we could compel God to do what we want.... Let us not have, therefore, an erroneous vision: it is not for us to capture the power of God to take personal profits from it, but much more to live, from day to day and in all circumstances, the law of love that Jesus has taught us.[108]

---

[106] Augustin Misago, "Evangelisation et Culture Rwandaise," *L'Eglise du Rwanda vingt ans après le Concile Vatican deux* (Kigali: Edition Palloti-Presse, 1987), p. 15.

[107] J.B. Gahamanyi, "Lettre Pastorale de Monseigneur Jean-Baptiste Gahamanyi, Evêque de Butare sur les Evènements de Kibeho" (July 30, 1983), reproduced in Maindron, *Des Apparitions à Kibeho*, pp. 227–34.

[108] Jean-Baptiste Gahamanyi, "Deuxième lettre pastorale de Mgr. Jean-Baptiste Gahamanyi, Evêque de Butare sur les Evènements de Kibeho," in *Dialogue*, no. 120 (January–February 1987): 60–8.

By 1992, the commissions had still not provided an opinion on the validity of the apparitions (which had declined in frequency for several years), but the church leadership had increased its efforts to control the associated popular piety. In 1991, a new organization, the Mouvement Marial Kibeho, was created to help organize pilgrimages to Kibeho and organize associated religious services. In addition, church officials increasingly sponsored events at Kibeho, both to expand their control over the piety and to benefit from it. Preaching at Kibeho in August 1992, Misago, who had become the bishop of the new diocese of Gikongoro, said:

I think it useful to recall in my turn that until now *none of the seers at Kibeho has yet been recognized officially* by competent ecclesial authorities. But it is important to recall as well that this same authority has already approved a public worship *(culte public)* at the site of the presumed apparitions....[109]

In other words, the official church did not accept the "miracles" (at least not yet), but if people wanted to express their own devotion and belief, they should do so through established means.[110] Naming Misago as bishop in 1992 may also have been a means of bringing the Marian devotions under control, since his pronounced sympathies for the movement would give him the legitimacy to restrict its independence and impose orthodoxy on it.

In the case of Charismatic Renewal, the church again tried to dampen its challenge to authority by incorporating it formally within the church institution. Pope Paul VI had recognized Charismatic Renewal as "a gift of the Holy Spirit," thus providing the movement official sanction, but also insisting on its institutional character. Rwandan church leaders tried to regularize and restrict its activity by placing a bishop and other sanctioned leaders in charge of its activity.[111]

Like state leaders, thus, Catholic leaders also followed a dual path to assure their authority. Responding to their critics, they sought to demonstrate greater independence and political engagement, but at the same

---

[109] Augustin Misago, "Les Apparitions de Kibeho," *Dialogue*, no. 161 (December 1992): 30–6.
[110] At the same time, church leaders made appearances at Kibeho to add to their own prestige among the masses or to gain support for their causes. I attended a mass held at Kibeho in November 1992 with several bishops in attendance; the mass, held at a time when the government was resisting a negotiated settlement to the War of October, called upon Mary to intercede in bringing peace to Rwanda.
[111] Mbonyintege, "Mouvements de spiritualité," pp. 315–16; Casas, "L'Action Catholique," pp. 200–1.

time they worked to reign in dissent. In addition to controlling the popular pietistic movements, the hierarchy used its power of appointment
and funding to assert authority over the church and limit the power of
critical clergy. Given the preponderance of Tutsi priests, this was no easy
task, but the church showed a willingness to promote Tutsi who dis-
tanced themselves from anti-regime sentiments. In some ways this was an
ideal tactic because it countered critics who accused the church of being
discriminatory, while it gave incentive for Tutsi priests to ally themselves
with the pro-Hutu power structure. Frédéric Rubwejanga, a Tutsi named
bishop of Kibungo in 1992, was remarkable only for his moderation,
much like the only other Tutsi on the Episcopal Council, Gahamanyi,
who had never been an advocate for Tutsi interests. Misago, named at the
same time as Rubwejanga, had little obvious sympathies for Tutsi.[112]

The various Protestant churches had similar conflicts within their
ranks. Lacking the tradition of pastoral letters, Protestant leaders nonetheless sought to engage in the political fray through public sermons,
speeches and other means. Like their Catholic counterparts, they took a
mixed position, both in support of limited reform and in support of the
regime. One way in which the Protestants sought to assert their political
engagement was in acting as neutral arbiters in the conflicts disturbing
the country. The All Africa Conference of Churches (AACC), in which
the EPR in particular was active, helped organize talks between the RPF
and the government. In August 1991, the AACC organized a meeting in
Nairobi with Rwandan refugees to attempt to discern the motives and the
source of support for the RPF. Separate meetings with representatives of
the RPF and the Government of Rwanda set the groundwork for direct
meetings between the warring parties in Paris and Dar es Salaam that led
to formal peace negotiations in Arusha during 1992 and 1993.[113]

Building on this model, Twagirayesu, as president of the Rwanda
Council of Churches (RCC), led an ecumenical effort to find a solution
to the political crisis within Rwanda in early 1992. In January 1992, as
anger over the new MRND government began to build and a sense of

[112] In 1999, the Rwandan government arrested Misago and charged him with genocide.
My own research in his diocese in 1995–96 found clear evidence of his cowardice in
the face of the genocide but no evidence of his direct involvement, as the prosecutors
have claimed. The Misago case seems, instead, to have served as a symbolic trial of the
Catholic Church for its complicity.

[113] Biziyaremye Gérard, "L'Eglise et l'engagement politique en général et au Rwanda,"
unpublished paper, Faculté de Théologie Protestante de Butare, April 1993; Cyanditswe
n'Itorero Peresibiteriyeni, "Ukuri Kubaka Igihugu."

crisis gripped the country, the RCC sponsored a meeting among the political parties, chaired by the prime minister. The Catholic hierarchy joined with the RCC to establish the Contact Committee to address the crisis. The committee consisted of ten individuals – three Catholic bishops and two Catholic priests, Twagirayesu and bishops of the Anglican and Methodist churches, plus one representative each from the Pentecostal and Seventh-Day Adventist churches, which were not part of the RCC and generally resisted inter-church cooperation. The committee contacted the various political parties within Rwanda, the refugees, and the RPF to determine the demands of each and to search for common ground. The church leaders acted as arbiters between the government and the political parties until the agreement was worked out in March 1992 for the multiparty government of transition. The Contact Committee disbanded after the new government took office, but it reassembled in November 1992 in response to ongoing political turmoil, met with members of the various political parties and issued a communiqué calling on political officials to avoid dominating their parties and all parties "refrain from violent protests, from acts of murder and assassination, and … suspend the youth associations transformed into militias."[114] This second initiative had little practical impact.

The role of neutral arbiter is a classic position for churches to take. This approach assumes that churches lack substantial political interests of their own and are above the political fray and that they can therefore help mediate between divided parties. While seeking a negotiated peace is a commendable goal, in the Rwandan case, this approach was problematic because the churches were *not* in fact politically neutral. The church leaders had clearly allied their institutions with the ruling regime and had an interest in preserving the existing structures of power, and thus in seeking a compromise with those opposed to the regime, they made no effort to assess the real sources of the conflict. In negotiating between the political parties, for example, the church leaders treated the participants as equal partners, ignoring the MRND's control of the military and its substantial use of violence and intimidation against the other parties.

As in the Catholic Church, Protestant leaders sought to quash rebellion in the ranks. As with the Kibeho movement, Protestant officials sought to bring the Abarokore under control. In the Presbyterian Church, for

---

[114] Agence France Presse, "Party Negotiations," in *Africa Research Bulletin*, February 1992, p. 10461; *Dialogue*, no. 162 (January 1993): 84–6; Des Forges, "Recent Political Developments;" Twagirayesu "La Politique: La Reflection de l'Eglise."

example, the Abarokore initiated a conflict in the early 1990s over the nature of baptism practiced by the church. Rwandan Presbyterians, like the Belgian Reformed missionaries who established the church in the country, practice baptism by sprinkling with water. One of the tenets of the *Abarokore* has been to support baptism by immersion, since a literal translation of the Greek word *Baptizo* is "to immerse" and immersion is practiced by Baptists, Pentecostals, and other Evangelical churches. In the 1990s, members of the movement placed pressure upon the church leadership to adopt immersion as the Presbyterian form of baptism, or at the least to endorse it as an option. Michel Twagirayesu, the president of the church, established a commission to discuss the nature of baptism, and it produced a document that urged compromise, but in the end, Twagirayesu took an uncompromising position, deciding definitively that the church was not going to change. He stated that not only would sprinkling be continued as the method of baptism, but that those who practiced immersion would not be Presbyterians in good standing. As with other conflicts, many people saw this as a symbolic conflict over authority within the church, as the Abarokore sought to shape the nature of religious practice while the head of the church asserted his authority.

6

"It Is the End of the World"

Christian Churches and Genocide (1993–1994)

It is the end of the world. Multi-party politics has sown hatred. There are only conflicts. Everything is linked to selfishness. Each one wants to depose the other so that he can eat too. But the past times cannot return.[1]

In the early months of 1992, President Habyarimana appeared on the defensive and seemed increasingly politically vulnerable. The opposition parties were united and were gaining substantial popular support, while the RPF posed a continuing threat to the regime. The international community was placing pressure on the government to move toward democracy. Rwandan civil society and opposition party activists, as well as foreign scholars who visited Rwanda at the time, were optimistic that Rwanda was on the threshold of a major political transformation.

The political transformation that ultimately did take place was not, however, what the scholars and activists had anticipated. The optimism that marked the establishment of the multiparty government of transition in March 1992 faded within only a few months and by early 1993 was replaced by frustration, disappointment, and fear. The failure of opposition politicians to change substantially the nature and direction of government made people increasingly cynical about the promises of politics. The escalation of the war marked by massive RPF invasions of northern Rwanda in June 1992 and February 1993 and the expansion of crime and political violence within Rwanda made the population increasingly fearful and uncertain and, thus, vulnerable to political manipulation.

[1] Interview in Nyanza, Butare, with 65-year-old man, December 28, 1992.

Hard-line supporters of the regime, people associated with the *akazu*, effectively redirected public frustration to serve their own interests by scapegoating the country's Tutsi minority. Using ethnicity as a wedge, the regime divided the opposition parties, co-opting large factions of each party into a broader reconfigured coalition united in opposition to Tutsi. They encouraged anxiety and paranoia in the general public to polarize the population along ethnic lines, and they identified the Tutsi and any Hutu who supported them as a threat to society. Ultimately, with nothing presenting an effective challenge, this logic of exclusion culminated in the genocide that began in April 1994. By the time a small group of military and government officials close to the regime set in motion their plans to eliminate their political opponents through a massive campaign of violence, the population was already so deeply divided, so full of fear, and so inured to violence that few were willing to oppose the plan and many were willing to support it.

The churches played an essential role in facilitating this descent into violence. As the primary voices of moral authority in Rwanda, the churches not only failed to speak out forcefully against the increasing exclusion of Tutsi and the growing violence against Hutu activists and Tutsi in the years leading up to the genocide but also lent strong support to the regime that was encouraging the exclusion and violence. Since the churches had a long history of engaging in ethnic politics and of encouraging loyalty to state authorities, Rwandans understood the failure of church leaders to criticize the regime and to decry ethnic scapegoating as an endorsement of the government's inflammatory anti-Tutsi policies. Because the churches did not use their influence to expose the government's responsibility for much of the expanding violence and insecurity, they left Rwandans vulnerable to manipulation by the regime's supporters who attributed the country's problems to the minority Tutsi. Although some individuals and groups within the churches spoke against the ethnic and political divides, theirs were isolated voices that the broader institutional churches not only failed to support but actively repressed as a threat to the established structures of church authority. Because church officials at all levels of the institutions refused to condemn specific instances of ethnic and political violence, even when church personnel and buildings were targeted, and because they encouraged continuing loyalty to the very state that was instigating this violence, many Rwandans concluded that ethnic and political violence was consistent with church teachings. The churches, thus, not only failed to provide an obstacle along the path towards genocide but actually helped to create a moral climate where genocide was possible. Since its inception in Rwandan, Christianity had consistently been, not a faith that preached brotherly love, but rather one that endorsed obedience to authorities, ethnic discrimination, and power politics. When the genocide finally occurred, thus, Christians, including some pastors and priests, felt little or no contradiction between their religious beliefs and their participation in the slaughter of Rwanda's Tutsi.

VIOLENCE AS RESISTANCE TO REFORM

Believing that their presence in government would allow them to engineer a successful transition to democracy, opposition party leaders in Rwanda fought intensely to force President Habyarimana to include them in the government. For Habyarimana and the *akazu*, however, the March 1992 assent to a multiparty government of transition represented a mere tactical ploy that would appease domestic and international critics without substantially changing the balance of power in the country. With the government of transition, Habyarimana intensified his practice of acceding to reforms in public in order to appease his critics while undermining the effect of the reforms behind the scenes in order to preserve the existing structures of power. The entrance of opposition politicians into the government took some of the fire out of the pro-democracy movement, while their presence in office offered Habyarimana and his supporters an opportunity to discredit their opponents.

Although the cabinet posts in the government of transition that took office in April 1992 were divided evenly between the MRND and the opposition parties, real power remained in the hands of the *akazu*. The MRND still held the key ministries of defense and interior, allowing the party to maintain control of the armed forces and the local administration. This continuing dominance coupled with the MRND ministers' refusal to cooperate with their opposition colleagues allowed them to thwart new initiatives and denied opposition ministers real control. In a September 1992 open letter to Habyarimana, Prime Minister Nsengiyaremye complained that the MRND was blocking government actions and thwarting efforts to reform the administration.[2] In November 1992, the minister of justice, a member of the Liberal Party, resigned claiming that MRND ministers refused to cooperate in efforts to restore security in the country.[3] Criticism came from within Habyarimana's own party as well. In

---

[2] Dismas Nsengiyaremye, reprinted in *Dialogue*, November 1992, no. 160, pp. 57–62.
[3] "Carnet 1er-30 novembre 1992," *Dialogue*, January 1993, no. 162, pp. 81–2.

July 1992, Christophe Mfizi, Habyarimana's former minister of information, published an open 15-page letter in French and Kinyarwanda addressed to the president of the MRND (Habyarimana) explaining his reasons for resigning from the party. Mfizi accused the regime of being dominated by a narrow clique, the "Zero Network," that:

> has methodically invested all of national life: political, military, financial, agricultural, scientific, educational, familial and religious. This nucleus considers the country as an enterprise from which it is legitimate to pull the maximum profit, thus justifying all sorts of policies. ... Rare are those who, these past years, could be promoted to an important post and/or remain there without maintaining relations of vassalage with a member of the Zero Network.[4]

Mfizi's critiques indicate that, despite political reforms, the *akazu* continued to dominate public life.

Even as they denied the opposition effective authority, Habyarimana's associates publicly held opposition politicians responsible for problems that arose in Rwanda after they assumed office, and they incited problems apparently with the explicit intent of discrediting the opposition parties and multiparty politics in general. The practice of provoking problems to undermine support for the opposition could be seen most clearly in the area of public security, which both political violence and an expansion of banditry compromised in 1992 and 1993. MRND party leaders used the youth wing of the party, the Interahamwe, "Those Who Attack Together," to intimidate their opponents and sow disorder. Along with activists from the extremist CDR, the Interahamwe harassed opposition politicians and civil society activists. They regularly interrupted opposition party rallies, provoking fights with supporters of the MDR, PSD, and PL. For their part, the opposition parties also began to use intimidation against regime supporters. Frustrated by the government's support for the Interahamwe and MRND, opposition parties, particularly the MDR and to a lesser extent the PSD, engaged in *kubohoza*, literally "to help liberate," the practice of forcing people to change their party membership through intimidation and violence. In many local communities, attacks and counterattacks by rival parties created an atmosphere of tension and fear.[5]

The Interahamwe became increasingly well organized during this period. Along with the CDR's youth wing, the *Impuzamugambi*, "Those with a Single Purpose," they received military training beginning in early

---

[4] Mfizi, "Le Reseau Zero," pp. 3–4.

[5] Des Forges, *Leave None to Tell the Story*, pp. 4, 54–7. See also the chapters on Nyakizu.

1992 that gradually transformed them into a civilian militia.[6] A letter published by the White Fathers on January 25, 1993, claims:

According to a circular emanating from the Ruhengeri MRND, and dated 18/1/1993, the MRND and CDR are preparing a "civilian coup d'Etat." To this end, these parties organize violent demonstrations blocking roads, setting up barricades and preventing all movement in some towns. ... In Kigali in certain quarters, the Interahamwe (MRND) and members of the CDR have systematically beaten people who did not have membership cards from the MRND or CDR.[7]

The impunity with which Interahamwe and CDR members were able to act encouraged some to step beyond the bounds of obviously political violence to engage in more general intimidation of the public through criminal activity, such as robbery and rape.

The armed forces also sought to support the regime by harassing its critics and intimidating the general population to discourage people from questioning the authority of the state. After the beginning of the War of October, the government expanded the military substantially, from 5,000 soldiers to more than 30,000.[8] This massive expansion allowed the regime to establish a military presence throughout the country. While the soldiers were ostensibly charged with maintaining order and preventing incursions by the RPF, in practice they terrorized the population, targeting in particular those they regarded as enemies of the regime, such as opposition party activists and Tutsi. They arrested numerous people they accused of supporting the RPF, torturing many and killing others. The armed forces set up roadblocks along major highways and walking paths, where they stopped both vehicles and people on foot to check identity and residence papers. Their official purpose was to search for RPF operatives, but they used these opportunities to monitor the population, bully people, and extract bribes. Like the Interahamwe, the armed forces became involved in acts of banditry, sometimes carrying out armed robbery while in uniform. Rape by soldiers was a serious problem, made all the more heinous by the high prevalence of HIV seropositivity among military personnel.[9]

The violence carried out by the militias and the armed forces served several purposes for the regime. First and most obviously, it attempted to

---

[6] Ibid.

[7] Missionaries of Africa, reprinted in *Dialogue*, March 1993, no. 164, pp. 43–4.

[8] Human Rights Watch Arms Project, "Arming Rwanda: The Arms Trade and Human Rights Abuses in the Rwandan War," (New York: Human Rights Watch, January 1994), p. 14.

[9] Africa Watch, "Talking Peace and Waging War," pp. 17–26; Africa Watch, "Beyond the Rhetoric: Continuing Human Rights Abuses in Rwanda" (New York: Africa Watch, June 1993), pp. 8–13; FIDH, et al., *Rapport de la Commission Internationale d'Enquête*, pp. 51–66.

frighten people away from opposing Habyarimana and the MRND. The armed forces clearly demonstrated their partisan affinities and presented a threat to anyone who publicly challenged the regime. Journalists, party activists, independent lawyers and judges, human rights organizers, and others identified with the opposition were arrested and tortured, had their homes broken into, and in some cases were assassinated. As Africa Watch reported at the time, "Tutsi and members of parties opposed to President Habyarimana's MRND live with the daily threat of death, injury, and the looting and destruction of their property."[10] A Belgian mission in mid-1992 that included respected Rwanda scholar Filip Reyntjens accused Habyarimana of being "encircled by crime." The mission claimed that the Zero Network had organized death squads to terrorize their enemies.[11] An International Commission of Inquiry that visited Rwanda in January 1993 uncovered evidence that the *akazu* had in fact organized death squads to carry out violence. They found proof linking assassinations and ethnic attacks to the highest levels of power.[12]

In addition to intimidating opponents, a second major purpose of violence was to undermine support for the opposition – and for multiparty government – by encouraging the impression that competitive politics incited insecurity. Crime had been increasing in Rwanda for several years, but after the establishment of the government of transition, the rate of crime, particularly violent crime, seemed to increase sharply. According to a number of people I interviewed, this rise in crime could be attributed to a growing reluctance of government officials to follow up on criminal acts by investigating and arresting those believed guilty. The population, frustrated with the failure of officials to act, increasingly turned to vigilante justice. After I witnessed a vigilante mob in one rural village beat a robber and rapist to death, I asked people why they had not called the officials. The nearly universal response was that the authorities would not act and that even if they did, the judicial system was faulty and would not keep perpetrators in prison.[13] An open letter by the White Fathers released in November 1992 made these points:

We can see violence of different types predominate ... Crimes and murders are committed across the country. Banditry is spreading everywhere making the

---

[10] Africa Watch, "Rwanda: Beyond the Rhetoric," p. 14.
[11] "Carnet 1er – 30 septembre 1992," *Dialogue* November 1992, pp. 55–6.
[12] FIDH, et al., *Rapport de la Commission International d'Enquête*, pp. 78–84.
[13] Interviews in Kirinda, Kibuye, September 9, 1992. I discuss this incident in greater detail in Chapter 7.

insecurity of people and goods reign. Some people incite ethnic and regional hatred. Authorities do not fulfill their role in assuring the peace for Rwandans, and refuse, often from fear or complicity, to punish those culpable of crimes, of robbery and other misdeeds. Rwandans erect themselves as judges and themselves punish (often by assassination) those whom they consider culpable.[14]

Some Rwandans with whom I spoke in 1992 and 1993 felt that if the government officials had wanted to reduce crime and violence, they were capable of doing so. After all, it was often the ruling party's youth wing and government soldiers who were involved in the crimes. Instead, the authorities helped to create a culture of impunity to serve their political interests. Some of the targeted crime intimidated opponents of the regime specifically, but untargeted crime also served to influence public opinion. Habyarimana, like many other military dictators, used to good end the popular belief that democracy breeds instability while military rule maintains peace and unity. After the 1973 coup, Habyarimana appealed for public support by promising to restore order, and following the establishment of the multiparty government in 1992, fostering disorder helped renew the popular distrust for competitive politics.[15]

While some Rwandans recognized the political machinations behind the rise in crime, many others did in fact blame multiparty politics, and the fact that the opposition parties engaged in *kubohoza* and other violent acts played into the hands of the regime, contributing to a general impression of declining order linked to multiparty politics. As one young man near Butare said, "You can see it is the end of the world. Everything has changed. All solidarity is diminished. Multiparty politics has cultivated animosity between people. I don't support multiparty government because it has sown conflict."[16] A middle-aged woman in Kibuye prefecture made a similar claim, "I want Habyarimana to continue to govern even though many people do not like his politics. Multiparty politics should not exist, because people want to kill their neighbors, want to burn the homes of their companions."[17] As supporters of the regime hoped, the rise in violence, both criminality and political violence, turned many people against democracy.

---

[14] Les Missionaires d'Afrique (Pères Blancs) réunis en assemblée à Remera-Ruhondo, le 20/11/1992, "Lettre ouverte à nos frères chrétiens engagés dans la politiques et la fonction publique." Mimeograph.
[15] Samuel Decalo's *Coups and Military Rule* claims that military rule is often justified as a means of maintaining public order in divided societies.
[16] Interview in Huye, Butare, Decembre 26, 1992.
[17] Interview in Biguhu, Kibuye, December 24, 1992.

Violence served a final important function in helping to "define the enemy"[18] and "exclude the victim," what Helen Fein argues was a precondition for the genocide of Jews and Armenians.[19] When he initially came to power, Habyarimana sought to gain popular support by putting an end to the ethnic violence that had so destabilized the country under Kayibanda. As the population became increasingly frustrated with and alienated from the regime, however, Habyarimana and his circle of supporters sought to regain their popular appeal by "playing the communal card,"[20] scapegoating the Tutsi minority while portraying themselves as the champions of the Hutu majority. Ideologues in the MRND and CDR exhumed the populist anti-Tutsi rhetoric of the First Republic, drawing upon the mythico-history of Rwanda that children learned in school, to portray the Tutsi as "foreigners" who had come to Rwanda from Ethiopia or Somalia to dominate the Hutu population. Given the chance to return to power, the ideologues argued, the Tutsi would again exploit and abuse the Hutu majority.[21]

This effort to define the Tutsi as an "essential outsider"[22] hit a chord with many people not simply because of the history of ethnic conflict in the country but also because of the War of October. The fact that a predominantly Tutsi rebel army was invading Rwanda, driving thousands of people from their homes and bringing destruction to the communities they entered, lent credence to the claims that the Tutsi wanted to regain their dominance over the Hutu and once again exploit them. While the RPF itself claimed to be interested in establishing a multiethnic democracy, the public heard from the Habyarimana regime that the RPF wanted

---

[18] This expression comes from Des Forges, *Leave None to Tell the Story*, p. 59.

[19] Fein, *Accounting for Genocide*, pp. 5–6. "It was not the roles they played, but the very existences of the Armenians and Jews that was constructed as alien. Both had been defined within recent memory similarly to pariahs outside the sanctified social order. Thus stigmatized, such groups are more readily redefined as strangers by the dominant group – strangers not because they are alien but because the dominant group was alienated from them by a traditional antipathy, Jew-hatred, or hatred of the infidel" (p. 6).

[20] This term comes from Human Rights Watch, *Playing the Communal "Card": Communal Violence and Human Rights* (New York: Human Rights Watch, 1995). The report, looking at cases ranging from Rwanda to Sri Lanka to the former Yugoslavia, asserts that "While communal tensions are obviously a necessary ingredient of an explosive mix, they are not sufficient to unleash widespread violence. Rather, time after time, proximate cause of communal violence is governmental exploitation of communal differences. ... [O]pportunism and the quest for short-term political gains drive governments to foment communal tensions ..." (pp. viii–ix).

[21] Des Forges, *Leave None to Tell the Story*, pp. 65–95, provides an excellent discussion of the propaganda used in the period leading up to the genocide.

[22] See Zukier, "The Essential 'Other' and the Jew."

to reinstall the monarchy. In CDR and MRND party meetings, in radio broadcasts, and in newspaper articles, regime supporters warned of infiltrators working for the RPF within Rwanda and suggested that Tutsi living in the country could not be trusted, because they sympathized with the RPF. The army general staff attributed to RPF infiltrators and their supposed accomplices in the country a series of bomb blasts in buses and markets, mine explosions along roads, and other apparently random attacks that killed a number of people beginning in early 1992 and continuing through 1993. Opponents of the regime argued that these explosions were in fact carried out by the Zero Network to create a sense of insecurity in parts of the country otherwise untouched by the war and to stir up sentiment against the RPF and those suspected of supporting it. A major RPF attack on northern Rwanda in early June 1992 that drove several hundred thousand people from their homes and led to the RPF occupation of a band of territory along Rwanda's border with Uganda in Byumba and Ruhengeri prefectures intensified public antipathy to the RPF.[23]

The idea that the Tutsi were an "Other" that should be feared and targeted for attack was emphasized by a series of ethnic massacres that began immediately after the initial RPF attack in October 1990. Attacks on Bagogwe Tutsi in Gisenyi in October 1990 killed over 300 and destroyed more than 500 homes, while attacks on Bagogwe in Ruhengeri and Gisenyi in January, February, and March 1991 killed several hundred more. Attacks in the Bugesera region south of Kigali in March 1992 killed at least 2,000. Just as the international human rights commission was concluding its investigation in January 1993, massacres killed several hundred people in Gisenyi and Kibuye. While the government portrayed each of these attacks as a spontaneous uprising of local Hutu, research by both Rwandan human rights groups and the international commission found that in each case the attacks had been organized by government and party officials, and in some cases they found evidence that approval for the attacks came from the highest reaches of power.[24]

These periodic massacres provided an important precedent for the 1994 genocide, serving as a dress rehearsal to test out methods later duplicated throughout the country. In most communities, the burgomaster or other MRND leaders called a public meeting at which they told

---

[23] Des Forges, *Leave None to Tell*, pp. 58–9, 65–95; Jean-Pierre Chrétien, *Rwanda: Les médias du génocide* (Paris: Karthala, 1995).
[24] Africa Watch, "Beyond the Rhetoric," pp. 5–8; FIDH, et al., *Rapport de la Commission Internationale d'Enquête*, pp. 18–50; ADL, *Rapport sur les Droits de l'Homme*.

the men in attendance that the commune was threatened by infiltrators. They charged those in attendance to undertake a "special *umuganda*," a special work, to "clear the brush," by which they meant wiping out those who threatened the security of the commune. While this was generally understood to mean Tutsi, the Bugesera massacres marked an important development in the nature of organized violence in that Hutu active in opposition politics were also identified as accomplices and targeted. In Bugesera as well, the radio and newspapers were used effectively to encourage participation. The Bugesera attacks followed several days of announcements on Radio Rwanda that a secret communiqué had been discovered that detailed plans by Tutsi in Rwanda to kill prominent Hutu. As later happened during the genocide, many Tutsi sought refuge at churches or other public buildings. In a few cases, anticipating a practice used widely in 1994, the burgomaster gathered Tutsi together so that they could be eliminated more easily.[25] These massacres helped to heighten ethnic tensions and to polarize the ethnic communities in Rwanda, planting fear in the hearts of Tutsi and demonstrating to Hutu that Tutsi, as well as Hutu who supported them, were enemies to be targeted.

CHURCH REACTIONS TO VIOLENCE

The reaction of the Christian churches toward the violence that spread through Rwanda in the early 1990s helped to create the social conditions that made genocide possible. Fein, who has sought to explain the differential rates of Jewish victimization in European countries under Nazi occupation, argues that churches played an important role in influencing how their societies reacted to Nazi plans for genocide. "Since the church is the institution claiming the monopoly of moral sanctions, the acts of its leaders should be sources of public definition of the situation and emergent norms in time of crisis."[26] Comparing a variety of European states, Fein finds that opposition by church leaders to discriminatory policy against Jews was a key factor in countries such as Bulgaria, France, and Romania where collaboration was limited:

Within the colonial zone [of Nazi occupation] ... church threats and protest operated directly to check government readiness to collaborate. The greater the church resistance, the fewer Jews became victims. By contrast, states in the

---

[25] Chrétien, *Rwanda: Les médias du génocide*, pp. 182–5; FIDH, et al., *Rapport de la Commission Internationale d'Enquête*.
[26] Fein, *Accounting for Genocide*, p. 46.

colonial zone with high Jewish victimization are states in which the dominant church was actively antagonistic towards Jews and/or failed to protest deprivation of their rights and liberties before the majority of them were held captive in the state's concentration camps.[27]

In other words, where church leaders opposed the early denial of rights and security of Jews, they were able to slow or halt the descent into genocide.

In the Rwandan case, some individuals and groups within the churches did speak out against the rising violence and the increasing scapegoating of Tutsi. The White Fathers published several open letters discussing declining security, specifically blaming government officials for failing to act and the MRND and CDR for engaging in violent acts meant to destabilize the state. The Catholic publications *Kinyamateka* and *Dialogue* published accounts of both criminality and political violence, often attributing these acts to the armed forces and Interahamwe.[28] Many priests, pastors, church employees, and active laity helped support the efforts of human rights groups that exposed the ongoing violence. The ADL, AVP, and LICHREDHOR received important church support, and parish priests and pastors served as important informants in human rights investigations.[29] When ethnic attacks occurred, churches frequently offered sanctuary to those threatened.

Those people and groups within the churches who actively opposed violence, however, were the proverbial voices crying in the wilderness. The dominant powers within the churches regarded those who opposed the regime as threats not only to public order but to their own authority within the churches, and the antagonism between the pro-reform and anti-government camps within the churches was widely known, though rarely displayed in public. Despite the small number of prophetic voices, the churches as national institutions failed effectively to expose the nature of the violence in the country and to mobilize against it. By refusing to condemn the scapegoating of Tutsi early on or to denounce the violent attacks against Tutsi that began in 1990, church leaders allowed ethnic tensions to escalate uninhibited. Worse, because of the well-known

---

[27] Ibid, p. 67.

[28] For example, in its July 1992 issue, *Dialogue* discusses the participation of soldiers in pillage and assassination in Kibuye and Gisenyi (pp. 56–7). In the December 1992 issue, *Dialogue* discusses orders given in October to assassinate Prime Minister Nsengiyaremye, the murder of a Catholic journalist and PL activist by a CDR mob, and an attempt to assassinate an MDR activist (pp. 55–7).

[29] C.f., ADL, *Rapport sur les Droits de l'Homme*.

pro-government and anti-Tutsi sentiments of some church leaders, their failure to speak out in defense of the Tutsi left an impression in many people's minds that they supported the actions of the regime in targeting the Tutsi. By failing to denounce the gradual exclusion of Tutsi from Rwandan society, by adding credence to government claims that the primary threat to Rwandan security came from the RPF and its supporters, by leaving in tact the public impression of their own antagonistic attitudes toward Tutsi, and by failing to identify the churches clearly as opponents to violence and sanctuaries for those in danger, church leaders helped to create a context in which genocide against Tutsi became morally acceptable.

Defenders of the churches might reasonably point out that church leaders did call for peace and reconciliation. Letters from the Catholic bishops, for example, spoke out against violence and in favor of ethnic harmony. In their letter following the October 1990 invasion, the bishops wrote, "At the ethnic level, our Christian solidarity ought to be manifested by good understanding, tolerance, and complementarily. All Rwandans, whatever ethnicity they are part of, have the right to live and grow in all tranquility in the heart of the national community."[30] Yet in this letter as in others, the bishops addressed ethnic and political conflict in only the most general terms. In the face of thousands of arbitrary arrests and the massacre of hundreds of Tutsi civilians in the days before this letter was written, the bishops' vague call for unity is drowned out by their strongly stated support for the government. In fact, none of the pastoral letters ever mentioned a specific political assassination or ethnic attack, nor did they provide any thorough analysis of the sources of the growing violence in Rwanda. The letters never held government officials, the armed forces, Interahamwe, CDR, or opposition parties specifically responsible for carrying out attacks or instigating violence. Instead, they implied that the conflicts in Rwanda were the fault of the general population rather than politicians and other national leaders.

As another example, in their pastoral letter for Lent in 1993, titled "Peace and Reconciliation for Rwandans," the bishops wrote,

Dear Christians, the motives of the war and the current insecurity influence one another and are very numerous. We are not going to cite them all. Let us point out only the most important in order to glimpse the route toward peace and reconciliation of which we have such a need today. Let us underline the lack of unity

---

[30] Les Evêques du Rwanda, "Heureux les Artisans de Paix," p. 5.

in difficult moments of the History of Rwanda, above all after changes of government and the nomination of leaders of the administration. We speak also of the
injustice, ethnic and regional discrimination that have characterized the sharing
of power. We mention again the limited respect accorded to the human person at
the point of spilling blood and, too often, that of innocents....

Dear Christians, present difficulties are the consequence of past negligence.
They are the consequence of a decision to let things go. They are the consequence
of greed and selfishness. They are the consequence of impatience that prevents us
from deepening whatever it might be. They are the consequence of our evasion
of the truth and our worship of lies. They are the consequence of the little love in
our relations marking such mistrust and selfishness.[31]

This analysis completely fails to address the institutional nature of the
violence in Rwanda. The letter mentions a history of division at times of
political change and the practice of ethnic and regional discrimination,
but it never specifies who is discriminating and against whom. It mentions no specific cases of discrimination or ethnic or political violence and
never holds those in power responsible for their role in supporting violence and discrimination. The letter never mentions, far less condemns,
the increasing exclusion and targeting of Tutsi. Instead, it approaches the
problems as manifestations of personal sin, of which all people seem to be
equally guilty. After mentioning that killing has become widespread, the
bishops write that, "The History of Rwanda is the work of all Rwandans.
The authors of crime as their passive witness are invited to repent and
to convince themselves that no one is authorized to be silent when the
children of God undergo an injustice."[32] The fact that the bishops never
address the massacres of Tutsi that took place in Kibuye and Gisenyi only
two weeks before the letter was issued is quite significant. In merely calling for reconciliation, for the coming together of the ethnic groups, the
bishops fail to address the increasing exclusion and isolation of Tutsi by
militant Hutu, acting with the support and direction of the government.
It should not, therefore, be surprising that many people read between the
lines and concluded that the bishops in fact supported government policies of ethnic scapegoating. As one witness told me:

All the bishops sign these letters, even when you know they don't represent their
ideas. The Catholic Church has written a letter condemning injustice and ethnic conflict, but when we have a specific example of an ethnic massacre as in
Bugesera, they don't speak out.

---

[31] Les Evêques Catholiques du Rwanda, "La Paix et la Reconciliation des Rwandais," Letter
Pastorale pour le Careme 1993, in *Recueil des Lettres et Messages*, pp. 255–7.
[32] Ibid, p. 256.

The failure of the Catholic bishops to address attacks on church personnel and church buildings proved particularly important in setting a precedent. Beginning with their failure to condemn the arbitrary arrests of several Tutsi priests at the start of the war in 1990 or to intervene on the priests' behalf, the bishops repeatedly refused opportunities to distance themselves and the Catholic Church from ethnic discrimination and the politics of violence. Likewise, the Catholic bishops made no attempt to defend Father Sibomana and the other journalists from *Kinyamateka* when they were taken to trial, even though the Episcopal Council itself published the paper. Even when church personnel were killed, such as Antonia Locatelli, an Italian volunteer with the Catholic Church in Bugesera who was shot a few days after contacting Radio France to report the massacres in March 1992, and Brother François Cardinal, a Canadian monk who had worked to empower urban youth and was murdered in November 1992, the bishops remained silent.[33] In Kibilira and Bugesera, Tutsi sought refuge in church buildings, but the bishops never openly supported the principle of sanctuary. When a church school at Muramba in Gisenyi was attacked in January 1993, the bishops' failure to defend the sanctity of the church sent a strong message to many people. Given the well-known support of the archbishop and a few other bishops for Habyarimana, the church's own practice of ethnic discrimination, and the fact that the four nuns at the school had pleaded for assistance and the bishop of Nyundo, Wenceslas Kalibushi had been turned away by the militia, many Rwandans read the bishops' failure to condemn government officials for organizing ethnic attacks or ordering assassinations, even targeting church personnel and buildings, as an endorsement of ethnic politics and the politics of violence.[34] A few bland and unspecific denunciations of violence making no attempt to hold accountable the government and its supporters for organizing the vast majority of violent incidents did nothing to counteract the church's long history of engaging in ethnic politics and seemed rather intended merely to appease critics, both internal and abroad.

The leaders of the Protestant and Seventh-Day Adventist churches were no more prophetic in addressing the deteriorating situation in Rwanda.

---

[33] "Carnet: 1er-31 mars 1992, *Dialogue*, no. 154 (May 1992): 54; ADL, *Rapport sur les Droits de l'Homme*, p. 221; "Hommage: Le Frère François Cardinal," *Dialogue*, no. 163 (February 1994): 29–32.

[34] Africa Watch, "Beyond the Rhetoric," pp. 5–6.

Lacking the tradition of pastoral letters, the leaders of these churches nevertheless had numerous opportunities to influence the public through less formal messages to their parishes, speeches at church conferences, radio broadcasts, visits to local churches, and other means. In general, the Protestant leaders, like their Catholic counterparts, failed to place themselves and their churches clearly in opposition to ethnic and political violence. They did not hold government officials accountable for organizing massacres and assassinations, and they never condemned specific instances of ethnic and political violence. In the Presbyterian Church, a commission appointed by the church president released a report in March 1992 that argued strongly against the popular belief in distinct ethnicities in Rwanda and claimed that, "Rwandans do not want [this ethnic conflict], but they are driven to it by the politicians who want only protect their power and who use force to promote their own interests . ..."[35] This letter, however, had no official standing and was not widely disseminated in the churches.[36]

By failing to explain the sources of the growing violence in Rwanda and failing to hold government officials accountable, church leaders allowed state officials to define the public discourse, and Habyarimana and his associates attributed declining security to two sources: the RPF with its Tutsi allies inside Rwanda and multiparty politics. Without guidance from their church leaders, many Rwandan Christians became increasingly alienated from the political process and increasingly fatalistic. Many of the Rwanda Christians I interviewed in 1992–93 interpreted the growing insecurity as a sign of the Second Coming. The type of apocalyptic messages I recorded in one Presbyterian sermon were not uncommon:

Our time is like the time of Noah. We should be prepared for the return of Christ. For example, here in Rwanda we are in a period like Noah's. There is war. People kill one another. The people in the family fight even against their brothers, because they are not in the same political party. Women of God become prostitutes. Christians must prepare for God to create another age. We prepare for heaven. We cannot be entangled in things of this earth must but be prepared for the moment of God's return.[37]

---

[35] Cyanditswe n'Itorero Peresubuteruyeni mu Rwanda, "Ukuri Kubaka Igihugu" (Kigali: EPR, March 1992). Translated form Kinyarwanda to French by Isaac Nshimiyimana.

[36] Michel Twagirayesu, "La Politique: La reflection de l'Eglise," lecture presented at Faculté de Théologie Protestante, Butare, April 2, 1993.

[37] From the sermon at Butare Presbyterian parish, November 29, 1992.

Many of the members of this parish seemed to accept this interpretation:

I consider these changes like the end of the world. It is predicted by the Bible. I do not want to be an adherent of any party. They are nothing but conflicts. If the elections are based on parties, I cannot participate in them. I am in the party of God.... I think these political changes anticipate a war inside the country.[38]

I find that it is the end of the world. It is a very bad situation. Multi-party politic does not give me any hope. I am not part of any political party and neither is my husband.[39]

Christians should not worry themselves with these changes [taking place in Rwanda]. It is the end. It is the prophecies that are accomplished.[40]

Such apocalyptic ideas were not confined to Protestants. Many Catholics embraced the apocalyptic messages from the apparitions of the Virgin Mary and Jesus at Kibeho. In the early 1980s, the shepherd Segatashya reported words attributed to Jesus:

In these times that are coming, these times that converge toward God, these are the times of testing, these times where each one will carry his cross. He who will be with me will suffer. He who takes the road to heaven, will march in suffering, until the day when he will rest, because from that moment there will be no more suffering. ... There are those who say that the world will not end. He who has created, did not do it to make it disappear. How will the earth disappear? How will it fall? How can it be overturned? Its fall will be caused by a fire coming from the center of the earth, then the earth will become an inferno of fire. Everything will be burned alive, whether it is trees or other living things.[41]

To many Catholics, the prediction of an approaching period of violence seemed to be coming true in the 1990s. During the 1990s, a substantial number of Catholics were also drawn into the Pentecostal Church, where teachings about coming catastrophe were more thoroughly embraced.

THE DESCENT INTO HELL

After the multiparty government took office in April 1992, the opposition political parties found themselves in a dubious position. Having accomplished many of the major goals of the democracy movement, including legalizing opposition politics and gaining representation in the

---

[38] Interview in Huye, Butare, December 24, 1992.
[39] Interview in Nyanza, Butare, with 32-year-old woman, December 22, 1992.
[40] Interview with 25-year-old man, Nyanza, Butare, December 27, 1999.
[41] Quoted in Maindron, *Des Apparitions à Kibeho*, pp. 154–5.

government, the drive for further reform lost momentum. Once in power, the MDR, PL, and PSD found that they quickly lost the popular allure that they had enjoyed as opponents of the regime and found themselves tainted by their presence in government. As part of the government, the very position of the MDR, PL, and PSD as "opposition" parties became questionable.[42] On taking office, the opposition parties were judged according to their performance, and with the economy continuing to decline, crime and violence expanding, and the war gaining in vigor, the public's high expectations were quickly extinguished. Habyarimana and his supporters adroitly exploited this situation, stimulating problems in order to tarnish the image of the new parties, but the parties brought much of the negative judgment on themselves. In the ministries, the handful of communal governments, and the one prefecture where they gained control, the opposition parties did not behave much differently than the MRND, distributing jobs and other benefits to their supporters, engaging in corruption, and failing to deliver on political promises. The use of *kubohoza* and other forms of violence by the opposition parties undermined their differentiation from the MRND.

In my research I found that by early 1993, much of the Rwandan population had soured on the promise of multiparty government. Even in opposition strongholds, many people expressed frustration with multiparty politics. A young man near Butare asserted:

These political parties should not exist, because they are only there to disturb people while they [those in the parties] profit from it. With a single party, we had peace, and here it is now, with troubles everywhere, misunderstandings between brothers since they are in different parties. They sing to us that they are going to give us water and electricity, but as for me, I do not believe it.[43]

An elderly man in Save claimed:

It is difficult to explain and even to understand. One group comes through saying that they are the ones who struggle for the good cause and for development, meaning for us poor people. They promise you miracles. You don't know which is right or wrong. The problem is that this causes troubles, wars between brothers, misunderstandings, whereas before these changes we had peace.[44]

---

[42] I nevertheless continue to refer to the PSD, PL, and MDR as opposition parties even after they joined the government, because this was the practice in Rwanda at the time and is how the parties continued to refer to themselves.

[43] Interview in Kinteko, Butare, January 20, 1993.

[44] Interview in Kiruhura, Butare, January 28, 1993.

During the course of 1993, Habyarimana and his supporters were able to capitalize on this public discontent to cripple the opposition parties. Although the president himself had charged the multiparty government with seeking a negotiated end to the War of October, the president and his allies used the negotiations to paint the opposition parties as soft on the RPF while presenting the MRND as defender of the Hutu masses. They continued to instigate massacres of Tutsi within Rwanda in order to heighten ethnic tensions and antagonize the RPF. As head of the PSD, Félician Gatabazi said, "Each time there are some difficulties (in the democratic process) there is a flare-up of tribal violence instigated by the regime, and the threats of civil war are used to justify the *status quo*."[45] Encouraging and then exploiting anti-RPF and anti-Tutsi sentiments, MRND and CDR leaders managed to divide the opposition parties and co-opt a substantial portion of their leaders and members in a newly reconfigured ruling coalition.

Acting on their charge to negotiate, representatives of the PL, MDR, and PSD met with representatives of the RPF in Brussels on May 29, 1992, followed by an official meeting between the government and RPF on June 6–8 in Paris. Perhaps wanting to improve its position for anticipated negotiations, the RPF launched a major assault on Byumba and Ruhengeri a few days later, occupying several communes and driving hundreds of thousands from their homes. Nevertheless, direct negotiations began in Arusha, and a cease-fire was signed on July 12 that went into effect on August 1. Habyarimana's supporters were disquieted by these developments, and in a radio address Habyarimana expressed his displeasure with the negotiators, whom he suggested had adopted "improvised positions." Nevertheless, the government and negotiators signed a first protocol in mid-August. Hardline Hutu responded with attacks on Tutsi in Gishyita and Rwamatamu communes of Kibuye, leaving some 85 dead and 500 homes destroyed.[46]

Peace talks continued, with protocols on power-sharing signed on October 30, 1992, and January 9, 1993, but again Habyarimana's forces offered resistance. The MRND ministers in the government released a letter in October expressing their lack of support, and the president denounced the accords in speeches on November 15 and again on January 25. Hard-line Hutu ideologues stepped up their anti-Tutsi

---

[45] Quoted in Prunier, *The Rwanda Crisis*, p. 144.
[46] Reyntjens, *L'Afrique des Grands Lacs en Crise*, pp. 202–4; Prunier, *The Rwanda Crisis*, pp. 149–50, 160–3.

rhetoric, as in the notorious November 22 speech in Kabaya, Gisenyi, by
Léon Mugesera, an influential MRND leader in which he claimed:

> Those we attack, don't call them the Patriotic Front, *Inkotanyi* [the indefatiga-
> ble]. Make the distinction. They are *Inyenzi* [cockroaches]. ... [The MDR, PL
> and PSD] have plotted to make Byumba prefecture fall to the enemy ... They
> have plotted to discourage the armed forces. ... The law is without equivocation
> on this point: "Any person who is guilty of acts seeking to reduce the morale of
> the armed forces will be punished with death." What are we waiting for? ... You
> know well that there are accomplices in this country. They send their children to
> the ranks of the RPF? These are the facts that have been reported to you. ... What
> are you waiting for to decimate these families and the people who recruit them?
> ... The fatal error we made in 1959, ... it was to let them [the Tutsi] get out. [...]
> [Their home] is Ethiopia, but we are going to find a shortcut for them, that is the
> Nyabarongo river [a tributary of the Nile]. I must insist on this point. We must
> react effectively![47]

Excerpts of this speech were broadcast on Radio Rwanda, and a cas-
sette was widely distributed. Only a few weeks later, in December 1992,
MRND and CDR activists launched another round of attacks in Kibilira,
this time, as in Bugesera, targeting both Tutsi and also Hutu opposition
party activists. The attacks picked up in intensity after the January 9
power-sharing protocol, spilling over into neighboring Kibuye and killing
an estimated 300. According Reyntjens, the massacres "were evidently
opposed to the [peace] process under way and constituted an attempt to
sabotage it."[48] The RPF responded on February 8 by breaking the cease-
fire with the largest attack on Rwanda, occupying a large swath of territory in Byumba, Ruhengeri, and Kigali-Rural and drawing quite near
Kigali itself. The RPF killed a number of civilians, targeting in particular
civil servants and their families, and hundreds of thousands more civilians fled the area of conflict, bringing the total number of displaced to
over one million, over a tenth of the population.[49]

The opposition parties found themselves in a more and more untenable
position, caught between the increasingly unpopular RPF and the increasingly militant and outspoken Hutu extremists. While the terms being
negotiated in Arusha were not wholly unreasonable, the hardliners in the
MRND and CDR opposed any plan to share power with the RPF – in fact,
they effectively opposed any agreement short of military victory – and

---

[47] Quoted in FIDH, et al., *Rapport de la Commission Internationale d'Enquête*, pp. 24–5.
[48] Reyntjens, *L'Afrique des Grands Lacs en Crise*, p. 205.
[49] Reyntjens, *L'Afrique des Grands Lacs en Crise*, pp. 204–6; Prunier, *The Rwanda Crisis*,
pp. 166–76; Des Forges, *Leave None to Tell the Story*, pp. 83–8.

they portrayed each attempt to reach a compromise as a betrayal of Hutu interests. In truth, the MRND was represented at the Arusha talks, but the hardliners Pierre-Claver Kanyarushoki and Colonel Théoneste Bagasora, did little more than observe and report back to their faithful while more moderate Defense Minister James Gasana signed onto the agreements.[50] By launching their February 1993 attack, the RPF seriously undermined the position of the opposition, ultimately enabling extremists to gain the upper hand. As Reyntjens writes, "While the offensive was an incontestable military success, it constituted without doubt a political error ... ."[51] Anti-Tutsi sentiments were not confined to the MRND and CDR, and, in fact, many within the opposition parties were uncomfortable with the negotiations, particularly a hardline faction of the MDR, which was, after all, the successor to Kayibanda's political party. The French, ever strong supporters of Habyarimana, increased their military presence in Rwanda and called on the opposition to form a common front with the government in opposition to the RPF. The opposition parties met with RPF representatives in Bujumbura in late February in an attempt to mend relations, and they released a joint declaration calling for a cease-fire, the withdrawal of French troops, a renewal of peace negotiations, and accountability for those responsible for massacres. After an early March 1993 meeting in Dar es Salaam, Prime Minister Nsengiyaremye announced a renewal of negotiations. Meanwhile, Habyarimana organized his own meeting with representatives of the MRND, CDR, MDR, PSD, and PL that issued a decree condemning the RPF attack, thanked the army, welcomed French support, condemned Uganda for assisting the RPF, and asked for the president, cabinet, and prime minister to coordinate efforts.[52] As Gerard Prunier wrote:

On the one side, even the most resolute and honest opponents of the regime began to fear that they had been naive and that, through their actions, they were running the risk of exchanging a Hutu military dictatorship for a Tutsi one. And on the other, both the genuine, basically unreconciled Tutsi-haters and the ambitious politicians who thought that there was new political mileage to be made out of deliberate Tutsi-bating moved to created a "new opposition" which would be both anti-Habyarimana and anti-Tutsi.[53]

---

[50] Prunier, *The Rwanda Crisis*, pp. 160–86; Reyntjens, *L'Afrique des Grands Lacs en Crise*, pp. 117–20, 204–11.

[51] Reyntjens, *L'Afrique des Grands Lacs en Crise*, p. 206.

[52] Prunier, *The Rwanda Crisis*, pp. 174–82; Reyntjens, *L'Afrique des Grands Lacs en Crise*, pp. 206–7.

[53] Prunier, *The Rwanda Crisis*, p. 180.

The crack that emerged between those in the opposition who sought negotiations with the RPF and those who viewed them as a danger to the Hutu population was soon to become a chasm that would split each of the parties into two and create a broad coalition united in ethnic solidarity against the Tutsi.

Throughout 1993, even as negotiations resumed in Arusha and the politicians moved the country officially toward peace, the military and its Hutu extremist allies moved Rwanda closer to expanded war. A January 1994 Human Rights Watch report, "Arming Rwanda," documented a massive importation of arms, such as 20,000 R-4 riffles and 20,000 hand grenades in October 1992, during the cease-fire. This import of arms from Egypt, South Africa, and elsewhere, funded largely by the French, continued in 1993.[54] Des Forges describes a massive jump in the import of machetes during this period as well, an estimated half million from January 1993 to March 1994. Meanwhile, the anti-RPF, anti-Tutsi, anti-opposition rhetoric of the extremists continued to heat up. In January 1993, a military group called AMASASU, which means bullet in Kinyarwanda,[55] issued an open letter to Habyarimana, arguing that the country needed to prepare for an RPF attack and calling for the organization of civilian self-defense. AMASASU apparently included Col. Bagosora and other members of the *akazu*, who were increasingly identifying with the extreme positions of the CDR and finding Habyarimana to be insufficiently hardline.[56] In April 1993, as a means of getting their message across more effectively, a group of hardliners created a new independent radio station, Radio-Television des Milles Collines (Radio-Television of the Thousand Hills, RTLM), which began broadcasting in early July.[57]

By mid-1993, the split in the opposition parties set the stage for a major reconfiguration of political power. The Nsengiyaremye government was originally mandated for a one-year term, which would have expired in April 1993 but was extended until July. The leadership of the MDR proposed continuing Nsengiyaremye in office, but Habyarimana instead named Agathe Uwilingiyimana with the support of Twagiramungu, president of the MDR. The MDR leadership responded by expelling both

---

[54] Human Rights Watch Arms Project, *Arming Rwanda*.
[55] The Alliance of Soldiers Provoked by the Age-old Deceitful Acts of the Unarists (Alliance des Militaires Agacés par les Séculaires Actes Sournois des Unaristes. Unarists refers to members of UNAR, the Union Nationale Rwandaise, the main Tutsi political party at the time of independence.
[56] Des Forges, *Leave None to Tell the Story*, pp. 96–109, 127–8.
[57] Chrétien, *Rwanda: Les médias du génocide*, pp. 63–9.

Twagiramungu and Uwilingiyimana, but the new government was installed nonetheless on July 19. A few days later, at a meeting of the MDR, the decision to expel Twagiramungu, Uwilingiyimana, and other officials who had accepted posts in the new government was endorsed by a large majority. Nevertheless, negotiators in Arusha, whose work was nearly complete, proposed Twagiramungu as prime minister in a new, expanded government.[58]

Two events ultimately finalized the realignment of political parties and set Rwanda down the path of genocide. First was the signing of the Arusha Peace Accords on August 4, 1993. The hard-liners' complaints centered around two provisions. The distribution of cabinet seats allotted only five seats for the MRND and none for the CDR, compared to nine seats distributed between the opposition parties, plus five seats for the RPF. With an MDR prime minister, the hard-liners feared that this plan would completely undercut their political dominance. Worse still for the hard-liners, the accords called for a 60:40 integration of troops, but with a 50:50 sharing of command posts. The idea that the RPF would have almost equal standing to the government forces was unthinkable to many of the extremists. With the peace accords finalized, a powerful group of military officers and politicians determined to see that the accords would never be implemented, and they had the sympathies of much of the population.[59]

The second major event that set the wheels in motion was the assassination of the first Hutu president of neighboring Burundi, Melchior Ndadye. Having taking office in July following Burundi's first multiparty presidential elections, Ndadye was killed in a coup attempt by Tutsi military officers on October 21, 1993. In the following weeks, attacks and counterattacks by Hutu militia and the Tutsi army killed at least 50,000 people in Burundi and drove 150,000 Tutsi to urban areas defended by the army and 300,000 Hutu across the border into Rwanda.[60] The assassination of Ndadaye gave credence to claims by the anti-Tutsi

---

[58] Reyntjens, *L'Afrique des Grand Lacs en Crise*, pp. 122–5; Des Forges, *Leave None to Tell the Story*, pp. 111–16.

[59] Des Forges, *Leave None to Tell the Story*, pp. 123–6; Reyntjens, *L'Afrique des Grand Lacs en Crise*, pp. 248–56; Prunier, *The Rwanda Crisis*, pp. 192–7.

[60] On the political situation in Burundi, see René Lemarchand, *Burundi: Ethnocide as Discourse and Practice*. On the assassination and the ensuing violence see, Fédération Internationale des Droits de l'Homme (FIDH), AfricaWatch, et al. "Rapport de la Commission Internationale d'Enquête sur les Violations des Droits de l'Homme au Rwanda Depuis le 1er Octobre 1990 (7–21 Janvier 1993): Rapport Finale." Paris: FIDH, March 1993.

ideologues in Rwanda that Tutsi could not be trusted and entering into agreements with them was dangerous. The Burundian Hutu refugees helped to arouse anti-Tutsi sentiment in many communities.

The significance of Ndadaye's assassination for developments in Rwanda cannot be overestimated. With the assassination of Ndadaye, the extremists intensified their efforts to prevent a transfer of power and establish a radical Hutu ethno-nationalist agenda for the country. RTLM, now reaching most of the country, broadcast alarming messages warning of the threat the RPF and its accomplices (*ibyitso*) in the country posed to Hutu and began to call for the elimination of enemies such as Prime Minister Uwilingiyimana. The opposition parties officially split, with a large portion of the MDR opposed to Twagiramungu creating MDR-Power and joining with smaller factions from the PL and PSD in an informal coalition known by the English name "Hutu Power" (sometimes written as it was pronounced in Kinyarwanda, "Pawa"). As Des Forges writes, "With the consolidation of Hutu Power, party allegiances faded before the imperative of ethnic solidarity: political life was reorganized around the two opposing poles of Hutu and Tutsi."[61] Hutu Power joined the CDR and MRND in radically escalating the organization of civil "self-defense" forces, providing military training to civilian militia groups throughout the country. The military expanded its distribution of arms to these civilian groups. While the extremist position may never have had the support of the majority of the country, the extremists very effectively used coercion to intimidate and suppress alternate views. Throughout the period leading up to the genocide, political assassinations, assaults, and other attacks targeting opponents of the extremist position continued to escalate. Those who supported the Arusha Accords, Tutsi and moderate Hutu, found themselves isolated and threatened. In contrast to the Hutu extremists, they had no militias and no arms. With the exception of a few brave politicians, human rights groups, and nongovernmental organizations (NGOs), the forces of democracy and moderation largely fell silent as the Hutu extremist forces laid the groundwork for genocide.[62]

Rwanda's churches had very little direct involvement in the political transformations that took place in 1993, at least at the national level. The Protestants helped to get the peace negotiations restarted after the February RPF assault, but the Contact Committee did not reconvene

---

[61] Des Forges, *Leave None to Tell the Story*, p. 139.
[62] Des Forges, *Leave None to Tell the Story*, pp. 134–40; Prunier, *The Rwanda Crisis*, pp. 198–206.

after its November 1992 declaration, and no other major initiatives were undertaken. The Catholic bishops, who had published a flurry of pastoral letters from 1990 to 1992, fell almost silent, issuing only two short, timid letters for Lent and Advent 1993 which received little attention, in part because their content was so thin. The leaders of Rwanda's churches failed to address the Ndadaye assassination.

A few voices in the churches in Rwanda continued to speak out. Most notably, Wenceslas Kalibushi, the bishop of Nyundo, and the priests of Kibuye and Gisenyi issued a letter in late December 1993 criticizing the government for distributing weapons to civilians.[63] The Catholic journal *Kinyamateka* voiced concerns about the deteriorating situation, and human rights groups appealed for international attention. On the eve of the genocide, Odette Kakuze, of the ARTC, a Catholic NGO for workers, wrote a letter to the African Synod, a major gathering of African bishops that began in Rome just days after the genocide began, that took the leaders of the Catholic churches in Africa to task for failing to sympathize with the poor:

You who are our pastors, how many times have you visited the people who are poor, sick, suffering? Do you known where they live, the condition of their houses, what they eat, the things they are in need of? Can you yourselves identify with their problems, the scale of these problem ... ? Why do you make friends only with the well-off people, the oppressors of the workers?

Your very affluent style of life (luxury cars, fashionable clothes, expensive houses) increases the gap between you and us ordinary people, and this adds to our lack of confidence in you. The Christians feel abandoned, whereas you and your priests ought to be the voice of the voiceless, the outcasts, and serve the common folk. Your neglect results in many Catholics switching over to the sects [new Protestant churches].[64]

On the whole, however, the churches were unwilling to use their influence to attempt to halt the descent toward genocide or to use their international connections to help warn the world of the impending disaster.

The reasons for the churches' reticence are complex. Some church personnel were in fact sympathetic to the radical anti-Tutsi sentiments of the CDR and Hutu Power. People such as Archbishop Nsengiyumva and EPR president Twagirayesu had strongly supported the regime for many

---

[63] Robert Block, "The Tragedy of Rwanda," *The New York Review* (October 20, 1994), p. 4.
[64] Odette Kakuze, "The Gap Between You and Us," quoted in *AMECEA Documentation Service*, ADS 17/1994, no. 424, September 15, 1994, p. 8.

years and had found their own authority challenged by progressive Tutsi and Hutu, the same type of people (sometimes the same people) who were challenging Habyarimana. Others were influenced by the February RPF attack and the Ndadaye assassination to harden their position. Anglican Archbishop Augustin Nshamihigo, a Hutu from Kigali who supported Habyarimana but was not fundamentally opposed to pro-democracy efforts, was deeply moved by the February attack, which affected thousands of people in his northern diocese, and he became vocal in his opposition to a settlement with the RPF.[65] Some Hutu who did not accept the demonization of Tutsi nevertheless felt that the threats to security required unequivocal support for the regime and the military. Still others simply followed wherever the political winds blew, in the tradition of Lavigerie, seeking to ally themselves with whomever appeared to be holding political power. When it looked as though a democratic transition was about to take place, people wanted to be on the side of the victors so that the church would remain in a strong position. Once it became clear that power had shifted decisively back to the *akazu* and its new allies, supporting the opposition and its demands was no longer expedient.

Whatever their reasons, at the local level if not in the national arena, many laity, church employees, and pastors and priests became involved in the creation of militia and other "civil self-defense" preparations that set the stage for genocide. For individuals who had found their authority within the churches challenged by the movement for democratization in the period 1990–92, the emergence of a broadly reconfigured network of power presented an opportunity for them to reassert their authority. Many political opportunists saw the shift in political power as a chance for personal advancement, and their efforts at self-promotion did not exclude church councils, basic Christian communities, and other church groups where they could increase their status and authority. The one place in Rwandan society where Tutsi did exercise some authority was in the churches, and thus churches could not be excluded from efforts to assert Hutu Power. Because the leaders of the Catholic, Presbyterian, Anglican, Baptist, and Free Methodist churches had all made clear their strong support for the regime and its opposition to the RPF and calls for national solidarity, people at the local level felt that their assertion of Hutu authority was consistent with church doctrines.

---

[65] This conclusion based upon an extended interview with Nshamihigo on August 6, 1992, and subsequent conversations with Twagirayesu in April 1993 and with Anglicans in Rwanda in 1996 and Nairobi in 1999.

Most of the people in the churches, perhaps even a majority of church members and personnel, were not supportive of the growing anti-Tutsi sentiment, but they were silenced by fear.[66] A majority of the Catholic priests and pastors in the main Protestant churches were Tutsi, and as such they could not take a lead in opposing anti-Tutsi racism without exposing themselves to danger. Whereas previously some Hutu colleagues, particularly in the south and center of the country, had been willing to take a stand on behalf of reform and against ethnic division, as the political climate changed, most became afraid of being labeled *ibyitso*. The few Hutu in the churches who continued to support progressive action on ethnic and political issues could not gain enough support to have an impact. For example, moderate Catholic bishops were no longer willing to join progressives Kalibushi and Thaddée Nsengiyumva to pressure bishops close to Habyarimana into a compromise, so the bishops simply said nothing. Tutsi and progressive Hutu in the church found themselves facing increasing opposition within the churches themselves.

THE GENOCIDE

It is unclear exactly when plans for the genocide were first drawn up, but Prunier suggests that extremists probably developed the idea of a widespread slaughter of opponents of the regime in late 1992 and that the idea gradually gained support and became more concrete.[67] Plans for genocide clearly were in place by late 1993, with lists of principal targets already drawn up, but no agreement to implement the plan had apparently been reached. Nevertheless, the situation was becoming explosive, with growing political violence, the expansion of the Interahamwe and other militia, and the distribution of arms. The pro-government, pro-Power newspapers and the increasingly popular RTLM issued more and more explicit calls for violence to eliminate *ibyitso* threatening the security of the country. While people may not have anticipated anything as extensive as the genocide, the signs of imminent violence were extensive. In fact, Des Forges listed thirty pages of warning signs between November 1993

---

[66] Research conducted by Scott Straus among confessed participants in the 1994 genocide indicated that fear, not ideology, was the greatest factor motivating participation in the violence (*The Order of Genocide: Race, Power, and War in Rwanda*, Ithaca: Cornell University Press, 2006). My own research in the period leading up to the genocide found fear to be an important factor influencing action and inaction alike.

[67] Prunier, *The Rwanda Crisis*, pp. 168–9.

and April 1994 that should have alerted the international community that a catastrophe was looming.[68]

Even in this context of impending doom, some aspects of the Arusha peace accords were implemented, but they served in some ways to add immediacy to the efforts of those who wanted to prevent the ultimate implementation of the accords. In November, United Nations troops who were to oversee the transfer of power arrived in the country. Among their first acts, United Nations Assistance Mission to Rwanda (UNAMIR) troops escorted, according to a provision in the accords, a 600-strong RPF battalion to Kigali, where they took up residence at the parliament building. The RPF troops were to offer protection to RPF politicians and oversee the establishment of the new transitional government, and in late December, three of the RPF ministers-designate arrived in Rwanda. However, the splits in the MDR and PL and continuing conflict over who should represent the parties in the new cabinet became an excuse for Habyarimana's failing to install the new government. With most opposition ministers in Uwilingiyimana's cabinet lacking the support of their parties, effective control of the country had fallen fully back into the hands of Habyarimana, the MRND ministers, and the military. A transfer of power was scheduled for February 10 but did not occur, and a week later the UN Security Council issued a call for the parties to decide on an implementation schedule.[69]

As the implementation of Arusha was repeatedly delayed, the supporters of the accord in Rwanda were increasingly suppressed. Assassins attempted to kill Twagiramungu on February 20, killing one of his bodyguards. When the MDR-Twagiramungu faction held a public meeting the next day in support of the installation of the new government, militants from MDR-Power attacked the meeting, causing a riot in Kigali that left eight dead. That night, the Minister of Public Works and Energy, Félicien Gatabazi, a moderate Hutu who was executive secretary of the PSD, the one party that had remained largely united in opposition to the Hutu ethno-nationalist extremism, was shot dead as he drove home in Kigali. The next day, Martin Bucyana, chairman of the CDR, was lynched when he drove through an angry mob in Gatabazi's home community just outside Butare that was demonstrating against Gatabazi's killing. Members of the CDR then rioted for several days in Kigali,

---

[68] Des Forges, *Leave None to Tell the Story*, pp. 143–72.
[69] Prunier, *The Rwanda Crisis*, pp. 192–206; Des Forges, *Leave None to Tell the Story*, pp. 141–67.

killing thirty-five people. In the next few weeks, Habyarimana insisted that the CDR had to be included in a transitional government, a proposition that the remnants of the opposition parties vehemently rejected. A transfer of power scheduled for March 25 was postponed; then another postponement took place on March 28. The international community, including Rwanda's neighbors, expressed frustration at the continued delays. On April 6, Habyarimana flew to Dar es Salaam for a meeting with regional leaders that was supposed to focus on Burundi, but instead turned to an attack on Habyarimana for failing to implement the Arusha agreement.[70]

As is now well known, the plane returning President Habyarimana and Burundian President Cyprien Ntaryamira from the meeting in Dar es Salaam was shot down as it approached Kigali airport, killing all aboard. Exactly who was responsible for firing the two missiles has never been firmly established, as various scenarios attributing the attacks alternatively to the RPF, Habyarimana's own presidential guard, and even European troops continue to be promulgated.[71] Within hours after the attack, members of the presidential guard and other elite troops spread out into the capital with lists of opposition politicians, civil society activists, and prominent Tutsi to kill. The presidential guard killed Prime Minister Uwilingiyimana along with ten Belgian UNAMIR soldiers charged with protecting her. Others killed on the first day included most of the PSD leadership, including party chief Frédéric Nzamurambaho; PL vice-president and minister of labor, Landwald Ndasingwa, along with his Canadian wife and two children; Minister of Information from the MDR, Faustin Rocogoza; president of the constitutional court and MDR sympathizer, Joseph Kavaruganda; human rights activist Charles Shamukiga; André Kamweya, journalist for the progressive newspaper *Rwanda Rushya*. Some targets, such as Twagiramungu, escaped only through shear luck, others through the assistance of those willing to risk their own lives through acts of bravery.[72]

The initial attacks focused on Kigali and a few areas of strong support for the regime, and the targets consisted primarily of those the

[70] Prunier, *The Rwanda Crisis*, pp. 206–12; Des Forges, *Leave None to Tell the Story*, pp. 163–72.

[71] Filip Reyntjens, *Trois j jours qui ont fait basculer l'histoire* (Paris: l'Harmattan, 1995), looks in great detail at the events surrounding Habyarimana's death and the beginning of the genocide.

[72] Prunier, *The Rwanda Crisis*, pp. 229–31; Des Forges, *Leave None to Tell the Story*, pp. 187–92, 199–201.

akazu viewed as leaders of the movements that challenged their authority. This included both opposition politicians who had resisted joining Hutu Power and leaders of organs of civil society, especially human rights activists and journalists. Some of the early targets included progressive elements in the churches. One of the first places the death squads hit on April 7 was the Centre Christus, a Jesuit retreat center which had a mission of seeking ethnic reconciliation and helping the poor and vulnerable. Around 7 A.M., a group of six soldiers arrived at the center and rounded up those present. They divided the Rwandans from the European priests and nuns, and in a separate room they shot all seventeen Rwandans, a mixed group of Hutu and Tutsi, including eight young girls there for a spiritual retreat.[73]

The diocese of Nyundo, which included Habyarimana's home prefecture of Gisenyi, had long been regarded as a haven for Tutsi in the Catholic Church, dating back to the 1950s when Kabygayi under Archbishop Perraudin became the center for the Hutu revolution. In the years leading up to the genocide, Bishop Kalibushi had distinguished himself as a moderate Hutu willing to support democratic reform, to criticize the regime, and to speak on behalf of Tutsi. As a result, the Nyundo Episcopal compound became one of the first targets outside Kigali. On April 7, many of the parish priests of the diocese were at the Episcopal center for a conference, and they were joined during the day by a number of Tutsi seeking refuge. The militia attacked at 5 P.M., killing around thirty people, including two priests. The refugees then moved to the bishop's residence, which they believed would be safer. The militia came there the next morning, demanded money, then kidnapped Bishop Kalibushi. They stripped him and took him to a common grave, but a military officer intervened, stopped the men from carrying out the execution, and transported the bishop to a safe house in Gisenyi. The next day, April 9, militia attacked the cathedral, breaking first into the sacristy, then entering the bishop's residence where they killed everyone they found, over three hundred, including eight priests. During the same period, militia also attacked the parishes of Rambura and Muramba, also in Nyundo diocese, killing priests there, and militia killed Father Evode Mwanangu in an attack on Rukoma parish in Kibungo. At the beginning of May, militia returned to the cathedral to attack refugees who had again gathered there. This time they burnt the

---

[73] Victor Bourdeau, "Une Semaine d'Horreur a Kigali," *Dialogue*, no. 177 (August–September 1994): 4–14.

cathedral and other Episcopal buildings, including schools, a dispensary, and a library.[74]

As the research in *Leave None to Tell the Story* makes clear, the killing advanced progressively, initially carried out by a small group in only a few areas, targeting a relatively specific group of moderate Hutu and Tutsi, and expanding only gradually to implicate more people, to focus more specifically on Tutsi, and to extend throughout the entire country. Even among the top military officers, government officials, and MRND leaders, many did not support the plan for genocide and sought to bring the violence to a close. "The leaders of the killing campaign had to invest considerable political and military resources to end opposition to the genocide ... ."[75] The leaders used intimidation and repression to eliminate some opponents, but they also relied heavily on ideological and political appeals to convince others of the necessity, efficacy, and legitimacy of the program of mass slaughter. In this process of ideological and political legitimization, churches played an important role. The strong support that national church leaders offered to the new government, even in the face of attacks on church personnel and buildings, gave moral sanction to the policies of violence. As Des Forges wrote:

Within the first twenty-four hours after the plane crash, it was clear that Tutsi clergy would be killed like any other Tutsi and, a day after that, it was evident that the churches would be desecrated by slaughter carried out at the very altar. Still, four days later, the Catholic bishops promised their "support to the new government." They asked all Rwandans to "respond favorably to calls" from the new authorities and to help them realize the goals they had set, including the return to peace and security. The bishops balanced the statement with a denunciation of troublemakers and a request to the armed forces to protect everyone, regardless of ethnic group, party or region.[76]

The leaders of other churches, notably the Anglican archbishop and the Anglican bishop of Kigali, issued similar calls to Rwandans for support of the government. Des Forges claimed:

By not issuing a prompt, firm condemnation of the killing campaign, church authorities left the way clear for officials, politicians, and propagandists to assert that the slaughter actually met with God's favor. [Newly installed president]

---

[74] Neno Contran, *They Are a Target: 200 African Priests Killed* (Nairobi: Paulines Press, 1996), pp. 65–123; Priests of the Diocese of Nyundo, "Des Rescapés du Diocese de Nyundo Temoignent," *Dialogue* (August–September 1994), no. 177, pp. 59–68.

[75] Des Forges, *Leave None to Tell the Story*, p. 263.

[76] Ibid, p. 245.

Sindikubwabo finished a speech by assuring his listeners that God would help them in confronting the "enemy." RTLM announcer Bemeriki maintained that the Virgin Mary, said to appear from time to time at Kibeho church, had declared that "we will have the victory."[77]

Beyond merely "leaving the way clear" for authorities to give religious sanction to the genocide, the churches played a major role in making Rwanda fertile ground for a genocidal program. As the history presented here should indicate, by actively playing ethnic politics and practicing ethnic discrimination, by allying themselves closely with state power and urging obedience to state authority, and by imbuing struggles for power within the churches with ethnic and political overtones, church personnel, from the bishops to the leaders of small Christian communities, created an environment where good, practicing Christians could kill their neighbors without feeling that they were acting inconsistently with their faith.

When the government relocated in the second week of April from Kigali, which was under siege by the RPF, to Gitarama, the Catholic archbishop, along with several other bishops, relocated to nearby Kabgayi, a move that many Rwandans saw as a sign of the church leadership's support for the new national leadership. On May 13, after the major massacres in the genocide were already over and the hunt for Tutsi survivors was underway, the leaders of Rwanda's churches finally issued a public declaration about the violence. In a joint letter, four Catholic bishops, five Anglican bishops, and the leaders of the Presbyterian, Free Methodist, and Pentecostal churches, expressed their condolences to those who had lost relatives, urged both sides of the conflict, both the RPF and the government, to stop the war and massacres, called on the United Nations to intervene, and urged Christians to refuse to participate in massacres. The church leaders never mentioned the ethnic nature of the violence nor labeled the massacres genocide, and they implied that the RPF and the government were equally responsible. Archbishop Nshamihigo was unwilling to sign even this mild letter.[78]

In addition to helping to provide moral sanction to the genocide, the churches also played a role in obfuscating the nature of events in Rwanda for the international audience. In their communication with international

---

[77] Ibid., p. 246.
[78] Hugh McCullum, *The Angels Have Left Us: The Rwanda Tragedy and the Churches.* (Geneva: WCC Publications, 1995), pp. 68–9; African Rights, *Death, Despair, and Defiance*, pp. 896–8.

church bodies, the Rwandan church leadership avoided acknowledging genocide and treating the violence instead as a simple effect of war that could be resolved through a peace agreement between the government and the RPF. In a letter to the head of the All Africa Conference of Churches in May, the assistant bishop of Kigali, Jonathan Ruhumuliza, wrote:

> After the setting up of a new government, we see that things are changing in a good way. The ministers are doing their best to bring back peace in the country although they are facing many problems ... The fightings around are still on there and we worry of what is happening; because the rebels are destroying every thing, killing everybody they meet while the Government is trying bringing peace in the country. Nobody was, is or will be happy of what happened. But we have to see what we can do so that human rights be considered. It is why we do appeal to everybody who can help to shout on our behalf so that nations understand that Rwanda needs peace and ask the Rwandese Patriotic Front and the Government to sit together, in prioritarizing the interests of the whole country first, stop fighting and put in action the Arusha agreements. The Churches tried their best, are still doing that, believing that God will help his people.[79]

A few weeks later, Ruhumuliza and Archbishop Nshamihigo held a press conference in Nairobi in which they attempted to explain events in Rwanda in a light highly sympathetic to the genocidal government, blaming the violence in the country on the RPF. According to a press report, Nshamihigo said, "I don't want to condemn one group without condemning the other one. ... Our wish is not to condemn, but to show the situation that is happening in the country."[80]

The organizers of the massacres spread the genocide into various local communities in a consistent fashion. They first sought to win the support of community leaders, including both political authorities and religious leaders. For example, at a meeting on April 18 in which the new prime minister and other national leaders sought to pressure into carrying out the slaughter the population of Gitarama Prefecture, which had resisted the genocide for two weeks, participants included burgomasters, local party leaders, and clergy. Without ordering those who attended the meeting to kill, they made clear that "continuing to resist the violence would have many costs and no rewards."[81] To support the efforts of local militia

---

[79] Letter (in English) from Rt. Revd. Jonathan Ruhumuliza, Coadjutor Bishop of Kigali to Revd. José Chipenda, dated May 12, 1994. Mimeograph.
[80] Mark Huband, in *The Observer*, June 5, 1994, quoted in African Rights, *Death, Despair, and Defiance*, p. 902.
[81] Des Forges, *Leave None to Tell the Story*, p. 274.

leaders and others who supported the genocide, the authorities generally sent in soldiers or national police. Violence began with limited initial attacks on Tutsi homes that were usually sufficient to drive most Tutsi into flight, after which community leaders then encouraged the Tutsi to gather in a central location, generally a church, but sometimes the communal office or a school, to facilitate their "protection." As a next step, the soldiers or militia eliminated those who might offer resistance, such as PSD party leaders or peasant organizers or other progressive elements. Finally, the militia gathered and, with the assistance of the armed forces, systematically attacked the church or other shelter to wipe out all inside. The attacks generally began with a barrage of gunfire and grenades, followed by attacks with machetes, spears, and other "white arms." With 20,000 to 30,000 people gathered in some places of refuge, killing everyone was an arduous task that often took several days. After the initial massacre in each community, the local government instituted a "civil self-defense" program, including barricades on roads and paths to prevent Tutsi from fleeing and patrols to seek out Tutsi who might be in hiding. The barricades and patrols involved a much larger portion of the population than the massacres, as in most communities all adult men were required to participate. Those who refused, such as Hutu men married to Tutsi women who feared leaving their wives unguarded at home, risked being labeled *ibyitso* and targeted themselves, and they almost certainly guaranteed that their homes would be searched and anyone hiding there would be discovered. Through these barricades and patrols, most Tutsi who had escaped death in the initial massacres were eventually found and killed, while a much larger portion of the population became implicated in the genocide.[82]

The churches played a mixed role in the execution of the genocide. As the discussion of Biguhu parish in Part II of this text indicates, some churches were viewed as stumbling blocks to the genocide and thus had to be neutralized as forces that could dissuade people from participation. This was particularly the case given the large number of Tutsi pastors and priests, who were often an early target of attack. At the same time, leaders of the genocide regarded churches as an excellent resource that could be exploited to support the killing. In many communities, community leaders capitalized on the concept of sanctuary, and the fact that Tutsi

---

[82] Des Forges, *Leave None to Tell the Story*, discusses this pattern in many communities. An excellent example is the case study on Nyakizu, pp. 353–431, chapters I helped research and whose initial draft I wrote.

had been granted refuge in churches from violence in the 1960s and in 1973, to entice Tutsi to gather in the churches to facilitate their slaughter. As Philip Gourevitch quotes one Rwandan, "This was a tradition in Rwanda. 'When there were problems, people always went to the church ... The pastors were Christians. One trusted that nothing would happen at their place.'"[83] In some cases, clergy and other church employees and lay leaders actively participated in the process of gathering Tutsi at the churches with the explicit knowledge that Tutsi would not be offered protection. As one woman in Kaduha, Gikongoro, told me, her priest forcibly took her from her home and attempted to turn her over to a mob preparing to attack the nearby church.[84] Clergy, evangelists, and catechists often had excellent knowledge of their local communities, and in many areas they helped identify who was Tutsi (as physical appearance was not a reliable judge) and where Tutsi lived.

In a few cases, clergy actively participated in directing the killings. The case of Father Wenceslas Munyeshaka, who offered militia access to Tutsi gathered at Ste. Famille Church in Kigali and provided lists of RPF sympathizers, has received much attention.[85] Philip Gourevitch details the case of Elizaphan Ntakirutimana, president of the Seventh-Day Adventist church in Kibuye, who helped organize the killings at the Adventist center Mugonero. Seven Adventist pastors gathered at Mugonero sent a letter to Ntakirutimana informing him that they were to be killed, but he reportedly responded, "You must be eliminated. God no longer wants you."[86] Father Robert Nyandwi remained active at Kaduha parish throughout the killings there and was seen sporting a pistol.[87] Many other clergy and church personnel participated in the patrols and barricades. In each of the communities in Butare, Gikongoro, and Kibuye where I conducted research on the genocide, I found examples of clergy who had led patrols or headed barricades. As community leaders, clergy frequently were included in the communal security committees that oversaw the "self-defense" efforts after the first massacres.

---

[83] Philip Gourevitch, *We Wish to Inform You*, p. 26.
[84] Interview in Kaduha, June 12, 1996.
[85] Bonner, "Clergy in Rwanda Is Accused of Abetting Atrocities;" Hammer, "Blood on the Altar."
[86] Gourevitch, *We Wish to Inform You that Tomorrow We Will Be Killed with Our families: Stories from Rwanda* (New York: Farrar Straus and Giroux, 1998), pp. 25–29, 32–43, quote p. 28. Ntakirutimana and his son were found guilty of genocide by the International Criminal Tribunal in Arusha.
[87] Africa Rights, *Death, Despair, and Defiance.*

Throughout the genocide, there were church people whose religious beliefs inspired them to resist the killing. On the first day of the genocide, Augustin Nkezabera, the Hutu priest of Muramba parish in Kibuye, refused to turn over to militia Tutsi who had sought refuge in his church and was cut down by a machete.[88] Ananie Rugasira, a Hutu priest who taught at the minor seminary of Kigali in Ndera, protected Tutsi who sought refuge in the seminary, including the rector who survived the genocide as a result of Rugasira's efforts. Militia killed him on April 9 when he barred the door of the building to them.[89] Jean-Bosco Munyaneza, the Hutu priest at Mukarange parish in Kibungo, opened his church to both Tutsi and moderate Hutu seeking refuge during the first week of the genocide. The militia who came to attack the parish on April 12 killed him when he confronted them, saying "If you want to kill, start with me."[90] One sixty-year-old Hutu nun in Gisenyi, Félicitas Niyitegeka, chose to die with the people she was protecting, even after her brother, an army colonel, offered to save her. She refused to abandon her charges, and on April 21 militia members transported her and a group of Tutsi to a cemetery where they shot them, saving her for last and offering even at the end to save her. She told them, "No, I no longer have a reason to live since you have killed my sisters." In a letter to her brother she wrote:

Brother Dearest, Thank you for having wanted to help me. But in place of saving my life in abandoning those of whom I have charge, forty-three people, I choose to die with them. Pray for us, that we will arrive to God's home, and say goodbye to our old mother and our brother. I will pray for you when I arrive in God's home. ...[91]

There were many lay people as well who, because of their religious beliefs, risked, and sometimes lost, their lives. Most people avoided public opposition to the genocide, since this would almost certainly result in death, but many resisted quietly by hiding Tutsi in their homes or businesses or transporting Tutsi to safe havens. One comment that I heard a number of times in testimonies of witnesses discussing resistance to the genocide was that someone saved Tutsi "because he was an *umurokore*," a member of the Abarokore movement or a member of the Pentecostal church. For example, in one story about a group of Tutsi children in

---

[88] Contran, *They Are Targets*, pp. 98–9.
[89] Contran, *They Are a Target*, p. 112.
[90] Contran, *They Are a Target*, pp. 89–90.
[91] Quoted in Nadine Donnet, "Le Massacre des Religieux au Rwanda," in Guiachaou, ed. *Les Crises Politiques au Burundi et au Rwanda*, pp. 702–4.

Butare who were threatened in early May when the genocide expanded to include Tutsi children and women married to Hutu, a Hutu policeman transported a large group of children to a location where they could be transported by the Red Cross to Burundi. The witness describing the policeman's actions explained simply, "He was a Pentecostal who opposed the massacres for religious reasons."[92] While not all Pentecostals or other *Abarokore* opposed the genocide, a disproportionate number, including soldiers and policemen charged with instigating the killing, resisted. This should not be surprising given two important factors about the Abarokore movement. First, the Abarokore were generally not integrated into the established structures of power. As discussed in Chapter 3, the Pentecostal Church was late in arriving in Rwanda, and it had never sought the same type of links to authority as the other churches, targeting its appeal instead to the poor and disenchanted. The Abarokore movement within established Protestant churches arose as a challenge to the structures of power. Second, the theological ideas of the Abarokore eschewed engagement in politics as corrupting. They taught a strict code of moral conduct that forbade engagement in corruption, even when it was urged by authorities. This emphasis on a higher law easily translated into resistance to actions that were endorsed by the state but that nevertheless appeared clearly to violate certain important tenets in the Bible. Muslims are also said to have participated much less willingly in the genocide and in particular to have resisted killing fellow Muslims.

In general, however, Christianity as a system of belief and Christian churches as institutions served more as a support for the organizers of the genocide than as a hindrance. While those clergy and other church personnel who actively participated in the killing were the exceptions, the churches nevertheless helped make genocide possible. As Doris Bergen argued about the churches in Nazi Germany, Christianity in Rwanda "did play a critical role, not perhaps in motivating top decision makers, but in making their commands comprehensible and tolerable."[93] After years of practicing ethnic discrimination and urging obedience to state authorities, Rwandan Christians understood the admonitions of their church leaders to "support the new government" as a call for them to participate in the genocide. While the church leaders never specifically called on church members to kill Tutsi, it is important to realize that even the chief organizers of the genocide, like Col. Bagasora, never used

[92] Interview in Butare, December 29, 1995.
[93] Bergen, "Catholic, Protestants, and Christian Antisemitism in Nazi Germany," p. 329.

such direct language. The appeal for participation was always couched in terms of "self-defense" and rooting out "accomplices." Statements that were bland on the surface were understood by Rwandans because of the historical context. The churches had helped to make identifying Tutsi as an "Other" understandable to people through their own practices of ethnic differentiation and discrimination. They helped to give legitimacy to actions initiated by the government and military by teaching obedience to authority and allying themselves publicly with the established powers.

Given the long history of the Rwandan churches' practice of ethnic discrimination and support for the government as well as church engagement in recent political struggles, it should not be surprising that many Christians believed that the genocide was consistent with Christian belief, that it even had the sanction of the churches. The case of Ngoma parish in Butare, where Christians went to pray before they went out to kill, was not isolated. The fact that people could desecrate church buildings and kill even at the foot of the altar or in the sacristy is not evidence of a lack of respect for Christianity or a shallowness of Christian faith. Instead it reveals the nature of Christianity in Rwanda as a politicized, conservative, discriminatory faith. While there were other visions of what Christianity should be that some people in Rwanda were actively advancing, the genocide helped to eradicate those other possibilities and to reassert churches as authoritarian institutions allied to an authoritarian state.

I do not mean to suggest that the churches alone could have halted the genocide if they had chosen to do so. Rather, I argue that the genocide was never a foregone conclusion and could have been stopped even once it began if actors in Rwanda and the international community had shown greater courage, compassion, and integrity. Churches could have played an important role in supporting those who resisted the genocide, in informing the world about what was happening in Rwanda, and in making genocide more difficult to execute. In the second section of this book, I contrast two local parishes to demonstrate the different paths that churches took. In Kirinda, the church helped to support the genocide and facilitated its execution. In Biguhu, in contrast, the church was a hindrance. This second parish represents the road not taken in Rwanda and suggests that if they had been more unified and effective in their resistance, churches might have helped to prevent the genocide from being as successful as it was. Along with an international community that was more interested in saving lives than in avoiding entanglement in an African conflict, churches offered the best possible source for preventing the Rwandan genocide.

PART II

"GOD HAS HIDDEN HIS FACE"

Local Churches and the Exercise of Power in Rwanda

Why dost thou stand afar off, O Lord?
Why dost thou hide thyself in times of trouble?
In arrogance the wicked hotly pursue the poor...
He sits in ambush in the villages;
in hiding places he murders the innocent.
His eyes stealthily watch for the hapless,
he lurks in secret like a lion in his covert;
he lurks that he may seize the poor,
he seizes the poor when he draws him into his net.
The hapless is crushed, sinks down,
and falls by his might.
He thinks in his heart, "God has forgotten,
God has hidden his face, he will never see it."

– from Psalm 10

INTRODUCTION TO PART II

The first part of this book has provided a social and political history of the churches in Rwanda in an attempt to explain how the churches became so deeply implicated in the 1994 genocide. I emphasized three main points. First, from the arrival of the first missionaries in Rwanda, the leadership of the Christian churches committed themselves to developing a close alliance between their institutions and the state. The success in winning converts and influence that the Catholic Church in particular achieved through the strategy of fostering an obedient population and engaging actively in power politics indelibly shaped the subsequent social engagement of both Catholic and Protestant churches. The principle of supporting public officials for the good of the church, even when the officials engage in reprehensible behavior, dates back to the earliest days of Rwandan Christianity.

Second, the churches have consistently participated in Rwanda's ethnic politics, playing a major part in shaping the very nature of ethnic identities in the country. Far from preaching the unity of all humankind, Rwanda's Christian churches have actively discriminated on the basis of ethnicity, first in favor of the Tutsi minority and later in favor of the Hutu majority. The churches objected to neither the harsh exploitation of the Hutu during most of the colonial era nor the massacres of Tutsi in 1959–1965 and 1973. During the period of political turmoil from 1990 to 1994, church leaders continued to support the regime and failed to condemn ethnic massacres, again supporting a public impression of the acceptability of ethnic politics. Although genocide was an extreme expression of ethnic hatred, it was not inconsistent with actions previously condoned, or at least tolerated, by the churches.

Third, churches are important centers of power in Rwanda, controlling substantial resources and influence, and that power has been guaranteed through a patron–client system parallel to and linked with the state patrimonial system. The attack on authoritarianism that emerged in Rwanda in the 1990s targeted not simply the state but the churches as well, seeking to democratize church structures and redistribute power – not only control over resources but spiritual power also. Just as state leaders who felt their positions threatened by the pressures for democratization turned to ethnic arguments to regain popular support and bolster their positions, some church personnel were also drawn to reactionary politics to bolster their own positions.

To make this final point more effectively requires turning from an analysis of churches as national institutions to a grassroots analysis of local parishes. The local community is where most people have their primary contact with the churches. The principal work with which churches justify their existence takes place in the parish – teaching and conversion, preaching the Word, administering the sacraments, gathering together the community of believers, providing charity – and the parish level, particularly in rural areas, is where one can most completely appreciate the significance of churches as social and political institutions.

A grassroots analysis quickly reveals that the conflict within Rwanda's churches was not one between the top and the bottom, that is, between the national church leaders and the local pastors and priests, but rather a conflict over competing visions of the very nature of Christianity and the role and operation of the church. In studying three Catholic and three Presbyterian local parishes in the prefectures of Butare in southern Rwanda, Kibuye in west-central Rwanda, and Ruhengeri in the north, I found that this competition was present in all of the parishes to some degree, regardless of denomination and location. In the following account, I focus on two contrasting parishes that most clearly highlight the two competing visions that were present to some extent in every parish and at every level of each denomination. The parish of Kirinda aptly demonstrates the historically dominant disposition of Rwanda's churches as instruments of the powerful. In this parish, a close alliance prevailed between church employees and local administrative and business elite. In fact, the church played a major role in helping to create a local elite and maintain its dominance over the general population through a patrimonial network. In contrast, in nearby Biguhu parish an alternative vision had become dominant, which pushed the church to ally itself with the less powerful, to seek to create opportunities for the marginalized and to break down the local system of patronage and privilege. In Biguhu, rather than serving to reinforce the existing system of power, the church presented a challenge to the dominance of local elites. Ultimately, this meant that the church in Kirinda was at the center of the genocide there, while the church in Biguhu was regarded as a hindrance and targeted by the genocide. Although I focus here on two Presbyterian parishes, the conflict over the nature of the church was the same in Catholic parishes. In all three of the Catholic parishes that I studied – the Butare Cathedral parish and Save in Butare and Kampanga parish in Ruhengeri – both of these tendencies could be seen to various degrees. Although I did not conduct parish-level case studies of other denominations, my comparative research suggests that I would have found similar findings in Baptist, Anglican, and Free Methodist parishes as well.

The conflict in Rwanda's churches that I describe in this section reveals important aspects of the general crisis that engulfed Rwanda in the years leading up to the 1994 genocide. As it manifested itself in Rwanda, the wave of democratization that swept across Africa in the 1990s was more than a simple argument over limited reforms to state institutions. Rather, it was a broad struggle over the distribution of power and its exercise within the country. For a brief moment in the first years of the decade, popular mobilization appeared to be on the verge of forcing a radical redistribution of power and reshaping of public life in Rwanda. Churches were both major instigators of the challenges to the status quo and targets of popular mobilization, as people sought to democratize power within the churches as well. The supporters of the status quo were eventually able to reorganize their system of support and reassert their power by redirecting public discourse to center on ethnicity, co-opting former opponents, and expanding their use of coercive force. This strategy ultimately culminated in the genocide. As the discussion in the next three chapters should demonstrate, churches were at the center of this struggle over the nature of power in Rwanda, both attacking the authoritarian traditions of the society and, in the end, facilitating the implementation of genocide.

7

Kirinda: Local Churches and the Construction of Hegemony

Situated along the banks of the Nyabarongo River, a primary tributary of the Nile, in a remote, heavily populated, agricultural region of west-central Rwanda, the parish of Kirinda serves as one of the primary centers for the Presbyterian Church in Rwanda (EPR). In 1907, King Musinga granted land and authorization to German missionaries from the Bethel Lutheran mission to establish two Protestant stations in Rwanda, including one on a hill called Kirinda in Nyantango, a region only recently incorporated into the Rwandan kingdom during the reign of Musinga's father.[1] Nyantango remained largely independent and rebellious. As Danielle de Lame writes, "The region of Kirinda was ... an enclave little assimilated into the administration of the central kingdom."[2] Hence, Musinga apparently hoped that locating a Protestant mission at Kirinda could contribute to his efforts to centralize his rule, just as the missions of the White Fathers in Rwaza and Nyundo had done.

Kirinda quickly became the main center for Protestant missionary activity in Rwanda. By the time the German Protestant missionaries were forced out of Rwanda during World War I, they had begun to gather a core of converts, counting sixty members in Kirinda, and had established a growing number of mission outposts around Rwanda.[3] With the departure of the missionaries, however, the congregation at Kirinda swiftly fell

---

[1] Rennie, "The precolonial kingdom of Rwanda," p. 31.
[2] Danielle de Lame, *Une Colline Entre Mille, ou le Calme Avant la Tempête* (Tervuren: Musée Royal de l'Afrique Central, 1996), p. 51.
[3] Twagirayesu and van Butselaar, *Ce don que nous avons reçu*, p. 71.

into decline. When David Delhove, a Swiss Seventh-Day Adventist began working in Kirinda in 1919, he found that:

In general the former Christians have not remained faithful in their belief. Many died during the famine of 1917–1918, many women and young girls have had sexual relations with soldiers, and some Christians have restarted the practice of polygamy or have returned to the worship of spirits.[4]

The Adventists remained in Kirinda only briefly before establishing a new station at Gitwe, much closer to the royal capital, Nyanza.[5]

After the Belgian crown requested that the Belgian Society of Protestant Missions in Congo (Société Belge de Missions Protestantes au Congo, SBMPC) begin operations in Rwanda, they made Kirinda the headquarters for their Rwanda mission. Several Belgian missionaries arrived in Kirinda in 1921 and, after restoring the church building, they began a school, an infirmary, a carpentry workshop, and a project to make rugs from banana fibers.[6] Each of these programs expanded slowly over the next several decades, making Kirinda a minor regional hub in an area removed from Rwanda's major trading and administrative outposts. In 1956, Kirinda's dispensary was expanded to become a hospital, and in 1962 the EPR founded a nursing school at Kirinda. For a time in the 1950s, Kirinda was home to a teachers' training school, but the school was subsequently moved to Remera. By 1960, Kirinda was educating 2,645 primary school students.[7] The Kirinda parish controlled a large tract of land and gradually expanded its land holdings and operations onto the large neighboring hill of Shyembe, where a small residential and commercial center developed. The activities of Kirinda parish continued to increase following independence in 1962, although many of the operations of the national church shifted to Kigali and to the other Presbyterian centers at Rubengera and Remera. The territory served by the parish, which initially included a vast area of west-central Rwanda, was diminished gradually as new parishes were established in neighboring communes in Kibuye, Gitarama, and Gikongoro. At the time that I began field research in Kirinda in 1992, the parish had approximately 4,000 members, most of whom lived in four sectors of southern

---

[4] Cited in Twagirayesu and van Butselaar, *Ce don que nous avons reçu*, p. 73.
[5] Linden and Linden, *Church and Revolution in Rwanda*, pp. 153–4; Gatwa and Karamaga, *Les autres chrétiens rwandais*, pp. 64–7.
[6] Twagirayesu and van Butselaar, *Ce don que nous avons reçu*, pp. 83–7.
[7] Gatwa and Karamaga, *La Présence Protestante*, pp. 42–52; Twagirayesu and van Butselaar, *Ce don que nous avons reçu*, pp. 121–30.

Bwakira Commune of Kibuye – Nyabiranga, Cyamatare, Murambi, and Shyembe.

THE CHURCH PRESENCE IN KIRINDA

The overwhelming majority of the population in Kirinda parish during the time of my research worked as peasant farmers who, characteristic of Rwandan social structure, lived not in villages but in isolated family dwellings surrounded by banana groves and fields of manioc, sorghum, and beans. The relatively high altitude in this region near the Zaire-Nile Crest produces a pleasant, cool climate, with abundant rainfall, but the swampy banks of the Nyabarongo support an abundance of mosquitoes, so malaria is endemic. The density of the population has encouraged overcultivation of the land and, coupled with the steepness of the hillsides where people live and farm, has resulted in severe soil degradation. Malnutrition has been prevalent in the area, and famine occurs periodically. In the early 1990s, some area streambeds were excavated in a search for trace amounts of gold, but the region is otherwise lacking in mineral resources. The area had no industry, and given the lack of resources and the fact that the nearest paved road lies over an hour's drive from Kirinda, the potential for industrial development has remained limited. Although the seat of Bwakira Commune lay a short walk from the parish, the government presence there was insignificant, and only a few commercial enterprises and homes surrounded the communal office. The church in Kirinda, therefore, represented the primary focus for economic activity in the immediate area. A brief review of the various activities sponsored by the parish in the years before the genocide can demonstrate the breadth and importance of the church's involvement in the local community.

A large parish church building constructed in the 1920s stands at the summit of Kirinda, the hill that provides the parish its name. On Sunday mornings, prior to the disaster of 1994, the sanctuary hosted several hundred children for Sunday school, then filled to capacity for a 10 A.M. worship service that continued until 1 or 2 o'clock in the afternoon. Each service included several scripture readings, songs by five to ten choirs, and a sermon from the parish pastor or one of the other ordained clergy stationed in Kirinda or, sometimes, an evangelist, an unordained church employee whose main task was recruiting and training new members. After the formal service ended and most of the faithful left, the *Abarokore* or "Saved," a group known in the community as the most ardent believers, stayed to sing, pray, and "witness" their faith until 4 or 5 o'clock in the evening.[8] On the other days of the week, the church sanctuary hosted catechism classes for children and adults, prayer meetings, choir practices, and occasional meetings for the local, regional, or national church, but the primary activity of the parish shifted elsewhere.

Because of its historic importance and the concentration of Presbyterians in the surrounding area, Kirinda remained central to the EPR, despite its remote location. One long building down the hill from the sanctuary housed both the parish office and the office of the Kirinda region, one of five regional divisions of the EPR. The regional president, an ordained minister, oversaw a number of parishes in Kibuye and Gitarama prefectures, including Kirinda. The Department of Theology for the national EPR lay a short distance from the parish offices. Before the genocide, a Dutch missionary couple, both ordained pastors, worked with a Rwandan pastor who directed the office to plan continuing education for Presbyterian pastors, to advise the church on theological questions, and to prepare church publications.

The offices of the Department of Women for the EPR lay just behind the church building. The director, who was the first ordained Rwandan woman, her assistant, a sister from an order of Protestant nuns, and their secretary oversaw Presbyterian women's groups throughout Rwanda. They sought out and distributed international financial assistance for women's groups, planned national women' meetings and workshops, prepared pamphlets, newsletters, and other materials for use in the EPR parishes, and also directed and oversaw women's activities in the Kirinda parish. A group of parish women raised chickens and rabbits in a fenced off area to one side of the office, and another group met each Tuesday to cultivate fields of pineapples and strawberries and make jellies in a building that housed a kitchen on the other side of the office. A large group of women met each Wednesday afternoon to make baskets in an open-air building just down the hill from the church. On Thursdays, a small group of young women from the church met at the women's office to sew tablecloths and other items. None of these activities was particularly remunerative, primarily because of the limited market, but some

---

[8] The conduct of religious services was a major difference between Catholic and Protestant churches. In contrast to the single long service that most Protestant churches held, Catholic masses were usually limited to an hour, but a number of masses were held each Sunday. This was in part necessitated by the larger general size of Catholic parishes, where several thousand people might attend mass on any given Sunday, in contrast to the several hundred at Protestant services.

items were sold locally and others were transported to an EPR-sponsored store in Kigali, so participants occasionally received a small payment that they could use to buy items such as clothing or to pay children's school fees. According to participants, the weekly meetings were also of value because they allowed women to come together to socialize, to pray, and to talk about their problems.[9]

Projet Agro-Pastorale et Artisanal de Kirinda (The Agro-Pastoral and Artisanal Project of Kirinda, PAPAKI) had an office down the hill from the church, next to the women's basket project. PAPAKI began in 1979 with a demonstration farm on 50 hectares of church land along the banks of the river in conjunction with a prefecture-wide Swiss-sponsored project, the Projet Agricole de Kibuye. Subsequently operated independently by the church in collaboration with Institute of Agricultural Sciences of Rwanda, ISAR, a small group of workers grew vegetables and raised cows, goats, pigs, rabbits, ducks, and chickens on the demonstration farm, testing new varieties of plants and new breeds of animals and demonstrating new farming and animal rearing techniques. With financial support from ICCO, a Dutch development agency, the demonstration farm in 1992–93 undertook the process of converting to a self-supporting, independent cooperative with the ten employees of the project becoming member-owners. In 1992, a group of fifteen women from the church took over some of PAPAKI's fields to cultivate in another independent cooperative.[10]

On another side of Kirinda hill, PAPAKI used Swiss development money to construct a silo for safely storing beans and sorghum. In a scheme typical for silos in Rwanda, participants bought an inexpensive membership and then were paid for the harvest they brought in. They were eligible later in the year to buy back beans and sorghum at a lower-than-market price. This allowed the nearly 300 participants to budget their consumption, to keep their harvests dry and insect-free, and to receive a lump sum of money that could be used for school fees or for necessary household purchases. The silo building also housed a mill and a small shop for seeds and agricultural implements. The silo and shop were a cooperative owned by the 133 original members who would have shared profits had any ever accrued.[11]

---

[9] Interview in Kirinda, June 29, 1992; interviews in Kirinda, July 8, 1992.
[10] Interview in Kirinda, September 5, 1992.
[11] Interview in Kirinda, September 5, 1992. As part of its development program, the Habyarimana regime established OPROVIA in the 1970s, a government agency that built

Another large project sponsored by PAPAKI was the *banque de chèvres*, the goat bank. Under this scheme, a family was given a goat whose manure could be used as fertilizer to enrich exhausted fields. Participants were required to return to the project the offspring of their goat. In the 1980s, the Ministry of Agriculture directed all communes to establish an animal program for poor farmers, and to fulfill this obligation the communal authorities in Bwakira asked PAPAKI to expand its program to the entire commune. With support from the commune and from ICCO, more than 700 families had received one or two goats.[12]

By 1992, two PAPAKI projects had fallen into serious decline. A men's mat-weaving project met irregularly and had attracted no new members for several years because of the difficulty in finding a market and the lack of profitability. *Médecine de Masse*, a project organized in cooperation with the hospital to teach principles of nutrition to families with children suffering from kwashiorkor had nearly stopped functioning. The project gave nutrition education to select peasants who could then organize educational meetings among their neighbors and other fellow peasants. As the director of PAPAKI explained:

> The project used to run well. There were grassroots health agents trained who came and got teaching on different subjects and then could go out into the hills to teach others. But then the government came in with a coordinated national program. They brought in a politicized teaching. When there was a meeting, politicians came. The grassroots health agents gained a position of status. They were given a shirt that was symbolic and set them apart. So other peasants stopped coming. ... There is still some education going on in the area, but people were not happy to receive an education that was not useful, so they stopped attending. The project still exists, but it functions badly.[13]

In 1992, the hospital had a nutritionist who worked with children so severely malnourished as to need medical attention, and some families continued to receive rabbits and other food supplements,[14] but the popular education of peasants no longer continued. The director of PAPAKI claimed that he was himself no longer able to attract peasants to farming

many silos and bought beans and sorghums under a similar strategy. By the 1980s, this program had fallen into decline, but many churches had picked it up and built their own silos or taken over OPROVIA silos. Johan Pottier, "Taking Stock: Food Marketing Reform in Rwanda, 1982–89," *African Affairs*, 92, no. 366 (January 1993): 5–31; Newbury, "Recent Debates," p. 202.

[12] Interview in Kirinda, September 5, 1992.
[13] Interview in Kirinda, September 5, 1992.
[14] Interview in Shyembe, September 12, 1992.

education sessions, because of the bad reputation that the project had given to popular education.[15]

In the domain of education, the Kirinda parish hosted several grade schools and three secondary schools. Near the church and the parish offices were a small grade school and also a Centre d'Enseignement Rural et Artisanal Intégré (Center of Integrated Rural and Artisanal Teaching, CERAI), a three-year technical high school run by the parish. Begun under a state initiative in 1985, the CERAI originally educated only girls in sewing, cooking, embroidery, and knitting, but added carpentry and car mechanics courses for boys in 1992–93. The Ministry of Education paid the salaries in the CERAI and grade schools, but the church directed hiring and administration and provided the facilities.[16]

In addition, the EPR operated two full six-year secondary schools in Kirinda. The Institut Presbytérien de Kirinda (IPK), began by initiative of the national EPR in 1981 with 50 students and steadily expanded, counting 429 students in the 1992–93 school year. The administration added a course of study in education to the original economics program, and the school gradually improved its facilities to include boys and girls dormitories, a large meeting hall and cafeteria, a new kitchen, and new, well-equipped classrooms. Teachers sent by churches and other international agencies from Switzerland, Belgium, the Netherlands, Germany, and the United States regularly taught at the IPK. In the 1992–93 school year an American Peace Corps volunteer, a German fulfilling national service requirements, and a Dutch woman working for the Mission Belge worked at the IPK. The exchange of personnel supplied teachers whose salaries were paid from abroad and helped build links between the IPK and foreign donors, allowing the school to obtain a computer, copy machine, truck, television, calculators, and other facilities. The Ministry of Primary and Secondary Education accredited the school in 1989, so that the state recognized IPK diplomas. To receive accreditation, the IPK had to submit to state regulation of the content and quality of its education. The church, however, continued to pay all of the expenses of the school, including salaries.[17]

Across the valley, attached to the hospital on Shyembe hill, stood the oldest of Kirinda's post-primary institutions, the Ecole des Sciences

---

[15] Interview in Kirinda, September 5, 1992.
[16] Interview in Kirinda with director of CERAI, September 3, 1992.
[17] Twagirayesu and van Butselaar, *Ce don que nous avons reçu*, p. 159; interview in Kirinda with principal, March 15, 1993.

Infirmières de Kirinda (ESI), a nursing school. Like the IPK, the ESI had benefited from international assistance in funds and personnel, including a German volunteer and (in conjunction with the IPK) a Dutch church volunteer in 1992–93. In contrast to the IPK, which attracted students from throughout Rwanda, the ESI focused primarily on students from within the area. In the 1992–93 school year, the ESI began a massive expansion of its student body under an initiative of the Ministry of Health. Because the director of the ESI accepted a challenge to train more nurses issued by the health minister, the ESI doubled the size of its 1992 incoming class, and the church began a project to construct a number of new classrooms for the school. As with the CERAI and the grade school, the church provided the buildings for the ESI, which therefore was considered a church school, but the state paid salaries and the Ministry of Health regulated the curriculum and the quality of education. The church hired the director and other administrators of the school, but the state hired teachers, and the Ministry of Education closely regulated the program of instruction.

The most substantial presence of the church on Shyembe was the Kirinda Hospital. The church began its first health dispensary in Kirinda in 1921. From 1949, the SBMPC in cooperation with the Belgian colonial administration expanded the medical work in the parish, and in 1956, with the arrival of a Belgian doctor, Kirinda's medical center was upgraded to a hospital. In 1992, the hospital had four doctors, extensive medical equipment, and a capacity of 150 beds. Kirinda hospital served as the official health center for four communes in Kibuye, Gitarama, and Gikongoro Prefectures. The hospital continued to receive physical and financial support from abroad, including a program that brought in Dutch medical specialists several times a year, but the administration and the majority of the financing were Rwandan. The primary financing came from the Ministry of Health, which paid half of the salaries, and most other funds came from fees collected from patients.

A large community surrounded the hospital and the adjacent ESI. The church built a number of homes on Shyembe to house medical personnel, teachers, students, and other church employees, and a number of private residences had been built in the town center as well. A substantial commercial district of shops, restaurants, and cabarets (the local term for bars that generally serve locally brewed beer) sprang up to serve the residents, students, and the many people who came to Shyembe to seek medical care or to attend to sick family members. Next to the hospital, the national women's office built a restaurant and cabaret, *Amahoro* (Peace), that served hospital patients, students, and others. The women's office later built a small hotel/dormitory, *Home Amahoro*, to house visitors to Kirinda and students at the ESI. Ostensibly the restaurant and hotel were a project to provide money for the women's work of the EPR, but they had not yet become profitable.[18] At one end of town was a community center, built with funding obtained from the Dutch embassy by a Dutch nurse who directed the ESI for more than twenty years and was retired in the community, that hosted a kindergarten, language classes, and various community events. At the other end of Shyembe, a large field hosted a weekly market for meat, produce, used clothing, and other goods. The Shyembe market gradually expanded in importance within the region and in the 1990s attracted merchants and consumers from as far away as Gitarama, more than one hour by car.

The parish of Kirinda counted over 4,000 members. It included a large number of hills in addition to Shyembe and Kirinda, but church life focused very clearly on the parish center. Like most parishes in Rwanda, Catholic and Protestant alike, Kirinda was divided into sub-parish units, basic Christian communities, intended to integrate members more effectively into the church. In Kirinda the basic Christian communities were relatively inactive. Each of the ten communities had a small chapel building used for children's Sunday school and weekly prayer services, but levels of participation were low, and the communities had little independent identity. The church-owned large tracts of land in the parish, with groves of trees, fields cultivated for the pastors, and grazing land for cattle, goats, and sheep, but development projects and other church activities were concentrated on church land around Kirinda and Shyembe.[19]

THE PARISH AND THE CONSTRUCTION
OF SOCIOECONOMIC CLASS

The work of the Kirinda parish extended far beyond the sacred tasks ascribed to churches by Western social theory to encompass many of the secular social, political, and economic activities of the area. The population in the region turned to the church not only for religious guidance, but also to receive health care, educate their children, participate in development projects, and on occasion receive food aid or other forms of relief assistance. Even local political and business activity centered around the

---

[18] Interview in Kirinda, June 29, 1992; interview in Kirinda, July 8, 1992; interview in Kirinda, September 4, 1992.
[19] Interview in Kirinda, July 29, 1992.

parish, and people had few options for economic and social opportunity outside the church. The greater a family's access to church resources, the greater their chances of improving their social and economic status. The church, thus, played a major role in creating socioeconomic class differentiation within the community.

One family I interviewed on numerous occasions in Kirinda provides an example of the centrality of the church in the economic lives of area residents. The family unit in question consisted of an elderly father and mother, a single adult daughter, another unmarried daughter with a child, and four grandchildren left orphaned by the death of a third child. Everyone in the family participated in cultivation, including the children, but the family's fields were on a steep hillside above the river and thus suffered from soil infertility; farming provided no excess food for sale on the market. To bring in money for school fees and other household expenses, the mother sold fried *beignets* (a fried dough pastry) at the local market each week. One daughter was a member of PAPAKI's silo cooperative, allowing the family to deposit and preserve its bean and sorghum harvests. The other daughter began working as a teacher at the IPK in 1991 and in 1993 was transferred to a salaried position as an agronomist in the parish. In the past, before the family had the benefit of a salaried employee, they received occasional food aid from the church. The parish thus was fully integrated into the economic program of this family, which included the silo cooperative, church employment, and food aid; even the sale of *beignets* was made possible by a market that owed its existence to the presence of the church. In addition, the family participated in religious services, and several members of the family sang in church choirs. The children studied in the church grade school.[20]

In a context of extremely limited resources, the local church served as a primary source of opportunities for earning an income in Kirinda. The church supplied salaried labor, day labor, and other earning opportunities, such as the various cooperatives, and it also supplied health care and education, factors important for creating other opportunities. The degree to which a family in Kirinda was able to access church resources went far in determining the family's economic position and social status. As Manning Marable claimed,

Poverty must be understood as a comparative relationship between those segments of classes who are deprived of basic human needs (e.g., food, shelter,

---

[20] Interview in Kirinda, September 11, 1992 and other interviews.

clothing, medical care) vs. the most secure and affluent classes within a social and economic order. ... The process of impoverishment is profoundly national and regional ... .[21]

While no one in Kirinda would be considered wealthy by Western standards, a large gap in the community existed between a small elite group that lived in comparative comfort and security and the mass of the population that lived in modest circumstances. While most people in the region had difficulty finding the small amounts of cash necessary to pay for clothing, school fees, and health care and a large portion of the population struggled even to provide sufficient food to feed their families, a small group lived in comparative luxury and ease, and most of these had gained their privileged position through connections to the church. In an overwhelmingly rural setting, the church and its schools and hospitals provided some of the only opportunities for salaried employment. This employment provided a steady income, in contrast to the uncertainty of day labor or the sale of agricultural and artisanal products. Professional positions – pastors, teachers, doctors, nurses – provided an income many times larger than the average annual income in the region, as well as quality housing, land to cultivate, and other perquisites, such as access to vehicles.

In addition to the formal salary and benefits, church employment provided many informal opportunities to make money, usually through illicit means and often by exploiting those with limited means. Examples of corruption by church personnel in Kirinda were abundant. The teachers at the schools, particularly the IPK, were widely accused of accepting bribes of beer, money, and sex in exchange for higher grades – and of requiring such bribes of students who needed to make up exams or needed other special consideration.[22] The principal condemned such practices in teachers' meetings, but he was himself accused of using his position for profit. According to several informants, he kept back 300 Rwandan francs at the end of one school year from each dormitory resident's 500 franc security deposit, ostensibly to pay for damages to property. In fact, the students claimed that no damage had been done to the property and no improvements were made during the school recess. They conjectured that the money was used to finance the principal's wedding festivities,

[21] Manning Marable, *How Capitalism Underdeveloped Black America* (Boston: South End Press, 1983), p. 54.
[22] Interviews in Kirinda, July 10, September 8, December 26, 1992.

whose opulence far exceeded anything his salary could have supported.[23] A number of informants also accused the principal of accepting bribes. One informant testified that, consistent with procedures for enrolling in the IPK, he wrote a letter in April requesting that a position be reserved for him, then in July he presented himself at the school officially to register. The director told him that the classes were full. "Then," the informant stated, "while I was still in the room, some others came in, and they gave the director money, and he let them enroll. He didn't even wait for me to leave the room! He took the money right in front of me and let them enroll!"[24]

A former principal at the IPK, a pastor, was transferred to an obscure EPR parish after evidence indicated that he had embezzled funds from the school. Financial irregularities apparently surfaced at his parish as well, but after a few years there, he was transferred back to Kirinda, this time as director of the Department of Theology for the entire EPR. Here once again he embezzled money, according to several other employees of the office. Before leaving for a church-funded English language program in Kenya in late 1992, he had a check for half of the theology department's supplies budget made out to him in order to purchase materials for the office in Kigali, but neither the supplies nor the money were ever subsequently seen.[25]

Another pastor, formerly president of the Kirinda region of the EPR, was transferred to a small parish after an incident involving the distribution of food aid. According to diverse sources, a large shipment of beans was sent to Kirinda from a European church to be distributed to the needy. According to a witness whose story was confirmed by several others:

The pastor distributed [the aid], and it was chaotic. They announced in church that there would be a distribution, and the peasants came to the parish office for three days hoping to get the aid, and they were sent away each day. In the end, there were *commerçants* who received 50 kilos [of beans] while the peasants received only 5 or 10 kilos.[26]

This pastor had a large family, and several informants claimed that he took a large portion of the shipment for personal use, as well as kickbacks

---

[23] Interviews June 24, July 10, September 9, 1992.
[24] Interview in Kinigi, Ruhengeri, August 3, 1992.
[25] Interviews in Kirinda, December 26, 1992; February 8, 1993.
[26] Interviews in Kirinda, September 9, 1993.

from the merchants. The abuse was so flagrant that the church leadership could not ignore the public outcry and transferred him as a punishment. But after less than a year in his new parish, he was transferred back to Kirinda, this time as chaplain for the IPK.

Nearly all of the administrators of church institutions conspicuously made expenditures that their salaries could not support, flaunting their wealth without attempting to mask the implication of its improper or illicit acquisition. A new director installed at PAPAKI in early 1993 found that most of the project budget for the year was gone, while, not coincidentally, the former director's property was undergoing expensive improvements.[27] In the early 1990s, the director of the hospital built a large home on Lake Kivu for his family. The director of the IPK kept large numbers of cattle in his home district, according to reliable sources there.

The higher economic standing of the salaried elite was emphasized by an ostentatious display of wealth. The homes of the elite were made of fired bricks, rather than the more common mud bricks and stucco, and nearly all had electricity and running water. Nearly all of the elite owned a number of cattle, the traditional symbol of wealth in Rwanda. While most area residents went to drink in dark, mud-walled private bars known as cabarets, where they passed around a calabash of home-brewed banana beer, the elite sat under the glare of electric lights on the cement porch of a chic bar, where they became publicly drunk on expensive bottled Primus and Mützig. The elite ate meat daily, rather than subsisting on the normal Rwandan diet of beans, bananas, sweet potatoes, and sorghum. To travel between Kirinda and Shyembe, the most important elite did not walk the steep and sometimes muddy paths down the hills and across the valley like the rest of the population but rather traveled in the vehicles belonging to the hospital, school, and local merchants. In Rwanda, wealth and girth were closely associated, and almost all of the prominent employees of the church in Kirinda were rotund.

The class position of the elite was emphasized not only in material terms but also in the exercise of power over subordinates. Several of the professors at the IPK demanded sexual favors of female students, and one of the pastors was widely said to be having an extramarital affair with a student at the IPK – even as his own children were attending the school. The parish pastor caused a minor scandal in June 1992 when, in

---

[27] Interview in Kirinda, March 22, 1993.

a drunken rage, he refused to pay his bar tab at a local cabaret and beat the woman bartender. That same week, the church, which owned the lease on the cabaret, evicted the woman, claiming a construction project necessitated it. Later, after considerable public criticism, the church again allowed the woman to rent the space, but at triple the rent.[28] While the members of the elite showed a level of disdain for those of subordinate classes in the community, those in the subordinate classes were expected to show deference and respect to the elite.

The glue that held the class system together in Kirinda lay in the ability of the elite to distribute benefits and opportunities to others. In conditions of extreme scarcity, access to church resources could mean the difference between struggling on a daily basis to find enough food, being unable to send children to school and unable to seek medical attention for illnesses or having a regular income and access to medical care and schooling for ones children. The pastors, the directors of the schools, the director of the hospital, and other elite had the ability to hire employees at various levels, including not only those in skilled positions (teachers, nurses, technicians, evangelists), but many people in unskilled positions (janitors, nightwatchmen, gardeners). In overseeing the budgets of their institutions, they had considerable latitude in determining where the money should be spent, who should supply vegetables for the school cafeteria for example or who should be contracted to build a new school building. The elite also hired people for household work, as cooks, nannies, and daylaborers on their fields. In addition to distributing employment opportunities, the elite distributed a variety of other benefits, such as deciding who should get school scholarships, what grades students would get, and whether an individual should pay for a visit to the doctor and how much. The pastors also had an additional power in providing access to spiritual benefits, being able to assure individuals of their salvation or, alternatively, predicting their damnation and encouraging their ostracism by the community.[29]

As in any patrimonial system, the more benefits individuals within the church were able to provide and the more clients they could gain, the greater their personal status and power. Individuals could calculate how to distribute benefits to most enhance their power. While they generally sought to support their families, their neighbors, and their home communities, the elite also supported one another in a reciprocal manner,

---

[28] Interviews in Kirinda, June 26, 1992, February 8, 1993.
[29] See Schatzberg, *Political Legitimacy in Middle Africa*, on the issue of spiritual power.

accumulating obligations from others that could later be called in. For example, when the daughter of the director of women's affairs ought to have failed out of the IPK based on both low grades and disruptive conduct, the principal instead saw that she was allowed to continue.

The greatest patron in the EPR was the president, Michel Twagirayesu, who was a native of Kirinda and, as such, provided many benefits to his home community. There was considerable rivalry within the EPR between the three historic centers of Remera, Rubengera, and Kirinda, and to maintain his power within the church, Twagirayesu saw that each of these communities received benefits, ranging from church jobs and scholarships to new construction projects to the location of church offices. For example, while the offices of theology and women's affairs were in Kirinda, the office of youth affairs was in Rubengera, the medical office was in Remera, and the development office and the national church headquarters were in Kigali. Residents of Remera and Rubengera, however, complained that Twagirayesu unduly favored Kirinda, providing a disproportionate number of jobs to people from his home community, and many people in Kirinda concurred. One former church official native to Kirinda claimed, "When [Nasson] Hitimana was church President, everyone was from Remera [his home community]. Under Twagirayesu, everyone was from Kirinda."[30]

Within Kirinda, Twagirayesu provided opportunities above all to members of his family and people from his hill just west of the parish at Gisovu. The director of development for the church was a member of Twagirayesu's family, as were the secretaries at the national church office in Kigali and even the kitchen staff at the restaurant of the women's project, Amahoro. Members of Twagirayesu's family were the first to be considered for receiving church contracts, scholarships, and other perquisites. One informant speculated that the continuing influence of the president of the church within the community stifled attempts to reform local church institutions and contributed to the sense of fatalism and malaise that predominated in the area:

Here change is hindered by the fact that everyone is from the family of Michel [the president of the EPR]. No one dares to oppose him. They just obey. Really it's sad. They knew the good moment here once, back in the 1960s and 1970s. But now ... .[31]

[30] Interview in Nairobi, August 1, 1999.
[31] Interview in Kirinda, February 8, 1993.

Of the pastors in Kirinda, the director of women's affairs, Rénate Ndayisaba, was probably the most influential. A native of southern Rwanda, a region with few Presbyterians and herself not having been raised Presbyterian, she did not have the same degree of family obligations as many others. Hence, she was able to distribute benefits more strategically, offering jobs and funding in ways that built obligations. She had, however, seen that several of her siblings as well as her children got into Presbyterian schools, and one of her sisters had married into Twagirayesu's family.

The principal at the IPK, Fidele Ntawirukanayo, was another powerful individual in Kirinda. A native of Biguhu, a neighboring parish (which is discussed in detail in Chapter 8), he hired several others from Biguhu as teachers, and students from other communities complained that Biguhu students received greater leniency in grades and were allowed greater flexibility in paying school fees. Students with outstanding debts were not allowed to take final exams according to school rules, but students from Biguhu were allowed to sit for exams even with large debts.[32] The Reformed Church of the Netherlands supplied scholarships intended for poor students at the IPK, but they were apparently distributed on the basis of personal connections to the principal and his teachers rather than according to financial need.

The director of Kirinda Hospital, Antoine Kamanzi, had greater hiring power than anyone else in Kirinda other than Twagirayesu. The hospital employed not only many doctors, nurses, technicians, and chauffeurs, but also many manual laborers for jobs such as cleaning, laundering, and gardening. Dr. Kamanzi was from far western Rwanda, along the shores of Lake Kivu, and he maintained connections there, but like Pastor Ndayisaba, he had built up considerable power within Kirinda through distributing benefits and acquiring obligations.

Church employees were not the only elites in Kirinda. The burgomaster, Tharcisse Kabasha, had served since 1973, when Habyarimana came to power, and he had amassed substantial power and wealth. A March 1993 public petition calling for his replacement accused Kabasha of a wide range of abuses of office. The petition claimed that he repossessed parcels of land from various individuals in the commune for his own use or for his friends to have cultivated, that his assistants gave official papers to his friends without hassle while requiring bribes from his enemies,

---

[32] Interview June 14, 1996.

and that taxes collected went straight into his pocket. According to the petition:

He has stolen the wealth of the commune. Today, the commune cannot even buy paper even though we pay our taxes. He does not fulfill his function as bailiff, he ignores the *doleances* of the population and furthermore, he puts himself above the law, without scruples he refuses to give out official papers, he drives out any-one he does not want in his commune.[33]

Kabasha also provided jobs to various relatives. The clerk of the com-mune was his cousin, while his son served as accountant for a state-run cooperative.

In addition to the burgomaster, several of the wealthiest people in the commune were shopkeepers and traders, who traveled to Kigali or Gitarama to bring back goods to sell at a substantial markup in the com-mercial centers at Kirinda and Bwakira. The elites within the business community and the local government were, however, closely linked to the church elite through relationships of reciprocity. Many of the business people were related to the church elite, and they supported one another. The church elite distributed business opportunities to local business peo-ple who in turn provided kickbacks and other benefits to the church per-sonnel. The burgomaster got support from the church personnel and in turn helped to enrich them and gave them easy access to government services. Prominent business people and government officials had their social status enhanced by being named to lay positions within the church, such as one reputed to be the wealthiest businessman in Kirinda, who also served as head of the Kirinda regional church council. The educated and those with salaried employment dominated the local church council, even though peasants with limited education constituted the large major-ity of the church members.

The class solidarity among the church, government, and business elites was reinforced through social contacts. These social contacts were symbolic of and strengthened the reciprocal ties between elites. On many evenings, burgomaster Kabasha joined the director of the hospital and another of the doctors, the principals of the IPK and the ESI and one or two of the professors, the director of women's affairs, the president of the Kirinda region, the pastor of Kirinda parish, and one or two busi-ness people at the restaurant Amahoro, the other elite bar at Shyembe,

[33] Letter from "the People of the Commune of Bwakira" to the President of the Commission of Control of Agents of the State," Bwakira, March 11, 1993.

or the cabaret at the parish. Not all of the elite were part of this social circle, but those who were generally shared reciprocal ties of cooperative business ventures, favors and obligations, and, in a number of cases, family ties.

Exclusion from this social circle usually reflected an absence of other reciprocal ties. Employment alone did not determine ones integration into the system of reciprocal ties, since some people in elite positions were not included. The agronomist who was director of PAPAKI, despite being a relatively prominent church employee, was not included, since he was a member of an opposition political party. While previously some Tutsi had been welcomed in this group, by 1992 the few Tutsi who worked at the schools or the hospital were generally not included. Similarly, Pastor Ndayisaba was the only woman regularly included in the group. Until early 1992, a Tutsi who was a native of Kirinda had been director of the Department of Theology, but he did not often participate in the elite social circle and by 1992 he was almost entirely excluded. In early 1992 he was transferred from his important post to a less prominent position as a parish pastor. Informants told me that he was transferred both because he was Tutsi and because he did not have connections to other community leaders. The degree of an individual's power depended not simply upon his or her position but how he or she used the position to develop reciprocal ties. Thus, Dr. Kamanzi, Pastor Ndayisaba, and IPK principal Ntawirukanayo enjoyed much greater power than the director of the ESI and Ernest Kariganya, the pastor of Kirinda parish, because these latter had not used their positions as effectively to gain debts of obligation from other people.

The rapid rise to prominence of one individual from Kirinda effectively demonstrates the manner in which reciprocal ties among the elite operated. Amani Nyilingabo was a distant relative of Twagirayesu, native to the same hill. In the late 1980s he worked as a domestic worker in the home of Ndayisaba and also did some day labor on church construction projects. Working for the church, he became acquainted with several expatriates associated with the church and used these connections to improve his social status. He eventually married Ndayisaba's younger sister. Shortly after this marriage, Nyilingabo was contracted to build an addition to the Biguhu dispensary, despite his lack of experience overseeing construction projects. This project was followed by contracts to build Home Amahoro, the hotel attached to Amahoro restaurant, a new set of classrooms at the IPK, and a major expansion at the ESI. Nyilingabo made a hefty commission off these contracts, and they also provided him access to other money-making opportunities. The Burgomaster Kabasha was a particularly close friend of Pastor Ndayisaba, and according to a widely circulated rumor, Kabasha, Ndayisaba, and Nyilingabo cooperated on a venture to mine gold and smuggle it out of the country. Kabasha allegedly supplied the necessary authorization, Nyilingabo organized the labor and transport, and Ndayisaba used her international connections to market the gold. While these rumors could not be independently confirmed, the evidence of illegal gold mining could be seen in creek beds throughout the area and the wealth the three partners displayed seemed to reinforce the rumors. Nyilingabo went from being a houseboy to one of the wealthiest people in Kirinda in less than five years. With the profits he made, he was able to buy four cars and trucks in as many years.[34]

POLITICS AND CLASS CONFLICT

The Presbyterian Church played an important part in creating and reinforcing class divisions in Kirinda. While supporting the dominant class position of a limited elite and providing little real opportunity for advancement to the majority of people in the parish, a patrimonial system within the church created dependency in the subordinate classes that limited their ability to challenge the system. The church was the major distributor of jobs, resources, and opportunities in the region, and the elite determined how those goods were distributed. Because poor families in the community had few other alternatives, they needed to maintain good relations with the elite so that members of their families could get jobs, so that if the family fell on hard times or had a medical disaster, they could turn to the church for assistance, and so that one or more of their children could get enough education to be able to rise out of poverty. While not everyone in the community could get a church job and not every child could receive a position in school and fewer still a scholarship to pay for their education, the possibility of gaining these opportunities – and the reality that people would have to rely on the church in case of disaster – forced the population generally to show at least public support for the status quo.

At the same time, the subordinate classes of peasant farmers, day laborers, and low-wage salaried workers did not blindly submit to domination

---

[34] I have discussed this case in some detail in my article, "Empowering the Weak and Protecting the Powerful: The Contradictory Nature of Churches in Rwanda, Burundi, and Congo," *African Studies Review*, 41, no. 1 (spring 1998): 49–72.

by the upper classes. What James Scott observed in the Malaysian village of Sedaka applies equally to Kirinda:

Those with power in the village are not, however, in total control of the stage. They may write the basic script for the play but, within its confines, truculent or disaffected actors find sufficient room for maneuver to suggest subtly their disdain for the proceedings. ... The resources the different contestants bring to this contest hardly bear comparison. The local elite nearly always has its own way in the economic life of the village. Given its sway over resources, it can also largely control public ritual life – that is, the "onstage" conduct of most of the poor in the community. Only "backstage," where gossip, tales, slander, and anonymous sabotage mocks and negates the public ritual order, does elite control fall away.[35]

People in Kirinda likewise employed numerous strategies to promote their personal interests and independence and to undermine the ability of the elite to exercise dominance over them. What is of particular interest is that in the early 1990s, the everyday forms of protest practiced by Kirinda's peasants became much more frequent and visible, moving as it were "onstage." Inspired by and linked to the broader process of social change taking place in Rwanda in which existing structures of power were being fundamentally challenged, the poor in Kirinda began to challenge more openly and forcefully the elite who exploited them.

A number of people I interviewed emphasized that the conditions of inequality and class differentiation in Kirinda had emerged only gradually. One expatriate who had been in Kirinda since the early 1960s claimed that the parish had once been much less class divided. In decades past, the parish had actively worked with the poor in an attempt to improve their conditions. "*Medicine de masse*, grassroots medical education, was begun long ago by the missionaries along with the [Rwandan] pastors. All the development programs of the women were started from the bottom. But now the church is more concerned with money."[36] According to this witness, the problem in the EPR in general and in Kirinda parish in particular was the entrenchment of leaders in office. As they held their positions for increasingly long periods, they developed greater power and enjoyed increasing benefits, and they had an interest in preserving their positions. "When Michel [Twagirayesu] began as president, he did a lot of good things. It is like in the political system. Habyarimana started

---

[35] James C. Scott, *Weapons of the Weak: Everyday Forms of Peasant Resistance* (New Haven: Yale University Press, 1985), pp. 26–7.
[36] Interview in Kirinda, February 8, 1993.

out well. But it is the power. Once they get it, they want to hold onto it."[37] As the witness suggests, the entrenchment of an elite in Kirinda to some extent mirrored the more general process of class differentiation in Rwanda, as a limited elite gained increasing wealth even as the masses of the population became increasingly impoverished.[38]

The formation of an elite class in Kirinda was, thus, a gradual process, and as in other parts of Rwanda, the population in Kirinda did not passively accept the abuse of office and concentration of wealth by the local elite but expressed their displeasure in various ways and found diverse means to undermine the authority of the elite. While publicly showing respect, peasants often belittled and insulted the elite behind their backs. *Radio bouche-bouche* served as an important means of undermining the authority of community leaders. Rumors spread widely about the embezzlement of funds or nepotistic hiring practices and also about the personal failings of individuals, their sexual improprieties, drunkenness, and family conflicts.[39]

When abuses of power became too flagrant, complaints sometimes went beyond mere gossip to open criticism and, ultimately, refusal to respect the authority of the abusive leader even in public. Such escalation of resistance had the power to force other elites to react, in order to preserve the stability of the general system of authority. For example, the Sunday after the parish pastor beat a barmaid in a drunken rage, the crowd at church was extremely restive during his sermon, gossiping loudly about his behavior rather than listening to his preaching. Public anger over his attempt to cover up his behavior by revoking the woman's lease forced him to allow her to reopen the bar a short time later. The public condemnation of the regional president's misappropriation of food assistance in 1991 forced the national church leadership to transfer him out of this position. Similarly, objections to the former director of the IPK's embezzlement of funds led to his transfer out of that position. At the IPK, a group of students organized during the 1991–92 school year to protest the favored treatment of Biguhu students. Although several of the leaders of the protest were expelled, the protest forced school administrators to mask more carefully the favoritism they showed, as it risked

---

[37] Ibid.

[38] Bezy, *Bilan socio-économique d'un régime.*

[39] James Scott, *Weapons of the Weak*, discusses at great length the ways in which the peasants of Sedaka, similar to those in Kirinda, challenged the prestige of the elite through rumor and storytelling.

angering the international funders of the school and leading to a cut in financial support.[40]

Because churches in Rwanda are ultimately voluntary organizations, parish members discontent with church leadership could, despite various pressures, vote with their feet and join another church. A number of former Presbyterians had left the Kirinda parish over the years to join the nearby Adventist or Pentecostal churches. As one informant explained to me, "the Kirinda church does not seem to have God in it. All the rich come dressed in their best clothes and sit in the front rows. We poor do not feel welcome."[41] The decision to leave the church, however, meant breaking ones patrimonialties. Once an individual left the church, he or she could no longer expect to receive church employment or assistance for his or her children in school. When a Dutch missionary couple arrived in Kirinda in 1992, they hired a gardener based on his experience, but local church leaders objected, because he had become a Pentecostal, and they insisted that he return to the Presbyterian Church or be fired. The man chose to return to the Kirinda church rather than lose his job.[42]

Many people who did not wish to risk similar ostracism tried to find ways to challenge the authority of church leaders from within the church. The strength of the *Abarokore* movement in the parish indicated a level of discontent with the church leadership. As when the *Abarokore* movement first emerged in Anglican parishes earlier in the century, it was a populist movement in Kirinda, with meetings directed by laity. The Sunday afternoon gatherings included congregational singing, individual prayers, personal testimonials, speaking in tongues, and other forms of popular participation. In their meetings, the *Abarokore* condemned the consumption of alcohol and tobacco, womanizing, and corruption, all offenses widely attributed to the local elite, including church leadership. The movement thus provided an implicit – and occasionally explicit – challenge to the church leaders. Participants in the movement were almost all peasant farmers, with only one teacher identified as an *Umurokore*.

With the legalization of opposition political parties in July 1991, class conflict in Kirinda assumed overtly political overtones. While the vast majority of Kirinda's population supported the MDR, which was based in neighboring Gitarama and had its greatest support in the central

[40] Notes from research assistant, September 1992; interview in Butare, March 25, 1996.
[41] Interview in Kirinda, A41
[42] Interview in Kirinda, December 26, 1992.

region of the country, Kirinda's elite supported the MRND and, later, the CDR. Having gained their privileged positions through the existing social system, the elite had a vested interest in preserving that system and thus supported the parties that were committed to maintaining the existing structures of power. While many people in Kirinda wore the red and black cap of the MDR or flew an MDR flag, the elite made no secret of their pro-MRND sympathies. EPR president Twagirayesu remained a member of the Kibuye regional committee of the MRND. Longtime Burgomaster Kabasha was a member of the MRND, but many people believed him to have CDR sympathies. After its formation in 1992, several local elite openly embraced the CDR, including IPK principal Ntawirukanayo, whom several students witnessed wearing a CDR cap at a rally in Kibuye town. Nyilingabo became head of the CDR chapter in the southern part of Bwakira. As a result, for the masses of the population, support for the opposition parties came to mean opposition to the local elite. A shift in national political power to the MDR could potentially undermine the power of the entrenched local elite and open up the possibility for other people to gain access to the resources of the church, state, and business. For many people in Kirinda, sporting an MDR cap meant thumbing their noses at the local elite.

The emergence of political party competition heightened the class conflict that was already present in Kirinda. It gave, in effect, an official blessing to challenges to existing structures of authority, allowing them to come out into the open. The lines between political party protest, class conflict, and simple criminality or hooliganism became blurred. During the long dry season of 1992, peasants in Kibuye and Gikongoro burned forests in a form of protest. Many of these forests had been planted as part of *umuganda*, communal public works, as erosion control and for general public use, but they had become sources of enrichment for communal authorities, who demanded calabashes of beer or other bribes in exchange for the right to use wood from the forests. Burning the forests expressed anger over *umuganda* and over corruption by public officials. Peasants angry with the extravagance and blatant disregard for the law among the wealthy set other privately owned forests ablaze. Around Kirinda, both communal and private forests were burned, as were some of the forests of the parish. One informant stated:

The forests of the parish were burnt because it is said that the parish possesses many parcels of land, spread over a wide area, while the population doesn't possess enough. Some people say it was done under the influence of the political parties, but in general it was simply some form of spitefulness, because even children burnt the parish woods.[43]

In 1992–93, Kirinda experienced a rise in the incidence of robbery, rape, and other violent crimes. Most of these crimes were committed by a loosely defined gang of unemployed youths from the community. With little land available to farm and without money to obtain an education, many young people in the area had become increasingly disaffected. Without money or land, they could not build a home, marry, and start a family. Some of these youths had gone to Kigali in search of employment but returned unsuccessful and more frustrated. These youths hung out in the commercial centers at Shyembe or Birambo, sometimes obtaining day labor, such as loading and unloading trucks for merchants, then using the money on alcohol and marijuana. They harassed people in the community and sometimes robbed individuals or businesses.

While at one level the destructive behavior of the youths who hung out in Kirinda was merely an expression of fatalism and nihilism, at another level, it had a political content, since it targeted primarily the elite of the community. As Donald Crummey claimed:

Crime is inherently a form of political protest, since it violates the law. Crime may be accompanied by many forms of consciousness. Where laws are clearly directed by one class against another, as is the case with laws inhibiting poaching or restricting access to forests or common lands, they engender a class-conscious defiance.[44]

In June 1992, someone tried to rob the parish pastor, striking him in the head with a brick.[45] On July 31, 1992, a gang of more than ten youths attacked the principal of the IPK and several of his drinking buddies on a day when he had returned from church offices in Kigali with the funds to pay the monthly salaries of the teachers. He was drinking at Amahoro with the director of the hospital, one of the IPK teachers, the president of the region, and several of their wives, when a fight broke out outside among a group of youths loitering in the commercial district of Shyembe. The director went outside to intervene, but the youths apparently turned

---

[43] Notes from research assistant, September 1992.
[44] Donald Crummey, "Introduction: the Great Beast," in Donald Crummey, ed., *Banditry, Rebellion, and Social Protest in Africa* (London: James Currey, 1986), p. 3. Crummey's edited volume makes a fascinating link between criminality and more recognized forms of political protest.
[45] Interview in Kirinda, July 29, 1992.

on him and the others, driving them back inside Amahoro, where they barricaded themselves in. The youths threw stones at the restaurant, breaking most of the windows. Before they dispersed, they broke glasses and bottles, which were expensive to replace in Rwanda. The teachers and regional president, who lived in Kirinda, were afraid to drive back along the roads, so they stayed that night at the home of the director of the hospital in Shyembe. The next day, gendarmes came to Kirinda and arrested three of the youths, while others fled.[46]

Because the MDR challenged the authority of the community elite, these youths identified with the opposition party. They supported the party's youth wing (Jeunesse Démocratique et Républicain, JDR) and participated in JDR rallies, which were frequently rowdy and sometimes degenerated into violence and looting. In some cases, youth from the JDR participated in *kubohoza*, acts of vandalism or violence committed in the name of the MDR to harass and hopefully forcibly convert members of the MRND.[47] In December 1992, Amuza Epimaque, the son of the wealthiest merchant in town and a friend were riding home on their motorcycle from drinking at Shyembe when they were attacked by four youths who threw a grenade that knocked them off of the bike. The youths came to rob the two, but fled when other people approached. Gendarmes were again called in, and three of the youths were arrested. The youths turned out to be natives of Kirinda who lived in Kigali, where they had gone to seek employment. The gendarmes claimed that their investigation revealed that the youths had been called to Kirinda by a local merchant, Emmanuel Habiyakare, who supplied them with six grenades and instructions to kill and rob six of the leading citizens of the community, including the burgomaster. The intended victims were all members of the MRND, while the merchant was in the MDR. The attack thus seemed to involve a mixture of motives – a criminal opportunity, personal vendettas, and political conflict – though facts of the case were challenged and the charges against Habiyakare were eventually dropped.[48]

In January 1993, the burgomaster became the target of a more obviously political attack. A rally for the MDR in Bwakira ended in a march to the communal offices, where the party supporters attacked the burgomaster

---

[46] Notes from research assistant, September 1992; interview in Kirinda, September 4, 1992.

[47] See discussion of *kubohoza* in Des Forges, *Leave None to Tell the Story*, pp.

[48] Interviews in Kirinda, December 26 and 27, 1992; Letter from the People of Bwakira, p. 5; Letter from Burgomaster Kabasha, no. 1.921/04.17.02, December 24, 1992.

and forced him to wear the red and black cap of the MDR and march to Birambo, the head of the sub-prefecture. According to those involved, the attack on Kabasha was in response to his eviction of a commerçant from the commercial district of Bwakira. After this incident, the government arranged for the burgomaster to be protected round-the-clock by gendarmes sent from the prefecture.[49]

The elite in Kirinda did not, of course, passively allow the various challenges to their authority – and their personal safety – to go without response. Just as they faced harassment, they subjected elite who were members of other parties to harassment. For example, the president of the MDR in neighboring Mwendo Commune, who was a math teacher at the ESI and lived at Shyembe, claimed that the water in his house was poisoned in early 1993.[50] The burgomaster and his friends began to gather their own group of young malcontents to carry out destructive acts in support of the MRND. According to the March 1993 public petition demanding Kabasha's ouster, "In the context of protecting his [illegal] acts and to harass the population, he has created a group of people charged with guarding his security. This group of troublemakers is based near the communal office. It is always near to intervene."[51] The petition claimed that the group attacked the home of the assistant burgomaster, who was a member of an opposition party, to force him to quit, while other assistants were transferred out of the commune.[52] Several church employees were also fired or transferred out of Kirinda. One Tutsi who had served as chauffeur for the hospital for a number of years was accused of financial improprieties in 1991 and fired, but he and a number of other people in the community felt that his firing was due to his ethnicity and his refusal to support the MRND. Similarly, the Tutsi director of the Department of Theology was demoted to a parish post outside of Kirinda in 1992.

As an additional tool to discourage challenges to the MRND, the pro-MRND elite regularly called upon the coercive power of the state to support their interests. Following the December 1992 grenade attack in Shyembe, the gendarmes called in by Kabasha from Kibuye arrested and

---

[49] Interviews in Kirinda, February and March 1993; letter from the People of the Commune of Bwakira, p. 5.

[50] Interview in Kirinda, March 21, 1993.

[51] Letter from the People of the Commune of Bwakira, March 11, 1993. The letter goes on to list the names of five men, apparently youths since their parentage is identified, and claims "there are others."

[52] Ibid, p. 4.

beat Habiyakare, the MDR commerçant, as well as his brother-in-law, the agronomist for Kirinda parish, another MDR supporter. They pillaged Habiyakare's home and beat him, before releasing him.[53] In each of the cases where the elite were threatened, gendarmes came from Birambo or Kibuye town to investigate and arrest perpetrators. When the level of violence in the community became sufficiently acute that the burgomaster and his supporters were in danger, a permanent protective force was stationed in the commune.

At the same time that the authorities intervened to protect the pro-MRND elite, they were slow to defend the general population. While the delinquent youth gangs associated with the JDR clearly posed a threat to community security, including the security of the elite, they also indirectly served the interests of the elite by discrediting the MDR and the transition to multiparty politics in general. Because their acts of theft and violence were not entirely restricted to the pro-MRND elites, the youth gangs were highly unpopular with the general population, and by associating themselves with the JDR, these youth gangs seemed to prove the claim put forth by both national and local MRND leaders that multiparty politics was disruptive and was contributing to declining internal security. By intervening only to protect their prominent supporters but otherwise allowing acts of violence to go unchallenged, the authorities sought to create nostalgia for the order that prevailed under single party rule.

A series of incidents in September 1992 reveal the ambivalent relationship between the community, the youth gangs, and the authorities:

A group of twenty young men situated themselves on the road to carry out together acts of banditry. They encountered business people who were coming from the market, since it was market day. They stole from them all the merchandise and all the money they had. There was also among the commerçants a girl who was going to be married three days after this, and they took her and forced her to have sex with them. They directed her to a small forest near the road, and because they were numerous, the girl did not have the strength afterward to walk, so she spent the entire night in the forest.[54]

The following day, the commerçants returned along with members of the girl's family and joined with people from the town to search out those

---

[53] Letter from the Population of the Commune of Bwakira, p. 5.
[54] Notes from research assistant, September 1992. I was a witness to this final vigilante killing and watched as a group of around one hundred men, women, and children beat the young man to death, each person taking a turn to hit or kick the body.

responsible for the crime. The group used sticks and stones and machetes to kill two of the bandits; two others were hospitalized.

The day after [these first vigilante attacks], they looked through the entire town searching for the one who was the chief of the bandits [Paul Nyandwi]. Around noon, they found this bandit and conducted him near the river Nyabarongo where he was killed by girls, women and men. He tried to jump into the river to escape. He was hit until he was dead. During these two days, no authority came to intervene. The communal authorities only intervened to conduct inquiries after the death of the third bandit.[55]

After I myself witnessed this vigilante killing of Nyandwi, I asked a number of people in the community, both participants and not, why no one had called in the authorities to arrest the bandits instead of the community's forming a vigilante mob. The nearly universal response was that the authorities would not act and that even if they did, the judicial system was faulty and would not keep the perpetrators in prison. In fact, Nyandwi had been threatening the town for some time and had been previously imprisoned but released.[56] While the vigilante killings thus clearly demonstrated a lack of faith in the authorities, they also challenged the position of the opposition parties both because of the nominal connection of the bandits to the MDR and because of the general decline of public order to which the youth gang had contributed.

The elite in Kirinda carefully used public fear and uncertainty to manipulate the population. While the majority of people in Kirinda had enthusiastically supported the advent of multiparty politics in 1991, by mid-1992 the general public had become disenchanted. The testimonies of several informants in the days surrounding the gang attack and vigilante killings demonstrate the impact these events had on people's impressions of multiparty politics:

It is better to respect the authorities. Before, people showed great respect to the burgomasters. The authorities have lost their honor. Banditry too. Before the multiparty government, there was not much banditry, stealing, raping of girls. Now there is banditry and delinquency. The war is one factor, but with multipartyism, the authorities are not sufficiently strong to combat it. They lack a voice. They can not stop it.[57]

[Multiparty politics] was good, but now it is bad. There is no longer an understanding among the population. People fight the politicians. Now someone can

---

[55] Ibid.
[56] Interviews in Kirinda, September 9–14, 1992.
[57] Interview in Kirinda, September 13, 1992.

kill and say that it is multipartyism. People consider themselves equal to the authorities. Here by the river there were people attacked on Monday. They stole from the commerçants. The women and girls were raped. This is the result of multiparty politics, the decline of order.[58]

The pro-MRND elite in Kirinda took advantage of the public's sense of insecurity and growing disenchantment with multiparty politics to strengthen their own position. A few days after the attack and vigilante killings, on September 14, 1992, the burgomaster convened a community meeting in Shyembe to discuss the security situation in the community with local government officials, church elite, and business people. At the meeting, they created a security committee, composed of the president of the Shyembe commercial center, the councilors of the two cells in Shyembe, the directors of the hospital, the ESI, and the IPK, and the pastor of Kirinda parish. Kamanzi, the director of the hospital, was elected chair, with Musa (Moise) Semilindi, the president of the commercial center as vice president, and Ntawirukanayo, the principal of the IPK as secretary. According to the burgomaster's letter informing the prefect of the meeting:

In this meeting, we studied together how it would be possible that security could be establish once more in the center. It was found that this could be possible but only if the commerçants utilize workers who are well behaved and who have the permissions [to work] from the commune. Around the center, there should be people to unload trucks who are well known and who behave well; the unemployed ought to leave the center.

The inhabitants of the center need to assure their security themselves and they ought to meet often. ....[59]

It is significant that all the members of this committee charged with overseeing the security of the sector were MRND stalwarts and powerful among the community elites. The unemployed youths to whom the burgomaster refers were the very malcontent youths who were harassing the elite in the name of the JDR.

The creation of a security committee of the sort set up in Kirinda was a common tactic throughout much of Rwanda as Habyarimana's supporters sought to reassert their control. These committees helped to organize

[58] Interview, September 9, 1992. It was at the conclusion of this interview conducted at the PAPAKI farm near the Nyabarongo that the lynch mob carrying the gang leader Paul Nyandwi passed by on their way to beat him to death.

[59] Letter no. 1.526/04.09.01/4 from Tharcisse Kabasha, the Burgomaster of Bwakira Commune, to the Prefect of Kibuye, dated October 7, 1992.

their communities in support of the regime and to identify political opponents as threats to public order. They did not, of course, immediately
garner the support of the entire population, but by setting themselves up
as defenders of order in an increasingly chaotic context, they did put the
supporters of the opposition on the defensive. Over time, discussions of
security threats focused increasingly on the RPF and on Tutsi, and these
committees eventually took the leading roles in organizing the genocide
in many communities.[60]

CONSTRUCTION OF HEGEMONY

In his prison writings, Antonio Gramsci discusses the establishment of
"hegemony of a fundamental social group over a series of subordinate
groups." According to Gramsci, the dominant social group emerges out
of a link developed between "structure" and "superstructure," that is,
between the economic system on the one hand and the political society
and civil society on the other. Various elements of the elite from business, government, and private organizations, form a unified social group
when they develop a consciousness of "the solidarity of interests of all
the members of a social class." The dominant group attempts to gain the
compliance of the masses of the population both by seeking their voluntary consent through economic incentives and ideological arguments and
by using the coercive power of the state. In periods of crisis, the equilibrium between the classes is challenged and overt class conflict emerges,
what Gramsci calls a "war of position," which under appropriate circumstances can become a "war of movement," or a revolutionary program.
During these periods of crisis, the dominant social group struggles to
reestablish equilibrium by co-opting other social groups and by asserting
new ideologies. Although the dominant group relies on the coercive force
of the state to support it, the ensuing conflict unfolds to a great extent
within the civil society, as ideologies compete for supremacy. Eventually
either the dominant group is able to redefine itself sufficiently to reestablish equilibrium or a new dominant class emerges.[61]

Gramsci's analysis helps to make sense of the process of class differentiation and conflict that I have described here in Kirinda, but that I
witnessed as well in the five other parishes. In Kirinda, the revolution of
1959 uprooted the existing class structure, opening up the possibility for

---

[60] Des Forges, *Leave None to Tell the Story.*
[61] Gramsci, *Selection from the Prison Notebook*, pp. 11–13, 106–14, 175–85.

new classes to emerge. Because of its access to resources and its ability to accord individuals with social status (or, to use Gramsci's term, prestige), the Kirinda church played an important part in the creation of a dominant class in the region. The church both created a religious elite (not purely clerical, but including many lay church employees) and supported elites in the realms of business and government. The religious elite, the bureaucratic class, and, to a much lesser extent, the business class,[62] developed their own systems of patronage, which linked them to the lower classes of farmers, day laborers, low-salaried and manual laborers, and small shopkeepers. During the 1970s and 1980s, the various elite groups in Kirinda both improved their positions vis-à-vis the subordinate classes and developed greater connections to one another. Both the government administrators and church elite helped family and friends gain business opportunities, thus largely creating the local business class to fill the void left by the departure of many Tutsi elite. The three elements of the ruling class developed increasing material and social connections with one another,[63] while they established hegemonic control over the masses by making them economically dependent, claiming to preserve order, and, to eliminate challenges to their hegemony, employing the coercive capacity of the state.

The role of the church in helping to create a local elite was present in all the parishes that I studied but was most pronounced in rural areas, where fewer competing social institutions exist, and in older parishes, where the church had been able to integrate itself into the community more thoroughly. Of the five other parishes that I studied, the one that most resembled Kirinda in terms of its social position was Save, the oldest Catholic parish in Rwanda, situated just outside the town of Butare. Like Kirinda, the parish of Save was a massive presence within its area, sponsoring not only numerous spiritual groups and activities but also a health center, schools, and development programs. The parish priest enjoyed extensive power because of his ability to hire and fire, distribute aid, and determine who could be baptized, married, and buried in the

---

[62] Robert Fatton, "Gramsci and the Legitimization of the State: The Case of the Senegalese Passive Revolution," *Canadian Journal of Political Science*, 19, no. 4 (December 1986): 729–50, claims that "the dominant fundamental group in Senegal is composed of three major factions" – the business class, which he identifies as the "weak link," the bureaucratic class, and the religious elite.

[63] Gramsci writes, "The three elements – religion ... State, party – are indissoluble, and in the real process of historico-political development there is a necessary passage from one to the other" (*Selections from the Prison Notebooks*, p. 266).

church,[64] and he developed an extensive patrimonial network in alliance with the leaders of the schools, medical center, and various monasteries based in Save. In my research in Save, many parishioners complained of corruption in the operation of the church and its services, and a substantial number had left the Catholic Church to join a Pentecostal, Seventh-Day Adventist, or Episcopalian parish. In the large area around Save parish, which included portions of four communes, the church was the real center of social, economic, political, and spiritual power.[65]

In contrast, in the two case studies I conducted in the urban community of Butare, I found the churches' role in creating the dominant class less pronounced because the university, research institutes, the government, large secular development projects, insurance agencies, banks, and industries all provided employment and opportunities for patronage. The Catholic Church was, nonetheless, an important player, with the bishop of Butare and various Catholic priests serving on communal and prefectural committees, while the local political and economic elite used the church to advance their own prestige and opportunities. For example, the burgomaster of Ngoma Commune, Butare's commune, sat on the parish council of Butare parish. The new Presbyterian parish in Butare, however, did not play an important role at all in the creation of an elite. Having been founded only in 1990, the parish had attracted primarily poor and relatively powerless people disaffected by other churches, including the Catholic parishes of Butare and Save, where they felt excluded from opportunities or witnessed corruption or, as several told me, felt that the church was too focused on material affairs rather than on spiritual life. Similarly, Kampanga Catholic parish in Ruhengeri was established only in 1986, and, even though located in a rural area, it had yet to become a major factor in local power politics. The parish had no full-time priest, being led instead by several expatriate sisters, and it had only a few social and economic activities. Most prominent politicians were members of other churches, including the burgomaster of Kinigi Commune, where the parish was located, who was an Episcopalian.

Scott provided an important corrective to Gramsci's treatment of hegemony as ideological domination, arguing that peasants consent to the

---

[64] Ellis and ter Haar, "Religion and Politics in Sub-Saharan Africa," discuss the importance of spiritual power in Africa, the power that the ability to impart blessings and other spiritual goods gives to individuals.

[65] I discuss the case of Save in greater detail in "Church Politics and the Genocide in Rwanda," *Journal of Religion in Africa*, 31, 2 (2001): 163–86.

status quo because they see no practical alternative to it, not out of ideological commitment arising out of "false consciousness."[66] In Kirinda, as in Scott's Sedaka, the peasants and other subordinate classes had historically complied with the elite largely out of fear of the consequences of refusing to do so. People knew that if they challenged authority – whether in the state or church – they risked being cut off from the material benefits the elite could distribute and, potentially, facing arrest, beating, and imprisonment. For most people, rebellion against the system seemed futile.

At the same time, ideological constraints to rebellion should not be entirely discounted. The example of Kirinda suggests that people did support their leaders at least in part because of the ideological justifications they offered for their dominance. After taking office in 1973, Habyarimana gained substantial public support by promising to establish order after more than a decade of ethnic conflict and by promising to guarantee the rights, particularly economic rights, of the Hutu majority. The fear of returning to the turmoil of the Kayibanda years and the sense that Habyarimana was helping to develop the country convinced many people to support the regime and its local representatives. Similarly, church leaders gained public support by portraying themselves as promoting the development of their parishioners. The peasants and other poor in Kirinda developed a sense of dependence on the church to assist them, which prevented them from taking independent initiative. The national director of development for the EPR explained how this dependent mentality limited the effectiveness of PAPAKI:

At Kirinda, there was a Swiss pastor who brought funding from the outside for the project. The people did not understand why the project was there. They saw it as a service provided for them. When the Swiss pastor left, the financing left. People now ask [the development office], "Why don't you give money for the project?" ... The funders developed a certain mentality among the peasants. They just gave in the past, and there was no understanding of why.

Since parishioners saw the church leaders as the only source of economic possibilities, they were reluctant to challenge them overtly. The sense of

---

[66] Scott, in *Weapons of the Weak*, chapter 8, argues that the peasants of Sedaka challenged the notions of justice and other ideological ideas of the elite but because of their material dependence on the elite and the possibility of retribution, including police action, they believed the status quo inevitable. This interpretation of hegemony is more convincing than Gramsci's claim that the masses consent to domination because of "the prestige (and consequent confidence) which the dominant group enjoys," (*Selections from the Prison Notebooks*, p. 12).

inevitability of the status quo, thus, was itself ideological, as the contrasting case of Biguhu in Chapter 8 will demonstrate. The elite actively cultivated a sense of dependence in the population as a means to maintain their status.

During the 1990s, the balance of power was challenged in Kirinda, as in the rest of the country, as Rwanda descended into crisis. Economic decline in the 1980s laid bare the degree to which the elites, on both a national and local level, were benefiting themselves rather than the general public. Exposure at the national level of the corruption and personal enrichment of government and military officials was mirrored at the local level in rumors and storytelling that challenged the excesses of the elite in Kirinda. The mere presence of economic crisis was not, however, sufficient to produce the type of open attack on elites that occurred in Kirinda.[67] In fact, the declining economy in some ways increased the dependence of the population, because their cash crops and agricultural surplus brought in less income. The public challenged the elite more directly in the 1990s – in Kirinda through sabotage (such as the burning of forests), criminal attacks, refusal to pay taxes and participate in *umuganda*, and ultimately political party activity – because the democracy movement contradicted the ruling class's claim to its inevitability. The international movement for political reform that swept through Africa beginning in 1990 inflamed "sentiments of independence, autonomy, and power" (to use Gramsci's phrasing), and the success of democracy movements both in Rwanda and elsewhere in gaining concessions from regimes, or even driving them from power, suggested to people the possibility for alternatives to the status quo. If the elite's claim to obedience from the subordinate classes rested on convincing them that they needed the elite's assistance for their own survival, then the emergence of opposition parties and of open criticism of the government undermined the existing class equilibrium by presenting the possibility for an alternative power structure to the status quo, one in which those currently disempowered might be able to gain greater control over their own lives and greater access to resources. While people had long been frustrated with the elite and quietly subverted their control, in the 1990s people felt empowered to confront the elite more

[67] Gramsci points out that the French Revolution "did not occur as the result of direct mechanical causes – i.e. the impoverishment of the social group which had an interest in breaking the equilibrium, and which did in fact break it. It occurred in the context of conflict on a higher plane than the immediate world of the economy; conflicts related to class "prestige" (future economic interests), and to an inflammation of sentiments of independence, autonomy and power" (*Selections from the Prison Notebooks*, p. 184).

directly, and these challenges created a serious threat to their continued dominance.

Ultimately, of course, the conflict between the classes in Rwanda did not result in another revolution. Instead, the elite reconfigured itself; it promulgated a reformulated ethnic ideology and co-opted many of its opponents into a new, more broadly based coalition, then sought to reinforce its dominance through a massive campaign of violence. As I discuss in greater detail in Chapter 9, the situation in Kirinda provides great insight into why Rwanda went down the road of genocide rather than the road of revolution. In Kirinda in 1992, members of the community saw criminality and corruption as the primary threats to their well-being, but over the next two years, the elite of Kirinda, using the organizational structures of the security committee, the political parties, and the communal government, and backed up by national political leaders and media, helped to transform public thinking in the community in a way that made genocide possible. By convincing enough people that the Tutsi and their sympathizers were the key threat to public order, the elite in Kirinda were able to regain popular submission to their dominance, and the church played a key role in helping to bring about this shift.

Before turning to a detailed analysis of how the elite accomplished this shift in public thinking, however, it is important to look at another community, Biguhu, a Presbyterian parish that resembles Kirinda in many ways, but that represents the road not taken and in particular shows how Christian churches might have helped Rwanda avoid the catastrophe that befell it in 1994.

FIGURE 7.1. Map of Rwanda.

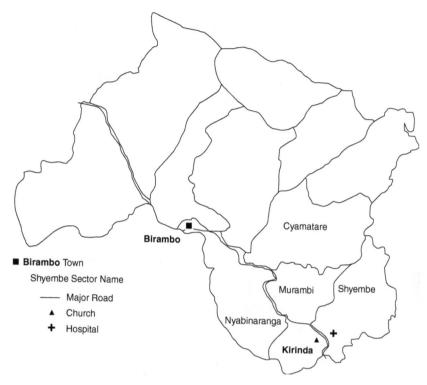

FIGURE 7.2. Map of Bwakira Commune.

8

Biguhu: Local Churches, Empowerment of the Poor, and Challenges to Hegemony

THE CHURCH IN BIGUHU

The Presbyterian parish of Biguhu lies a moderate distance west of Kirinda in what was then Mwendo Commune of Kibuye Prefecture in west central Rwanda. The Presbyterian Church established a presence at Biguhu in the 1950s when Kirinda parish designated the area as a "field of evangelism." In 1967, the EPR elevated Biguhu to parish status, making it the ninth Presbyterian parish in the country. At that time, they constructed a modest church building at the summit of Biguhu hill and a parsonage just behind. The activities of the parish gradually expanded to include a health center, a technical school, and a variety of development services, and Biguhu gained some prestige within the denomination, producing several prominent church leaders and benefiting from the presence of several missionaries. A small commercial and residential community focused around the church developed on Biguhu and several neighboring hills. The prominence of Biguhu both within the church and as a regional center, however, was limited by its inaccessibility.

Mwendo Commune, the political unit that included Biguhu at the time of the genocide, was less densely populated than many other rural areas of Rwanda, with a population density of 285 people per square kilometer in 1991 – compared, for example, with neighboring Bwakira where the population density was 343 people per square kilometer[1] – but

---

[1] République Rwandaise, *Recensement général de la population et de l'habitat au 15 août 1991: Résulats provisoire* (Kigali: Service National de Recensement, December 1992). The most densely populated regions of Rwanda, such as the communes surrounding the

the commune's location along the continental divide between the Congo River and the Nile severely limited its capacity to support agriculture, so overpopulation remained a serious problem. The hills in Mwendo are especially high and steep-sided, particularly in sectors closest to the Congo-Nile Crest, leaving much of the land too steep to cultivate and other areas subject to severe soil degradation. As a result, poverty in the region was severe, and famine occurred regularly. As one farmer told me, "This is an unproductive region. You plant your farm, you work hard, but you harvest almost nothing."[2]

The economic prospects of the area around Biguhu parish were further limited by its remote location. Lying at the southern end of Mwendo commune, Biguhu was initially accessible only by foot, but two roads were constructed in the 1970s, one linking Biguhu to the seat of the subprefecture, Birambo, the other linking Biguhu to Kirinda, running along the Nyabarongo River that divided Gikongoro Prefecture from Kibuye. This second road, though much more direct, had fallen into disrepair by the early 1990s and was passable only by foot or motorcycle. The Gitarama–Birambo–Kibuye road ran through the northwest corner of Mwendo commune, but Biguhu itself was an hour's drive from the road, while the nearest paved road was more than two hours away.[3] After heavy rains, the road to Birambo became nearly impassable. Because no public buses or "taxis" (minivans used as private buses) served Biguhu even in good weather, and because most people lacked access to a private car, traveling out of the community generally required several hours of walking, either north to Birambo or east to Kirinda.

Despite its isolation, Biguhu became a fairly important center for the Presbyterian Church. The church building at the summit of Biguhu hill housed the church offices, Sunday worship services, catechism classes, Bible studies, and various church meetings. A technical school, the buildings for several development projects, and houses for the pastor, teachers, and other church employees were clustered around the parish hall.

---

southern city of Butare – Huye, Mbazi, and Shyanda – have population densities of 705, 639, and 645 people per square kilometer, respectively.

[2] Interview in Biguhu, December 23, 1992.

[3] Two roads connected Kibuye city to the center of the country, the better and more widely traveled linked Kibuye to the capital directly through Gitarama and bypassed both Mwendo and Bwakira communes. The Gitarama–Birambo–Kibuye road was a secondary route that provided access from Kibuye to Butare and the south of the country and passed through Kirinda. In the 1990s, Kibuye was the only prefecture without any paved highways, though a project to pave the main Gitarama–Kibuye road was underway when the war stopped progress in 1994.

A health center stood on an adjoining hill, and a minor commercial center, with small shops and homes and an open square where a weekly market was held, lay a short distance further up the road.

In contrast to Kirinda, however, the activities of Biguhu parish were much less centralized. The parish covered a large area that included parts of five sectors – Ruganda, Shoba, Rucura, Biguhu, and Gisayura – and many church members lived more than an hour's walk from the parish center. The parish was divided into fifteen basic ecclesial communities (BECs), known as chapels, each with its own program of activities, community council, and chapel building. Each community held weekly prayer and Bible study meetings, Sunday school for children, and, most weeks, a Sunday worship service; the entire church membership gathered in the main sanctuary only on the first Sunday of each month and for Easter and Christmas services. Many of the chapels also sponsored development projects. Three evangelists and six catechists assisted the parish pastor in overseeing the activities of the basic communities, but community members themselves organized and directed most chapel community activities.[4]

Other than the parish hall, the largest church presence on Biguhu Hill was the health center. In 1980, the medical service of the EPR established a health center on a hill adjoining Biguhu, only the fourth Presbyterian health center in the country. The national church improved and enlarged the health center at Biguhu in 1989, constructing new buildings and expanding the center's health programs and staff. By 1992, the center served approximately one hundred patients per day, provided beds for ten to twelve patients, offered educational programs three times per week, and maintained a nutritional program that served fifty people per day and provided food supplements to thirty children. The center employed four nurses and two additional staff. The state paid the salaries of two of the nurses, but the operations of the center were otherwise supported through fees, donations from the EPR, and charitable contributions. Compassion, a nongovernmental organization based in the United States, provided funding and food assistance for the nutritional center.[5]

As with the religious activities of Biguhu church, the educational and development activities of the parish were decentralized, encouraging active participation and grassroots organization within the community. In response to a government initiative in the 1980s, the Biguhu parish

---

[4] Interview in Kirinda, June 16, 1992.
[5] Interview in Biguhu, July 11, 1992.

began a CERAI. The Biguhu CERAI offered a three-year, post-primary, general technical education to both male and female teens. The church constructed classrooms for the CERAI near the parish center along the road to the health center, and it provided housing for the director and some of the teachers. The government paid all of the salaries and regulated the curriculum. The church also operated, with government financial assistance, six grade schools scattered throughout the territory of the parish. People within the parish identified primary education as an important priority of the pastor.[6]

Biguhu parish's most extensive programs were in the domain of economic development. A carpentry shop, located just behind the church building, was constructed in 1988 with a grant from the Reformed Church of Belgium that also covered the cost of carpentry tools. The shop produced high-quality, hand-made, hand-tooled furniture, primarily on commission from people in the surrounding area. Begun with four employees, the shop added two workers in 1990 and four more in 1992 to accommodate a growing business. The ten employees, who had all finished CERAI, came from the Biguhu area, although not all were Presbyterians. A cooperative association of the employees, Cooperative des Jeunes Menuisiers (Cooperative of Young Carpenters, COJEM) owned and directed the shop.[7]

A large brick silo building stood along the road between the CERAI and the health center. The silo was built with money from the Swiss Reformed Church and had bins for storing beans, soybeans, and sorghum. Members, those who purchased a 50-franc (about 1992 US$0.15) annual membership card, could sell their harvest to the cooperative. The silo cooperative then sold the beans, soybeans, and sorghum at a price far below seasonal market value, though higher than the purchase price. While anyone could buy from the silo, members were given preference. If the stocks ran out, the cooperative could purchase additional stock, saving consumers money by buying in bulk. In 1992, the silo cooperative had 412 members. In addition to the food stock, the silo ran a small store that sold farming supplies such as fertilizers, seeds, and hoes. In principle, profits would be distributed among the members, but in practice returns

---

[6] One person said that the church, "advised before the school year begins for all Christians who have children in the home having reached the age to begin primary school to be certain that they enroll, because if you do not send them, you risk creating delinquency and banditry" (Gituntu, December 26, 1992).

[7] Interviews in Biguhu, July 10, 1992.

from sales went to cover salaries and other operating expenses, and the silo had never shown a profit.[8]

The carpentry shop and the silo were cooperatives owned and operated by their members and technically independent of the church, but they were projects initiated by the parish, and they continued to receive advice and technical support from the church's economic development program, the Service de Développement Rural de Biguhu (SDRB). The EPR founded the SDRB in 1983 with a five-year grant provided jointly by the United Church of Belgium and the Belgian government. A Belgian agronomist initially directed the program, and then a Swiss missionary couple took over in 1986. The couple worked with a Rwandan agronomist who in turn took over as director at the end of their three-year term in 1989.[9] He directed the SDRB until his murder in April 1994.

The SDRB supported a wide range of programs. It attempted to combat erosion, which is a severe problem in the area. The SDRB operated two model fields, where new crops were introduced and peasants were trained in new farming techniques. For example, the SDRB ran a small agroforestry project where it cultivated several fast-growing leguminous trees to provide alternatives to eucalyptus, a non-indigenous tree that, although popular because of its rapid growth, depletes soils and contributes to erosion. Farmers could see in the model fields how the trees could be used for soil erosion prevention, firewood, fertilizer, and animal fodder and could obtain saplings free of charge. The model fields also demonstrated radical terracing, a means of preventing erosion and allowing farming on steep terrain by setting up narrow fields in steps up the hillside.

The silo and carpentry cooperatives were only two of thirty cooperative societies supported by the SDRB. Other groups produced honey, raised cattle and marketed milk, raised chickens and rabbits, and cultivated communal fields. The SDRB also encouraged the formation of savings and rotating *tontines*, credit societies. These tontines gathered a small group of people, generally neighbors, who each contributed a sum on a weekly or monthly basis. Each week or month one member of the group, determined through a random method or according to need depending on the group's rules, received the entire pot. Each member was thus able to obtain periodically a large sum of money that could be used

---

[8] Interview in Biguhu, July 11, 1992.

[9] Géras Mutimura, "Le passé et l'avenir du Service de Développement Rural de Biguhu," mimeograph, December 1992. Interviews July 10, 1992; February 7, 1993.

to pay school fees, to buy clothes, or to invest in a business venture of some sort. Many of the cooperative groups grew out of the basic ecclesial communities, the chapels, helping to expand the focus of these groups beyond prayer, Bible study, and worship to more material concerns. The cooperatives, however, did not limit their membership to Presbyterians but were open to anyone in the community, though the majority of participants were Presbyterians.[10]

The six most active cooperative societies in Biguhu – the silo, carpentry shop, three farming and animal-raising cooperatives, and a farming and honey-producing cooperative – joined together in 1991 to form an *intergroupement*, an association of associations, Twishyire hamwe Bahinzi Borozi Turengerane (Farmers and Animal Raisers Joining Together to Help Themselves, TWIBATURE). TWIBATURE had gradually assumed responsibility for some of the activities formerly directed by the SDRB, while the SDRB focused increasingly on agricultural education and on supporting the formation of new cooperative societies.[11]

One particularly successful effort supported by TWIBATURE was a "Bank of Solidarity." Previously the nearest bank to Biguhu was several hours' hike away in Birambo, the seat of the sub-prefecture. This made depositing money or obtaining a loan an inconvenient and time consuming process – and a stumbling block to associations wishing to obtain money for capital expenditures. Many peasants, particularly women, had difficulty obtaining credit in traditional banks, including the public bank set up specifically to support development. Hence, in 1988 the SDRB supported the founding of a cooperative bank. Initially controlled by COPARU, a farming cooperative for people in Ruganda Sector, when the bank grew too large for a small group to manage effectively, it was turned over to the six associations in TWIBATURE. In conjunction with TWIBATURE the bank was directed by an association of 274 members, but anyone in the area was free to use the bank.[12]

In 1992 the bank had 272 savings accounts that earned 2 percent interest on deposits, including thirty-eight accounts for associations. Loans were given for a term of one year at 24 percent interest. Individual loans ranged from 20,000 to 30,000 Rwandan francs (US$130–200 in 1992). As the director of the bank explained, "Most loans are used for agriculture

---

[10] Interviews in Biguhu, July 10, 1992, and February 7, 1993.
[11] Interviews in Biguhu, July 11, 1992; December 22–24, 1992; Mutimura, "Le passé et l'avenir."
[12] Interview in Biguhu, December 22, 1992.

and to pay school fees for students in secondary schools. Sometimes the loans are used to buy animals or for construction, but most are used for agricultural purposes."[13] Associations could take out larger loans. For example, COPARU took out a 150,000 FRw loan to buy goats and build stables for livestock, and COJEM, the carpentry cooperative, took out a 75,000 FRw loan to buy cattle and goats. The bank gave out approximately fifty loans each year and, according to the bank's administrator, enjoyed an extremely high rate of repayment. Nevertheless the bank cooperative had moved toward encouraging people to create associations to obtain loans rather than seeking loans as individuals, along the lines of the Grameen Bank model,[14] because the groups provided a security network to guarantee repayment, thus protecting both the debtors and the bank. By 1992, many of the loans were being given to tontines. An office for the bank was built at the back of the SDRB director's home.[15]

STRUCTURES OF POWER AND EMPOWERMENT IN BIGUHU

In the Biguhu area, as in other rural communities, the church occupied a dominant position in the economy. The church, health center, and CERAI provided the only major employment in the area outside of the retail trade. In contrast to Kirinda, however, where the church helped to create and reinforce class divisions through its distribution of employment and resources, the church in Biguhu played a role in helping to bridge the gap between the rich and the poor and helping to prevent the emergence of the hegemonic control of a single elite group. Although salaried church employees certainly enjoyed benefits such as free housing, one rarely encountered in Biguhu ostentatious display of wealth of the type regularly exhibited in Kirinda. Furthermore, my research assistants and I heard almost no complaints of corruption in Biguhu. Instead, residents spoke warmly of the honesty and good intentions of their pastor, the SDRB agronomist, school teachers, and other church elite.

---

[13] Interview in Biguhu, December 23, 1992.
[14] The Grameen Bank is a large and highly successful development project in Bangladesh that loans small amounts of money to small groups, primarily of women, who are collectively responsible to see that the loans are repaid. Cf., Susan Holcombe, *Managing to Empower: The Grameen Bank's Experience of Poverty Alleviation* (Atlantic Highlands, NJ: Zed Books, 1998); David Bornstein, *The Price of a Dream: The Story of the Grameen Bank and the Idea that Is Helping the Poor to Change Their Lives* (Chicago: University of Chicago Press, 1997).
[15] Interiews in Biguhu, December 23, 1992.

A variety of factors explain why Biguhu failed to develop a system of reciprocal exchange between elites and instead developed a culture that emphasized social equality rather than hierarchies of status. One factor was the relatively recent creation of Biguhu compared to the Kirinda parish. Because it was not one of the historic centers of the church, Biguhu had not produced a large number of pastors and others who had risen to national prominence within the church, and the patrimonial system had not had as much time to develop and become entrenched. The church had, however, produced a few prominent individuals, including the national director of the Rwandan Bible Society and the principal of the IPK, who was deeply involved in Kirinda's patrimonial system. Furthermore, the elite group in Kirinda had emerged only in the 1970s and 1980s, after Habyarimana's coup, when the Biguhu parish was already in existence.

Another contributing factor was Biguhu's relative poverty as a parish. While Kirinda had several national offices, a large hospital, and other programs that brought in substantial resources, Biguhu's programs were relatively modest. The parish simply had fewer jobs to distribute and other resources to attract clients to a patrimonial system. This relative poverty does not, however, explain why the resources that were available were not used to develop reciprocal ties among the elites and to establish dependence on the part of the masses. As Mahmood Mamdani's idea of "decentralized despotism" suggests, isolation and poverty do not prevent the development of strongly authoritarian and patrimonial social structures.[16]

The emergence of a distinction between Kirinda and Biguhu, thus, seems to have been due not simply to material differences between the two parishes but also to ideological or theological differences. Over the years, the Biguhu parish had developed an egalitarian ethic that emphasized the equality of all Christians, the rights of the poor to expect a better life, and the need for community solidarity and cooperation. This ethic seems to have developed as a result of both influential individuals who promoted these ideas and also the institutions that they set up. All of the factors mentioned in Chapter 4 as important changes in Rwanda's churches in the 1980s – the emergence of liberation theologies, ideas of sustainable development, decentralized church structures, and the proliferation of lay organizations – could be witnessed in Biguhu and seemed to have shaped the church there into a more progressive institution.

---

[16] Mahmood Mamdani, *Citizen and Subject: Contemporary Africa and the Legacy of Late Colonialism* (Princeton: Princeton University Press, 1996).

Biguhu had been served by several pastors who had played an important part in promoting the interests of the poor and encouraging them to join together to support one another. Pastor Stéphane, who came to Biguhu in 1992, fit this mold quite well. He was a respected intellectual who had traveled and studied in Europe, yet he maintained a relatively modest aspect. Parishioners praised him for the example of Christian living he presented by addressing them with kindness and respect and not taking advantage of them for his personal gain. As one example of his relationship with the peasantry, Pastor Stéphane owned a pickup truck that he used regularly to transport those who needed the attention of a doctor from the Biguhu health center to Kirinda hospital. While it was customary for those with vehicles to charge high rates for transporting people, Pastor Stéphane asked only that riders contribute as much as they were able to the cost of fuel. As he passed through the countryside, he let peasants hitch a ride on the truck bed or in the cab, if there was room, without charge.

Pastor Stéphane's sermons and other theological messages showed the influence of new theological ideas that he had developed through his studies and through earlier employment in the EPR Department of Theology. His teachings emphasized responsibility to help those in need and, in contrast to most pastors, who avoided controversial topics, directly addressed current social and political issues of the day. For example, in his sermon on Christmas, probably the most widely attended service of the year, the pastor used the story of Jesus' humble birth to discuss the failures of multipartyism:

You Christians who are fighting for political parties, do not be like [the rulers of Jesus' day]. On the contrary, seek you first the kingdom of God. Do not respond with violence to those parties that trick you into going wherever, to do whatever. They run behind things that seem useless rather than accepting the search for God who gives peace! You men who are free, leave these things, because it is high time to receive Jesus Christ as your savior. There are people who are pushed to do evil to their neighbor. Leave these things, because the Word of God does not ordain that each should fight against his comrade. ...

The Banyarwanda say, *Imana y'irirwa ahandi igataha i Rwanda* ["God passes all the day elsewhere but returns to Rwanda for the night."] This proverb describes for us how God loves Rwanda, with all of these problems our country has known, even though there has been violence that is not inexplicable.

You Christians be prudent. You can follow the path of the political parties, but it is ultimately not the political parties that show you the path to follow. The Bible tells us: Happy are the poor because they will come to God. Happy are the poor in heart for they will be saved. Happy are the poor who weep because it is they who will have their eyes wiped dry by the spirit. Happy are the oppressed, for they will have eternal life.[17]

In other words, those who are being persecuted – such as Tutsi and human rights activists – are on the side of God. In contrast to the Abarokore, who preached complete rejection of political party membership and involvement in the political process as inherently corrupting, Pastor Stéphane did not discourage participation in parties but urged that people be directed by a higher law that forbids certain types of conduct, such as the use of violence.

In addition to promoting political moderation, Pastor Stéphane also urged people to be charitable and concerned for one another. Speaking to a catechism class for adults who were to be baptized in the church, Pastor Stéphane first reminded them of the proverb, "The riches of the stupid are eaten by sorcerers."[18] Then he encouraged them to use their resources wisely to help those in need:

As Christians we have to give offerings to help the poor – not only the gifts that you are required to bring at baptism. There are some people who forget after their baptism that as Christians they are called to charity. But as Christians, we must keep giving to the poor. For example, it is the time for sorghum harvest now, and you can bring some of your harvest to share with those who do not have enough.[19]

In the interviews I conducted in the community, many people were proud that they had themselves contributed from their own harvest to the church, and in Biguhu, unlike in Kirinda, there was little fear that the assistance was being misused to help those already privileged. Instead, people seemed confident that their aid went to help widows and orphans and the sick.

The significant point here is not the personal characteristics of Pastor Stéphane but the manner in which he was received by the members of the parish. In fact, his calls for charity and community followed in the tradition of pastors who had served the parish in the past. The founding pastor of the parish, Oscar Rwasibo, had served the community for nearly twenty years, and he had worked hard to shape the character of the congregation. He was known as a humble man who lived simply and worked

[17] Sermon, December 25, 1992.
[18] Catechism class in Biguhu, July 9, 1992.
[19] Address to adult catechism class, July 10, 1992.

hard. The congregation came to expect a similar character from subsequent pastors. When one of the original pastor's successors in the early 1990s attempted to act more like a typical pastor, enriching himself and maintaining distance from his parishioners, the people in the community rebelled and refused to support him. Eventually community complaints forced the national EPR office to transfer him out of the parish.[20]

The employees of the development projects had also played a major role in the construction of an egalitarian ethic in Biguhu. Like many development projects in Rwanda, the SDRB was founded in 1983 in a manner that many development experts today would criticize as patrimonial and unsustainable. The office of development of the EPR and the international donors established a set of objectives for the project, and an outside organizer, a Belgian, came into the community to implement them. The project was run *by* the church *for* the peasant farmers in the community who, as a consequence of its method of implantation, had little connection to the project. Hence, the SDRB initially had little impact on the community, and when the outside organizer left, the project fell swiftly into decline.[21]

The Swiss couple who came to restart the project in 1986 changed its focus to allow greater peasant participation and to foster a greater sense of ownership among participants. The couple presented themselves as facilitators for development work in the area and as sources of information rather than as the directors of the project, and therefore they sought to turn the operation and direction of the SDRB over to the peasants themselves. They offered training in their areas of expertise, the husband teaching methods of alternative farming and fighting erosion, the wife teaching carpentry and cabinetmaking. They created an administrative council composed of representatives from each of the groups, the parish, the EPR development office, and the commune, and this council assumed responsibility for setting the SDRB program.[22]

The Swiss couple also hired as an assistant a Rwandan agronomist, Géras Mutimura, who took responsibility for the project when the couple returned to Switzerland in 1989. Mutimura continued the process of converting the SDRB into a grassroots, peasant-run association. He encouraged each of the SDRB groups to become an independent cooperative,

[20] Interviews in Biguhu, December 22, 1992; February 6, 1993; in Kirinda, July 15, 1992; and Johannesburg, South Africa, August 1998.
[21] Mutimura, "Le passé et l'avenir;" interview December 22, 1992.
[22] Interview, December 22, 1992.

owned and directed by participants rather than by the church or the SDRB and urged collaboration between the cooperatives, such as the formation of TWIBATURE, believing that these small intergroup organizations would be better able to innovate and take independent initiatives than the larger SDRB council. The administrative council selected two peasant organizers from within the community to assist the director and support the operation of the various cooperatives.[23]

Mutimura explained the philosophy of development behind his activities:

The work with the peasants of Biguhu has been based on non-directivity. The peasants are considered the motors of their own development. The agents of the SDRB have stimulated peasant initiatives and have supported peasant participation. The approach to the work rests on a commitment to self-development of the individual within the group.[24]

This approach sought to avoid repeating the failures of earlier development programs in Africa, which encouraged dependence on outside support and initiative and disregarded the knowledge of local residents, sometimes leading to environmental or other disasters. Hence, the project offered information and new technologies and products and assisted groups with problems, such as marketing, but the director left the initiative for new programs and other innovations to the groups themselves and to individuals. For example, the model fields were a method of introducing new crops and new farming techniques, but no effort was made to force farmers to adopt them. The agronomist provided information, and if farmers liked what they saw in the model fields, he would explain to them how to imitate the methods or provide seeds or seedlings.

The people of Biguhu held Mutimura in high regard, because his philosophy of development was reflected in his personal comportment. He had received a secondary school degree in Zaire, worked with Europeans, and traveled to Italy for a month in 1992 for training, but he consciously sought to approach peasants as equals. He owned a motorcycle to travel around the large parish, but he did not own a car, and despite the extensive development expenditures in Biguhu since he started working there in 1986, he had not acquired obvious wealth buying cattle or land or building a home; the few nice possessions he owned, such as a camera and stereo, had been given as gifts from the Swiss couple. The local

---

[23] Mutimura, "Le passé et l'avenir;" interviews July 10, 1992; December 22, 1992.
[24] Mutimuta, "Le passé et l'avenit du SDRB."

population respected him for his integrity and his strong advocacy of their concerns.[25]

Mutimura tried to set a good example of tolerance and modesty. For instance, when a man jokingly told Mutimura's daughter as we walked past to watch out because the *umuzungu*, the white man, would get her, a common joke in Rwanda, Mutimura stopped and very quietly confronted the man. He explained that even though it was a joke, it was dangerous to teach children to think of themselves as different from the whites, because that plants the seeds for a sense of inferiority. According to people in the parish, he took the same approach to ethnic chauvinism when he heard it. He confronted people gently, and patiently explained why the problem in Rwanda was not the Tutsi but rather the wealthy elite, Tutsi and Hutu alike, who exploited the poor. According to one anecdote that I heard, the agronomist went to a wedding at the house of a peasant and, according to custom, he and other elite present were offered the few chairs as a sign of respect, while the peasants sat on the ground. He refused to take a chair and told the farmer hosting the marriage that the people he should show respect to were his neighbors and family. After all, if he ran into trouble, none of these elite would come to help him out, but instead he would have to depend upon the people he had seated on the ground, his neighbors, friends, and family.

The point of this discussion is not that agronomist Mutimura or Pastor Stéphane or other leaders of Biguhu parish were saints but rather that they promulgated through both their words and actions an ideology that valued the worth of each individual and that opposed hierarchy, exploitation, and oppression. Both men had embraced theological ideas and Biblical interpretations similar in some ways to Latin American Liberation theologies, regarding God as particularly concerned about the plight of the oppressed and the poor. They also were influenced, Mutimura in particular, by modern ideas of sustainable development that emphasized fighting against poverty and raising the standards of the poorest citizens rather than just increasing aggregate national wealth. Eschewing the class privileges that they would otherwise have enjoyed, they sought to empower the peasant farmers in the community to overcome fatalism and act for their own development.

One important factor that shaped the nature of the Christian message proclaimed in this parish was a history of Tutsi leadership. The founding

[25] Interviews December 22–24, 1992; February 6–7, 1993.

pastor had been a Tutsi, as were both Pastor Stéphane and agronomist Mutimura. As Tutsi in the post-revolutionary period, these men were by definition socially marginal to at least some degree, which made it possible for them to empathize with other marginal groups in society, such as poor farmers, women, single mothers, Twa, and other groups. Tutsi leadership is not, of course, sufficient to explain the emergence of a populist theology, as many parishes had Tutsi leadership but did not promote democratic ideas. In fact, many Tutsi did not embrace populist ideas but instead struggled to overcome their marginalization and gain acceptance among the elite. In Rwanda as in other settings, the mere experience of marginalization does not necessarily produce sympathies for other oppressed groups but merely makes developing those sympathies somewhat more possible. In several other parishes I studied, Tutsi leaders had not embraced a similar philosophy, while some of those who did, like Father Sibomana, were Hutu.[26]

The public acceptance of the egalitarian philosophy in Biguhu was furthered not only by the advocacy of people like Stéphane and Mutimura but by the institutions that they set up. Both the parish's fourteen chapels and the numerous development cooperatives brought together members of the Biguhu community in autonomous organizations that they themselves ran. The vigorous basic ecclesial communities allowed laypersons to take substantial responsibility for organizing and sustaining their own spiritual lives. An administrative committee ran each, and members shared responsibilities for organizing scripture reading and leading prayers. Each development cooperative had a board of directors, and the largest had subcommittees for administration, accounting, and other purposes. Members of the cooperatives elected their employees, such as the director of the bank and the administrator of the silo. The chapels and cooperatives thus provided members with practical experience in democratic process and offered many opportunities for people to take leadership roles. Such experience in self-organization and empowerment undoubtedly affected people's attitudes toward power and authority.

Popular involvement in the church and in development organizations and the egalitarian philosophies promoted by church leaders had

---

[26] When I presented my research on this case to a class at the University of Rwanda in 1996, several students conjectured that only Tutsi had been able to become progressive in Rwanda, because of their experience of marginalization. This perspective underestimates both the number of Tutsi who rejected populist ideas and the number of Hutu who embraced them.

a substantial impact on the community. The peasants in Biguhu displayed a greater awareness of their capacity to improve their own conditions of life than did their counterparts in other communities, who looked to the church or the government or the international community to provide opportunities for them. People in Biguhu did not regard the church as a source of wealth. As one farmer said, "The church cannot do much to help the poor. The church is poor too here, because the people are poor."[27] While this belief that the church is poor might seem a negative reflection on the church at first glance, it in fact demonstrates several important points. First, people understood that they themselves composed the church. Second, rather then being dependent upon the church as an outside entity to assist them, people believed that, as members of the church, they had to assist themselves and their neighbors. Several quotes from interviews in Biguhu demonstrate this attitude:

The role of the church in addressing the problems [of the region] is very difficult, because it is poor. ... Christians must help one another, this is the word from the leaders of the church. A Christian ought to visit his fellow who is sick or who is facing all sorts of problems.[28]

The church helps some people who have houses that need roofs repaired. Certain youths come to cover their houses. Also, when there is a widow or widower without children, the church can help. When there is someone who dies without family, the church can put up the funds for a burial. ... People go to the church [for help] because it is nearby, but the commune is far away. People are afraid of the authority of the state. You can go to the church to get assistance without encountering problems.[29]

How can the church assist us when it is itself poor? The advice the church often gives is this: Give to the poor if you are more rich than they.[30]

The population in Biguhu had a strong sense of community responsibility. Despite their poverty, many members of the parish gave generously of their harvests to help the destitute (widows and orphans in particular) or the war refugees. In 1991, the youth group, which involved nearly 200 young people, began a program of assisting the poor by providing them with labor. The group gathered each Wednesday to work for a needy family, to till their land or repair their home.[31]

[27] Interview in Biguhu, December 24, 1992.
[28] Interview in Biguhu, December 26, 1992.
[29] Interview in Biguhu, December 24, 1992.
[30] Interview in Kirinda, December 28, 1992.
[31] Interview in Biguhu, December 23, 1992.

A commercial venture launched by TWIBATURE in 1992 demonstrates the degree to which the participants in the projects were inspired to take initiative for their own development. The six member organizations of TWIBATURE pooled their funds to purchase a boutique in the commercial district of Biguhu to market their goods, raise funds, and circumvent the exploitative commercial system. Wealthy farmers from the area owned most of the approximately twenty shops and cabarets in Biguhu that sold soap, detergent, cloth, candles, palm oil, tomato paste, and other household necessities, and they contributed to an economic system that allowed the rich to gain wealth at the expense of the general population. Most of the shop owners held large tracts of land, which allowed them to leave fields periodically fallow and thus to preserve or rejuvenate the soils and so gain higher output. They also generally owned cattle that provided manure for fertilizer that further increased the productivity of the land. In contrast, poor farmers had to maintain all of their fields constantly in cultivation, thus denuding the soils, and they did not generally have animals to provide fertilizer. The majority of farmers in the area had difficulty raising sufficient food to supply their families, yet they often needed to sell part of their harvest or to rent or sell parcels of land to obtain cash. The local merchants benefited from this situation both because they bought the farmers' harvest at discount rates and because a good portion of the money was then returned to them when the poor farmers bought products from their stores.[32]

In buying a shop, the peasants in TWIBATURE sought to act as their own middle person and thus to return the profits from the purchase of necessities to the groups that they themselves controlled. The store bought the inputs needed by the various associations – seeds for cabbage and carrots, hoes, products for the carpentry shop, plastic jars for honey, veterinary supplies – and sold honey and other products made by the cooperatives. The store also sold Bibles and newspapers brought from the capital and gave out pamphlets on AIDS and on Christian marriage to those who purchased items. The initiative for the store arose from within TWIBATURE, and the member associations provided the funds to purchase the building.[33]

The experience that peasants in Biguhu gained in organizing themselves and the greater financial security and group solidarity that they

[32] On the problems of food availability and distribution in Rwanda, see Pottier, "Taking Stock."
[33] Interviews, July 10–11, 1992.

enjoyed as members of the cooperatives made it possible for them to defend their interests and assert their rights more effectively. A conflict that arose in the silo cooperative demonstrates the degree to which the poor in Biguhu were willing and able to defend their interests. In the silo cooperative, the vast majority of members were poor farmers, but merchants and others whose primary income did not derive from agriculture also cultivated fields and used the silo. As is often the case in cooperative associations, because of their level of education and economic power, the non-peasants were initially represented disproportionately on the administrative council of the silo. When, however, evidence of embezzlement surfaced around 1990, the peasants joined together and voted to remove the non-peasants from the council and replace them with peasants.[34] The original situation, in which the wealthy used the silo to improve their position, fits well the role that Peter Uvin argued development programs generally played in Rwanda during this period.[35] Yet the actions taken by the small farmers to increase their power demonstrate that the reinforcement of the class system was not inevitable. With their small scale and democratic organization, cooperatives provided opportunities for common people to empower themselves, particularly when they had the support of a powerful institution like the local church.

As a result of the factors discussed in the preceding text, in Biguhu little evidence existed of the development of a hegemonic group. The church, business, and government elite did not maintain particularly strong social ties, and many factors served to break down the barriers between people of different income levels. Without recourse to illegal or quasi-legal financial ventures, the income differential between church employees and the peasants was much less extreme than in many places. The proliferation of independent development projects created economic opportunities for many people who might otherwise have faced dire impoverishment. Many of the projects made it possible for peasants to purchase livestock, the traditional symbol of prosperity in Rwanda and a valuable tool for revitalizing denuded soils. They also provided employment to a number of peasants, including the carpenters, directors of the bank and silo, workers on the cooperative farm, and assistants to the SDRB who all received small salaries that augmented their families' agricultural income. While the projects did not make people wealthy, they did create opportunity for a number of people, and they also helped protect members

[34] Interview in Biguhu, December 22, 1992.
[35] Uvin, *Aiding Violence*, pp. 82–101.

from exploitation by the wealthy. The silo, for example, was designed to protect members from the cruelties of the market which ordinarily forced them to sell their produce at a low price at harvest when supply was abundant only to buy some of it back at a much higher price later when demand was high.[36] Positions of authority both within the cooperatives and in church groups were not, as in Kirinda, the exclusive domain of the elite. For example, the administrator of the silo was a single woman in her 30s from a poor farming family. She also served as president of the church youth group in which capacity she was the primary organizer of the weekly youth work projects for the poor.[37] Similarly, the director of the Bank of Solidarity was a peasant farmer chosen for his honesty and leadership skills despite his lack of elite status in the community.[38]

In short, the church in Biguhu served as a hindrance to the concentration of wealth, status, and power by a small elite in the community and helped to equalize conditions, socially and economically. The church helped to provide both an institutional and ideological basis from which the masses of the population could challenge injustice and exploitation. While community concerns focused primarily on local conditions, the church activities also raised the consciousness of the population about national political issues and linked them to national networks. The SDRB worked closely with Iwacu, a center in Kigali that provided training and support for cooperatives throughout the country.[39] Various cooperative members from Biguhu went to workshops and conferences at Iwacu as representatives of the SDRB and its constituent programs. The Biguhu silo sold memberships to a national cooperative for farmers, *Twibumbe Bahinzi*, that provided a national support network to members. The agronomist, Mutimura, was an outspoken member of the PSD, the party that had most identified itself with the plight of the poor, and the fact that the cooperative store sold pro-opposition newspapers suggests that these sentiment were shared by others.

Challenges to the status quo and public support for opposition parties put those local political leaders and business people linked to the regime on the defensive. The councilor of Shoba sector, who was also vice-president of the Biguhu parish council, complained that, "With all

---

[36] David Waller, *Rwanda: Which Way Now?* (Oxford: Oxfam, 1993); Newbury, "Recent Debates," p. 210; Pottier, "Taking Stock."
[37] Interview in Biguhu, December 23, 1992.
[38] Interview in Biguhu, December 23, 1992.
[39] Cf., Iwacu, "Rapport d'Activitiés 1992," Kigali 1993.

of these political changes, this period is difficult for me, since I am in the MRND and everyone says that those of us in this party are fools."[40] Obviously, the fact that someone should hold a prominent position in both the government and the church indicates that the Biguhu parish did not entirely refrain from reinforcing status, but many elite did perceive the church as a threat. Supporters of the regime tried to thwart the church's efforts to support empowerment of the population, but their efforts were only partially successful. For example, in mid-1992, the SDRB sent a farmer to Kigali for training at Iwacu in a program of political education that the center had initiated part of its attempt to develop civil society.[41] The seminar informed participants about their political rights and responsibilities in the new multiparty system, not advocating any particular political party over another but rather explaining the workings of the system and the rights to organize and to vote according to conscience rather than according to the dictates of the local political and economic (and spiritual) elite. Participants were expected to return to their home areas and educate fellow peasants. Before Biguhu's representative at this training event even returned from Kigali, however, the burgomaster of Mwendo Commune contacted the director of the SDRB to inquire about the program and to declare that the peasant *animateur* would not be allowed to meet with the peasants in the commune. According to the director, the political authorities were afraid that the program could result in the development of a peasant political party that could provide a fundamental challenge to the existing structure of power.[42]

Biguhu was not immune to the tensions that were gripping the rest of the country. Letters from the burgomaster of Mwendo to the prefect of Kibuye in 1992 and 1993 indicate an expansion of violence. An October 1992 security report described several recent violent incidents near Biguhu. On September 30 in Shoba sector, three men beat a woman who died several days later. After a communal official in Muko commune of Gikongoro had written an open letter warning the people of Mutuntu sector of potential banditry at Mukungu market, a group of eight men arrived in Mutuntu from Muko on September 30, 1992, intending to prospect for gold in the area. Although they had the appropriate travel

[40] Interview in Biguhu, December 28, 1992.
[41] IWACU, "Rapport d'Activités 1992."
[42] Interview in Biguhu, July 11, 1992.

papers and had checked in with the local officials, some residents accused them of being bandits who were planning an attack. All eight plus the Mwendo resident in whose home they had stayed, were lynched. Finally, On October 3, an unidentified group burned the home of a woman in Ruganda sector.[43] Numerous additional violent incidents over the next year testify to a deteriorating security situation throughout the commune, though most incidents seem to have centered on Kigoma sector, where the communal office for Mwendo was located.[44]

While community leaders in Biguhu could hinder mobilization of the masses, they had difficulty organizing the population toward their own ends, because people were well informed politically and had developed a level of class solidarity. Many of the cooperatives were multiethnic and included non-Presbyterians, facts that members proudly declared. The population of Biguhu was thus more resistant to ethnic mobilization than were people in most other communities. Many parish members regarded the church as a unifying source. The impressions of one woman I interviewed were shared by many others:

The church tells people that the members should stay united and should not fight one another. Christians must act with love. Christians must not go to fight their brothers. If you are a Christian, you can participate in politics, but you can also decide not to, and politics should not cause people to fight.[45]

As we shall see in the next chapter, this had tangible implications for the conduct of the genocide in Mwendo Commune. The community in Biguhu was not well organized to carry out the massacres, and Biguhu parish was regarded as a hindrance to the plans of those who organized the genocide. Hence, the parish buildings did not become a location for massacres, and people from outside Biguhu had to intervene to organize the slaughter of Biguhu's Tutsi population. During the genocide, the church and its programs became targets for violence and destruction.

---

[43] Letter no. 0.425/04.17.02, from Gabriel Muragizi, Burgomaster of Mwendo, addressed to the Prefect of Kibuye, concerning "Report of those who were killed, houses burned in Ruganda sector" (Raporo y'abntu bishe, Inzu yahiye mori Segiteri Ruganda), Mwendo, October 2, 1992, found among papers in Office of the Prefecture, Kibuye.

[44] Letters from the burgomaster discuss, for example, burning of forests in Kigoma sector in February 1993, a revenge murder in March, another murder and an attack on the Kabageni market in August, the burning of a mill and homes as well as another murder in September.

[45] Interview in Biguhu, December 23, 1992.

LOCAL CHURCHES AND EMPOWERING THE POOR

According to Gramsci, transformations of the structures of power must be preceded by ideological transformations. New groups can gain supremacy only after they have developed a vision for society that the population finds compelling. According to Gramsci:

the supremacy of a social group manifests itself in two ways, as "domination" and as "intellectual and moral leadership". ... A social group can, and indeed must, already exercise "leadership" before winning governmental power (this indeed is one of the principal conditions for the winning of such power) ... .[46]

In Kirinda, the expansion of political freedoms initiated by the democracy movement in the early 1990s made protest against the powerful in the community possible, but the protest that occurred was disjointed and often expressed itself through violent and destructive means. While the population of Kirinda was discontent with the status quo and blamed the established leadership for their problems – and once the loss of authority allowed, the hidden transcript surfaced as public challenges to the status quo – no ideological alternative emerged to provide a plausible vision of a more just potential structure of power. In other words, a crisis arose in Rwanda in which the conditions for class struggle (or "war of position") existed, but intellectual and moral leadership was not sufficiently developed in places such as Kirinda for a new social group to gain power.

The case of Biguhu demonstrates the degree to which churches had the potential to help provide the intellectual and moral leadership necessary for a revolutionary restructuring of society. Church leaders such as the development workers and pastors offered an ideological and theological justification for the assumption of power by the lower classes. The numerous church groups and development cooperatives created an institutional basis from which common people felt more secure to assert their interests. For those in Biguhu involved in the church and its development activities, a vision of a plausible alternative structure of power existed. The moral and intellectual leadership of those sympathetic to the interests of the poor farmers in Biguhu made the population there less susceptible to the efforts by supporters of the existing regime to reassert their own dominance through the ideology of ethnic fear and hatred.

---

[46] Gramsci, *Selections from the Prison Notebooks*, p. 57.

The transformations democratizing churches that I discussed at the end of Chapter 4 and that could be seen clearly in the case of Biguhu affected parishes throughout Rwanda to varying degrees. Many pastors and priests encouraged compassion and charity for the poor but made no theological critique of the system that created poverty, and even the most radical church people in Rwanda did not embrace the marxist revolution promoted in Latin American Liberation Theology. Many clergy were slow to implement structural reforms to decentralize church activities, and even where BECs were present, clergy did not necessarily allow them to function independently. Further, development projects were not inevitably progressive, as they could easily becomes tools within a patrimonial structure. Farming cooperatives, for example, depended on the commune or the church to provide land to cultivate, and this made them open to abuse. Many development projects continued to be implemented in a paternalistic manner, and even formally autonomous grassroots cooperatives were subject to manipulation by elites and integration into patrimonial networks.[47]

Nevertheless, the important changes that began taking place in Rwanda's churches as early as the 1970s had affected to some degree virtually every Christian parish in the country by the early 1990s. The sermons in Biguhu were exceptional within my research for directly addressing ethnic and political party conflict, but the injustices of poverty and the sympathies of God for the poor were common themes for sermons and homilies. For example, a homily delivered at the Catholic cathedral in Butare at the 11 A.M. Sunday mass frequented by the Catholic elite included the following:

Regarding wealth, Jesus sees that those are happy who don't seek wealth. Can it be true that there are people who don't seek to be rich? There are people who steal and kill to become rich. But Jesus himself served as an example. The rich are just people, too. And Jesus shows that you don't have to be rich to be valued as a person... People think that if you suffer it is because God is not with you, but Jesus says otherwise. God is with those who suffer. People think that if you are not successful, God is not with you, but Jesus says otherwise.... The man who has a lot of money but who has abused people to get it, who has stolen or cheated, is he happy? The robbers, are they happy? No. The rich are not happy.... If you don't follow Jesus' word, you are not a Christian. Jesus has provided these lessons to guide our behavior. If you seek only wealth, if you fight others, you are not a Christian.[48]

---

[47] Uvin, *Aiding Violence*, makes this point powerfully.
[48] Homily, 11 A.M. mass, Butare cathedral, January 31, 1993.

While nothing so systematic as the theologies of liberation in Latin America developed in Rwanda, many poor church members that I interviewed in both Catholic and Presbyterian parishes had a surprisingly clear idea that in the conflict between the rich and the poor, God was on the side of the poor. I heard repeatedly from people that "the church is for the poor," even in parishes where church leaders acted as though the church existed for their personal benefit. For example, a few women from the basket project in Kirinda told me in an interview that the main problem in the project was finding a market for their baskets and that only the woman pastor who oversaw the project helped deal with this and other problems. A few minutes later they told me that the church was for the poor, because it helped them with this project. When I asked them how they could say the church helped the poor and helped their project in light of their prior statement that none of the male leaders of the church helped them, one of the women told me: "What we mean is, for example, when you are sick or when you have no money, the people in the church can pull together and plant your fields or repair your home or give you food."[49] In other words, the church helping the poor might mean the poor joining together to help themselves, because the church was as much for them as it was for the rich. Another woman told me, "The church makes it possible for the poor to diminish their misery a little. The church helps the poor, not only the rich. The church is for everyone."[50] The theological idea that God and the Church are for the poor implied not simply that the poor would be rewarded in Heaven but that the poor had rights in this world and that society had certain responsibilities toward them. I found it ironic that the poor used the teachings they heard in Sunday sermons about the injustice of exploiting the poor to condemn the very pastors and priests who gave the sermons for failing themselves to live up to those teachings.

By the 1990s, development projects had become a standard feature of parish life, even in the most hierarchical and patrimonial parishes. Although these groups could become integrated into the patrimonial structures, they also provided opportunities and increased the options available to the poor. Among the primary benefits for participants in development groups was the social solidarity they fostered among members. Even where development projects made little money, they helped to create a network of mutual support among participants, an important factor because the breakdown in traditional social networks since the

---

[49] Interview in Kirinda, July 8, 1992.
[50] Ibid.

revolution made people more vulnerable to patrimonial exploitation. The opportunity to work and talk together with others who shared common problems and interests provided participants with ideas for addressing their problems and offered moral and sometimes material support. One woman in a Caritas farming cooperative in Butare explained why she preferred participating in a Catholic-sponsored group over simply receiving a handout. "You can't always receive and receive. You have to do something for yourself. And it's important to work together. It's not just the harvest we take in. When we come together, we share ideas, we talk about our problems. We help each other."[51] Participants in other projects expressed an appreciation for the assistance that they expected they would receive from group members were they to fall sick or otherwise have emergency needs.

Many church groups specifically targeted marginal social categories, such as women, the handicapped, orphans, street children, people with AIDS, and Twa. Single mothers have historically suffered severe social ostracism in Rwanda,[52] but churches had organized specific projects for them. One woman explained why she had remained in the single mothers' group at the Presbyterian parish in Butare despite its limited financial return:

When we were in the countryside, we had a lot of problems [because of the social prejudice against single mothers] and no opportunities. Here we work together and pray together to God to help us. ... The church helps us not only in the project, but it helps us with prayer and in keeping us in good company.[53]

Churches, thus, brought together categories of people with limited status and power so that they could support one another, which helped reduce their vulnerability to exploitation by more powerful and higher status social groups.

The social unity that church groups provided served as a basis for the poor and marginalized more effectively to assert their rights and defend their interests. Johan Pottier noted a similar potential in a secular cooperative that he observed in Butare in 1986. The debates that he recorded provided:

a forum for challenging established cultural convention. This convention demands of resource-poor people, women and men, that they refrain from pursuing

---

[51] Interview in Butare, January 10, 1993.
[52] C.f., Taylor, *Milk, Honey, and Money*, pp. 130–1.
[53] Interview in Butare, October 9, 1992.

genuine knowledge or material success; aspirations that run counter to the "natural order." Rwanda's cooperative movement, as I experienced it, constitutes a new, powerful challenge – a force which has arrived to stay.[54]

Pottier found that the cooperative movement in Rwanda was creating particular opportunities for women, even as men tried to use the system to reinforce their dominant social position.

While many of the attributes of the church groups I studied were similar to those of secular development cooperatives, the spiritual power that people felt they derived from participation in church groups was particularly important and should not be overlooked. Even many groups that were formally autonomous and included people from various churches began their meetings with prayer and hymn singing. One woman in Kirinda explained why people turned to the churches rather than the state to organize development groups:

Some people prefer [to participate in] church projects, because they can pray in them. When there is a problem, the church will assist you. It also helps us fight poverty. When you pray you forget the problems of the family. The state easily forgets the poor. But in the church, we are all together.[55]

While prayer and religious practice can provide an escape from problems, it can also empower, filling people with confidence in their own capacity, and it can educate, raising people's consciousness about their exploitation and about the social situation. Another woman explained that she participated in the Kirinda basket-weaving project:

because we come together to pray and we work together and we earn money. ... There is no future for agriculture, because the soil is not fertile. There is not much else to earn money. There are few parcels of land, and they are infertile. ... The church during the worship service explains the situation that causes our poverty. It teaches.[56]

Finally, development projects, including those in the churches, also provided financial advantages for people. A few projects, like the carpentry workshop in Biguhu, yielded significant profits that could help to lift participants out of poverty. Most provided participants with only small

[54] Johan Pottier, "Debating syles in a Rwandan co-operative: reflections on language, policy and gender," In Ralph Grill, ed., *Sociological Review Monograph* no. 36, pp. 41–60, citation p. 58.
[55] Interview in Kirinda, July 10, 1992.
[56] Interview in Kirinda, July 10, 1992.

supplements to their income. More importantly, though, most offered a degree of financial security for people that limited their vulnerability to exploitation. People who ran into difficulties could expect assistance from their group that could help avoid their falling into debt or being forced to sell off land or produce. Many development projects, including many church projects, were intentionally designed to free the poor from exploitative economic arrangements. For example, silo projects like those in Kirinda and Biguhu helped maintain a fair price for produce. A 1993 Oxfam report explains:

Poverty ... makes farmers vulnerable to merchants who buy their crops at rock-bottom prices when the family is most desperate (often just before harvest). To rub salt in the wound, the same merchant may then sell back the crop to the farmer, at a far higher price, several months later when the harvest is over and food is scarce once more.[57]

The silos sought to end such exploitative practices, and in doing so, they limited the ability of the privileged to enrich themselves and presented a challenge to existing structures of power.

Various church organizations, including development cooperatives, gave participants practical experience in democracy. People who found their choices limited in most aspects of their lives by poverty and by authoritarian government had an opportunity in church groups to choose their leaders and to set their own agenda. While many groups reinforced the existing social structure, as groups proliferated in the 1980s, the opportunities for new people to enhance their status by becoming an officer in an organization increased. If religious groups have been an important factor in the expansion of democracy, as Huntington, Witte, Monga, and others suggest,[58] I would contend, based on the example of places like Biguhu, that this goes far beyond the influence of bishops over the process of political reform to the promotion of democratic values and independent thinking at the local level.

The fact that people were also gaining greater control over their religious lives was significant as well. The basic ecclesial communities, religious movements like the Abarokore, and other church groups gave Christians increasing opportunities to define their beliefs and to shape

---

[57] Waller, *Rwanda: Which Way Now?* p. 24.
[58] John Witte, "Introduction," in John Witte, ed., *Christianity and Democracy in Global Context* (Boulder: Westview, 1993), pp. 1–13; Huntington, *The Third Wave*; Monga, *Anthropology of Anger*.

their own rituals. What Harri Englund notes about Dedza villagers in Malawi applies in Rwandan villages as well. "Christianity is a valued and internal aspect of villagers' own relationships, not a force that derives exclusively from, or is monopolised by, the parish. Local church politics comprises a thriving scene of Catholic groups and offices."[59]

Some church leaders, like those in Biguhu, encouraged the growing autonomy of church members. Others, like those in Kirinda, regarded it as a threat and sought to reassert authority – in political, economic, social, and religious realms alike. The relationship to the process of reform ultimately shaped how various churches became integrated into the genocide that sought to crush the democratic fervent in the country. In the next chapter, I show the divergent roles of the Presbyterian parishes in Kirinda and Biguhu.

[59] Harri Englund, "Between God and Kamazu: the transition to multiparty politics in central Malawi," in Richard Werbner and Terence Ranger, eds., *Postcolonial Identities in Africa* (London and New Jersey: Zed Books, 1996), pp. 107–35, citation p. 123.

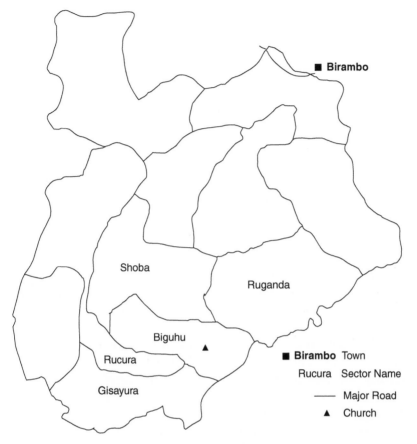

FIGURE 8.1. Map of Mwendo Commune.

9

"Commanded by the Devil"

Christian Involvement in the Genocide in Kirinda and Biguhu

By early 1993, the sense of tension in both Kirinda and Biguhu had risen to an alarming level. The threat of violence was palpable, and yet the fault lines in the communities had not yet taken a clearly ethnic form. Instead, the divisions remained more class-based and political. The gang of unemployed youths who threatened the peace of Kirinda identified with the MDR and continued to focus their anger against the Hutu elite, who were identified with the MRND and CDR. The key to understanding how the genocide became possible in these communities lies in explaining the diversion of public discontent and anger from the pro-Habyarimana Hutu elite to the Tutsi and other Habyarimana opponents. Ultimately, during the genocide in Kirinda, it was the very youths who had once harassed and robbed the Hutu elite who carried out the slaughter of local Tutsi under the Hutu elite's direction. In Biguhu, this ethnicization of community conflict was never fully accomplished, so that the community surrounding the parish never became a center for the genocide. Instead, Biguhu's Tutsi were lured outside the community and killed there. The structures of power in the two communities helped to determine their readiness to participate in the genocide, and the churches

The information for this chapter is based on data that I gathered in 1995–96 while in Rwanda with Human Rights Watch/Africa. I returned to Kirinda several times and interviewed a number of Tutsi survivors of the genocide as well as Hutu. In addition, I searched through the offices of Bwakira Commune and Kibuye Prefecture and copied several hundred relevant documents. Some of these documents were later entered into evidence in the International War Crimes Tribunal for Rwanda in Arusha. I was not able to access the archives in Mwendo but did conduct interviews with people from Biguhu.

played an important part in shaping those structures. While the church as such in Kirinda did not instigate the killings there, church personnel were intimately involved, church structures facilitated the organization of the community, and the church helped lend moral authority to those who carried out the massacres. In contrast, the church in Biguhu served as a hindrance to the political officials in Mwendo who wanted to organize massacres in the commune.

KIRINDA

In Kirinda in 1992, members of the community considered criminality the primary threat to public order, and they blamed the growing criminality on the decline in public unity and in respect for authority associated with multiparty politics. In this location, far from the frontlines of the war, people regarded the war as only a minor source of insecurity. Over the next two years, however, the elite of Kirinda, using the organizational structures of the security committee, political parties, communal government, and church, backed up by national political leaders and media, helped to transform public thinking in the community in a way that made genocide possible. They continued to identify the opposition parties as a threat to security, but they increasingly sought to do so by associating the parties with the RPF and the war. According to their claims, RPF agents operating in the community, both opposition politicians and Tutsi, were instigating the problems. By convincing enough people that ethnicity was the key threat to public order, the elite in Kirinda were able to regain popular compliance to their dominance.

Although there was some history of ethnic violence in the community, the ethnic argument was slow to take hold in Kirinda in the 1990s. In 1973, a truckload of Hutu students from other schools came to drive the Tutsi students out of the ESI, and some of the Tutsi in Kirinda were killed in subsequent attacks, a fact to which Tutsi in the community still referred in the 1990s as evidence of the potential for violence there. Through most of its history, however, Kirinda had been a relatively welcoming place for Tutsi.[1] The Presbyterian Church had historically employed a large number of Tutsi pastors, and many Tutsi had worked in Kirinda. The rate of intermarriage in the community was high. Particularly after the

---

[1] Interview in Kirinda, April 2, 1996.

outbreak of the War of October in 1990, however, the elite in Kirinda publicly embraced an anti-Tutsi stance – in contrast to the local opposition parties, that sought to appeal across ethnic lines and enjoyed broader public support.[2]

The elite had diverse motivations for their anti-Tutsi attitudes. Some who owed their personal success to the current system viewed the recent political turmoil as a threat to their positions, and they came to view the RPF and Tutsi more generally as the main instigators of the unrest. Many sought to maintain or advance their positions within the patrimonial network by aligning themselves ideologically with Twagirayesu, who was known not only to have a close association with Habyarimana and the MRND but to strongly dislike the RPF and have little love for Tutsi. Some informants from Kirinda claimed that a number of the elite embraced the PAWA agenda because of their own mixed ethnic origins. By expressing hatred for Tutsi, individuals could negate suspicions that they were themselves Tutsi. Because of the preponderance of intermarriage and the historically flexible nature of identity in Rwanda, just who was Tutsi and who was Hutu according to lines of patrilineal heritage was not always clear. Amani Nyilingabo, for example, was thin with narrow features and, along with other members of the Twagirayesu family, was widely rumored to have Tutsi blood.[3]

The anti-Tutsi attitudes originally limited to the elite gradually gained acceptance in Kirinda over the course of 1993 through a series of events. The roots of the shift in community fault lines from political and class division to ethnic division can be traced back to the anti-Tutsi violence of August 1992 and January 1993 and the RPF offensive in northern Rwanda that began in February 1993. Ethnic attacks first occurred in Kibuye in the communes of Gishyita and Rwamatamu along the shore of Lake Kivu. Fights between members of the MRND/CDR and the MDR in July took on an ethnic character, and in August 1992 MRND/CDR partisans attacked Tutsi, killing at least six, burning 500 homes, and displacing 5,000 people.[4] The ethnic massacres that began in December

---

[2] The local MDR leader told me, "All the ethnic groups are part of the MDR. PARMEHUTU-MDR [the original version of the party under Kayibanda] was violent because it responded to violence. But now the job is to construct unity. The MDR has tried to stop the violence. It is the behavior of people afraid of losing their power." Interview in Kirinda, March 23, 1993.

[3] Interviews in Kigali, July 31, 1992; Kirinda, March 21, 1993.

[4] ADL, *Rapport sur les Droits de l'Homme au Rwanda*, pp. 236–64. Also see letter from Prefect Clément Kayishema to the Minister of Interior, dated August 24, 1992.

1992 in Gisenyi Prefecture spread into Rutsiro commune of Kibuye prefecture in January, following MRND rallies held throughout the prefecture on January 21.[5] While these massacres in Gishyita, Rwamatamu, and Rutsiro, did not directly affect either Bwakira or Mwendo Communes, their proximity raised the level of anxiety among local Tutsi, giving the expanding social conflict in the country an ethnic character. That anti-Tutsi violence could occur anywhere in Kibuye despite its strong affiliation with opposition parties demonstrated the potential for violence to spread into other parts of the prefecture and defied the widely held perception of the conflict to that point as largely political and regional in nature.[6] The Rutsiro massacres particularly upset the people of Bwakira, as rumors spread that MRND and CDR militia were planning to attack local Tutsi. In several sectors, the MDR organized the population to defend local Tutsi in late January and early February, blowing whistles and beating drums to warn people of the threat, though Burgomaster Kabasha insisted that the rumors of an imminent attack were unfounded.[7]

Partly in response to these massacres, the RPF broke a self-imposed cease-fire and launched a major offensive into northern Rwanda on February 7, 1993. The RPF quickly occupied Ruhengeri town, then swept down through Byumba and into northern Kigali-Rural prefecture, coming within striking distance of Kigali. This attack displaced hundreds of thousands of residents from Ruhengeri, Byumba, and Kigali-Rural, including families of several students at the IPK and ESI. In the aftermath of this attack, the Hutu elite in Kirinda began to adopt more overtly anti-Tutsi rhetoric. A group of Hutu students, led by several from the centers of MRND support in the northern prefectures, began to harass Tutsi students at the IPK, and the principal of the IPK, who was reportedly a member of the CDR, apparently supported them. A Tutsi student, "Paul," at the IPK reported to me about several incidents at the school in

[5] Africa Watch, *Beyond the Rhetoric: Continuing Human Rights Abuses in Rwanda* (New York: Human Rights Watch, June 1993), pp. 5–6. Also, fax 002/04.09.01, from Clément Kayishema to MINITER, dated January 21, 1993.

[6] Kimonyo, *Rwanda*, points out the importance of the MDR's PARMEHUTU heritage as a source of mobilization. In Kibuye, however, I found that the MDR presented itself as more a regional party, self-consciously multiethnic, until mid-1993.

[7] Letter from Kabasha to the Prefect of Kibuye, no. 0170/04.09.01/4, Bwakira, February 15, 1993, and attached security report dated February 4, 1993. Kabasha wrote that "Everywhere, people are talking about people who beat drums during the night, saying that the Tutsi will be attacked." He goes on to thank the prefect for sending gendarmes to insure his personal security.

which the school administration and the group of students targeted Tutsi students:

Karemera, head of the MRND [in Kibuye],[8] passed by Kirinda at least two times per week after the attack at Ruhengeri. Fidele [the principal] organized a group in the school to do a screening of the Tutsi at the school. The head of the group was a student from Gisenyi in the 6th class. The first time, they chose eleven whom they accused of being Inkotanyi. The director called us into his office. He asked us how we were organizing to massacre the students at the school.[9]

Following this incident, the pro-MRND group sponsored an initiative to replace Paul as head of the 5th form, because he was Tutsi. As he testified:

After this incident, the principal tried to get the students to push me out of my position as president of the class. "David" [a European teacher] said that we should have new elections. After these elections, those who were against me were only eight out of forty-one. The others were for me, so I remained leader of the class. But a student at the meeting announced where David overheard, "This democracy should not be practiced here in Rwanda. I'm going to show you. I'm going to kill you along with Paul." David went to get the principal. The principal, after seeing that the situation had gotten too extreme, he covered up his intentions, saying, "Paul can continue."[10]

The refusal of the students to reject a class president solely because he was Tutsi reflected a general unwillingness in the community at this time to perceive the Tutsi as a threat. Despite the general hatred for the RPF and the long-standing tensions between Hutu and Tutsi, political and class differences remained more important to the Hutu masses. Nevertheless, local Tutsi, especially Tutsi students, themselves became increasingly afraid for their lives.[11]

As insecurity continued to expand throughout 1993, much of it contained political or class, rather than ethnic, overtones. The communal archives in Bwakira contain a series of letters and reports in which Burgomaster Kabasha accuses his political opponents of inciting insecurity. A running battle between Kabasha and Emmanuel Habiyakare, a Hutu storekeeper and MDR leader in Shyembe, went on for months.

---

[8] Édouard Karemera was an MRND deputy in the National Assembly from Kibuye. Guichaoua, *Les crises politiques au Burundi et au Rwanda*, p. 763.

[9] Interview in Butare, March 23, 1996.

[10] Interview in Butare, March 25, 1996.

[11] Several Tutsi students from the IPK came to speak with me in late 1992 and early 1993 to ask my advice on whether they should flee the country.

In December, Kabasha had Habiyakare arrested on apparently false accusations, but after his release, Kabasha continued to complain about him and his associate Emmanuel Nsengimana as security threats. In March, he again accused them of being behind a grenade explosion and of organizing an attack against the councilor of Murambi sector (which includes Kirinda). In response, they circulated a petition addressed to the president calling for Kabasha's removal.[12] Kabasha made a similar set of accusations against François Ntawiha, a teacher in Nyabiranga sector, whom he accused of organizing a gang to harass MRND members in January and February 1993.[13] Ntawiha wrote to the prefect in his own defense, denying any involvement in attacks and claiming instead to being framed by another teacher in his school, Anastace Munyakinani, an MRND member.[14] A month later, Munyakinani wrote a letter to the judicial officials in Birambo claiming that he himself was now threatened by attackers who wanted to kill him.[15] Other letters in the file from this period include civilian complaints of robberies by soldiers and requests from Kabasha for police assistance in responding to additional attacks on MRND members. In one letter of particular interest, a resident of Bwakira wrote complaining of being threatened by the presidents of the MRND and CDR as a Tutsi, but he wanted to clarify that he was in fact a Hutu.[16] Most violence, however, seems to have been political in nature, and the MDR and MRND/CDR engaged in *kubohoza* against one another, battling along ideological lines. Within a few months, however, these two groups would begin to unite against a common perceived enemy: the Tutsi "collaborators" with the RPF.

Nationally the Arusha Accords, signed in August 1993, were the turning point that served to split the opposition parties and reorganize support for President Habyarimana along largely ethnic lines, thus setting the stage for the genocide.[17] In Kirinda, however, it was the assassination of Burundian President Ndadaye that was the catalyst for redrawing political lines. While the Arusha Accords were generally unpopular with

---

[12] Letter from Kabasha to prefect of Kibuye, no. 0242/04.09.01/4, dated Bwakira, March 9, 1993; letter to president, March 11, 1993.
[13] Letter from Kabasha to Prefect of Kibuye, no. 0470/04.09.01/4, dated Bwakira.
[14] Letter from Ntawiha François to the Prefect of Kibuye, dated Nyabiranga, May 15, 1993.
[15] Letter from Anastace Munyakinani to Premier Substitu Parquet Birambo, June 1, 1993.
[16] Letter to Procurer of Kibuye, dated March 8, 1993.
[17] Des Forges, *Leave None to Tell the Story*, pp. 123–40; Prunier, *The Rwanda Crisis*, pp. 174–91, 198–206.

the local population, they did not in themselves bring people to support Habyarimana. The assassination of Ndadaye, however, convinced many Hutu of the validity of the warnings that they had heard from MRND and CDR leaders – and even from some leaders of the MDR – that the Tutsi were actually intent upon seizing complete power and dominating the Hutu. I quote at length a Tutsi student at the IPK whose testimony suggests the event that helped to turn the tide toward the pro-Habyarimana PAWA coalition and against the Tutsi:

The principal [Fidele Ntawirukanayo] was in Europe, in Switzerland. At his return – I even remember the date, the 25th of October, the day around the celebration of the army – on his return, he went immediately to Birambo without first stopping at Kirinda. A group of MDR youth stopped him on the road between Kirinda and Birambo. [...] He had a white car, a Hyundai. The youth stopped him and engaged him in conversation. He called on the help of students from the school. The manager took the car and went to get students to come protect him. The group left with machetes – the prefect took them out of stock – and they went to protect him. The group chosen was the same [as those who had harassed the Tutsi students earlier in the year] except for those who had graduated. It was directed by Samuel Baragwize, the dean. The group took him to Shyembe rather than Kirinda. [...]

He was taken to Shyembe. Coming to the school, [the group] said that the director was attacked by a gang organized by the group of Tutsi, but this time it was 14 of us. Imagine! We knew nothing about this! We didn't even know when he was returning! They went to contact the director of the hospital [Dr. Antoine], Amani [the head of the CDR]. It was 8 P.M. He [the principal] came to his office with the manager and the prefect of discipline. They called the students out, one by one. This time the principal was surrounded by guards with machetes, and scythes, and sticks.

First, he called D.F., then F.F., then me, at about the time when studies had finished, around midnight, when I was already in bed. Arriving there, I found a group of six people who had been interrogated. He said, "Paul, you are the leader, president of the Red Cross, and in the 6th form. Explain to me how you supported the people who killed Ndadaye." I was astonished. I had no idea about these things. The group [of Tutsi students] was frightened, because of what happened. The second question: "Explain to me how you are organizing a massacre here at the school?" I said, "Fourteen people?" because he had a list of fourteen. [The school had over 400 students]. The third question, he asked me if we organized a demonstration of joy about the death of Ndadaye culminating with the attack on the principal. I said I was not Murundi, I had no family there, I had never been there. He said if I didn't explain, he said, he would make me explain. I said, "Mr. Principal, I am a good Catholic. I have many responsibilities. How many times have I sacrificed for the school? I get up at 3 A.M. to transport the sick [as head of the Red Cross]. You have never in two years complained of my work. And now you have these huge accusations." I said, "You have asked me about nothing that I know anything about."

He sent us to the dormitory. We saw all the weapons. The whole dorm was awake. We were afraid there were CDR everywhere around. We stayed awake together outside the dormitory. In the morning, I went to Pastor M. [the Dutch missionary] to explain the situation. He understood. The principal organized a meeting with the leaders of the school with these fourteen. He said we needed to debate the problems. We were angry and demanded to know who had told him these things, since he was in Europe. [...] I said, "I see that all fourteen are Tutsi. Why?" [...] Fidele said that he had stopped the coup. He said that if these things continued, there would be retribution.[18]

This attack on the principal seems to have been the crucial turning point in Kirinda, in which the pro-Habyarimana elite began to redirect public discontent from themselves to local Hutu who remained loyal to the opposition and, above all, to Tutsi, whom they effectively defined as a threat to the community. In the context of the unpopular Arusha Accords and the national outrage over Ndadaye's assassination, the idea of an uprising involving the opposition parties and directed by Tutsi seemed credible. While the local Hutu population did not like the Habyarimana regime, they also did not like the RPF, which had, after all, been attacking the country for four years, driving thousands of people from their homes, and ruining the economy, and they objected to the significant share of power given to the RPF by the Arusha Accords. The fact that Hutu believed that most Tutsi sympathized with the RPF added to their distrust of their Tutsi neighbors. Since the Tutsi youths accused of organizing the attack on the principal were from outside the community, they were even more suspect. Because these students were not from Bwakira, community members could not disprove the claims of Ntawirukanayo and Nyilingabo that they were RPF spies.

Whether the attack on the principal actually had any connection to Ndadaye's assassination is unclear, but by defining the attack as a Tutsi-organized manifestation of support for Ndadaye's murder, Ntawirukanayo, Nyilingabo, and their supporters were able to portray themselves as the defenders of Hutu interests and the anti-Habyarimana opposition as pro-RPF traitors to Hutu interests. This incident created an incentive for MDR and PSD supporters to ally themselves with the pro-Habyarimana PAWA wings of their parties. While not all local MDR and PSD activists aligned themselves with the PAWA faction in their parties, the public increasingly viewed allegiance with MDR-Twagiramungu as support for the RPF. In other words, while previously most people in

[18] Interview in Butare, March 23, 1996.

Kirinda had opposed Habyarimana because they regarded his regime as having unfairly favored the northern prefectures while neglecting Kibuye and other central and southern prefectures, the attack on the principal helped to redefine opposition to Habyarimana as support for the RPF. Community fault lines did not become completely ethnic in nature at this time, but the political divisions in the community took on an increasingly ethnic character that set the stage for ethnic-based violence six months later.

The youths who participated in the attack had an incentive to shift their allegiance so as not to be viewed as traitors. The youths were not drawn to the MDR by ideological commitment to democracy or to ethnic or regional unity but rather out of discontent with the status quo and a desire to express their frustration and rage, and the youths did not wish to be characterized as pro-RPF or pro-Tutsi. Since the MDR nationally had split, this shift in allegiance did not require a radical jump from opposing the MRND to joining it but merely a less radical affiliation with the PAWA wing of the MDR. The PAWA elite sought to tap into this frustration by offering an alternative focus for their anger. Although militia training that began in other communities at this time seems not to have been conducted in Kirinda, by cultivating a cooperative relationship with these youths, Nyilingabo and Ntawirukanayo sought to co-opt the youth and transform them from an antisocial youth gang into a violent resource that they could direct toward their own purposes.

During this period, as ethnic and political tensions mounted in the community, the church offered no moral guidance to parishioners. With the two most prominent lay employees of the church – the directors of the hospital and the IPK – along with several important lay church leaders, such as Nyilingabo, directing the accusations against Tutsi, the silence of the pastors regarding ethnic conflict was interpreted by many people as an endorsement. The open support for Habyarimana and the MRND from the president of the Presbyterian Church, who remained highly influential in his hometown (if for no other reason than for his power of hiring and firing and for distributing church funds), and the well-known pro-Habyarimana sentiments of the president of the Kirinda region of the church added to the popular impression that the church supported the PAWA agenda. While the pastor of the parish did not seem to have personally supported PAWA, he failed to articulate his opposition from the pulpit. Hence, the stage was set for people in Kirinda to participate in the massacre of Tutsi without being hindered by the knowledge that their actions were in opposition to church policy.

BIGUHU

While Biguhu was not entirely sheltered from the rising ethnic conflict and deteriorating public order, the community did not experience the same degree of political realignment and heightened ethnic and political tensions as Kirinda, and the Presbyterian parish played a central role in fostering a different environment. In contrast to Kirinda, Biguhu did not have a large reserve of disaffected unemployed youths who could be transformed into a militia. Church development projects helped to increase employment opportunities and, even if they were not particularly profitable, effectively integrated a number of young men into the community. Those unemployed youths who were not involved in projects generally gravitated toward Birambo, Kirinda, or Kigali, where opportunities for day labor were greater and where community divisions created a more fertile environment for gang activity. Since the CERAI served only a local population, Biguhu had no students from northern prefectures who could be mobilized to support the regime, as they had in Kirinda.

Perhaps more importantly, in contrast to Kirinda, where the church leaders set an example of ethnic intolerance, both Hutu and Tutsi church leaders and employees in Biguhu continued actively to oppose ethnic divisions and to decry class divisions and exploitation. A week after the January 1993 ethnic violence in Rutsiro came to public attention, the pastor of the Biguhu church explicitly denounced ethnic divisions as inconsistent with God's plan and ethnic and political violence as un-Christian in a sermon preached before the monthly gathering of the entire congregation:

There are Christians who think all things they do are allowed. Some husbands mistreat all the people in their care. There are husbands who are drunk, wives who are drunk. And these people don't think that they are sinners. It is possible for them to come to church thinking that they are holy. But Christians can be thieves, they can be drunks. Those who sin would be better to know that they sin. We must examine ourselves. We are in a period of multipartyism. We must ask whether injuring others is not sin? Can you hurt others and say you are Christian? It is possible that Christians look at their neighbors and say that they are not brothers? We must examine ourselves. ...

People today are led on paths of evil. There are those who kill their brothers. Can these people expect to receive eternal life if they do not recognize their sin and repent? Isaiah 1:12–13 says, "Bring no more vain oblations; incense is an abomination to me; the new moons and sabbaths, the calling of assemblies, I cannot away with; it is iniquity, even the solemn meeting." We must come into the church having a good heart.

God has not created all these ethnicities. God created a single person. People created ethnicity later. God does not teach us to divide from one another. Those who do evil, each will be saved by his actions. In Romans 14:12 it is written, "So then every one of us shall give account of himself to God." What do you want to show God? Hate? Jealousy? What do you display before God? You hide nothing before God. As Peter said, "Leave me, I'm a sinner." We must imitate Peter, tell God we are sinners and ask forgiveness.[19]

The direct denunciation of ethnic and political violence from the pulpit in Biguhu in this and others was unique among the six parishes I studied during my fieldwork in 1992–93. While the impact of such sermons on the parishioners is difficult to demonstrate, those in attendance at these services could not have left believing that their church was unified in supporting the president and the anti-Tutsi rhetoric of his supporters. The fact that the pastor was himself Tutsi would certainly have affected how parishioners received the message, but his forthright condemnation of ethnic violence made it more difficult for people under his care to assume that ethnic hatred was consistent with Christian teachings. The pastor's condemnation of ethnic violence as un-Christian could not in and of itself prevent ethnic violence from taking place, but it might dissuade some people from joining in the killing and it could certainly impede the use of church structures to support it.

Certainly Biguhu was not spared entirely from mobilization of support for PAWA. Some people in the community, including active Presbyterians, supported the CDR, MRND, and the PAWA faction of the MDR. But while PAWA organizing in Bwakira centered on Kirinda, basing itself in part within church institutions, PAWA organizing in Mwendo centered on Birambo and on the office of the burgomaster, while the Biguhu parish represented more an obstacle to effective PAWA organizing than a support.

KIRINDA AND BIGUHU MOVE TOWARD GENOCIDE

When President Habyarimana's plane went down on April 6, 1994, the conditions that could allow the citizens of Kirinda to carry out genocide were already in place, while the level of ethnic polarization and pro-government community mobilization in Biguhu lagged behind. I find no evidence to suggest that PAWA leaders in either community were aware of plans by national leaders to carry out a large-scale massacre of Tutsi

---

[19] Sermon, Biguhu Parish, February 7, 1993.

and moderate Hutu, but local leaders in Kirinda had effectively followed the example of the national PAWA establishment in seeking to win over the Hutu masses by identifying local Tutsi as a threat to security and presenting themselves as the defenders of Hutu interests against the alleged effort by the RPF and its opposition allies to reestablish Tutsi rule. The anti-Tutsi, anti-opposition rhetoric broadcast on RTLM helped strengthen the claim of a Tutsi threat, as did the pronouncements by politicians opposed to the Arusha Accords. In Kirinda, the alliance between religious, business, and church leaders within the PAWA movement created a strong base for mobilizing community support, and the cooptation of the local youth gang into the youth wing of the PAWA movement provided a coercive force that silenced voices of opposition. A similar organization based in Birambo included Mwendo Commune, but the population within Biguhu parish was only partially integrated into it.[20]

The IPK was a particularly important base of operation for the local PAWA movement, with the principal able to mobilize easily a core group of PAWA students and with the presence of non-local Tutsi creating an excellent tool for inciting public fear of a Tutsi threat. When Martin Bucyana, chairman of the CDR, was lynched in Butare in February 1994, the pro-CDR students at the IPK used the opportunity to level threats once again against Tutsi students at the school. "The death of Bucyana will be followed by other deaths," one Hutu student told the Tutsi. One Tutsi student traveled to Kigali to report to the president of the Presbyterian Church, Twagirayesu, about the deteriorating security conditions at the school.[21] When Habyarimana's plane crash actually set the wheels of genocide into motion, however, both the IPK and the ECI were on Easter break, so there were no students present. Instead, Kirinda was at the time hosting a national meeting for Presbyterian pastors, so Twagirayesu and a number of other Presbyterian pastors and church leaders were staying in the dormitories at the ECI and in other lodgings throughout the community.[22]

For the first several days after Habyarimana's death, the plan for the genocide seems to have been unclear even to the top political authorities in Kibuye. Violence, some of it specifically ethnic in nature, broke

---

[20] Letter no. 002/04.09.01, from Clément Kayishema to the Minister of the Interior, April 10, 1994, "Sécurité dans la Préfecture Kibuye." Marked "Secret Confidentiel." From files at Prefecture Office Kibuye.
[21] Interview in Butare, March 25, 1996.
[22] Interview in Kirinda, April 2, 1996.

out almost immediately in various parts of Kibuye, but government authorities and gendarmes initially intervened to stop the violence and restore peace. According to an April 10 letter from Clément Kayishema, the prefect of Kibuye,

> Since the death of the President of the Rwandan Republic Major General Juvénal Habyarimana 6/04/94, Kibuye Prefecture has suffered from an interethnic (Hutu-Tutsi) tension, this tension degenerated into an open conflict on the night of 7/4 to 8/4/94 in Rutsiro Commune at the commercial center of the Zaire-Nile Crest. Currently the most affected communes are: ...
> -Rutsiro above all Gihango Sector and Murunda Parish. There were six recorded deaths, including a priest from Murunda Parish [killed on the night of April 8]. Recently in Bwiza and Kagano Sectors a tension also is signaled. There was pillaging at first, but currently where the tension began it seems to have subsided. The administrative authorities intervened, and there were several arrests.[23]

Of more direct significance to Mwendo and Bwakira, the prefect reported attacks in Birambo:

> -the center of Birambo. There were two deaths of shopkeepers with pillaging. Most of the criminals have been arrested (11). The administrative authorities and the gendarmes intervened, but currently tension is not diminishing.[24]

In the attached security report, the prefect offers greater details of the attack in Birambo that took place on the night of April 7:

> -a shopkeeper named Kazungu originally from Bwishyura Sector Gitesi Commune was pillaged by bandits from Birambo who afterward killed him.
>   -the Tutsi commerçants and teachers gathered at the ENP (girls) [high school] run by the sisters. Damien Kirusha is present as well.[25]

While the report does not specify the ethnicity of Kazungu, the fact that Birambo's Tutsi sought refuge at the school strongly suggests that he and Etienne, another shopkeeper attacked, were Tutsi. According to the report, the next day the local authorities sought out and arrested those responsible for the attacks in Birambo:

> Mwendo Commune: -arrest of 11 criminals who robbed and killed Kazungu as well as robbed the store of Etienne of Birambo (originally from Mwendo at

---

[23] Letter no. 002/04.09.01, from Kayishema to the Minister of the Interior.
[24] Ibid.
[25] "Rapport sur la Sécurité dans la Préfecture Kibuye," marked "Confidentiel," annex to letter no. 002/04.09.01, p. 2.

Ngange). The IPJ [police investigator] of the Birambo prosecutor's office was afraid to conduct an investigation, which is why the criminals were brought to Kibuye [town].[26]

Violence broke out in Kibuye prefecture almost immediately after Habyarimana's death, but it had not yet assumed a distinctly ethnic character. Those who initially felt threatened and sought refuge in most Kibuye communities included not only Tutsi but non-PAWA members of the opposition, since PAWA activists had previously targeted both Tutsi and prominent anti-Habyarimana Hutu. The prefect reported that on April 8 in Kibuye town, "the Tutsi and the partisans of the party MDR-Twagiramungu are in flight toward Karongi; also the deputy Ndindabo from the PSD."[27] Government officials themselves were not yet prepared to endorse ethnic violence as official policy but instead associated ethnic attacks with general lawlessness and saw them as a threat to public order. The prefect reported to the interior minister:

Honorable Minister, in making a close analysis, the cause of troubles would be:

-an already existing Hutu-Tutsi interethnic tension in certain regions (Gishyita and Mabanza)
    -a group of bandits who turn up after there is a small event that occurs. These groups exist nearly throughout the Prefecture (Gishiyita, Mubuga, Rubengera, Birambo, Kirinda, Zaire-Nile Crest) and they are the first to stir up situations. It should also be remarked that bad intentioned people use these bandits to distribute information or to initiate troubles. That which proves this is that this is the same group that turns up at different incidents.[28]

In nearly all reported cases of violence and pillage during these first several days, communal and prefecture authorities intervened to restore order and arrest those responsible. Either the decision to extend the genocide throughout the country had not yet been made, or the prefect of Kibuye and his burgomasters had not yet been informed of the plan to systematically eliminate Rwanda's Tutsi.[29] Within only a few days of this letter

---

[26] Ibid, p. 5.
[27] Ibid, p. 3. Ndindabo, a deputy in the national assembly, was Hutu.
[28] Letter no. 002/04.09.01, "Sécurité dans la Préfecture Kibuye," p. 2.
[29] Alison Des Forges in *Leave None to Tell the Story* argues that the leadership of the country following Habyarimana's death was not unanimous in supporting genocide. "The leaders of the killing campaign had to invest considerable political and military resources to end opposition to the genocide and they did so, belying their assertion that they were trying to halt the slaughter. They killed or removed some of the dissenting soldiers and officials and intimidated others into compliance. They left other opponents

and security report, the administration would shift its policy from intervening to prevent ethnic violence and looting to working with the "bad
intentioned people" and organizing the very "groups of bandits" that the
prefect here denounced to carry out the massacre of Kibuye's Tutsi.

The flight of displaced people into Kibuye helped heighten tensions,
moving the prefecture toward genocide. Some Tutsi displaced from
Ramba Commune in Gisenyi had been in Rutsiro since the violence
against the Bagogwe more than a year earlier, but new refugees from
Kayove Commune in Gisenyi began to arrive in Rutsiro and Mabanza
on April 9. Civilian militia also began to attack Tutsi in Muko Commune
of Gikongoro on April 9, sending Tutsi refugees into Mwendo. While
only 150 refugees from Muko were reported on April 10, by April 11 the
number had risen to more than 1,000. By April 10, Mabanza had 3,000
refugees, while the numbers in Rutsiro were unknown, since violence
had already begun there, the IPJ, a policeman, and the communal forester
were killed, and phone lines were cut.[30] Since the refugees were nearly all
Tutsi, they became an immediate target for the PAWA militia and contributed to efforts by PAWA leaders to raise fears in the local population
of a possible Tutsi attack. With the RPF having renewed its attack and
with RTLM announcing that Tutsi within Rwanda were mobilizing to
support the RPF, the appearance of several thousand unknown Tutsi
refugees could be viewed as a threat. As a result, their presence helped
to polarize the ethnic communities and raised the level of threat against
local Tutsi.

The prefect of Kibuye reported on April 10 that in "Mwendo tension
has begun to rise since the arrival of the displaced from Muko Commune.
They are currently 150."[31] According to the burgomaster, "The inhabitants

---

of the slaughter in place, but destroyed their effectiveness ..." (p. 263). The effort to gain
broader support by focusing the killing specifically on Tutsi began on April 11–12, with a
call on Radio Rwanda for unity by Froudauld Karamira, leader of MDR-Power, and the
Ministry of Defense's denial of division among Hutu in the military: "The enemy is the
same. He is the one who has always been trying to return the monarch who was over-
thrown" (quoted in Des Forges, p. 203). Kayishema, as a member of the MRND-allied
Christian Democratic Party, seems to have been a fairly marginal member of the government coalition, and having served as prefect for only two years, was not "in the loop," not
part of the central decision-making group that decided upon the genocide. Once he was
informed of the decision – or perhaps once he saw the way the winds were blowing – he
clearly supported the efforts to exterminate the Tutsi, as testimony in his trial before the
International Criminal Tribunal for Rwanda makes clear.

[30] Notes from "Réunion de Conseil de Sécurité Elargi du 11 Avril 1994," Janvier Tulikumwe,
rapporteur.

[31] Letter no. 002/04.09.01, "Sécurité dans la Préfecture Kibuye."

of Muko threaten to pursue these displaced people."[32] In the afternoon of April 9, "Pastor Michel Twagirayesu President EPR who is at Kirinda signals that there are many displaced coming from Muko to the center called Gituntu at Mwendo and that the Pastor responsible for the region is threatened."[33] By April 10, violence began in Mwendo:

-in Gashari Sector, houses began to burn, but the gendarmes intervened.

  -in Gisayura Sector tension is serious, a cow was killed.

  -the displaced from Muko located at the commune are gathered at the primary school. Information spreads that these displace from Muko have been threatened by a group of bandits from the center Kizanganya.[34]

With the presidential guard, soldiers, and militia having begun ethnic and political massacres in Kigali on April 7, the murder of ten United Nations Belgian soldiers, and the renewal of an RPF advance on the capital, most foreign embassies ordered an immediate evacuation of their citizens. On April 10, two caravans left Kibuye for Bujumbura under military guard. All but one of Kirinda's expatriates evacuated in a caravan that passed through Butare.[35] In the past, the Tutsi in the community had appealed to the Dutch missionary couple and foreign teachers at the ESI and IPK whenever they felt threatened, and their intervention had frequently helped restore calm. Their departure from Kirinda thus eliminated a potential constraint on those who regarded the Tutsi as a threat, though events in other communities demonstrated that this restraint was not sufficient to prevent genocide from taking place.

With massacres beginning on April 10 just across the river from Biguhu in Muko and with violent incidents already beginning in Mwendo, the Tutsi in Biguhu feared that, given their proximity to the violence and their isolation, they were vulnerable to attack. Hence, a number of the Tutsi from Biguhu left the community on Monday, April 11, to seek refuge in Kirinda, where they believed they would be safer. Kirinda remained calm, a larger number of Tutsi lived there than in Biguhu, and Stéphane and other Tutsi hoped that the church would use its powerful presence in Kirinda to supply refuge. Pastor Stéphane explains his reasons for leaving Biguhu:

When I saw that they were beginning to kill people at Gikongoro, I wanted to go to Kirinda. I had a home there. I thought that I would be protected there. I

---

[32] "Rapport sur la Sécurité dans la Préfecture Kibuye," p. 5.
[33] Ibid.
[34] Ibid., p. 6.
[35] Annexe to "Rapport sur la Sécurité dans la Préfecture Kibuye."

was born there. I took Géras and his family, a teacher and her family, and Géras' brother-in-law, and we went to stay in my house [in Kirinda].[36]

While Mwendo began to be overrun with refugees fleeing Gikongoro, Kirinda began to receive not only Tutsi refugees, such as those from the Biguhu parish, but also another type of refugee – Hutu fleeing the renewed war. Around the time that Géras and Pastor Stéphane arrived in Kirinda, the wives of several military officers arrived from Kigali along with a military guard. They took up residence at a house for medical personnel at the ESI.[37] While some of the Presbyterian pastors who had been in Kirinda at the outbreak of fighting were able to return to their parishes, others, especially those from Kigali, chose to stay because of the fighting around Kigali.[38] A number of these, such as Twagirayesu and the director of development, were originally from the Kirinda parish. Hence, Kirinda became host to a number of refugees, but because the schools were in recess, plenty of housing was available.

THE GENOCIDE IN KIRINDA AND BIGUHU

The exact process by which the decision was made to carry out genocide in Bwakira and Mwendo communes remains unclear. However, that those who carried out the attacks did not do so under their own initiative seems apparent. There appears to have been careful coordination among community leaders who planned the attacks according to a pattern followed throughout much of the country. They first established roadblocks along the roads to regulate movement and prevent the proposed targets from fleeing. Then they encouraged Tutsi to gather at central locations by organizing attacks on Tutsi homes while at the same time promising protection to Tutsi at designated sites. Once the Tutsi were gathered, they organized and armed mobs, composed of the local militia and generally with military backing, to attack the sites of refuge. Concentrating the Tutsi facilitated their slaughter, since it meant having to attack and force entry into only one location rather than multiple, and it helped prevent the Tutsi from escaping.[39]

According to testimonies that I gathered from people who were present in the area during the genocide, the sub-prefect of Birambo along

---

[36] Interview in Kigali, May 20, 1996.
[37] Interview in Kirinda, April 25, 1996.
[38] Interview in Kirinda, April 2, 1996; interview in Kigali, May 20, 1996.
[39] Des Forges, *Leave None to Tell the Story*, pp. 205–16, describes this pattern.

with the burgomasters of Mwendo and Bwakira played the leading roles in organizing the communes, working closely with the security committees in each community and with other leading citizens. In Kirinda, these included the principal of the IPK, director of the hospital, several of the pastors, the hospital pharmacist, the councilors of Nyabiranga and Shyembe sectors, and several business people. The sub-prefect may have received the order to carry out massacres, either from the prefect or directly from Kigali, and passed it along to the burgomasters and security councils, or he might have taken initiative himself, seeing the massacres organized in Gikongoro and following on the general directives of national political leaders that, from April 11, clearly identified Tutsi as the target.[40]

As a first measure of control, the sub-prefect and burgomaster organized barriers at the bridge over the Nyabarongo that linked Kibuye to Gitarama and another at Gisovu, along the road between Kirinda and the center of Bwakira where an important hydroelectric power station was located. Kabasha held a public meeting at Gisovu and another at Shyembe on April 11 or 12 (informants were unclear of the exact date) to inform the community of security measures and enlist their support. The roadblocks were established after these meetings and initially manned by local supporters of PAWA, particularly the youth, whom the communal authorities and security committees supplied with arms.[41]

Meanwhile, the security committees began preparations for the massacre of Tutsi. In Kirinda, the leaders of the security committee, consisting of the hospital director, IPK principal, and the president of Shyembe commerce center, Moise Semilindi, along with Amani Nyilingabo, the head of the local CDR chapter, began to mobilize the population. According to one informant, "There was a meeting on April 11 organized by Amani. This was when they organized plans to attack the Tutsi."[42] They supplied the youth gang, now reconstituted as a militia, with arms. According to several witnesses, Semilindi supplied funds to buy machetes and oversaw their distribution to the militia. The president of the EPR, Michel Twagirayesu, and several other members of his family, including Amani, took leading roles in organizing the community as well.[43] During the day of April 13, some of the community leaders visited the homes of Tutsi

[40] Des Forges, *Leave None to Tell the Story*, pp. 201–4.
[41] Interview in Kigali, May 20, 1996; interviews in Gisovu, May 21, 1996.
[42] Interview in Kigali, November 27, 1995.
[43] Interview in Kigali, May 20, 1996; interview in Kirinda, May 22, 1996.

in the community to encourage them to seek refuge in central locations where they could be protected – the ESI, for those at Shyembe; the parish for those at Kirinda. One woman reports that Amani came to convince her neighbor, Tito, to come to the ESI:

Amani came to Tito and put his arm around him and said, "Come to the school. You are from Shyembe like us. We will protect you." My greatest regret is that I did not take Tito's four children into my arms to protect them, but we never thought that Amani would kill children.[44]

The recommendations to seek refuge were reinforced by the threat of violence. Sometime on April 12, Athanase, the pastor who was president of the church region in Mwendo, was killed there, and his family fled to Kirinda and took refuge at the parish. In the evening of April 13, crowds attacked Tutsi homes throughout Shyembe, Murambi, and Nyabiranga sectors. While these attacks do not seem to have caused any fatalities, they clearly sought to scare Tutsi into leaving their homes and gathering at the designated sites. Pastor Stéphane explains that the people staying in his home fled to the ESI only after they were attacked:

We stayed Tuesday and Wednesday [April 12 and 13]. But we began to be threatened. A large group of people came, around thirty, at about 7 P.M. They threw rocks through the windows, the doors. That same night, they took the car of Tito, and they tried to burn the car. When they were being attacked [at Tito's home], we fled to the ESI. We scattered, but afterward we went to the school where Twagirayesu and some other pastors were staying. We were there Wednesday and Thursday night.[45]

A young Tutsi woman, "Georgette," who was living near the nursing school with several other young women reported:

That night we heard an explosion just behind us, at the home of Tito. We later found out that it was a grenade that they had thrown into the house. A little while after that, the crowd came to our house, and they began to throw stones through the windows. We fled out a back window. Most people went to take refuge at the ESI, but I went to hide at the home of a friend.[46]

While most of the Tutsi of Shyembe fled to the ESI, some living near the parish fled to the church. Others who lived closer to Bwakira town fled

---

[44] Interview in Kibuye, April 25, 1996.
[45] Interview in Kigali, May 20, 1996.
[46] Interview in Kigali, November 27, 1995.

to the communal office. Some, however, like the informant above, did not go to the central locations but instead stayed in their homes or sought other hiding places.

Once the Tutsi were gathered, the community leaders sought to account for everyone who was there, apparently so that they could determine who had not come and also to make certain, once the killing had begun, that none of the Tutsi were missed. Pastor Stéphane reports how the community leaders came on April 13 and took the names of everyone gathered at the ESI:

What makes me sad still: Twagirayesu, Malachie [accountant at the hospital], Antoine Kamanzi, the doctor, and Marcel [the director of the ESI], they came and asked the names of the children, their names and sex, so they could give them food. There were about fifty people – Tito, some nurses, Augustin. We gave them the list, thinking they would get something to eat. But Wednesday and Thursday, there was no food.[47]

Fearing that they were vulnerable to attack, the refugees in the ESI put a padlock on the door to the dormitory.

The Massacres in Kirinda

The killing in Kirinda began on Thursday, April 14, around 5 P.M., when Nyilingabo led the youth gang that was now reconstituted as a death squad on an attack of the hospital. They killed two Tutsi workers, Gahima and Augustin, as well as several Tutsi patients.[48] A few hours later, they attacked the ESI. Pastor Stéphane witnessed the attack:

Thursday evening Amani [Nyilingabo] and a gang of youths came. There were soldiers, too, who had been stationed in Kirinda. Thursday evening around 9 P.M., they came. They had whistles and made cries. We had closed the door. We had put our own lock on the door. They broke down the door at the dormitory. We were in prayer, because we knew it was the last moment of life. ... A group of about twenty entered, with Amani in the lead, the boy from the pharmacy first, and the youth from the community. Musa had given money to buy machetes. ... They began to chop at people there in my presence, Amani and the youths he brought with him. They had machetes, knives, guns, grenades. I was to the side by the door, and I slipped out the door. It was God who pushed me there. I went over the enclosure. ... When I ran, they followed me. "Stéphane flees!" They said,

---

47 Interview in Kigali, May 20, 1996.
48 Interview in Kigali, May 20, 1996.

"Leave him, we'll get him tomorrow morning." I asked myself, will they get me this morning?[49]

Armed gangs attacked and killed Tutsi throughout the parish that night. Géras offered money to Doctor Kamanza to hide him and his family, but he and his wife and baby daughter were taken and killed that night as well. His older daughter, Candide, survived and was taken to Kirinda hospital, where she was killed several weeks later.[50] That same night, another armed gang apparently led by the principal of the IPK attacked and killed a small group who had sought refuge at the parish at Kirinda.[51] A militia also attacked Tutsi households just up the road from the parish in Gisovu, although in this community, it appears that few of the Tutsi had fled to central locations. One Tutsi woman reported, "They came with a list of those to kill. My name was on it. They came by with a group and tried to force their way into the house."[52] Despite the attack, the informant's Hutu husband was able to prevent her being killed that night.

The Massacres in Mwendo

The genocide in Biguhu followed a somewhat different path than in Kirinda, centered much less on the church and more on the communal office. Tutsi refugees from Muko commune began pouring into Mwendo on April 9, gathering at various locations, such as Kugituntu parish in Mutuntu sector and the Mwendo communal office in Kigoma sector. On April 10, a gang from Birambo set fire to Tutsi homes in northern Mwendo, while other violent incidents took place along the border with Gikongoro, and violent incidents increased over the next several days, spreading into other areas of the commune. By April 11, refugees had begun to arrive from Musebeya and Musange communes of Gikongoro, bringing the number of displaced Tutsi into the thousands, while Mwendo's own Tutsi began to flee their homes, seeking refuge as well.

---

[49] Interview in Kigali, May 20, 1996.
[50] Interview in Kigali, May 20, 1996; interview in Kirinda, April 2, 1996.
[51] Details on the attack on the parish are somewhat more sketchy, since there were apparently no survivors and I did not speak to anyone who was willing to admit to being an eyewitness. Two of my informants, however, independently provided similar accounts of events there: interview in Kigali, May 20, 1996; interview in Kirinda, April 2, 1996.
[52] Interview at Gisovu, May 21, 1996.

Community leaders did not encourage Tutsi to gather at Biguhu, perhaps because they feared that the church's success at building community solidarity would inhibit church members from committing atrocities there. With the pastor and other parish leaders having fled, the parish seemed less secure, so most of the Tutsi living in the community followed the example of the refugees from Gikongoro and fled to the communal office, where they were housed in a grade school. The burgomaster appears to have been the key organizer of the attacks in Mwendo. As the former pastor from Biguhu claims, "The burgomaster changed people's ideas."[53]

The refugees from Biguhu stayed at the communal center of Mwendo for several days, then on April 15 the burgomaster sought to divide the crowd of thousands gathered at his office. He sent the people from around Biguhu back to their community, telling them to go to the church for refuge. This was, however, a trap. An armed militia group was waiting along the road between Mwendo center and Biguhu for the Tutsi to pass. When they came, the militia surrounded them and slaughtered them. "There was so much blood that the burgomaster's car slid on the road when he drove by later."[54] The armed gang then descended on Biguhu parish and killed the one family that had sought refuge there as well as several other families they found nearby. The gang then destroyed the large, two-story brick home of the agronomist, a church-owned building that had served as headquarters for the cooperative bank and other SDRB projects. Over the next several days, death squads attacked and killed thousands at the communal office and many thousands more in Birambo.

Survivors' Tales

The majority of Tutsi from Kirinda and Biguhu were killed in the massacres on April 14 and 15. Some Tutsi, however, managed to escape being killed in this first wave of massacres. Most Tutsi wives married to Hutu men were initially spared. Other Tutsi were sheltered by friends – or even, in some cases, by near strangers. Still others made their way to places of refuge, such as the Catholic parish of Kabgayi.

After seeing his family slaughtered before his eyes and fleeing the dormitory, Pastor Stéphane hid in the darkness for several hours. From his hiding place, he heard the attackers load the bodies of their victims

---

[53] Interview in Kigali, May 20, 1996.
[54] Interview in Kigali, May 20, 1996.

into the merchant Semilindi's flat-bed truck and transport them to the Nyabarongo. Several hours later, he left his hiding place to find refuge in Gitarama:

At 3 A.M., I left to go toward Gitarama. At the river, there was a barricade that the sub-prefect of Birambo and Kabasha [the burgomaster of Bwakira] had put up. It was well guarded, but the guards had drunk much. They were asleep. I passed the bridge, then I left the road, walking along the hills to avoid the barricades. Luckily, it was calm in Gitarama.

He briefly hid in the home of a sympathetic Hutu nurse,[55] then fled to the Adventist center at Gitwe, "But the pastors there said, 'No, we are threatened ourselves.'" So he continued on to Murama near Nyanza. "The burgomaster there welcomed us. He was very nice. I had no money. There were people who gave us money, and we were able to buy sweet potatoes. But after three days there, we were threatened. The burgomaster there began to change his face." Eventually Stéphane fled to the home of a student he knew whose family harbored him for the next three months, first in a hole in their wall, then on the roof, which was hidden by a banana plantation.[56]

  Georgette, a young woman who worked at the IPK, fled to the home of Margarite, the parish agronomist, a former teacher at the school. Margarite's family lived just behind the parish building on a steep hillside from which they had an excellent view of people approaching. "All my other colleagues and friends turned against me." She stayed there for several days, but people came to look for her, so she was moved. For the next three months, she moved around to the homes of various friends of Margarite's father, moving always under the cover of night.

Fidele, the principal of the IPK, he suspected that I was being hidden by Margarite. So he sent his domestic worker to go search for me, but someone got word to Margarite, and I was moved. If they had found me there, they would have killed Margarite and her family as collaborators.[57]

After three months, when most of the population had fled, Georgette emerged from hiding. "My eyes hurt from the light after so much time indoors, and I could barely walk because my legs were so uncertain."[58]

[55] Interview in Masango, Gitarama, November 26, 1996.
[56] Interview in Kigali, May 20, 1999.
[57] Interview in Kigali, November 27, 1995.
[58] Interview in Kigali, November 27, 1995.

She eventually made her way back to her home community of Muko and found that of her entire extended family only two young second cousins had survived.

REGULARIZING LIFE UNDER WAR

The bulk of the killing around Biguhu and Kirinda was finished within only a few days. Public authorities then had two immediate concerns – establishing a civil defense against the perceived Tutsi threat and restoring a semblance of order within the community, particularly seeking to contain the violent energy unleashed by the genocide. Following the large-scale massacres, the first concern of PAWA leaders was to seek out Tutsi who had survived the initial massacres. Knowing that some people from Kirinda had fled into Gitarama, those who had organized the massacres at Kirinda and Shyembe organized an attack the following day, Friday, April 15, on Masango Commune of Gitarama. The population of Masango, however, organized to repulse the attack, committing itself at this point to defending its Tutsi population.[59] Witnesses from Gisovu in Murambi Sector of Bwakira, reported that the militia from Nyabiranga Sector attacked under the leadership of the counselor. "They killed there and then came here."[60]

To ensure that Tutsi in hiding could be uncovered and that those seeking to flee could not escape, the security committees quickly established two security measures. First, they expanded the number of roadblocks throughout the territory so that every route of escape would be blocked, and they organized the population around each barricade to work as guards. Anyone wishing to pass had to show an identity card to prove that they were not Tutsi and, once regulations on movement were put into place, had to show their *laissez-passer*. The barrier guards searched vehicles that passed to make certain that there were no hidden Tutsi and no guns or other arms. Second, the security committees organized nightly patrols in each community. These patrols were ostensibly intended to monitor the territory to prevent RPF agents from passing through, but they were actually employed as death squads that searched

---

[59] Interview in Masango, May 25, 1996. A similar pattern occurred just to the south, where mobs that had completed massacres in Gikongoro attacked Butare Prefecture. While these mobs were initially repulsed, intervention from national leaders forced leaders in the resistant prefectures to support the genocide or face death themselves. See, Des Forges, *Leave None to Tell the Story*, pp. 439–44.

[60] Interviews in Gisovu, May 21, 1996.

homes for hidden Tutsi and stopped Tutsi from escaping under the cover of night. As one witness testified, "Other Tutsi neighbors were killed as they were fleeing. They had hidden left and right. The Interahamwe hunted them."[61]

Both the roadblocks and patrols required extensive community organization and participation. The churches played an important part in supporting these activities. In Kirinda, people who had risen to prominence within the church as pastors, church employees, or lay leaders assumed responsibility for organizing the barricades and patrols. The family of Twagirayesuused the influence gained through the Presbyterian Church to organize the population around Kirinda. According to several witnesses, a relative of Twagirayesu who had served as director of a church department in Kigali organized the nightly patrols in Gisovu.[62] As one witness reported, "During the genocide, all the family of Twagirayesu were devils. They all killed."[63] Other people prominent within the church, such as Nyilingabo and Ntawirukanayo, likewise took leading roles in organizing the roadblocks and patrols.

While seeking to guarantee civil defense and complete the genocide by flushing out and eliminating survivors, public authorities were also concerned about containing the violence that they had unleashed and reestablishing a degree of public order. After distributing arms widely in the population and involving a large number of civilians, including volatile youth gangs, in targeted attacks on those they defined as "enemies," public authorities feared losing control over the population and watching violence become generalized. The roadblocks and patrols not only provided a defense against the perceived Tutsi threat, but also helped to channel and contain the violent energy unleashed by the genocide. They allowed the disaffected youth and other disgruntled people in the community to expend their violent energies in officially sanctioned activities while at the same time regulating the use of violence.

The written records I uncovered in the Bwakira communal office indicate a strong concern with reestablishing order after the massacres. Burgomaster Kabasha held public meetings in each of the sectors of the commune from April 20 through April 26, to discuss security concerns, including the appropriate policies for running roadblocks and nightly

---

[61] Interview in Gisovu, May 21, 1996.
[62] Interviews in Gisovu, May 21, 1996.
[63] Interview in Kirinda, April 2, 1996.

patrols.[64] Notes from the meetings of the Bwakira communal council and from the communal security committee in April and May reveal an overriding interest in resolving conflicts in the commune. In the April 29 communal council meeting, the burgomaster requested that, given the war in Kigali, the political parties in the commune unite in order to guarantee victory. He called upon people with unauthorized arms to return them to the commune, and he asked that the violence in the commune diminish, because it might endanger international aid. "Those who are dead are dead, but those who remain have a right to live." Finally, he requested that councilors provide a list of all those dead, and declared that their property was the possession of the state.[65] A number of these points were reiterated in a security committee meeting a week later, particularly the fear that continued killings would jeopardize international assistance. This point is particularly interesting for understanding the position of the church in the community, since most international assistance that came to Bwakira came through the churches.[66] At a May 24 meeting, the burgomaster addressed the issue of land left by those dead or in refuge, ordering that each community establish a committee to oversee and guard the land. The sorghum from these fields was to be sold and the money used to support the army.[67] The burgomaster was clearly concerned that conflict could break out among Hutu over the distribution of land and other property of dead Tutsi.

The concerns for establishing public order were common to the prefecture, as several letters from the prefect indicate:

Honorable Minister,

I have the honor of transmitting in annex to the present, the report on security in Kibuye Prefecture for the period 11/4/94 to 30/4/94. This period was characterized by: interethnic (Hutu-Tutsi) killings throughout nearly all the prefecture, a massive displacement of people and livestock, pillaging; the destruction of houses of habitation, the destruction of public properties (churches, schools, ...).

Calm has been re-establish progressively since 25/04/94 and people begin to attend to their habitual occupations. Meetings of pacification have been held at the prefectural, communal and sectoral administrative levels.[68]

---

[64] Letter no. 0.293/04.09.01/4 from burgomaster of Bwakira to all sector councillors and cell leaders, April 19, 1994.
[65] Handwritten notes from Bwakira communal council, April 29, 1994.
[66] Handwritten notes from meeting of Bwakira Security Committee, May 5, 1994.
[67] Handwritten notes from communal council meeting, May 24, 1994.
[68] Letter no. 0286/04.09.01 from the prefect to the minister of interior, May 5, 1994.

In a letter dated April 30, 1994, the prefect urged all parts of the prefecture to institute training for the population participating in patrols and roadblocks:

In view of the security situation that prevails in the country, the Rwandan government has decided to organize a civil protection of the population.

This civil protection will be done by the population itself in the cells and sectors and will aid notably in:
-the organization and control of patrols and barriers
-the maintenance of vigilance against the infiltration of Inkotanyi by the regular control of hidden passages[69]

He held meetings in May with administrative authorities to institute the civil defense program.

The authorities expended considerable energy to restore calm and normalize life, while at the same time seeking to involve the population in self-defense. On May 3, 1994, Prime Minister Kambanda toured Kibuye and held a public meeting with prominent people from throughout the prefecture to discuss "security in Kibuye Prefecture (message of pacification)."[70] President Sindikubwabo, toured the prefecture on May 16.[71] The records at the communal and prefectural level reveal various steps taken to return public life to normal, ranging from seeking a military escort to protect a shipment of beer and soda to Kibuye "given the penury of beverages in the prefecture,"[72] to reports from various public services on the personnel still present and alive and their degree of functioning,[73] to copies of passes issued to people seeking to travel outside their home commune. The school inspector for Bwakira ordered the reopening of schools in June.[74]

---

[69] Letter no. 0281/04.09.01 from the prefect of Kibuye to all burgomasters, April 30, 1994.

[70] Letter no. 0282/04.09.01 from prefect of Kibuye to members of prefecture council, et al., April 30, 1994.

[71] Unnumbered, handwritten letter from prefect to minister of the interior, no date, but apparently from late June.

[72] Letter no. 023/04.09.01 from the prefect of Kibuye to the commandant de place of the gendarmerie, May 4, 1994.

[73] "Compte rendu de la réunion de concertation enter les chefs de service à la Direction Régionale des Services Agricoles de Kibuye en date du 27–04–1994," handwritten notes; letter from Director of Ecole de Droit et Administration, Birambo, to School Inspector, July 2, 1994.

[74] Letter from School Inspector Ndamyabeza Adrien to principles and school directors, no. 08.03/7/701/88, dated Bwakira June 6, 1994.

Ultimately, the desire to establish calm and the paranoid concern for self-defense proved contradictory. Despite efforts to normalize life under war and to keep the population under control, public order began to deteriorate. Conflicts broke out over how to distribute the property of those killed. The roadblocks offered opportunities for participants to harass and rob passersby, and the patrols became instruments for carrying out personal vendettas. A man whose house was across the road from the barricade at Gisovu testifies, "They stopped cars there, sacked passersby. They profited from the situation to steal. Their main objective was to steal. ... In May stores were reopened, but they had nothing. ... If there was a boutique open, the Interahamwe stole their goods."[75] The Bwakira communal council complained in May of people killing Tutsi without first consulting the authorities. In mid-May a soldier was killed in Murambi. According to the burgomaster:

The soldier who was probably on leave asked his friend to show him the Inkotanyi who remained. They went and took a child in a family that had legal problems with the friend of the soldier. The inhabitants [of the area] came to their aide and captured the solder. They beat him to death.[76]

In June the burgomaster asked the councilor of Shyembe sector to protect the children of Mujawashema, because he had researched and found that they were Hutu since their father's identity card was Hutu.[77] The prefect complains in other letters of militia from various sectors and communes combating one another. Yet even after all of the evidence of the unmanageability of civilian violence, the burgomaster was still in late June reiterating the importance of maintaining barricades and patrols and "cutting the brush" in search of the enemy.[78]

In a late June letter, the prefect discussed some of the problems disturbing the peace of the prefecture:

Honorable Minister, I will not pass in silence the problems posed by the population in the security meetings and on which they would like government to give direction. These problems could degenerate into conflicts. They concern:

---

[75] Interview in Gisovu, May 21, 1996.
[76] Letters from Kabasha to the commandant of Kibuye no. 0.313/04.09.01/1 dated Bwakira, May 13, 1994, and to the Minister of the Interior, 0.314/04.06 dated May 5, 1994.
[77] Letter from Kabasha to Councillor of Shyembe, no. 0359/04.05/3, dated Bwakira June 21, 1994.
[78] Letter from Kabasha to councillors of all sectors, no. 0.354/04.09.01/4, dated Bwakira, June 20, 1994.

1. Clandestine meetings of the political parties. Example: replacing deputies.
2. The sharing of property left by the refugees or the disappeared at the time of the trouble of April-May 94. It will be necessary to propose formulas conforming with the laws in force.
3. The punishments to inflict on people not participating in the rounds (daytime or nocturnal) and at the barricades for diverse reasons such as:
   -Men having Tutsi wives (not leaving them for fear that they will be killed)
   -People who do not want to leave the pillaged goods.
   -People who simply do not want to participate.
   It is among these categories of people that the population condemns as "ibyitso" [traitors].[79]

As the RPF advanced across the country, refugees from the fighting fled to Kibuye, contributing to security problems. They began to arrive in Bwakira in large numbers in late April, and by June there were over 20,000 refugees gathered in Kirinda and Birambo.[80] Witnesses report that the refugees changed the political climate in the area, joining in patrols and barriers, but also getting into conflicts with the local population.[81] As the RPF took more territory and moved closer, the number of displaced continued to mount. On June 2, RPF troops took Kabgayi, the Catholic center where some of Kirinda's Tutsi had taken refuge. Then on June 13, the interim capitol in nearby Gitarama fell, putting Kirinda on the front line. The RPF was more interested in pushing south to Butare and north to Ruhengeri and Gisenyi, so fighting never reached Kibuye prefecture. Instead, during the last week of June, French troops in "Operation Turqoise" occupied both Mwendo and Bwakira communes. During August, with the French troops preparing to withdraw and fears of RPF retribution high, the population of Kirinda moved *en masse* through the French zone of protection in southwestern Rwanda to Zaire, where they settled together in a refugee camp near Bukavu. Kirinda's elite left in their vehicles, while others followed on foot. In the camp, the residents of Kirinda reconstructed the village, with the social and political structure intact. Many of Kirinda's population stayed in this camp for more than two years, until attacks by Laurent Kabila's Democratic Alliance for Congo/Zaire and RPF closed the camps in late 1996. Some people then fled into the interior of the country, while the rest of the population returned to Bwakira.

---

[79] Unnumbered, handwritten letter from prefect to minister of the interior, no date, but apparently from late June.
[80] Ibid.
[81] Interview in Gisovu, May 26, 1996.

ANALYSIS

Because, in the final analysis, a majority of the Tutsi from both Kirinda and Biguhu parishes were killed in the 1994 genocide, a reader might rightfully wonder whether the distinction I have emphasized in my account between the "preferential option for the poor" and church integration into the hegemonic bloc is of any real significance. Further, in neither community did the church, as such, instigate the genocide. And yet, it is my contention that the churches in these communities did play an important part in determining the readiness of the community for genocide. While in Kirinda, both the church structures and its moral leadership helped make the community fertile ground for the program of mass murder, in Biguhu the church made genocide more difficult to carry out.

In Kirinda, the church was at the center of a patrimonial structure that organized support for an elite that included not only church employees but also local business people and state functionaries. This elite group enjoyed high salaries and generous benefits and also enriched itself through embezzlement, bribery, and other forms of corruption. The masses of the population continued to participate in this patrimonial system, because they were economically dependent on it and saw no other alternatives. They did, however, find ways to express their discontent through other means, and during the 1990s, as economic problems, war, and changing international conditions created a crisis, not only did these everyday forms of resistance became more open and more serious, but more organized and ideological challenges to the existing patrimonial structure also emerged. The adoption of ethnic arguments by the local elite aimed to reassert hegemonic control by shifting the justification for public support from economic dependence to the preservation of order and defense of ethnic interests. Church personnel embraced anti-Tutsi rhetoric, because they felt that both their personal positions of power and the broader patrimonial structure were threatened. The conspicuous anti-Tutsi sentiments of prominent church employees in the period leading up to the genocide helped to legitimate hatred of Tutsi, and the leadership of hospital director Kamanzi, IPK principal Ntawirukanayo, and particularly prominent lay leader Nyilingabo in gathering the Tutsi and then organizing the killings on church property helped give moral sanction to the massacres. The involvement of these men and several of the pastors in organizing patrols and barriers assured the general population of the moral acceptability of involvement in the so-called "civil self-defense" programs that acted as death squads.

The role the church in Biguhu played in empowering the poor – by creating economic opportunities and greater economic security, promoting
class unity, and providing an alternative ideological framework, one that
exposed exploitation and encouraged self-empowerment – made the local
population less vulnerable to elite manipulation. In contrast to Kirinda,
the population of Biguhu was not easily swayed by ethnic arguments, and
once the genocide was in motion, officials in Mwendo apparently did not
feel that they could rely on the people of Biguhu to carry out the massacres. Biguhu's Tutsi were of course killed nevertheless, but they were
killed in spite of the church not with the assistance of the church. The
destruction of the home for the agronomist and office of the bank of solidarity, following the massacre of Tutsi, served as a physical symbol of the
smashing of the church as a source of progressive change and support for
peasant interests. The demolition of the building, a solid two-story brick
building originally constructed as a home for the missionaries, forcefully
asserted that the church in Biguhu represented not an ally of the poor but
a bastion of Tutsi subversion.

While I have presented Kirinda and Biguhu as representing two contrasting visions of churches as institutions in Rwanda, the two tendencies to empower the weak and to protect the powerful were present to
some extent in every parish I studied, whether rural or urban, whether
Catholic or Protestant. Almost all public officials in Rwanda participated in a church, and many served on church boards or other positions that enhanced their status. Many churches distributed jobs and
benefits on a patrimonial basis. Even decentralized church structures
involved in charitable activities could be integrated into the patrimonial network. In both Kampanga Catholic parish in Kinigi, Ruhengeri,
and Save Catholic parish near Butare, assistance to the poor was distributed through the basic ecclesial communities. My research assistant at Kampanga investigated the names of those who had received
assistance in cultivating their fields or building a home from one BEC
and found that one man was a merchant who owned a mill and large
tracts of land, sufficient to produce excess potatoes to sell. Another
was a wealthy widow who owned cattle, goats and sheep and a large
tract of land. Another widow who received assistance in constructing
a new home also had livestock and land, as well as wealthy children
who could assist her.[82] In Save a man who was head of a Catholic BEC

---

[82] Interviews in Kinigi, Ruhengeri, August 12, 1992 and August 28, 1992.

before converting to the Seventh-Day Adventist church admitted that he received benefit for helping others:

When I was Catholic, I worked for the church helping the poor. We gave them clothes, food, blankets, and even that house over there of a widow was built with help from the church. I'm the one who advised them that there was a woman who needed help. In reality, I myself profited as well. People gave me beer, money, or came to work in my field so that they could stay on the list [of those to receive assistance].[83]

At the same time, nearly every parish in Rwanda had development projects that created opportunities for the poor, many parishes had decentralized their structures, and popular lay movements were widespread. Women's groups and youth groups almost all focused not only on spiritual matters but on economic ventures as well. In the young Butare Presbyterian parish, the youth group had started raising pigs to sell for profit. In Save, each BEC had a branch of the Youth of Mary, a group that, among other things, volunteered to assist the poor, carrying water, collecting wood, and working fields for a poor family each month. The Butare Catholic parish had a range of economic projects that they had supported with loans, from a farming cooperative to a sewing workshop to a tea boutique. My research found no evidence that this assistance had been distributed in a patrimonial fashion, and the assistance had clearly helped participants crawl out of dire poverty.

My point, then, is not that there were "good" and "bad" parishes, as even in Kirinda, development projects such as the women's basket project played some role in empowering participants, while in Biguhu the church sometimes reinforced the status of the elite and helped to create class divisions. Rather, my point is that a conflict was ongoing within the churches over how power should be exercised in the church. The historically dominant position of the churches as patrimonial structures, allied to the state and practicing ethnic discrimination was being increasingly challenged by an alternative vision of the churches as allies of the poor, promoting equality and class solidarity and seeking to decentralize and redistribute power. Most of the established church leadership, both at the national and local levels, embraced ethnic ideologies at least in part as a means of quashing the radical tendency within their churches. Allowing the church to become an advocate for the poor threatened their own elite

[83] Interview in Shyanda-Kinteko, Butare, January 29, 1993.

status while portraying the church as a supporter of "civil self-defense" against a Tutsi threat allowed the preservation of patrimonial structures.

In short, the churches in Rwanda were sites of conflict – class, political, ideological, religious, and ultimately ethnic conflict. As Gramsci's analysis would predict, a period of crisis in Rwanda allowed alternative configurations of power to attempt to assert themselves within the civil society, in the churches but also in a range of other organizations, such as human rights groups, women's groups, and development cooperatives. The ruling classes sought to reconfigure their power and reassert their dominance by co-opting some people who were challenging them, which they did using ethnicity as a wedge, and by using coercion, using violence against not only Tutsi but also some moderate Hutu. The growth of a vibrant civil society did not guarantee a revolutionary shift in power arrangements, because the elite used ethnicity as an ideology to co-opt or disempower civil society. The churches, thus, were not peripheral to this struggle but at its center. Taking the two case study parishes, while it may be in part coincidental that the leading Tutsi in Biguhu were killed in Kirinda, it is nonetheless significant. Twagirayesu in particular regarded the position advocated by people such as Stéphane and Géras as a threat to his authority within the church. His and his allies' active support for the genocide in Kirinda was in part an assertion of their position within the EPR, locally, regionally, and nationally. A similar situation occurred in many other parishes and in other churches. Churches were centers of considerable power in Rwanda, and the contest for power within the churches helps explain, in part, church involvement in the 1994 genocide.

CONCLUSION

Churches and Accounting for Genocide

In the half century since the systematic massacre of Jews in Europe under Nazi rule, the idea of the uniqueness of the Holocaust has become an important subject of debate. Many scholars, activists, and survivors feel that the Holocaust was such a cataclysmic event of such profound significance that it cannot be compared to other historical events without insulting the memory of those who died.[1] As Elie Wiesel has claimed, "The Event remains unique, unlike any other product of history, it transcends history."[2] In other words, the Holocaust was so terrible that it surpasses human capacity for explanation.

A similar sentiment has emerged in the aftermath of Rwanda's 1994 genocide. During my work for Human Rights Watch in 1995–96 in which I helped investigate the causes and methods of the genocide, I encountered many Rwandans who claimed that the massacre of Tutsi was so extreme and so terrible as to exceed human capacity for explanation. As

---

[1] Steven T. Katz, for example, wrote, "the Holocaust is phenomenologically unique by virtue of the fact that never before has a state set out, as a matter of intentional principle and actualized policy, to annihilate physically every man, woman, and child belonging to a specific people. A close study of the relevant comparative historical data will show that only in the case of Jewry under the Third Reich was such all-inclusive, noncompromising, unmitigated murder intended." ("The Uniqueness of the Holocaust: The Historical Dimension," in Alan S. Rosenbaum, ed., *Is the Holocaust Unique? Perspectives on Comparative Genocide*, Boulder: Westview Press, 1996, pp. 19–38), citation pp. 19–20. See also, Michael R. Marrus, *The Holocaust in History* (New American Library: New York, 1987); Avishai Margalit and Gabriel Motzkin, "The Uniqueness of the Holocaust," *Philosophy and Public Affairs*, 25, no. 1 (Winter 1996): 65–83.
[2] Cited in Christopher Shea, "Debating the Uniqueness of the Holocaust," *Chronicle of Higher Education*, May 31, 1996.

Catholic lay leader Laurient Ntezimana demanded in the documentary *A Republic Gone Mad*:

Is it possible to explain such things? Is it possible to explain? How can you explain a horror like Auschwitz? Is it possible? I don't think so. Sometimes things surpass human reason. Things descended to the depths of the utterly unimaginable. Unimaginable. You can understand the wickedness but not something so dreadful and so long, because it lasted three months. In the end, everyone allowed themselves to be carried along. Everyone. That is what I cannot explain. Everyone ended up being swept along, even the best of them. They all ended up accepting the unacceptable. That is what I cannot understand.[3]

With due deference to such sentiments, which I encountered repeatedly during my research, the question of how such a terrible thing as the genocide in Rwanda was possible is exactly what I have attempted to explain, at least in part. Specifically, I have sought to explain how such brutal violence could be possible in a country where Christianity is such an important influence. As a practicing Christian myself, the conclusion that the very prevalence of Christianity in Rwanda – a conservative, hierarchical, bigoted variety of Christianity – helps explain why genocide did occur fills me with anguish.

As a comparative analysis of violent conflicts around the globe unfortunately reveals, the massacre of Tutsi in Rwanda was neither unique nor inexplicable, but rather a particularly appalling and extreme form of a phenomenon that has become all too common: ethnic scapegoating. A number of scholars have observed that ethnic conflict has become increasingly widespread in recent decades. While analysts previously believed that such conflicts were a feature of scarcity and isolation, and thus characteristic of underdeveloped countries,[4] most scholars today admit that "the rising tide of cultural pluralism"[5] has affected even many supposedly "developed" and "civilized" countries. From the Basque separatist movement in Spain to the rise of neo-Nazis in Germany to the continuing conflict over multiculturalism in the United States, increasingly today,

---

[3] Laurient Ntezimana, speaking in Luc de Heusch and Kathleen de Bethune, *A Republic Gone Mad, Rwanda 1894–1994* Simple Production RTBF-Television Belge, 1996.

[4] As recently as 1997, H.D. Forbes sought to revive Montesquieu's contention that the diminishment of international isolation, specifically through commerce, diminishes intergroup conflict. Forbes, *Ethnic Conflict: Commerce, Culture, and the Contact Hypothesis* (New Haven: Yale University Press, 1997).

[5] Crawford Young, ed., *The Rising Tide of Cultural Pluralism: The Nation-State at Bay?*(Madison: University of Wisconsin Press, 1993).

"Ethnic conflict is a worldwide phenomenon."[6] Not only is ethnic conflict not confined to the Third World, but in addition ethnic conflicts can no longer be thought of as purely domestic political concerns, not simply because of the international moral obligation to prevent massive loss of life, but also because of the growing danger of ethnic conflicts spilling across borders and provoking international wars, as occurred in Central Africa, where the genocide in Rwanda gave rise to massacres and eventually civil war in neighboring Congo.[7]

Polish lawyer Raphael Lemkin first used the term "genocide" to explain Hitler's policy of massacring Jews during World War II. Lemkin defined genocide as "a coordinated plan of different actions aiming at the destruction of essential foundations of the life of national groups, with the aim of annihilating the groups themselves."[8] Largely through Lemkin's efforts, the United Nations adopted the Convention on the Prevention and Punishment of Genocide in 1948, committing the international community to prevent governments in the future from implementing plans to annihilate segments of their population based on their identity, giving international support to the post-Holocaust pledge of "never again."[9] What exactly qualifies as genocide has since been widely debated,[10] but the international obligation to prevent genocide, along with other manifestations of ethnic violence, has gained gradual acceptance, even as the international community has been slow to move in the face of recurrent atrocities.

In recent years, diplomats, activists, and scholars of international affairs have placed substantial emphasis on how to predict and prevent deadly conflicts like the genocide in Rwanda.[11] In providing a detailed

---

[6] Donald L. Horowitz, *Ethnic Groups in Conflict* (Berkeley: University of California Press, 1985), p. 3.

[7] C.f., David A. Lake and Donald Rothchild, eds., *The International Spread of Ethnic Conflict: Fear, Diffusion, and Escalation* (Princeton: Princeton University Press, 1998).

[8] Raphael Lemkin, *Axis Rule in Occupied Europe* (Washington: Carnegie Endowment for International Peace, 1944), p. 79.

[9] Samantha Power, *"A Problem from Hell:" America in the Age of Genocide*, New York: Basic Books, 2002, pp. 17–78 presents a vivid account of Lemkin's work on international law against genocide.

[10] See discussions of the genocide debate in Frank Chalk and Kurt Jonassohn, *The History and Sociology of Genocide: Analyses and Case Studies* (New Haven: Yale University Press, 1990), pp. 8–32; Fein, *Genocide: A Sociological Perspective*, pp. 1–25; Leo Kuper, *The Pity of It All: Polarisation of Racial and Ethnic Relations*, (Minneapolis: University of Minnesota Press, 1977), pp. 277–86.

[11] See for example, the Carnegie Commission on Preventing Deadly Conflict's extensive research in recent years now collected on a CD-ROM, *Preventing Deadly Conflict*

analysis of the role of Christian churches in supporting (and to a lesser extent opposing) the genocide, I hope that this text helps further understanding of the importance of religion as a factor in the success or failure of ethnic violence. In contrast to some conflicts, like the Holocaust and the Armenian genocide, or more recent violence in Lebanon, India, Southern Sudan, the former Yugoslavia, Sri Lanka, and Northern Ireland, in Rwanda religion did not serve as an ascriptive identifier to single out a minority for exclusion and eventual slaughter. Yet Christian churches were intimately involved in Rwanda's genocide nevertheless. The genocide in Rwanda was a program organized by powerful individuals, primarily in the military and government, but its success required extensive popular participation, and I maintain that churches were a key factor in encouraging public involvement. My research in Rwanda in 1995–96 revealed a variety of reasons why Rwandans chose to participate in the genocide. Some people were motivated primarily by greed, wanting to pillage from their Tutsi neighbors. Many participated primarily because they feared the consequences of failing to do so. Some acted out of obedience to authorities, who told them to participated. Others had a long-standing hatred of Tutsi and were in fact motivated by ethnic hatred. Some, like the youth whom Nyilingabo employed in Kirinda, were malcontents with little respect for life who relished the opportunity to terrorize innocent people. The most powerful motivation, however, was fear. By controlling the flow of information in the aftermath of Habyarimana's death and the advance of the RPF across the country, the regime helped to convince people that killing Tutsi was a defensive act. How killing unarmed children, women, and the elderly could be understood as defensive may be difficult to conceive, but fear clearly distorted many people's perception, and the insistence of authorities that no one be spared seemed to have had its effect.

Churches played an important role in helping to make participation in the killing morally acceptable, whatever the individual reasons for participation. While Tutsi were never defined as heretics or infidels, the churches were extremely powerful and influential institutions in Rwanda, and their majority voice gave moral sanction to the killings as

(New York: Carnegie Commission on Preventing Deadly Conflict, 1999). See also Susanne Schmeidl and Howard Adelman, *Early Warning and Early Response*, Columbia International Affairs Online, 1998; Robert I. Rotberg, *Vigilance and Vengeance: NGOs Preventing Ethnic Conflict in Divided Societies* (Washington: Brookings Institution Press, 1996).

an acceptable form of political engagement. In broad historical terms, the churches bear responsibility for the ethnic violence because of their role in helping to intensify ethnic divisions in Rwanda, encouraging obedience to political authority, and legitimating both state power and ethnic discrimination. But the churches bear more immediate responsibility as well. Political accommodation and ethnic discrimination continued into the post-independence era, with churches continuing to ally themselves closely with political authorities and continuing to actively play ethnic politics. Church leaders clearly demonstrated their support for the regime that eventually carried out the genocide. They not only failed forcefully and effectively to condemn ongoing ethnic scapegoating and violence, but they actively practiced ethnic discrimination themselves.

In analyzing churches at both the national and local levels, I have attempted to demonstrate how intra-church conflicts also contributed to church involvement in the genocide. These intra-church conflicts divided neither along denominational lines between Catholics and Protestants nor between levels of the churches, between the church hierarchies and grassroots. Instead, two broad, informal alliances cut across the many levels and organizations within each of Rwanda's churches.[12] There existed a fairly developed and coherent coalition of people within the churches who benefited from the status quo and therefore had an interest in preserving it. Church personnel enjoyed high status and had numerous opportunities to enrich themselves and their families. They commonly maintained strong reciprocal ties with business and bureaucratic-political elites. In fact, pastors, priests, bishops, and lay employees of the churches constituted an important element of the dominant socioeconomic group at all levels of Rwandan society, and the churches played an important role in constructing and maintaining the hegemony of the dominant group. Churches were well integrated into the structures of power in the country, and the patrimonial networks that ran through the churches played a major role in linking Rwanda's population into the dominant

---

[12] Robert Wuthnow, in *The Restructuring of American Religion: Society and Faith Since World War II* (Princeton: Princeton University Press, 1988) argues that the significance of religious denominations as political actors in the United States has declined and, thus, social scientists should look at alliances of interest that cut across denominational divisions, such as the informal coalition that has developed between conservative Protestants, Catholics, and Jews on issues like abortion and gay and lesbian rights or the coalition of liberals of various confessions on issues like the nuclear freeze. In Rwanda, I found a similar declining significance of denomination and emergence of cross-denominational coalition.

system. Individuals integrated into this structure received benefits that helped to defuse opposition to a system that created gross social and economic inequalities.

At the same time, beginning in the 1980s another more loosely connected network of individuals and groups had emerged within the churches that sought to challenge existing structures of power, both religious and secular. Church institutions and organizations offered substantial opportunities to contest the exploitative nature of Rwanda's social, economic, political, and religious systems. Many individuals and groups within the churches actively promoted the interests of the peasants, the poor, women, single mothers, Twa, and other socially marginal and exploited categories. Parish pastors and priests, teachers, development workers, church administrators, and even some bishops decried the injustice of the existing system that limited opportunities for a vast majority of Rwanda's people. Basic ecclesial communities, parishes, religious orders, development offices, and lay groups all sponsored initiatives to create opportunities for the poor and to shield them from the exactions of the system.

Churches offered opportunities for people whose poverty severely limited their economic choices and whose subordinate social and political status limited their influence over the shape of the community and conduct of the state to organize and make free choices. BECs, parishes, and lay organizations provided possibilities for people in similar situations – peasant farmers, women, single mothers, unemployed youths – to meet together, share insights on problems, develop systems of mutual support, and create a sense of solidarity. Economic opportunities provided by the churches and church groups allowed some people to break out of the patrimonial networks upon which they previously depended for financial support. The groups also provided occasions for individuals who were otherwise disenfranchised to participate in elections, to contribute to making decisions that directly affected the way they lived their lives, and even to assume leadership roles. The impact of this could be empowering, helping to transform the way that participants perceived themselves in relationship to their surroundings, convincing many of their capacity to change their material and social circumstances.

In addition to the practical and experiential contributions that churches made to the rise of a challenge to the status quo, they also provided important ideological arguments that could be used to counter the dominant hegemony. Sermons, prayer groups, and Bible studies all presented religious and Biblical justification for the poor to demand a better existence. While no clearly articulated conception of the appropriate structure and organization of political and social institutions had yet emerged in Rwanda, there was a growing sense among the masses that the existing system was unjust and should be replaced by something with a less powerful and less pervasive state, where individuals and communities could enjoy greater autonomy and greater opportunity. The churches, I contend, played a major role in creating this emerging alternative vision that undermined the existing system of consensual domination.

The alternative network that emerged within the churches not only helped inspire Rwanda's movement to demand democratic reform of state structures but also created a challenge to structures of authority within the churches themselves. Development cooperatives reduced the vulnerability of poor farmers to exploitation by the rich but simultaneously limited the ability of the pastors, teachers, and other church employees to accumulate wealth through illicit means. As people enjoyed increasing autonomy in their religious activities in BECs and lay movements, they were more reluctant to accept the spiritual authority of religious leaders and became increasingly critical of their misbehavior. Within the Presbyterian church, an increasing number of members talked about the need for Twagirayesu to retire. Similarly, many Catholics hoped for Archbishop Nsengiyumva's retirement. Church leaders were finding exercising authority within their own churches more difficult, as people were increasingly refusing to respect their orders. I heard repeatedly in the interviews I conducted in 1992–93 that churches were themselves being democratized, and church personnel supported ethnic violence, repression of the democracy movement, and, eventually, genocide in part because of fears of losing control over their institutions and access to the benefits and privileges that they had until then enjoyed.

If churches had established patrimonial structures that were integrated into national structures of power, why did church leaders at the apex of these patrimonial systems allow the emergence of challenges to the status quo? The answer is complex. At one level, the autonomous space created by the churches is an inevitable factor of religious observance. Beliefs cannot ultimately be forced upon people. As James Scott states, "In as much as religion represents a system of meaning, it cannot be coerced."[13] People can be forced to behave in a particular way, but they remain free

[13] James Scott, "Hegemony and the Peasantry," *Politics and Society*, 7, no. 3 (1977): 267–96.

to believe as they choose. They may endow religious symbols with meanings quite at variance with the meanings intended by those who created the symbols. Because belief is a central focus of religious institutions and practices, the fact that it cannot ultimately be coerced constitutes an important source of autonomy within churches.

Second, as they have operated in Rwanda, churches are at least to some extent voluntary organizations. People could choose to participate in whichever church they preferred or in no church at all, though admittedly heavy pressure exists for individuals to be members of at least some religious group. Both Catholic and Protestant churches are present in nearly all parts of the country, with several Protestant denominations often existing within one community, creating substantial options for religious participation. Church leaders depended to some extent upon membership for their power and their access to resources, and therefore, they could not afford indefinitely to drive away members. As Jean-François Bayart states, "the sacred market is particularly volatile, and sensitive to the strategies of the 'little people' or the counter-elites who are frustrated by the established order."[14] The fact that people can come and go from churches with some degree of freedom forces those who benefit from people's participation to offer them reasons to participate. Health and education services helped draw some people to the churches in Rwanda. Financial possibilities from employment, development projects, and aid distribution also attracted participants. But the resources available to the churches were limited, despite support from foreign donors; the churches simply did not have the capacity to buy universal support. The threat of attrition forced leaders to be sensitive to the desires of the membership.[15]

Third, changing material conditions in Rwanda forced churches to reform in order to remain relevant. Increasing overpopulation and soil degradation contributed to steadily declining standards of living for peasants. The majority of people in Rwanda found it increasingly difficult to meet the nutritional needs of their families, much less pay for school fees that could help raise the prospects for their children. These declining conditions made people less and less tolerant of corruption and personal

---

[14] Jean-François Bayart, *The State in Africa: The Politics of the Belly* (London: Longman, 1994), p. 191.

[15] For further discussion of the religious marketplace, see Rodney Stark and Laurence R. Iannaccone, "A Supply-Side Reinterpretation of the 'Secularization' of Europe," (September 1993).

enrichment by the elite. By offering development groups where people believed they could improve their fortunes and by preaching messages that called upon an end to poverty, church leaders could appeal to people and attract members.

Fourth, the international factor was extremely important. The Roman Catholic Church and many European and American Protestant denominations have demonstrated a strong commitment in recent decades to supporting economic development in the Third World. They supply financial assistance to churches such as those in Rwanda and expect that it be spent according to stipulations that they establish. Church leaders depend on this influx of money from abroad to enrich themselves and support their patrimonial networks and must therefore be responsive to the demands of the donors. International church development agencies have increasingly placed pressure on churches in the Third World to liberalize and democratize their development programs. In the past several decades, an international trend within churches has encouraged greater lay participation in leadership and other spheres of church life, and international church organizations pressured Rwandan churches to respond to this trend.

Missionaries were also an important influence in Rwanda. The sympathies of many missionaries, driven by idealistic principles and rarely integrated into local structures of power, lay with the less fortunate, and these missionaries were often critical of the church hierarchies and church structures. They helped to create an autonomous space, controlled by neither the indigenous church leaders nor the state, and they played an important part in supporting the emerging press, human rights groups, and development cooperatives.

Fifth, theological and moral ideas were a powerful motivating force. Certainly the Christian message, like any system of belief, can be interpreted in many ways, but the growth of liberation theologies in the past several decades has had a profound impact in Africa. Regardless of the actual practices of the churches and their employees, people at all levels of Rwandan Christianity acknowledged that the churches had a responsibility to care for the poor, and not a single person I interviewed in either the Presbyterian or Catholic churches claimed that this care should be limited to spiritual ministry and ignore the physical (though there were some who objected to the relative emphasis given to development and evangelism). Even church pastors who profited from embezzling part of the funds designated for development projects claimed to believe that they had a responsibility to assist the less fortunate. The belief that God

called on Christians to take up the cause of the exploited was a powerful motivator for a significant number of people within the Rwandan
churches to act against their own class interests and fight against a system
that in many ways benefited them.

While those integrated into the church patrimonial networks allowed
(or could not prevent) the changes in theology, structure, and development strategy that fostered the emergence of challenges to their power,
they did not accept these challenges passively. They supported state
restrictions on religious "sects" that limited the religious options for people, keeping the "sacred market" from being a truly free market. They
implemented reforms in structures (e.g., the transformation of BECs)
and policies (e.g., greater local control over development) to appease
their domestic and international critics, but at the same time they sought
to integrate new church organizations and movements into their patrimonial structures. As the government cracked down on dissent, the
targets included not only opposition party leaders but civil society activists, many of whom were church personnel. By remaining silent, even
as they urged the population to support the embattled regime, church
leaders gave tacit consent to attacks on church personnel, such as the
murder of Brother Cardinal. Ultimately, church leaders embraced ethnic
chauvinism not only because they supported political authorities who
adopted an anti-Tutsi ideology but because it was a means of co-opting
people back into the patrimonial network. By defining Tutsi as a threat,
church leaders were able to appeal to their members along lines of ethnic
solidarity and shatter the emerging class solidarity that was challenging their control. Few of the activists in development programs, wom-
en's groups, or human rights groups were thus co-opted, but during the
course of 1993 and early 1994, many of these groups lost their popular
support, as people became increasingly preoccupied with concerns over
declining security and, in particular, the threat posed by the RPF and
its allies. Ultimately many of the activists were targets of the genocidal
violence. The ideology of ethnic chauvinism combined with the use of
coercion thus effectively reasserted the ruling class's hegemony. This was
as true in the churches as anywhere else in Rwandan society. If many
people were driven by fear to participate in the genocide, as I argue, the
churches played an important part in fostering that fear, making clear
that they themselves viewed Tutsi sympathizers as a danger and that they
were more interested in reestablishing control over society than in supporting those who might be victimized.

EXPANDING THE POLITICAL

To understand the implication of Rwanda's churches in the 1994 genocide requires focusing not simply on the alliance of churches with the
state, as important a factor as it was, but also understanding churches as
inherently political organizations. Churches are not merely relevant as
interest groups capable of supporting or challenging state policy. Instead,
they are powerful institutions that distribute substantial resources. If we
understand politics to involve the struggle over "who gets what, when,
how,"[16] then churches are necessarily political institutions.

According to instrumentalist theories of social and cultural conflict,
public leaders may seek to intensify ethnic polarization as a means of
unifying potential supporters. These ethnic entrepreneurs seek to raise
the salience of one central social identity at the expense of other identities that have tended to create social bonds.[17] René Lemarchand argues,
for example, that violence against the Hutu majority of Burundi has been
used as a means of unifying a deeply divided Tutsi population.[18] Similar
arguments could be made about Russia, the former Yugoslavia, India,
Indonesia, and many other sites of conflict.

Scapegoating Tutsi was, I contend, a means used by a limited elite in
Rwanda to attenuate the growing importance of cross-cutting class and
political divisions that threatened their hold on power and to unify a substantial portion of the population under the banner of ethnic solidarity.
The bonds of class and politics that undermined support for the ruling
elite affected structures of power within the churches as well, and the
effort to unify the Hutu majority along ethnic lines also encompassed the
churches. Most of the changes in the churches that challenged the established structures church power within the churches and ultimately helped
to support the movement for democracy were not overtly connected to
the exercise of state power. In fact, the struggles over church leadership,
efforts by peasants to gain control of their own development projects,
and challenges to the authority of pastors had almost nothing directly to
do with the state. And yet, I assert that these struggles were intrinsically

---

[16] Harold Laswell, *Politics: Who Gets What, When, How* (New York: Meridian Books,
1958). This definition is surprisingly rarely applied by political scientists, who choose
instead to focus on state institutions.
[17] C.f., Kuper, *The Pity of It All*, pp. 247–75; Crawford Young, *The Politics of Cultural
Pluralism* (Madison: University of Wisconsin Press, 1976).
[18] Lemarchand, *Ethnocide as Discourse and Practice.*

political. In studying the mixed record of religious groups as both supporters of violence and peacemakers, Scott Appleby notes the pluralism that exists within religious groups.[19] The effort to control this pluralism explains in part church support for genocide in Rwanda.

The process of "democratization" that shook the foundations of state power in Africa in the early 1990s swept through other social institutions as well. Naomi Chazan argues that the state "constitutes merely one of many possible foci of social action. ... Politics, power and control are not necessarily coterminous with the state."[20] She defines politics as "the competition for access and control over resources" and power as "the capacity to control resources."[21] I would expand these definitions to suggest that politics consists of competition between individuals and groups over their perceived interests – not only economic interests, but also physical, psychological, and moral or spiritual – and power is the capacity for people to realize their perceived interests. Churches are political institutions not simply because they influence the state, but because they help people accumulate resources, increase the social status of individuals and groups, and provide support for people to pursue their vision of "the good life."[22] Churches are important repositories of power that assist in the project of subjugating one class of people to another and can assist, as well, in the liberation of one class from the subjugation of another. Quite significantly, churches can help people formulate a new social and political vision.

A number of authors have made arguments in favor of a broader understanding of what constitutes the political. Aili Tripp, for example, has powerfully argued that discussions of civil society in Africa have generally failed to take into account the ideas of feminist scholars who have challenged the public/private dichotomy common to liberal political analysis. As a result, discussions of democratization in Africa have ignored the contributions of women, whose activities usually do not fit within the narrow sphere of formal middle class organizations. Tripp argues that the

---

[19] R. Scott Appleby, *The Ambivalence of the Sacred: Religion, Violence, and Reconciliation* (Lanham: Rowman and Littlefield, 2000).

[20] Naomi Chazan, "Patterns of State-Society Incorporation and Disengagement in Africa," in Donald Rothchild and Naomi Chazan, eds., *The Precarious Balance: State and Society in Africa* (Boulder: Westview Press, 1988), pp. 121–48.

[21] Ibid, p. 123.

[22] In his interesting study of Egyptian politics, Raymond Baker draws upon Aristotle to argue in a similar vein that politics is the process by which people come together to pursue their visions of "the good life." Raymond William Baker, *Sadat and After: Struggles for Egypt's Political Soul* (Cambridge, MA: Harvard University Press, 1990), chapters nine and ten.

orientation of women's groups around issues relevant to feeding and caring for families did not distract the groups from "meaningful" political action but actually led them into political involvement.[23]

The argument for a broader understanding of politics has been made in contexts outside of Africa as well. Frances Fox Piven and Richard Cloward's classic study *Poor People's Movements* looks at social movements in the United States during the depression of the 1930s and the civil rights era in the 1950s–70s. The authors argue that the influence of these mass movements arose not from their involvement in formal political channels (such as elections and organized protests) but from their ability to cause social and economic disruptions that often occurred outside the boundaries of formal political organizations. Piven and Cloward contended that the political impact of social movements cannot be understood by studying only the activities that follow traditional political channels, such as the activities of movement organizations. Instead, analysis must be conscious of the fact that the effectiveness of a social movement derives from factors that lie outside the scope of what is normally considered appropriate for political analysis – strikes, riots, truancy, and other actions that are not overtly directed against the state.[24]

According to James Scott in *Weapons of the Weak*, studies of resistance among the peasantry have focused on "organized, large-scale protest movements that appear, if only momentarily, to pose a threat to the state," the type of movement "with names, banners, tables of organization, and formal leadership."[25] In contrast, Scott's study focused on the activities of peasants in a remote part of Malaysia. In order to promote their own interests, these peasants subverted in small, almost imperceptible ways the social and political order imposed upon them, using what Scott terms "everyday forms of resistance." Like Piven and Cloward, Scott recognized that activities outside of formally organized political movements can have substantial political impact, even when they are not overtly directed at the state apparatus. According to Scott's observations:

Resistance is not necessarily directed at the immediate source of appropriation. Inasmuch as the objective of the resisters is typically to meet such pressing needs

---

[23] Aili Mari Tripp, "Rethinking Civil Society: Gender Implications in Contemporary Tanzania," in John W. Harbeson, Donald Rothchild, and Naomi Chazan, eds., *Civil Society and the State in Africa* (Boulder: Lynne Rienner, 1994), pp. 149–68.

[24] Frances Fox Piven and Richard A. Cloward, *Poor People's Movements: Why They Succeed, How They Fail* (New York: Pantheon, 1977).

[25] Scott, *Weapons of the Weak*, p. xv.

as physical safety, food, land, or income, and to do so in relative safety, they simply follow the line of least resistance.... Multiplied many thousandfold, such petty acts of resistance by peasants may in the end make an utter shambles of the policies dreamed up by their would-be superiors in the capital.... Just as millions of anthozoan polyps create, willy-nilly, a coral reef, so do thousands or individual acts of insubordination and evasion create a political and economic barrier reef of their own.[26]

In Rwanda, the human rights groups, newspapers, student groups, and associations of intellectuals that directly and obviously addressed the state were only the most obvious manifestations of a broader challenge to structures of authority, the tip of an iceberg of social and political transformation. Peasants organizing farming cooperatives to create an alternative system of support to the exploitative patrimonial network, the refusal to participate in *umuganda* and *animation*, the burning of communal forests, the creation and expansion of movements of popular piety, the ostracizing of corrupt public officials, pastors, and business people, the uprooting of coffee trees, the growth of armed robbery and other crimes, and many other developments that took place in Rwanda in the late 1980s and early 1990s all represent aspects of a single broad trend. Like the obvious democracy activism, these myriad forms of resistance sought to express the frustration of the people with the exercise of power in the country and concretely to force a decentralization of power, to assert and obtain greater freedom of action in the lives of individuals and in the organization of communities.

Churches around the globe have supported movements in favor of the democratization of state structures, but their own authoritarian structures and practices have also been challenged as part of the democratization process. As John Witte explained in his introduction to *Christianity and Democracy in Global Context*:

Democracy also challenges the structure of the Christian church. While the church has preached liberty and equality in the community, it has perpetuated patriarchy and hierarchy within its own walls. While the church has advocated pluralism and diversity in the public square, it has insisted on orthodoxy and uniformity among its members. The rise of democracy has revealed the seeming discordance of such preaching and practice. It has emboldened parishioners to demand greater access to church governance, greater freedom from church discipline, greater latitude in the definition of church doctrine and liturgy.[27]

---

[26] Ibid, pp. 35–6.
[27] Witte, "Introduction," pp. 12–13.

In Rwanda, just as the movement for democratization of state institutions challenged the authority of the Habyarimana regime, the movement for democratization of the churches challenged religious authorities. In both cases, arousing ethnic hatred and suspicion served to win back popular compliance, if not active support, for the established system, allowing the elites in church and state to reconfigure their power. The genocide in Rwanda was a program implemented by an embattled elite, primarily military and governmental but with the support of religious elites, who hoped to reassert their authority by wiping out opponents and redirecting public discourse to focus on ethnicity rather than on corruption, exploitation, or class inequality.

GENOCIDE AND CIVIL SOCIETY

Some scholars have suggested that the end of the Cold War has led to a reemergence of ancient conflicts between ethnic and religious groups, since the Super Power rivalry and its associated threat of nuclear annihilation no longer keeps conflicts in check.[28] This perspective implies that societies are naturally conflictual and need a strong state to maintain order. Robert Kaplan, for example, has cited Rwanda as an example of the danger of foreign powers weakening the state by imposing democracy on divided societies,[29] implying that the decline of the state naturally leads to the explosion of deadly communal conflicts.

The case of Rwanda suggests the fallacy of regarding genocide as a natural product of social divisions. My analysis should have made clear that the genocide in Rwanda was a carefully orchestrated attempt by an embattled elite to preserve their power. Attacks on Tutsi beginning in 1990 were not spontaneous but organized by government and military officials. In the period leading up to April 1994, the military trained and armed civilian militia and drew up lists of people to kill. Political speeches, hate radio, and newspapers exaggerated and distorted the threat posed by the RPF and denounced Tutsi and moderate Hutu as dangerous traitors. After Habyarimana's demise, death squads launched the genocide by methodically killing people who had challenged the structures of

---

[28] Samuel Huntington, "The Clash of Civilizations?" *Foreign Affairs*, 1993, 72, 3:22–49; and *The Clash of Civilizations and the Remaking of World Order* (New York: Simon and Schuster, 1996).

[29] Kaplan writes that, "The demise of the Soviet Union was no reason for us to pressure Rwanda and other countries to form political parties ... ." Robert Kaplan, "Was Democracy Just a Moment?" *The Atlantic Monthly*, 1997, 280, 6:55–76.

power. The policy of massacres spread through the country only gradually through the intentional efforts of government and military officials. In most communities, government officials oversaw the plans for carrying out massacres, and armed military or police began the killing. Even after the violence in Rwanda began, organizers of the genocide had to intervene repeatedly to guarantee that the genocide was fully accomplished.[30]

In short, genocide in Rwanda was never inevitable. The leaders who chose to implement a program of genocide could have chosen other political actions, and those who supported the program and participated in the killing could have made other decisions as well. My purpose in writing this book has been to explore one factor in the equation that led to genocide in order to understand not only what actions churches took that helped lead Rwanda into disaster but why the churches acted as they did. As I have argued, church support for genocide is explained in part by the desire for church leaders to unify their followers along ethnic lines and to thereby eliminate institutional divisions that were threatening their power.

Defenders of the churches have contended that even though churches were involved at some level, they could not be truly responsible, because they were targeted in the violence as well. As I hope I have clarified, the fact that churches were both targets of the genocide and participants does not mean that they were neutral. On the contrary, the churches were a major battleground between the forces supporting revolutionary social change and those defending the authoritarian status quo. For the genocide to be successful, required not only to neutralizing the progressive voices within the churches but regaining the churches as a clear ally of the status quo. The supposed "attack on the church," was in many ways a battle *within* the churches between the two tendencies that I have outlined. As in the case of Kirinda, where pastors, church employees, and lay leaders organized the murder of their fellow church members, the people who attacked church buildings that housed Tutsi refugees were generally members of the parish they were attacking. The leaders of the massacres were usually church members seeking to assert their own authority against a perceived threat, both in the political system and in the church, which they had redefined into ethnic terms.

The fact that churches were so deeply divided and became sites of such severe conflict should dissuade anyone from regarding churches and

---

[30] This is the central point of Des Forges, *Leave None to Tell the Story.*

other organs of civil society in overly romantic terms. The tragedy of Rwanda confirms Gramsci's conceptualization of civil society as a site of contestation between classes, not an inherently democratic and egalitarian space. According to Gramsci, in most societies civil society was the most important source of domination,[31] and only in times of crisis did it become a potential source of revolutionary organization. The expansion of civil society in Africa has not by itself produced a collapse of ruling class power, as the ruling classes have found ways to employ the civil society to serve their interests. Churches in Rwanda did challenge ruling class hegemony during the period of crisis in the early 1990s, but they also contained key members of the elite who strengthened their power within the churches by focusing public discourse on a "Tutsi menace."[32]

Although community leaders organized the genocide, the fact that most of the killing was actually done by common people, such as poor peasants and unemployed youths, is particularly troubling. Although reasons for participation were complex, ideology was clearly at least one important element, whether the ideology of obedience to authority, ethnic hatred, or self-defense, and popular participation suggests that people are in fact susceptible to ideological manipulation at some level. Playing the "communal card" sadly remains an effective means of gaining mass popular support.[33] My own study of Kirinda diverges from Scott's Sedaka in this regard, as the elite of Kirinda who had faced increasing challenges to their authority used ethnic chauvinism effectively to regain voluntary compliance from a substantial portion of the population. Whatever their individual reasons for choosing to participate, the fact that the churches gave moral sanction to the genocide freed people to act. The attitude of the churches toward ethnic politics and ethnic discrimination reassured those who were motivated by the anti-Tutsi ideologies. Even those who did not hate Tutsi but feared the RPF and were convinced that they had to kill local Tutsi to defend themselves took comfort from the support the churches showed to the genocidal government. And for those who acted merely out of obedience, the church once again offered support. In Rwanda, unfortunately, the Golden Rule taught by the churches was not "love your neighbor as yourself," but "obey those in authority."

---

[31] "The state was only an outer ditch, behind which there stood a powerful system of fortresses and earthworks … ." Gramsci, *Selections from the Prison Notebooks*, p. 238.

[32] My findings are thus consistent with those of Stpehen Ndegwa, *The Two Faces of Civil Society*, in which he observes that civil society groups can provide important alternatives but that leaders actively seek to co-opt and control them.

[33] Human Rights Watch, *Playing the "Communal Card."*

Before writing off the masses as hopelessly gullible and civil society as hopelessly co-opted, however, it is advisable to return to the case of Biguhu. The fact that ethnic arguments were not effective in winning the support of the population here and that civil society was never co-opted suggests the limits of the strategy of ethnic chauvinism. In Biguhu, a clearly articulated alternative existed to the ruling hegemony. People in Biguhu were conscious of the ways in which they were being exploited by the elite, and the fact that Hutu and Tutsi had worked closely together in various groups made it more difficult for Hutu to accept that their Tutsi friends were in fact their enemies. In Kirinda, in contrast, public discontent existed, but it was not channeled in productive directions, and there was no clearly articulated alternative to the status quo. Biguhu shows the potential that churches offered for charting a different course for Rwanda's future. Where church patrimonial structures were weak and not integrated with the state and where the church had empowered the population to defend their interests, people were in fact much less vulnerable to manipulation. Biguhu suggests that even if churches could not have stopped the genocide, they could have made it more difficult and possibly less successful.

RELIGION AND GENOCIDE

In reaction to criticism following the genocide in Rwanda, some church officials, including Pope John Paul II, have contended that individual Christians acting on their own initiative were culpable for the genocide but that the churches as institutions bear no responsibility.[34] Although it is fair to consider who, exactly, can act in the name of a church, my analysis should suggest that however one wishes to define "the church" in Rwanda, whether by its leaders, its doctrines, or its membership, one will find culpability. Most of the people who killed in Rwanda were professed Christians, and many of these Christian killers believed that their actions had the blessing of the official church. What this suggests is not, as some observers have suggested, insufficient conversion to Christianity. Instead it suggests something about the nature of the Christianity to which the Rwandan population adhered.

Since their inception, the Christian churches in Rwanda, both Catholic and Protestant (with the partial exception of the Pentecostal church),

---

[34] "Pope Says Church Not to Blame in Rwanda." This letter was written by Cardinal Ratzinger who has since been named Pope Benedict XVI.

had taught obedience to state authority as a primary virtue. Churches had allied themselves publicly and proudly with the state, both during the colonial era and after. Since their foundation, Rwanda's churches had also legitimated ethnic chauvinism through their rhetoric and by practicing ethnic discrimination themselves. In the years that led up to the 1994 genocide, most church leaders continued to urge their members to support the Habyarimana regime, even after it was shown to be responsible for organizing ethnic attacks. Under domestic and international pressure, church leaders issued a few statements vaguely condemning ethnic violence, but most people did not take these statements seriously and instead believed that the continuing statements of support for the regime were the true position of the churches. Even after the massacres began, church leaders urged support for the new regime that was then organizing the killing. In short, the theology of both Catholic and Protestant churches in Rwanda, as expressed both through history and through the ongoing statements and actions of church officials, tolerated violence and ethnic chauvinism, taught obedience to authority, and condemned challenges to the status quo. It should not be surprising, therefore, that Christians killed in good conscience.

Religious institutions can be distinguished in part from other public institutions by their association with the sacred. Churches, as religious institutions, assert a right to exercise moral authority, and their stated purpose for existence is to direct the spiritual lives of members. When they act, they claim to be acting under divine sanction. If religious groups clearly and forcefully denounce social conflicts, their intervention can help to diminish the intensity of violence or to prevent it altogether, even if it is sponsored by the state. The forthright denunciation of ethnic violence by church leaders in Kenya in 1992–93 helped to prevent that violence from expanding and becoming more severe.[35] Clear denunciations of violence by church leaders in South Africa similarly helped to prevent the liberation struggle there from becoming more violent. Religious opposition was able to hinder the implementation of genocide even in states under German occupation in World War II.[36]

---

[35] Agnes C. Abuom, "The Churches' Involvement in the Democratisation Process in Kenya," in Hizkias Assefa and George Wachira, eds., *Peacemaking and Democratisation in Africa: Theoretical Perspectives and Church Initiatives* (Nairobi and Kampala: East African Educational Publishers, 1996), pp. 95–116.

[36] Fein, *Accounting for Genocide*.

In cases like Rwanda where the moral weight of religious institutions works in favor of violence, the results may be tragic. The churches in Rwanda helped to set a moral climate in which participation in genocide was an acceptable behavior. Alternative voices in the churches, those calling for human rights, economic development, and democratization of church structures, were ostracized by church leaders, and among the first acts of the genocide was for the regime that benefitted from the support of church leaders to target these sources of opposition, such as the Jesuit Centre Christus in Kigali. As the genocide unfolded, church members heard nothing form their leaders that would contradict the established belief that targeting Tutsi *ibyitso* was consistent with Christian belief.

To many people, such horrific behavior on the part of ordinary citizens as took place during the Rwandan genocide cannot be explained in simple human terms. As one man from Gisovu in Kirinda parish told me:

What we saw in this country surprised us, too. These were things commanded by the devil. There were people who were good, who stayed calm. But there were others who were Interahamwe. These were everywhere in the country. Everywhere they went, they sowed disorder, killed people, stole cattle, pillaged.[37]

He was not alone in believing that only the devil could be at the root of such appalling crimes.

Whether the devil had a hand in the Rwandan genocide or not is a question best left to theologians, but in answer to Laurient Ntezimana's question of how it is possible to explain how so many people could be swept up in such an unimaginably dreadful event, I would argue that understanding the role of the churches goes a long way in providing an explanation. The Christian churches in Rwanda set themselves up as the moral authorities of society, and in that capacity, they helped to make genocide morally acceptable. Those people who challenged this position, who called on the churches to follow a different vision, in playing a prophetic role and standing up for justice, those people were themselves ostracized and eventually targeted for murder. When religious groups are willing to provide moral sanction to otherwise unacceptable acts, they can help to make those acts acceptable.

If the world is to avoid other Rwandas and other Holocausts, then religious people around the globe must consider their own faith. The failure of the churches in Rwanda reflects on Christian churches throughout

---

[37] Interview in Gisovu, 1992.

the world and should inspire Christians everywhere to ponder their own beliefs and to analyze their own institutions to ensure that they do not similarly exclude and condemn. Religion has the capacity to prevent violence, but it also has the capacity to facilitate programs of violence and to add to their intensity. Whether plans for genocide succeed or fail depends in part on the attitude of religious groups. Let Rwanda stand as a warning to the world that, even as they can inspire people to act courageously and ethically, if religious institutions become too closely tied to state power, they have the capacity to legitimize abhorrent state actions. Religious groups can help people accept the unacceptable, and this is what ultimately is necessary for genocide to occur.

Bibliography

Abuom, Agnes. "The Churches' Involvement in the Democratisation Process in Kenya." In Hizkias Assefa and George Wachira, eds. *Peacemaking and Democratisation in Africa: Theoretical Perspectives and Church Initiatives.* Nairobi and Kampala: East African Educational Publishers, 1996, pp. 95–116.

Adelman, Kenneth Lee. "The Church-State Conflict in Zaire: 1969–1974." *African Studies Review,* 18, no. 1 (April 1975): 102–16.

African Rights. *Rwanda: Death, Despair, and Defiance.* Revised edition. London: 1995.

Africa Watch. "Beyond the Rhetoric: Continuing Human Rights Abuses in Rwanda." New York: Africa Watch, June 1993.

"Rwanda: Talking Peace and Waging War, Human Rights Since the October 1990 Invasion." New York: Human Rights Watch, February 27, 1992.

Aguilar, Mario I. *The Rwanda Crisis and the Call to Deepen Christianity in Africa.* Nairobi: AMECEA Gaba Publications, 1998.

Ake, Claude. "Rethinking African Democracy." *Journal of Democracy,* 2, no. 1 (Winter 1991): 32–44.

American Embassy, Kigali. "Rwanda, Foreign Economic Trends and Their Implications for the United States." November 1979.

Antón, Angel. "Postconciliar Ecclesiology: Expectations, Results and Prospects for the Future." In René Latourelle, ed., *Vatican II: Assessment and Perspectives Twenty-five Years After (1962–1987),* vol. I New York: Paulist Press, 1989, pp. 407–38.

Appleby, Scott R. *The Ambivalence of the Sacred: Religion, Violence, and Reconciliation.* Lanham: Rowman and Littlefield, 2000.

"Archbishop Carey's Visit to Rwanda: Rwanda Church Voice 'Silent' during Massacres, Carey Says." *Ecumenical News International,* May 16, 1995.

Association Rwandaise pour la Défense des Droits de la Personne et des Libertés Publiques (ADL). "Rapport sur les Droits de l'Homme au Rwanda, Septembre 1991–Septembre 1992." Kigali: ADL, December 1992.

"Avant-projet de la Charte Politique Nationale." *Le Relève*, no. 154 (December 28, 1990–January 3, 1991).

Baker, Raymond William. *Sadat and After: Struggles for Egypt's Political Soul.* Cambridge: Harvard University Press, 1990.

Baroin, Catherine. "Religious Conflict in 1990–1993 Among the Rwa: Secession in a Lutheran Diocese in Northern Tanzania." *African Affairs*, 95 (1996): 529–54.

Bartov, Omer, and Phyllis Mack, eds. *In the Name of God: Genocide and Religion in the Twentieth Century.* New York and Oxford: Berghahn Books, 2001.

Bayart, Jean-François. *The State in Africa: The Politics of the Belly.* London: Longman, 1994.

"La Fonction Politique des Eglises au Cameroun." *Revue Francais de Science Politique*, 23, no. 3 (June 1973): 514–36.

"Les Eglise chrétiennes et la politique du ventre: le partage du gâteau ecclésial. *Politique Africaine*, no. 35 (October 1989): 3–26.

Bedford, Julian. "Rwanda's Churches Bloodied in Genocide." *Reuters*, October 18, 1994.

Bergen, Doris L. "Catholics, Protestants, and Christian Antisemitism in Nazi Germany." *Central European History*, 27, no. 3 (Summer 1995): 329–49.

Twisted Cross: The German Christian Movement in the Third Reich. Chapel Hill: University of North Carolina Press, 1996.

Berger, Iris. *Religion and Resistance: East African Kingdoms in the Precolonial Period.* Butare: Institute National de Recherche Scientifique, 1981.

Berryman, Phillip. *Liberation Theology: The Essential Facts about the Revolutionary Movement in Latin America and Beyond.* New York: Pantheon Books, 1987.

Bézy, Fernand. *Rwanda, 1962–1989: Bilan socio-économique d'un regime.* Louvain-la-Neuve: Institut d'Etudes de Développement, January 1990.

Bigangara, Jean-Baptiste. *Le Fondement de l'Imanisme ou Religion Traditionelle au Burundi: Approche inuistique et philoshophique.* Bujumbura: Expression et valeurs africaines burundaises, 1984.

Biloa, Marie-Roger. "Institutions, le président et les autres." *Jeune Afrique*, no. 1526 (April 2, 1990): 36–8.

Bizimana, Jean Damascène. *L'Église et le Génocide au Rwanda: Les Pères Blancs et le Négationnisme*, Paris: L'Harmattan, 2001

Biziyaremye, Gérard. "L'Eglise et l'engagement politique en général au Rwanda." Unpublished paper, Faculté de Théologie Protestante à Butare, April 1993.

Block, Robert. "The Tragedy of Rwanda." *The New York Review*, October 20, 1994.

Boff, Leonardo. *Ecclesiogenesis: The Base Communities Reinvent the Church.* Queson City, Philippines: Claretian Publications, 1986.

Bonner, Raymond. "Clergy in Rwanda Accused of Abetting Atrocities: French Church Gives Refuge to One Priest." *New York Times*, July 7, 1995: A3.

Borer, Tristan Anne. *Challenging the State: Churches as Political Actors in South Africa, 1980–1994.* South Bend, IN: University of Notre Dame Press, 1998.

Bornstein, David. *The Price of a Dream: The Story of the Grameen Bank and the Idea that Is Helping the Poor to Change Their Lives.* Chicago: University of Chicago Press, 1997.

Bourdeau, Victor. "Une Semaine d'Horreur a Kigali." *Dialogue*, no. 177 (August–September 1994): 4–14.

Bowen, Roger W. "Genocide in Rwanda 1994: An Anglican Perspective." In Carol Rittner, et al., *Genocide in Rwanda: Complicity of the Churches?* St. Paul: Paragon House, 2004, pp. 37–48.

Bratton, Michael, and Nicholas van de Walle. "Neo-Patrimonial Regimes and Political Transitions in Africa." *World Politics*, 46, no. 4. (1994): 453–89.

Bujo, Benézét. *African Theology: Its Social Context.* Nairobi: Paulines Publications, 1999.

Carnegie Commission on Preventing Deadly Conflict, *Preventing Deadly Conflict.* CD Rom. New York: Carnegie Commission on Preventing Deadly Conflict, 1999.

Casas, Jean. *L'enfant des milles collines.* Paris: Les Editions du CERF, 1991.

"L'Action Catholique." In Comission Episcopale pour le clergé, *L'Eglise au Rwanda vingt ans apres le Concile Vatican II.* Kigali: Edition Palloti-Presse, 1987, pp. 179–217.

Centre de Recherches Universitaires du Kivu. *Lyangombe Mythe et Rites: Actes du Deuxieme Colloque de CERUKI.* Bukavu: Editions du CERUKI, 1976.

Cernea, Michael. "Farmer Organizations and Institution Building for Sustainable Development." *Regional Development Dialogue*, 1987: 8.

Chalk, Frank, and Kurt Jonassohn. *The History and Sociology of Genocide: Analyses and Case Studies.* New Haven: Yale University Press, 1990.

Chazan, Naomi. "Patterns of State-Society Incorporation and Disengagement in Africa." In Donald Rothchild and Naomi Chazan, eds. *The Precarious Balance: State and Society in Africa.* Boulder: Westview Press, 1988, pp. 121–48.

"Africa's Democratic Challenge." *World Policy Journal*, 9, no. 2 (Spring 1991): 279–307.

Chrétien, Jean-Pierre. *Le défi de l'ethnisme: Rwanda et Burundi: 1990–1996.* Paris: Karthala, 1997.

ed. *Rwanda: Les médias du génocide.* Paris: Karthala, 1995.

Burundi, L'Histoire retrouvée: 25 ans de métier d'historien en Afrique. Paris: Karthala, 1993.

Chua-Eoam, Howard. "Of Death and Defiance: Hate Kills Burundi's Religious Fighter for Peace." *Newsweek*, September 23, 1996.

"Churches in the Thick of Rwandan Violence." *The Christian Century*, 112, no. 32 (November 8, 1995): 1041–2.

Communauté Rwandaise du France, La. "Memorandum sur la crise politique actuelle au Rwanda." Paris, December 1990.

"Communautés ecclésiale de base: Une Eglise communion de communautés missionaire et authentiquement africaine." *Missi*, no. 508 (February 1989): 52–7.

"Constitution de la République Rwandaise." Kigali: service de la Législation de la Présidence de la République Rwandaise, November 24, 1962.

Contran, Neno. *They Are a Target: 200 African Priests Killed.* Nairobi: Paulines Press, 1996.

Conway, John S. "Between Pacifism and Patriotism – A Protestant Dilemma: The Case of Freidrich Siegmund-Schultze." In Francis R. Nicosia and Lawrence D. Stokes, eds. *Germans Against Nazism: Nonconformity, Opposition and Resistance in the Third Reich.* New York: Berg, 1990, pp. 83–117.

Crummey, Donald. "Introduction: The Great Beast." In Donald Crummey, ed., *Banditry, Rebellion, and Social Protest in Africa.* London: James Currey, 1986, pp. 1–29.

Cyanditswe n'Itorero Peresubuteruyeni mu Rwanda. "Ukuri Kubaka Igihugu." Kigali: EPR, March 1992.

de Gobineau, Arthur. *The Inequality of Human Races.* New York: G.P. Putnam's Sons, 1915.

de Heusch, Luc, and Kathleen de Bethune. *A Republic Gone Mad, Rwanda 1894–1994.* Film. Simple Production RTBF-Television Belge, 1996.

de Lacger, Louis. *Le Ruanda: Aperçu historique.* Kabgayi, 1939, 1959.

de Lame, Danielle. *Une Colline Entre Mille, ou le Calme Avant la Tempête.* Tervuren: Musée Royal de l'Afrique Central, 1996.

Deane, Herbert A. *The Political and Social Ideas of St. Augustine.* New York: Columbia University Press, 1963.

Decalo, Samuel. *Coups and Army Rule in Africa: Motivations and Constraints.* New Haven: Yale University, 1990.

Des Forges, Alison L. *Leave None to Tell the Story: Genocide in Rwanda.* New York: Human Rights Watch and Paris: Fédération Internationale des Ligues des Droits de l'Homme, 1999.

"The Ideology of Genocide." *Issue: A Journal of Opinion.* 23, no. 2 (1995): 44–47.

"Rwanda." In Cynthia Brown and Farhad Karim, eds., *Playing the Communal Card: Communal Violence and Human Rights.* New York: Human Rights Watch, 1995, pp. 1–17.

"Recent Political Developments in Rwanda," unpublished paper, March 1992.

"'The Drum Is Greater than the Shout': The 1912 Rebellion in Northern Rwanda," In Donald Crummey, ed., *Banditry, Rebellion and Social Protest in Africa.* London: James Currey, and Portsmouth, NH: Heinemann, 1986, pp. 311–31.

"Defeat Is the Only Bad News: Rwanda under Musinga (1896–1931)." Ph.D. Dissertation, Yale University, 1972.

Diocese de Butare. "Statistiques Annuelle Diocese de Butare, 1990."

Direction Générale de la Politique Economique. *L'Economie rwandaise: 25 ans d'efforts (1962–1987).* Kigali: Ministère des Finances et de l'Economie, 1987.

Donnet, Michel. "Les C.E.B., lieu de liberation des pauvres?" *Dialogue*, no. 141 (July–August 1990): 33–50.

Donnet, Nadine. "Le Massacre des Religieux au Rwanda." In André Guichaoua, ed. *Les crises politiques au Burundi et au Rwanda.* Lille: Université des Sciences et Technologies de Lille, 1995, pp. 702–4.

Durning, Alan B. "Action at the Grassroots: Fighting Poverty and Environmental Decline." World Watch Paper 88. Washington: World Watch, 1989.

Ellis, Stephen, and Gerrie ter Haar. "Religion and Politics in Sub-Saharan Africa." *The Journal of Modern African Studies*, 36, no. 2 (June 1998): 175–201.

Englund, Harri. "Between God and Kamazu: The Transition to Multiparty Politics in Central Malawi." In Richard Werbner and Terence Ranger, eds. *Postcolonial Identities in Africa*. London and New Jersey: Zed Books, 1996, pp. 107–35.

Ericksen, Robert P. "A Radical Minority: Resistance in the German Protestant Church." In Francis R. Nicosia and Lawrence D. Stokes, eds. *Germans Against Nazism: Nonconformity, Opposition and Resistance in the Third Reich*. New York: Berg, 1990, pp. 115–35.

Evêques Catholiques du Rwanda, Les. "Lettre Pastorale sur la parenté responsable." Reproduced in *Dialogue*, no. 129 (July–August 1988): 6–26.

"Le Christ, Notre Unité." Kigali: Pallotti-Presse, April 1990.

"Comme je vous ai aimés, aimez-vous les uns les autres." Kigali: Conférence Episcopale du Rwanda, March 2, 1991.

Fatton, Robert, Jr. *Predatory Rule: State and Civil Society in Africa*. Boulder: Lynn Rienner Publishers, 1992.

"Gramsci and the Legitimation of the State: The Case of the Senegalese Passive Revolution." *Canadian Journal of Political Science*, 19, no. 4 (December 1986): 729–50.

Fédération Internationale des Droits de l'Homme (FIDH), Africa Watch, et al. "Rapport de la Commission Internationale d'Enquête sur les Violations des Droits de l'Homme au Rwanda Depuis le 1er Octobre 1990 (7–21 Janvier 1993): Rapport Finale." Paris: FIDH, March 1993.

Fein, Helen. *Genocide: A Sociological Perspective*. London and Newbury Park: SAGE, 1993.

Accounting for Genocide: National Responses and Jewish Victimization during the Holocaust. New York: The Free Press, 1979.

Femia, Joseph V. *Gramsci's Political Thought: Hegemony, Consciousness, and the Revolutionary Process*. Oxford: Clarendon Press, 1981.

Forbes, H.D. *Ethnic Conflict: Commerce, Culture, and the Contact Hypothesis*. New Haven: Yale University Press, 1997.

Freedman, Jim. *Nyabingi: The Social History of an African Divinity*. Butare: Institute de Recherche Scientifique, 1984.

Funga, François. "Espacement des naissance... et apres?" *Dialogue*, no. 104 (May–June 1984): 56–64.

"Condamnés au Multipartisme." *Dialogue* no. 144 (January–February 1991): 51–7.

Gager, John G. *The Origins of Anti-Semitism: Attitudes Toward Judaism in Pagan and Christian Antiquity*. Oxford: Oxford University Press, 1983.

Gahamanyi, Jean-Baptiste. "Deuxieme lettre Pastorale de Mgr. Jean-Baptiste Gahamanyi, Evêque de Butare sur les Evénements de Kibeho." *Dialogue*, no. 120 (January–February 1987): 60–8.

Gakwaya, Straton. "L'Eglise Catholique au Rwanda, 1962–1987." *Dialogue*, no. 123 (July–August 1987): 46–58.

Gatwa, Tharcisse. *Rwanda Eglises: Victimes ou Coupables: Les Eglises et l'idéologie ethnique au Rwanda 1900–1994.* Yaounde: Editions CLE and Lomé: Editions Haho, 2001.

"Eglises protestantes." *Vivant Univers*, no. 357 (May–June 1985): 40–1.

Gatwa, Tharcisse, and André Karamaga. *La presence protestante: Les autres Chrétians rwandais.* Kigali: Editions URWEGO, 1990.

Gautier, Mary L. "Church Elites and the Restoration of Civil Society in the Communist Societies of Central Europe." *Journal of Church and State*, 40, no. 2 (Spring 1998): 289–317.

Gifford, Paul. *African Christianity: Its Public Role.* London: Hurst and Company, 1998.

ed. *The Christian Churches and the Democratisation of Africa.* Leiden: E.J. Brill, 1995.

"Some Recent Developments in African Christianity." *African Affairs*, 93 (July 1994): 513–34.

Goujon, Emmanuel. "Two Rwandan Priests Given Death Sentences over Rwanda Genocide." *Agence France Press*, April 18, 1998.

Gourevitch, Philip. *We Wish to Inform You that Tomorrow We Will Be Killed with Our Families: Stories from Rwanda.* New York: Farrar Straus and Giroux, 1998.

Government of Rwanda. "Recensement Général de la Population et de l'Habitat au 15 Août 1991." Kigali: April, 1994.

Gramsci, Antonio. *Selections from the Prison Notebooks.* New York: International Publishers, 1971.

Gravel, Pierre Bettez. *Remera: A Community in Eastern Rwanda.* The Hague and Paris: Mouton, 1968.

Green, Reginald Herbold. "Christianity and Political Economy in Africa." *The Ecumenical Review*, 30, no. 1 (January 1978): 3–17.

Guichaoua, André, ed. *Les crises politiques au Burundi et au Rwanda..* Lille: Université des Sciences et Technologies de Lille, 1995.

Gutierrez, Gustavo. *A Theology of Liberation: History, Politics, and Salvation.* Maryknoll, NY: Orbis Books, 1988.

Hammer, Joshua. "Blood on the Altar: Rwanda: What Did You Do in the War, Father?" *Newsweek*, September 4, 1995, p. 36.

and Marcus Mabry. "Victim or Mass Murderer? The United Nations wants Rwandan pastor living in Laredo tried for Genocide. First a Texas judge must agree." *Newsweek*, February 9, 1998, pp. 56–7.

Harrison, Paul. *The Greening of Africa: Breaking Through in the Battle for Land and Food.* New York: Penguin, 1987.

Harroy, Jean-Paul. *Rwanda: De la féodalité a la démocratie, 1955–1962.* Brussels: Hayez, 1984.

Hastings, Adrian. "Christianity and Revolution." *African Affairs*, 74, no. 292 (July 1975): 347–61.

Haugen, Gary. Rwanda's Carnage: Survivors describe how churches provided little protection in the face of genocide." *Christianity Today*, February 6, 1995, p. 52.

Haynes, Jeff. *Religion and Politics in Africa.* Nairobi: East African Educational Publishers, and London: Zed Books, 1996.

Hehir, J. Bryan. "Catholicism and Democracy: Conflict, Change and Collaboration." In John Witte, Jr., ed., *Christianity and Democracy in Global Context*. Boulder: Westview, 1993, pp. 15–30.

Helbig, Danielle. "Rwanda: de la dictature populaire à la démocratie athénienne." *Politique Africaine*, no. 44 (December 1991): 97–101.

Heremans, R. *L'éducation dans les missions des Peres Blancs en Afrique centrale (1879–1914)*. Brussels: Editions Nauwelaerts, 1983.

and Emmanuel Ntezimana, eds. *Jounal de la Mission Save, 1899–1905*. Ruhengeri: Editions Universitaires du Rwanda, 1987.

Higiro, Jean-Marie Vianney. "Kinyamateka sous la 2e République." *Dialogue*, no. 155 (June 1992): 29–39.

Hilsum, Lindsey. *Rwanda: The Betrayal*. London: Blackstone Films, 1996.

Hirschman, Albert O. *Exit, Voice, and Loyalty: Responses to Decline in Firms, Organizations, and States*. Cambridge: Harvard University Press, 1970.

Hochschild, Adam. *King Leopold's Ghost: A Story of Greed, Terror, and Heroism in Colonial Africa*. New York: Houghton Mifflin, 1998.

Hoffman, Peter. "Problems of Resistance in National Socialist Germany." In Franklin H. Littell and Hubert G. Locke, eds. *The German Church Struggle and the Holocaust*. San Francisco: Mellen Research University Press, 1990, pp. 97–113.

Holcombe, Susan. *Managing to Empower: The Grameen Bank's Experience of Poverty Alleviation*. Atlantic Highlands, NJ: Zed Books, 1998.

Horowitz, Donald L. *Ethnic Groups in Conflict*. Berkeley: University of California Press, 1985.

Horowitz, Irving Louis. *Taking Lives: Genocide and State Power*, 4th ed. New Brunswick: Transaction Publishers, 1997.

Human Rights Watch. *Playing the Communal "Card": Communal Violence and Human Rights*. New York: Human Rights Watch, 1995.

Human Rights Watch Arms Project. "Arming Rwanda: The Arms Trade and Human Rights Abuses in the Rwandan War." New York: Human Rights Watch, January 1994.

Huntington, Samuel. *The Third Wave: Democratization in the Late Twentieth Century*. Norman: University of Oklahoma Press, 1991.

"The Clash of Civilizations?" *Foreign Affairs*, 73, no. 3 (summer 1993): 22–49.

The Clash of Civilizations and the Remaking of World Order. New York: Simon and Schuster, 1996.

Hyden, Goran. "Religion, Politics, and the Crisis in Africa." UFSI Reports, no. 18.

No Shortcuts to Progress: African Development Management in Perspective. Berkeley and Los Angeles: University of California Press, 1983.

Information, and Public Relations Office, Belgian Congo and Ruanda-Urundi. *Ruanda-Urundi: Geography and History*. Brussels, 1960.

Itangishaka, Bernard. "Pour la défense du revenu du paysan." *Dialogue*, no. 130 (September–October 1988): 26–36.

IWACU, Centre de Formation et de Recherche Cooperative. "Rapport d'Activités 1992." Kigali, 1993.

Johnston, Sir Harry. *The Uganda Protectorate*, vol. 2. London: Hutchinson, 1902.

Joseph, Richard. "The Christian Churches and Democracy in Contemporary Africa." In John Witte, ed., *Christianity and Democracy in Global Context.* Boulder: Westview, 1993, pp. 231–47.

"Class, State, and Prebendal Politics in Nigeria." *Journal of Commonwealth and Comparative Politics*, 21, 3 (1983): 21–38.

Kagame, Alexis. *La Poésie Dynastique au Rwanda.* Brussels: Institute Royale du Congo Belge (IRCB), 1952.

Le code des institutions politiques du Rwanda précolonial. Brussels: IRCB, 1952.

Les organisations socio-familiales de l'ancien Rwanda. Brussels: IRCB, 1954.

L'Histoire des armées bovines dans l'ancien Rwanda. Brussels: ARSOM, 1963.

Kagarlitsky, Boris. *The Thinking Reed: Intellectuals and the Soviet State: 1917 to the Present.* London and New York: Verso, 1988.

Kaïdi, Hamza. "Economie quand le café ne paie plus." *Jeune Afrique*, no. 1526 (April 2, 1990): 42–3.

Kalibwami, Justin. *Le catholicisme et la société rwandaise, 1900–1962.* Paris: Présence Africaine, 1991.

Kalilombe, Patrick A. "Cry of the Poor in Africa." *AFER*, 29, no. 5 (October 1987): 202–13.

Kaplan, Robert. "Was Democracy Just a Moment?" *The Atlantic Monthly*, 280, no. 6 (December 1997): 55–76.

Karamaga, Andre. *Dieu au pays des mille collines.* Lausanne: Edition du Soc, 1988.

"Les églises protestantes et la crise rwandaise." In Guichaoua, André, ed. *Les crises politiques au Burundi et au Rwanda.* Lille: Université des Sciences et Technologies de Lille, 1995, pp. 299–308.

Kasfir, Nelson, "State, Magendo, and Class Formation in Uganda." In Nelson Kasfir, ed., *State and Class in Africa.* London: Frank Cass, 1984, pp. 1–21.

Katz, Steven T. "The Uniqueness of the Holocaust: The Historical Dimension." In Alan S. Rosenbaum, ed., *Is the Holocaust Unique? Perspectives on Comparative Genocide.* Boulder: Westview Press, 1996, pp. 19–38.

Kelly, Joseph. "The Evolution of Small Christian Communities." *AFER*, 33, no. 3 (June 1991): 108–20.

Kimonyo, Jean Paul. Rwanda: Un Génocide Populaire. Paris: Karthala, 2008.

Klotchkoff, Jean-Claude. "Méfaits d'une dépendance: Une économie dominée par l'agriculture." *Jeune Afrique*, no. 1551 (September 19–25, 1990): 55–6.

Kuper, Leo. *The Pity of It All: Polarisation of Racial and Ethnic Relations.* Minneapolis: University of Minnesota Press, 1977.

Lake, David A., and Donald Rothchild, eds. *The International Spread of Ethnic Conflict: Fear Diffusion, and Escalation.* Princeton: Princeton University Press, 1998.

Laswell, Harold. *Politics: Who Gets What, When, How.* New York: Meridian Books, 1958.

Latourelle, René, ed. *Vatican II: Assessment and Perspectives Twenty-five Years After (1962–1987).* New York: Paulist Press, 1989.

"L'Esprit et le sel: Recherches sur l'histoire de l'Eglise au Rwanda par un groupe de travail de l'Ecole de Théologie de Butare." Butare: Ecole de Théologie, 1978.

"Le pouvoir commence à se partager." *Imbaga,* April 1992.

Lemarchand, René. *Burundi: Ethnocide as Discourse and Practice.* Cambridge: Cambridge University Press, 1994.

Rwanda and Burundi. New York: Praeger, 1970.

Lemkin, Raphael. *Axis Rule in Occupied Europe.* Washington: Carnegie Endowment for International Peace, 1944.

Lernoux, Penny. *People of God: The Struggle for World Catholicism.* London: Penguin Books, 1989.

"Les Communautés ecclésiales de base: Une Eglise communion de communautés missionaire et authentiquement africaine." *Missi* (February 1989): 52–7.

Lewin, Moshe. *The Gorbachev Phenomenon: A Historical Interpretation.* Expanded ed. Berkeley and Los Angeles: University of California Press, 1988 and 1991.

Lewis, Peter. "Political Transition and the Dilemma of Civil Society in Africa," *Journal of International Affairs,* 46, no. 1 (Summer 1992): 31–54.

Lewy, Guenter. *The Catholic Church and Nazi Germany.* New York: McGraw-Hill, 1964.

Ligier, Louis. "Lay Ministries' and Their Foundation in the Documents of Vatican II." In René Latourelle, ed., *Vatican II: Assessment and Perspectives Twenty-five Years After (1962–1987),* vol. II. New York: Paulist Press, 1989, pp. 160–76.

Linden, Ian. "The Churches and Genocide: Lessons from the Rwandan Tragedy." *The Month,* 28 (July 1995): 256–63.

and Jane Linden. *Church and revolution in Rwanda.* New York: Africana Publishing Company, and Manchester: Manchester University Press, 1977.

Lobinger, Fritz. "Christian Base Communities in Africa and Brazil." *AFER,* 29, no. 3 (1987): 149–53.

Longman, Timothy. "Congo: A Tale of Two Churches." *America,* 184, no. 11 (April 2, 2001): 12–13.

"Church Politics and the Genocide in Rwanda." *Journal of Religion in Africa,* 31, no. 2 (May 2001): 163–86.

"Empowering the Weak and Protecting the Powerful: The Contradictory Nature of the Churches in Rwanda, Burundi and Congo." *African Studies Review,* 41, no. 1 (Spring 1998): 49–72.

"Zaïre: Forced to Flee: Violence Against the Tutsis in Zaïre." Human Rights Watch Short Report, New York, 8, no. 2 (A), July 1996.

Lorch, Donatella. "The Rock that Crumbled: The Church in Rwanda." *New York Times* (October 17, 1994): A4.

Luneau, René. *Laisse aller mon peuple! Eglises africaines au-dela des modeles?* Paris: Karthala, 1987.

Lungu, Gatian F. "The Church, Labour and the Press in Zambia: The Role of Critical Observers in a One-Party State." *African Affairs,* 85, no. 336 (July 1986): 385–410.

MacAfrica, Jé. "World Should Condemn Africa's Biggest Massacres." *African Christian* (1988): 4–5.

MacGaffey, Janet. *Entrepreneurs and Parasites: The Struggle for Indigenous Capitalism in Zaire.* Cambridge: Cambridge University Press, 1987.

Magnani, Giovanni. "Does the So-Called Theology of the Laity Possess a Theological Status?" In René Latourelle, ed., *Vatican II: Assessment and Perspectives Twenty-five Years After (1962–1987)*, vol. I. Mahwah: Paulist Press, 1989, 568–633.

Maindron, Gabriel. *Des Apparitions à Kibeho: Anoonce de Marie au Coeur de l'Afrique.* Paris: O.I.E.L., 1984.

Malyomeza, Théophile. "Ces sects religieuses qui nous interpellent." *Dialogue*, no. 125 (November–December 1987): 22–41.

Mamdani, Mahmood. *Citizen and Subject: Contemporary Africa and the Legacy of Late Colonialism.* Princeton: Princeton University Press, 1996.

Maquet, Jacques J. *The Premise of Inequality in Rwanda: A Study of Political Relations in a Central African Kingdom.* London: Oxford University Press, 1961.

Marable, Manning. *How Capitalism Underdeveloped Black America.* Boston: South End Press, 1983.

Margalit, Avishai, and Gabriel Motzkin. "The Uniqueness of the Holocaust," *Philosophy and Public Affairs*, 25, no. 1 (Winter 1996): 65–83.

Marrus, Michael R. *The Holocaust in History.* New York: New American Library, 1987.

"Martyrs of Rwanda, The." *The Tablet.* (June 25, 1994): 791.

Mbembe, Achille. *Afrique Indocile.* Paris: Karthala, 1988.

Mbonimana, Gamiliel. "Christianisation indirect et cristallisation des clivages ethniques au Rwanda (1925–1931)." *Enquêtes et Documents d'Histoire Africaine*, 3 (1978): 125–63.

Mbonyintege, Smaragde. "Mouvements de spiitualité et récent dévotions poulaires au Rwanda." In *L'Eglise du Rwanda vingt ans apres le Concil Vatican deux.* Kigali: Editions Pallotti-Presse, 1987, pp. 311–30.

McCullum, Hugh. *The Angels Have Left Us: The Rwanda Tragedy and the Churches.* Geneva: WCC Publications, 1995.

Melson, Robert. *Revolution and Genocide: On the Origins of the Armenian Genocide and the Holocaust.* Chicago: University of Chicago Press, 1992.

Mfizi, Christophe. *Les lignes de faite du Rwanda Indépendant.* Kigali: Office Rwandais d'Information, 1983.

"Le Réseau Zéro," Open letter to the President of the MRND. Kigali: Editions Uruhimbi, July–August 1992.

Mfizi, François-Xavier, "Les Temoins de Jehovah." Ecole de Théologie de Butare, 1985–1986.

Ministry of Planning, Republic of Rwanda. "3ieme Table Ronde des Aides Exterieurs au Rwanda." Kigali, 1982.

Misago, Augustin. *Les Apparitions de Kibeho au Rwanda.* Kinshasa: Faculté Catholique de Kinshasa, 1991.

"Evangelisation et Culture Rwandaise." In *L'Eglise du Rwanda vingt ans apres le Concil Vatican deux.* Kigali: Editions Pallotti-Presse, 1987.

Misser, François. "Rumpus in Rwanda." *New African* (August 1990): 20.

Monga, Celestin. "Civil Society and Democratisation in Francophone Africa." *The Journal of Modern Africa Studies*, 33, no. 3 (1995): 359–79.

The Anthropology of Anger: Civil Society and Democracy in Africa. Boulder: Lynne Rienner, 1996.

Mugambi, J.N.K. "African Churches in Social Transformation." *Journal of International Affairs*, 50, no. 1 (Summer 1996): 194–221.

Mugesera, Antoine. "L'Irresistible poussée démocratique." *Dialogue*, no. 144 (January–February 1991): 129–43.

"Multipartisme? Pourquoi pas! Une interview du president Juneval Habyarimana." *Jeune Afrique*, no. 1551. (September 19–25, 1990): 47.

Munyatugerero, François-Xavier. "Oui au multipartisme." *Jeune Afrique*, no. 1560 (November 21–27, 1990): 7.

"Dérapages de moins en moins contrôlés." *Jeune Afrique*, no. 1562 (December 5–11, 1990): 29.

Munyembaraga, Narciss. "Développement socio-économique: Problèmes et perspectives." *Vivant Univers*, no. 357 (May–June 1985): 10–15.

Mutaganzwa, Charles. "La liberté de presse, essai d'interpretation conjoncturelle." *Dialogue*, no. 147 (July–August 1991): 51–61.

Muzungu, Bernardin. *Le Dieu de nos peres.* In three volumes. Bujumbura: Presse Lavigerie, 1974, 1975, and 1981.

Mvukiyehe, Etienne. "Sensibilisation au probleme demographique rwandais." *Dialogue*, no. 45 (July–August 1974): 47–58.

Nahimana, Ferdinand. *Le blanc est arivée, le roi est parti: Une facette de l'histoire due Rwanda contemporain, 1894–1931.* Kigali: Printer Set, 1987.

Ndahiro, Tom. "The Church's Blind Eye to Genocide in Rwanda," in Carol Rittner, et al, *Genocide in Rwanda: Complicity of the Churches?* St. Paul: Paragon House, 2004, pp. 229–49.

Ndegwa, Stephen. *The Two Faces of Civil Society: NGOs and Politics in Africa.* West Hartford: Kumarian Press, 1996.

Newbury, David, and M. Catharine Newbury. "Rethinking Rwandan Historiography: Bringing the Peasants Back In." Paper prepared for Colloquium Series, Program in Agrarian Studies, Yale University, April 3, 1998.

Newbury, M. Catharine. "Rwanda: Recent Debates Over Governance and Rural Development." In Goran Hyden and Michael Bratton, eds., *Governance and Politics in Africa.* Boulder: Lynne Reinner, 1992, pp. 193–219.

"The Resurgence of Civil Society in Rwanda." Paper prepared for conference on Civil Society in Africa, Hebrew University, Jerusalem, January 5–9, 1992.

The Cohesion of Oppression: Citizenship and Ethnicity in Rwanda, 1860–1960. New York, Columbia University Press, 1988.

"Dead and Buried or Just Underground? The Privatization of the State in Zaire." *Canadian Journal of African Studies*, 18, no. 1 (1984): 112–14.

Nezehose, Jean Bosco. *Agriculture rwandaise: Problématique et perspectives.* INADES-Formation-Rwanda, 1990.

Ngirira, Mathieu, and Nzitabakuze Jean Bosco. *Le Rwanda à la croisée des chemins.* Butare, June 1991, 74–5.

Nicosia, Francis R., and Lawrence D. Stokes, eds. *The German Church Struggle and the Holocaust*. San Francisco: Mellen Research University Press, 1990.

Ntamahungiro, Joseph. "Se reconcilier avec le Peuple." *Dialogue*, no. 147 (July–August 1991): 35–50.

"Oui au Multipartisme." *Dialogue*, no. 144 (January–February 1991): 59–73.

"Sans morale pas de démocratie." *Dialogue* no. 128 (May–June 1988): 26–38.

Ntezimana, Emmanuel. "Principes essentiels et conditions préalables à la démocratie." *Dialogue* no. 144 (January–February 1991).

Nyandwi, Damien. "Que les Parties Politiques S'interessent Normalement aux Problèmes actuelles du Pays: Que les Partis Nous Disent Ce Qu'ils Vont Faire au Lieu de Nous Tromper." *Imbaga*, no. 10–11 (February–March 1992).

Office National de la Population. "Rwanda 1983 Enquête sur la Fécondité." Kigali: ONAPO, 1983.

Le Problème Démographique au Rwanda et le Cadre de sa Solution. Kigali: la Présidence du MRND and ONAPO, 1990.

O'Hara, Thomas. "Rwandan bishops faltered in face of crisis." *National Catholic Reporter*, September 29, 1995.

Overdulve, C.M. *Le defi des pauvres: De la fonction diaconale de l'Eglise au Rwanda*. Butare: Faculté de Théologie Protestante, 1991.

Pages, A. *Un Royaume Hamite au centre de l'Afrique: Au Rwanda sur les bos du lac Kivu*. Brussels: Van Campenhout, 1933.

Parratt, John. *Reinventing Christianity: African Theology Today*. Grand Rapids, MI: William B. Eerdmans Publishing and Trenton, NJ: Africa World Press, 1995.

Paternoste de la Mairieu, Baudouin. *Le Rwanda: son effort de développement: Antécédents historiques et conquêtes de la révolution rwandaise*. Brussels: Editions A. De Boeck, 1981.

Phayer, Michael. "The Catholic Resistance Circle in Berlin and German Catholic Bishops during the Holocaust." *Holocaust and Genocide Studies*, 7, no. 3 (Fall 1993): 216–29.

Piven, Frances Fox, and Richard A. Cloward. *Poor People's Movements: Why They Succeed, How They Fail*. New York: Pantheon, 1977.

"Pope Says Church is Not to Blame in Rwanda." *New York Times*, March 21, 1996: A3.

Pottier, Johan. "Taking Stock: Food Marketing Reform in Rwanda, 1982–89." *African Affairs*, 92, no. 366 (January 1993): 5–31.

"Debating Styles in a Rwandan Co-operative: Reflections on Language, Policy and Gender." In Ralph Grill, ed., *Sociological Review Monograph*, no. 36, pp.41–60.

"Pour le multipartisme et la démocratie." *Dialogue* no. 144 (January–February 1991): 144–50.

Power, Samantha. *"A Problem from Hell:" America and the Age of Genocide*. New York: Basic Books, 2002.

Priests of the Diocese of Nyundo. "Des Rescapés du Diocese de Nyundo Temoignent." *Dialogue* (August-September 1994): 59–68.

"Priests Sentenced to Death for Rwanda Massacre." Associated Press, April 20, 1998.

Prunier, Gerard. *The Rwanda Crisis: History of a Genocide.* New York: Columbia University Press, 1995.

"L'Uganda et le F.P.R." *Dialogue,* no. 162 (February 1993): 3–18.

"Radioscopie de la nouvelle presse rwandaise." *Dialogue,* no. 147 (July–August 1991): 69–80.

Rau, Bill. *From Feast to Famine: Official Cures and Grassroots Remedies to Africa's Food Crisis.* London: Zed Books, 1991.

Rennie, J.K. "The Precolonial Kingdom of Rwanda: A Reinterpretation." *Transafrican Journal of History,* 2, no. 2 (1972): 11–54.

République Rwandaise. *Recensement général de la population et de l'habitat au 15 août 1991: Resultats provisoire.* Kigali: Service National de Recensement, December, 1992.

Reyntjens, Filip. *Trois jours qui ont fait basculer l'histoire.* Paris: l'Harmattan, 1995.

L'Afrique des Grandes Lacs en Crise: Rwanda, Burundi: 1988–1994. Paris: Karthala, 1994.

"Rwanda: Economy." In *Africa South of the Sahara: 1993.* London: Europa Publications, 1993, pp. 680–82.

"Rwanda: Recent History." In *Africa South of the Sahara: 1993.* London: Europa Publications, 1993, pp. 678–9.

Pouvoir et Droit au Rwanda: Driot Publique et Evolution Politique, 1916–1973. Butare: Institut National de Recherche Scientifique, 1985.

Rittner, Carol, John K. Roth, and Wendy Whitworth. *Genocide in Rwanda: Complicity of the Churches?* St. Paul: Paragon House, 2004.

Rotberg, Robert I. *Vigilance and Vengeance: NGOs Preventing Ethnic Conflict in Divided Societies.* Washington: Brookings Institution Press, 1996.

Rubenstein, Richard L., and John K. Roth. *Approaches to Auschwitz: The Holocaust and its Legacy.* Atlanta: John Knox Press, 1987.

Rumiya, Jean. "Ruanda d'hier, Rwanda d'aujourd'hui." *Vivant Univers,* no. 357 (May–June 1985): 2–8.

Rutayisire, Paul. *La christianisation du Rwanda (1900–1945): Méthode missionaire et politique selon Mgr. Léon Classe.* Editions Universitaires Fribourg Suisse, 1987.

Rutembesa, Faustin, Jean-Pierre Karegeye, and Paul Rutayisire. *Rwanda: L'Église catholique à l'épreuve du génocide,* Greenfield Park: Les Editions Africana, 2000.

Rwabukwisi, Viateur. "Relations juridiques entre l'Etat rwandais et les confessions religieuses en matier socio-sanitaire." *Imbonezamuryango,* no. 12. (August 1988): 17–20.

"Rwanda: Defiant Protestants Jailed." *Africa Report* (January–February 1987).

"Rwanda: Entre la peur et l'anatheme." *Dialogue,* no. 125 (November–December 1987): 3–7.

"Rwanda/Uganda: A Violent Homecoming." *Africa Confidential,* 31, no. 21 (October 12, 1990): 1–3.

"Rwandan Churches Culpable, says WCC." *The Christian Century,* 111, no. 24 (August 24–31, 1994): 778.

Safi, Protais. "La formation du lacait chrétian." In *L'Eglise du Rwanda vingt and apres le Concile Vatican deux.* Kigali: Edition Pallotti-Presse, 1987, pp. 153–66.

Sanders, Edith R. "The Hamitic Hypothesis: Its Origin and Functions in Time Perspective." *Journal of African History*, 10, no. 4 (1969): 521–32.

Saul, John. "'For Fear of Being Condemned as Old Fashioned': Liberal Democracy vs. Popular Democracy in Sub-Saharan Africa." *Review of African Political Economy*, 24, no. 73 (1997): 339–53.

"Liberal Democracy vs. Popular Democracy in Southern Africa." *Review of African Political Economy*, 24, no. 72 (1997): 219–36.

Schatzberg, Michael. *Political Legitimacy in Middle Africa: Father, Family, Food.* Bloomington, IN: Indiana University Press, 2001.

The Dialectics of Oppression in Zaire. Bloomington, IN: Indiana University Press, 1988.

Schmeidle, Susan, and Howard Adelman. *Early Warning and Early Response.* New York: Columbia International Affairs Online, 1998.

Schonecke, Wolfgang. "The Role of the Church in Rwanda." *America* (June 17, 1995).

Scott, James. *Weapons of the Weak: Everyday Forms of Peasant Resistance.* New Haven: Yale University Press, 1985.

"Hegemony and the Peasantry." *Politics and Society*, 7, no. 3 (1977): 267–96.

Secrétariat Général des Evêques Catholiques du Rwanda. *Recueil des Lettres et Messages de la Conference des Evêques Catholiques du Rwanda Publiés Pendant la Period de Guerre (1990–1994).* Kigali: Sécretariat Général, 1995.

Sells, Michael A. *The Bridge Betrayed: Religion and Genocide in Bosnia.* Berkeley: University of California Press, 1996.

Semana, Emmanuel. "Politiques et programmes de population dans le monde et au Rwanda." *Imbonrzamuryango*, no. 12 (August 1988): 5–11.

Service d'Appui à la Coopération Canadienne. "Profil socio-économique de la femme rwandaise." Kigali: Réseau des femmes oeuvrant pour le développement rural, May 1991.

Shea, Christopher. "Debating the Uniqueness of the Holocaust." *Chronicle of Higher Education.* May 31, 1996.

Shelah, Menachem. "The Catholic Church in Croatia, the Vatican and the Murder of Croatian Jews." *Holocaust and Genocide Studies*, 4, no. 3 (1989): 323–39.

Sibomana, André. *Hope for Rwanda: Conversations with Laure Guilbert and Hervé Deguine*, London: Pluto Press, and Dar es Salaam: Mkuki na Nyota Publishers, 1999.

Sigaud, Dominique. "Genocide: le dossier noir de l'Eglise rwandaise." *Le Nouvel Observateur.* February 1–7, 1996: 50–1.

Sigmund, Paul E. *Liberation Theology at the Crossroads: Democracy or Revolution?* New York and Oxford: Oxford University Press, 1990.

"Sin and Confession in Rwanda." *The Economist*, January 14, 1995: 39.

Sirven, Pierre. *La sous-urbanization et les villes du Rwanda et du Burundi.* Published by the author: 1984.

Smith, Helmut Walser. "Religion and Conflict: Protestants, Catholics, and Anti-Semitism in the State of Baden in the Era of Wilhelm II." *Central European History*, 27, no. 3 (Summer 1995): 283–314.

Speke, John Hanning. *Journal of the Discovery of the Source of the Nile.* London: William Blackwood and Sons, 1863.

Straus, Scott. *The Order of Genocide: Race, Power, and War in Rwanda.* Ithaca: Cornell University Press, 2006.

Taylor, Christopher C. *Milk, Honey, and Money: Changing Concepts in Rwandan Healing.* Washington: Smithsonian Institution Press, 1992.

Theunis, Guy. "Le rôle de l'église catholique dans les événevments récents." In Guichaoua, André, ed. *Les crises politiques au Burundi et au Rwanda.* Lille: Université des Sciences et Technologies de Lille, 1995, pp. 289–98.

Thibeau, Josette. "Le Rwanda: Ombres et lumiéres." Brussels: Commission Justice et Paix, February 1991.

Thomas, Norman E. "Church and State in Zimbabwe." *Journal of Church and State,* 27, no. 1 (Winter, 1985): 113–33.

Tincq, Henri. "Le fardeau rwandais de Jean Paul II." *Le Monde,* May 23, 1996.

Tolotti, Sandrine. "Le Rwanda retient son souffle." *Croissance,* no. 356 (January 1993): 34–9.

Toynbee, Arnold J. A Summary of Armenian History Up to and Including 1915." In Viscount J. Bryce, ed. *The Treatment of Armenians in the Ottoman Empire: Documents Presented to Viscount Grey of Falloda, Secretary of State for Foreign Affairs.* London: H.M.S.O., 1916, pp. 593–653.

Tripp, Aili Mari. "Rethinking Civil Society: Gender Implications in Contemporary Tanzania." In John W. Harbeson, Donald Rothchild, and Naomi Chazan, eds. *Civil Society and the State in Africa.* Boulder: Lynne Rienner, 1994, pp. 149–68.

"Gender, Political Participation, and the Transformation of Associational Life in Uganda and Tanzania." *African Studies Review,* 37, no. 1 (April 1994): 107–31.

Twagirayesu, Michel, and Jan van Butselaar, eds. *Ce don que nous avons reçu: Histoire del'Eglise Presbetérienne au Rwanda (1907–1982).* Kigali: Eglise Presbetérienne au Rwanda, 1982.

"Two Priests Condemned to Death." All Africa News Agency, April 27, 1998.

"Uganda/Rwanda: Picking up the Pieces." *Africa Confidential,* 31, no. 23 (November 23, 1990): 5–6.

Uvin, Peter. *Aiding Violence: The Development Enterprise in Rwanda.* West Hartford: Kumarian Press, 1998.

Vail, Leroy. "Introduction: Ethnicity in Southern African History." In Leroy Vail, ed., *The Creation of Tribalism in Southern Africa.* Berkeley and Los Angeles: University of California Press, 1989, pp. 1–19.

Van Hoyweghen, Saskia. "The Disintegration of the Catholic Church in Rwanda: A Study of the Fragmentation of Political Religious Authority." *African Affairs,* 95, no. 380 (July 1996): 379–402.

Van Overschelde, A. *Mgr L.P. Classe.* Kabgayi, 1945.

van't Spijker, Gerard. *Les Usages Funéraires et la Mission de l'Eglise.* Kampen: Uitgeversmaatschappij J.H. Kok, 1990.

Vansina, Jan. *L'évoltion du royaume rwanda des origines a 1900.* Brussels: Academie Royale des Sciences d'Outre-Mer, 1962.

Le Rwanda Ancien: Le royaume nyinginya. Paris: Karthala, 2001.

Vidal, Claudine. *Sociologie des passions.* Paris: Karthala, 1991.

"Le Rwanda des Anthropologues ou le fétchisme de la vache." *Cahiers d'études africaines.* 9, 1969, pp. 389–401.

Voegelin, Eric. *The History of the Race Idea: From Ray to Carus* in *The Collected Works of Eric Voegelin,* vol. 3. Baton Rouge: Louisiana State University Press, 1998.

Waller, David. *Rwanda: Which Way Now?* Oxford: Oxfam, 1993.

Walsh, Peter. *Prophetic Christianity and the Liberation Movement in South Africa.* Pietermaritzburg: Cluster Publications, 1995.

Watson, Catharine. "Exile from Rwanda: Background to an Invasion." Washington: The U.S. Committee for Refugees, February 1991.

"War and Waiting." *Africa Report* (November/December 1992): 51–55.

Witte, John, Jr., ed. *Christianity and Democracy in Global Perspective.* Boulder: Westview Press, 1993.

Wuthnow, Robert. *The Restructuring of American Religion: Society and Faith Since World War II.* Princeton: Princeton University Press, 1988.

Young, Crawford. *The Rising Tide of Cultural Pluralism: The Nation-State at Bay?* Madison: University of Wisconsin Press, 1993.

Young, Crawford, ed. *The African Colonial State in Comprative Perspective.* New Haven: Yale University Press, 1995.

Zahn, Gordon C. "Catholic Resistance? A Yes and a No." In Franklin H. Littell and Hubert G. Locke, eds. *The German Church Struggle and the Holocaust.* Detroit: Wayne State University Press, 1974, pp. 203–37.

German Catholics and Hitler's Wars: A Study in Social Control. New York: Sheed and Ward, 1962.

Zarembo, Alan. "The Church's Shameful Acts: Many Rwandans Refuse to Return to Sanctuaries Where Blood Was Spilled." *Houston Chronicle,* January 29, 1995.

Zuiker, Henry. "The Essential 'Other' and the Jew: From Antisemitism to Genocide." *Social Research,* 63, no. 4 (Winter 1996): 1110–54.

Zürcher, Erik J. *Turkey: A Modern History.* London: IB Taurus and Company, 1993.

Index

BOOKS IN THIS SERIES